Diplomatic Departures

Canada and International Relations
Kim Richard Nossal, Brian L. Job, and Mark W. Zacher, General Editors

The Canada and International Relations series explores issues in contemporary world politics and international affairs. The volumes cover a wide range of topics on Canada's external relations, particularly international trade and foreign economic policy.

1   David G. Haglund, ed., *The New Geopolitics of Minerals: Canada and International Resource Trade*
2   Donald McRae and Gordon Munro, eds., *Canadian Oceans Policy: National Strategies and the New Law of the Sea*
3   Theodore H. Cohn, *The International Politics of Agricultural Trade: Canadian-American Relations in a Global Agricultural Context*
4   Russell S. Uhler, ed., *Canada-United States Trade in Forest Products*
5   A. Claire Cutler and Mark W. Zacher, eds., *Canadian Foreign Policy and International Economic Regimes*
6   Andrew F. Cooper, Richard A. Higgott, and Kim Richard Nossal, *Relocating Middle Powers: Australia and Canada in a Changing World Order*
7   Lawrence T. Woods, *Asia-Pacific Diplomacy: Nongovernmental Organizations and International Relations*
8   James Rochlin, *Discovering the Americas: The Evolution of Canadian Foreign Policy towards Latin America*
9   Michael Hart, with Bill Dymond and Colin Robertson, *Decision at Midnight: Inside the Canada-US Free-Trade Negotiations*
10 Amitav Acharya and Richard Stubbs, eds., *New Challenges for ASEAN: Emerging Policy Issues*
11 Donald Barry and Ronald C. Keith, eds., *Regionalism, Multilateralism, and the Politics of Global Trade*
12 Daniel Madar, *Heavy Traffic: Deregulation, Trade, and Transformation in North American Trucking*
13 Elizabeth Riddell-Dixon, *Canada and the Beijing Conference on Women: Governmental Politics and NGO Participation*
14 Nelson Michaud and Kim Richard Nossal, eds., *Diplomatic Departures: The Conservative Era in Canadian Foreign Policy, 1984-93*
15 Rosalind Irwin, ed., *Ethics and Security in Canadian Foreign Policy*

Edited by Nelson Michaud
and Kim Richard Nossal

Diplomatic Departures:
The Conservative Era in Canadian
Foreign Policy, 1984-93

UBCPress · Vancouver · Toronto

This book is printed on acid-free paper that is 100% ancient forest free (100% post-consumer recycled), processed chlorine free, and printed with vegetable based, low VOC inks.

ISBN 0-7748-0864-0 (hardcover)
ISBN 0-7748-0865-9 (paperback)

National Library of Canada Cataloguing in Publication Data

Main entry under title:

Diplomatic departures

  (Canada and international relations, 0847-0510; 14)
  Includes bibliographical references and index.
  ISBN 0-7748-0864-0 (bound); 0-7748-0865-9 (pbk.)

  1. Canada – Foreign relations – 1945- I. Michaud, Nelson. II. Nossal, Kim Richard. III. Series.

FC630.D56 2001   327.71'009'048   C2001-910937-7
F1034.2.D59 2001

This book has been published with the help of a grant from the Humanities and Social Sciences Federation of Canada, using funds provided by the Social Sciences and Humanities Research Council of Canada.

UBC Press acknowledges the financial support of the Government of Canada through the Book Publishing Industry Development Program (BPIDP) for our publishing activities.

Canadä

We also gratefully acknowledge the support of the Canada Council for the Arts for our publishing program, as well as the support of the British Columbia Arts Council.

Set in Stone by Bamboo & Silk Design Inc.
Copy editor: Joanne Richardson
Proofreader: Deborah Kerr
Printed and bound in Canada by Friesens

UBC Press
The University of British Columbia
2029 West Mall, Vancouver, BC V6T 1Z2
(604) 822-5959
Fax: (604) 822-6083
E-mail: info@ubcpress.ca
www.ubcpress.ca

Contents

Foreword / vii
Barbara J. McDougall

Acknowledgments / xiii

Acronyms / xv

Part 1: Introduction

1 The Conservative Era in Canadian Foreign Policy, 1984-93 / 3
Nelson Michaud and Kim Richard Nossal

2 Architects or Engineers? The Conservatives and Foreign Policy / 25
Denis Stairs

Part 2: Policy Issues

3 Leaving the Past Behind: The Free Trade Initiative Assessed / 45
Brian W. Tomlin

4 Continental Drift: Energy Policy and Canadian-American Relations / 59
Tammy L. Nemeth

5 Shades of Grey in Canada's Greening during the Mulroney Era / 71
Heather A. Smith ⟹ Acid Rain

6 A Northern Foreign Policy: The Politics of Ad Hocery / 84
Rob Huebert ⟹ Arctic Sovereignty

7 Big Eyes and Empty Pockets: The Two Phases of Conservative Defence Policy / 100
Norrin M. Ripsman

8 The Conservative Approach to International Peacekeeping / 113
Manon Tessier and Michel Fortmann

9 Mulroney's International "Beau Risque": The Golden Age of Québec's
Foreign Policy / 128
Luc Bernier

10 Explaining Canada's Decision to Join the OAS: An Interpretation / 142
Gordon Mace

11 Good Global Governance or Political Opportunism? Mulroney and UN
Social Conferences / 160
Andrew F. Cooper

12 How Exceptional? Reassessing the Mulroney Government's Anti-Apartheid
"Crusade" / 173
David R. Black

13 Liberal Internationalism for Conservatives: The Good Governance
Initiative / 194
Paul Gecelovsky and Tom Keating

Part 3: The Policy-Making Process

14 The Conservatives and Foreign Policy-Making: A Foreign Service View / 211
J.H. Taylor

15 Adding Women but Forgetting to Stir: Gender and Foreign Policy in the
Mulroney Era / 220
Claire Turenne Sjolander

16 Ethnic Groups and Conservative Foreign Policy / 241
Roy Norton

17 Bureaucratic Politics and the Making of the 1987 Defence White Paper / 260
Nelson Michaud

18 Opening Up the Policy Process: Does Party Make a Difference? / 276
Kim Richard Nossal

19 Diplomatic Departures? Assessing the Conservative Era in Foreign Policy / 290
Nelson Michaud and Kim Richard Nossal

Appendices

A Chronology of Events, 1984-93 / 297
B Photo Gallery / 301
C Foreign Policy Appointments, 1984-93 / 311

Bibliographical Essay / 313

Contributors / 316

Index / 319

Foreword

Barbara J. McDougall

It is a pleasure to introduce this collection of essays on the foreign policy of the Progressive Conservative government of Brian Mulroney, for it is time that we examined the historical record in a dispassionate and scholarly way. I say this not merely out of partisan pride, although I am very proud of our many accomplishments, from human rights in South Africa, to taking Canada's seat at the Organization of American States for the first time, to free trade, to calling early for action in the Balkans, to the Haiti intervention. Rather, I welcome an assessment of the Conservative record because it demonstrates that the roots of much of Canada's contemporary foreign policy can be found in the changes that came about during the Tory period – particularly in the last few years of Prime Minister Mulroney's leadership, when the world was undergoing such profound changes, and new ground had to be broken with almost every decision.

To paraphrase the Chinese proverb, as a government we lived in interesting times. Indeed, they were often tumultuous times. When we started in 1984, the world had not much changed over the preceding thirty years: it was frozen in a Cold War, divided between a democratic West, an undemocratic East, and a mostly undemocratic South. Security concerns were those that had existed since the late 1940s: the possibility of nuclear war over Europe, the Middle East, and Korea. In economic affairs the mindset was also traditionally nationalist and defensive, and, in some countries, overtly protectionist. The information revolution and the globalization of commerce were still on the horizon. Social or non-traditional issues like the environment and the role of women were only beginning to find their way onto the international agenda. In short, it was a world that William Lyon Mackenzie King, or even Sir Robert Borden, would have recognized.

But change came rapidly. Mikhail Gorbachev launched perestroika and glasnost and set in train events that he could not have anticipated. In 1989 Berliners from East and West scrambled to meet atop a wall that for nearly thirty years had kept people apart. The Cold War ice broke up and so, incredibly, did the Soviet Union and its empire. As a result, one of the world's two superpowers was unceremoniously consigned to history, Europe was reunited, and fifteen new independent countries were born. There was a resurgence of nationalism. And democracy, for so long the privilege of developed countries, became an achievable goal for peoples all over the world. Apartheid in South Africa, that great blot on the conscience of humanity, was at last swept away.

An equally profound change involved the computer-driven revolution in how business was conducted and how people communicated. Power and wealth came to be measured by the ability to use new knowledge-based technologies rather than by what was dug out of the ground, grown, or manufactured. Governments found themselves contending with powerful market forces and with non-governmental actors, now organized on a global scale. By the time the Conservatives left office in 1993 it was a new game entirely – one in which the old rules, attitudes, and policy instruments were no longer adequate.

By 1993 we were also looking at a greatly expanded international agenda. Security no longer just meant alliances, armies, and nuclear weapons: it had come to include protection from environmental damage, terrorism, health pandemics, drug trafficking, illegal migration, and other evils that could only too easily cross borders. Foreign policy no longer just meant the interests of states, but also the interests of groups that transcend international borders – women, children, and Aboriginal populations. This brought new bureaucratic and civil society players into the game, changing the face of diplomacy forever.

It is easy to forget how radical these changes were. Equally radical were the policy departures. To some extent, this was a function of having to respond to events. While international crisis management was a daily requirement for us, certain principles always guided our responses to these momentous events. The Conservative approach to foreign policy was interventionist and activist; we sought to shape change and create the new structures that are a key part of our international approach today.

First – as I think it should be – we took an active role in the hemisphere. The free trade negotiations, and later those by which Mexico was brought in to create the North American Free Trade Agreement (NAFTA), were an affirmation of one obvious fact: for economic purposes we are an integral part of North America, and we needed to develop rules-based arrangements that would allow us to shape our relations with the United States and our Latin American partners. No longer could we sit in a corner, trying to fight off protectionist sallies from south of the border.

Canadian business, sensing the rapidly changing environment, was confident that it could prosper under free trade. By and large it did, in some cases spectacularly so: in the 1990s Canada benefited from a long-running

US bull economy while Mexico-Canada trade enjoyed solid growth. And a useful by-product was the strengthened partnership between government and the private sector – a partnership that developed through the sectoral advisory groups that helped develop the Canadian position in the free trade negotiations. In effect, we helped put "Team Canada" on the ice – years before it started to go on tour.

If we were going to rethink our relationship with the US, it made sense to rethink our relations with the rest of the hemisphere. Joining the Organization of American States (OAS) made Canada a full participant in hemispheric affairs. By the time I attended my first OAS meeting in 1991, all the countries of the hemisphere (except Cuba) were democracies. I was welcomed with open arms by my Latin American colleagues, who were genuinely pleased that the Canadian chair was no longer empty. We managed to exercise considerable influence in the OAS in those days. At our insistence, the OAS established a Unit for the Promotion of Democracy. We were also instrumental in the adoption of the Santiago Declaration, which bound countries to take joint action in the event that democracy was threatened in any member country.

It was that declaration that was the foundation for OAS – and later UN – intervention in Haiti. We played a leadership role following the overthrow of Haiti's president Jean-Bertrand Aristide in a military coup. We worked hard to keep the OAS coalition together, to bring in the United Nations, and to ensure that the United States remained engaged. Our actions underlined our commitment to the hemisphere and reinforced our continuing effort to promote democracy.

The political earthquake in Europe in 1989 demanded a strong response by Canada. With one in seven Canadians claiming eastern European ancestry, there was obviously a strong domestic interest in the dramatic events that were taking place. But the stakes in Europe were always high, and Canada did its share – and more – in providing economic assistance to eastern Europe, Russia, and the other countries of the former Soviet Union. In per capita terms, Canada was at the forefront of all Western donors. We knew that there was not enough money to transform an entire way of life in such a large and highly populous region. But our actions were driven by optimism about the overthrow of communism. That optimism may not have been well founded, but, at the time, it united the developed democracies in a concerted and genuine effort to consolidate democracy and build free markets throughout former communist countries.

We shifted our military engagement in Europe once the Soviet threat disappeared, withdrawing our armed forces from Germany. While our North Atlantic Treaty Organization (NATO) allies were concerned, in our minds this was a realistic move given the changed political climate and our own limited resources. We knew we could not be everywhere, and we chose to demonstrate our commitment to Europe through substantial participation in the UN mission to the Balkans, where we played a central role.

We also withdrew from Cyprus, after twenty-eight years of patrolling the boundary between Greeks and Turks on that island. We concluded that peacekeeping was never intended to be a permanent condition; however, if it were going to be so, then others would have to share the burden. We also convinced the secretary-general of the United Nations to instigate peace talks among the fractious parties to the dispute – not, I must say, without some cajoling. Those talks did not reach a successful conclusion, but they marked the first effort in over twenty years to resolve the impasse.

I am particularly proud of our activism with regard to improving the lot of women throughout the world. We began to tie our aid programs to ensure participation by women and to monitor the progress made in recipient countries. We began to insist that recipients of Canadian aid increase the role of women in development assistance programs, and we began to monitor progress in this respect. We participated actively in the Nairobi Conference and its follow-up. An impressive number of women occupied foreign policy posts during the Mulroney years. These included external affairs, international trade, national defence, environment, energy, employment and immigration, and communications – all senior portfolios. Women were also made ministers of external relations with responsibility for the Canadian International Development Agency, and a woman was appointed to be associate minister of national defence. And women were appointed as heads of missions so that they could lead by example. These women included Louise Fréchette, who was appointed as our permanent representative at the United Nations. These were genuine breakthroughs at the time, and they set the stage for permanent improvements.

A second area of pride is the environment. Not only did Canada play a leading role at the United Nations Conference on the Environment and Development in Rio de Janeiro, but we also fostered better environmental practice through our aid programs. We reactivated the Great Lakes Commission and played a leading role in convincing the US to become more activist on environmental issues.

A third area of pride involves putting la Francophonie on a sound footing and establishing a more cooperative relationship between the federal government and Québec. The pinnacle was the 1987 Francophonie summit in Québec City. That summit, along with the 1987 Vancouver Commonwealth summit, also advanced the international agenda in a number of key areas, such as debt forgiveness, advancing the North/South dialogue, and promoting human rights, especially the struggle against apartheid.

One of the proudest achievements of the Conservative era in foreign policy was the leadership role we played in the promotion of democracy and pluralism. The ultimately victorious fight against apartheid was, in many ways, the centrepiece of this policy thrust. But it was not the only string to the Mulroney government's human rights bow. Our strong reaction to the events in Tiananmen Square in June 1989 was adopted despite bureaucratic resistance in Ottawa. The government continued to engage China at a ministerial level, but by cancelling visits at the prime ministerial level, we clearly signalled that it was not "business as usual." We followed much the same path with Cuba, and in 1991 we cut off aid to Indonesia following the Dili massacre in East Timor. Canada was also a strong proponent of the 1988 Harare Declaration, which set new standards for political governance in Commonwealth countries. The original legal and technical meeting that began the process that created the International Criminal Court was staged in Vancouver in 1992. In short, there was a determination to seize the moment to work for a better world in what I consider to be the best traditions of Canadian voluntarism and internationalism.

We were deeply committed to multilateralism. In addition to the Commonwealth, la Francophonie, and the OAS, Canada's increasingly important relationships with Asian countries were reflected in a more active role in the Asia-Pacific Economic Cooperation (APEC) forum and in the partnership structure of the Association of Southeast Asian Nations (ASEAN). The United Nations, of course, remained the centre of our multilateral activity, particularly after the end of the Cold War, as much of the hope for the "New World Order" – now there's a quaint phrase no longer much in use! – was vested in the United Nations. Canada played a distinguished role on the Security Council under the leadership of Ambassador Yves Fortier and was influential both in Secretary-General Boutros Boutros-Ghali's *Agenda for Peace* and in an important reform initiative that did bring some bureaucratic improvements but that later, alas, stalled.

I have no doubt betrayed my own view that much of lasting importance in Canadian foreign policy was, in the end, accomplished. Needless to say, I remain very proud of the record of the government of Prime Minister Mulroney in foreign policy and equally proud to have been a part of that government. But now it is time to let the contributors speak. I look forward to their judgment.

Acknowledgments

Most of the chapters in this volume were initially presented at a conference we organized in Hull in November 1999. We are most grateful to the members of the Ottawa Branch of the Canadian Institute of International Affairs (CIIA) for their contributions to the conference at which these papers were initially discussed. Many of the CIIA's Ottawa Branch members are serving or retired civil servants, and thus many of those who attended the Hull conference were often personally acquainted with the issues and events explored in this volume. Their willingness to share their recollections, add their perspectives to the analyses, and dispute conclusions with which they disagreed contributed considerably not only to the conference in Hull, but also to this book. Our deep appreciation as well to the three former policy-makers from that era who took time out of busy schedules to give keynote addresses to the conference – Barbara McDougall, who held a number of portfolios in the Mulroney Cabinet, including secretary of state for external affairs; Thomas Hockin, who cochaired the Special Joint Committee on Canada's International Relations; and J.H. (Si) Taylor, who was the under-secretary of state for external affairs between 1985 and 1989.

A number of papers presented at the conference subsequently appeared as part of a special issue of *Études internationales* that we guest edited and entitled "Nécessité ou innovation? Vers une redéfinition de la politique étrangère canadienne, 1984-1993" (31, 2 [juin 2000]). Our thanks to the editor of *Études* and the Institut québécois des hautes Études internationales at Université Laval for inviting us to edit this issue and for permission to present the English versions of these papers in this collection.

Special mention should be made of the financial assistance provided by the Centre for Foreign Policy Studies at Dalhousie University. All scholars in Canada know that institutional support can make a crucial difference to academic pursuits, and we are most grateful to our colleagues at Dalhousie for making that difference.

This book has been published with the help of a grant from the Humanities and Social Sciences Federation of Canada, using funds provided by the Social Sciences and Humanities Research Council of Canada. We owe yet another debt of gratitude to the Social Sciences and Humanities Research Council of Canada, however. The SSHRCC not only provided the financial assistance that made the Hull conference possible through conference grant 646-99-0062, but it also supports the ongoing research programs of so many of the participants in this project. The council has a far greater impact on scholarly inquiry in Canada, and ultimately on our understanding more of both ourselves and the world around us, than those who provide it with its resources often seem to know.

Finally, we would like to thank all those at UBC Press who worked so hard on this book: Emily Andrew, our editor, for being an unfailing source of encouragement and support from the outset of this project; Joanne Richardson, our copy editor, for dealing with twenty different contributors with both sensitivity and care; and Holly Keller-Brohman and Darcy Cullen, in the production department, for transforming the millions of ethereal bytes we sent them into this more enduring form.

NM and KRN
Québec City and Hamilton, July 2001

Acronyms

ABM	Anti-ballistic missile
ACCT	Agence de coopération culturelle et technique
ADI	Air Defense Initiative
ADM	Assistant deputy minister
ADMP	Air Defence Modernization Program
AES	Atmospheric Environment Service
ANC	African National Congress
APEC	Asia-Pacific Economic Cooperation
ASEAN	Association of Southeast Asian Nations
ASW	Anti-submarine warfare
AWACS	Airborne Warning and Control System
AWPPA	Arctic Waters Pollution Prevention Act
BCNI	Business Council on National Issues
CCFPD	Canadian Centre for Foreign Policy Development
CF	Canadian Forces
CFCs	chlorofluorocarbons
CFE	Conventional Forces in Europe
CFMSA	Committee of Foreign Ministers on Southern Africa
CHOGM	Commonwealth Heads of Government Meeting
CIAV	International Support and Verification Mission – Central America (Comisión Internacional de Apoyo y Verificación)
CIDA	Canadian International Development Agency
CIIA	Canadian Institute of International Affairs
CMA	Canadian Manufacturers' Association
CSCE	Conference on Security and Cooperation in Europe
CSO	Civil society organization
DEA	Department of External Affairs
DEMR	Department of Energy, Mines and Resources
DFAIT	Department of Foreign Affairs and International Trade

DND	Department of National Defence
DoD	Department of Defense (United States)
DOE	Department of Environment
DRIE	Department of Regional Industrial Expansion
EAITC	External Affairs and International Trade Canada
EC	European Community
EEZ	Exclusive Economic Zone
EPG	Eminent Persons Group
FAO	Food and Agriculture Organization
FCCC	Framework Convention on Climate Change
FEMA	Foreign Extraterritorial Measures Act
FIRA	Foreign Investment Review Agency
FTA	Free Trade Agreement
G-7	Group of Seven
GATT	General Agreement on Tariffs and Trade
GDP	Gross Domestic Product
HOP	Head of Post
ICBM	Intercontinental ballistic missile
ICJ	International Court of Justice
IEA	International Energy Agency
IMF	International Monetary Fund
INF	Intermediate-range nuclear forces
ITC	Industry, Trade and Commerce
MAI	Ministère des Affaires internationales
MFO	Multinational Force and Observers
MNE	Multinational enterprise
MOI	Memorandum of Intent
MRI	Ministère des Relations internationales
MTAP	Military Training Assistance Program
NAC	National Action Committee on the Status of Women
NAFTA	North American Free Trade Agreement
NATO	North Atlantic Treaty Organization
NDP	New Democratic Party
NEP	National Energy Program
NGO	Non-governmental organization
NORAD	North American Aerospace Defence Command
NORPATS	Northern patrol flights
NORPLOY	Northern deployment of naval vessels
NPCSD	North Pacific Cooperative Security Dialogue
NSC	National Security Council (United States)
OAS	Organization of American States
ODA	Official development assistance

OECD	Organisation for Economic Co-operation and Development
ONUCA	UN Observer Group in Central America (Grupo de Observadores de las Naciones Unidas en Centroamérica)
ONUVEN	UN Observer Mission to Verify the Electoral Process in Nicaragua (Misión de observadores de las Naciones Unidas encargada de vigilar el proceso electoral en Nicaragua)
PC	Progressive Conservative
PCO	Privy Council Office
PMO	Prime Minister's Office
PQ	Parti Québécois
SADCC	Southern African Development Coordination Conference
SAPs	Structural adjustment programs
SCEAIT	Standing Committee on External Affairs and International Trade
SCOND	Standing Committee on National Defence
SDI	Strategic Defense Initiative
SELA	Latin American Economic System
START	Strategic Arms Reduction Talks
UN	United Nations
UNCED	UN Conference on the Environment and Development
UNCLOS	UN Conference on the Law of the Sea
UNDOF	UN Disengagement Observer Force (Golan Heights)
UNEP	UN Environment Program
UNFICYP	UN Force in Cyprus
UNGOMAP	UN Good Offices Mission in Afghanistan and Pakistan
UNIIMOG	UN Iran-Iraq Military Observer Group
UNITAF	Unified Task Force (Somalia)
UNMOGIP	UN Military Observer Group India-Pakistan
UNOSOM	UN Operation in Somalia
UNPROFOR	UN Protection Force (Yugoslavia)
UNTAG	UN Transition Assistance Group (Namibia)
UNTSO	UN Truce Supervision Organization (Palestine)
USSR	Union of Soviet Socialist Republics (Soviet Union)
USTR	US Trade Representative
WMO	World Meteorological Organization
WSO	World Sikh Organization

Part 1
Introduction

1
The Conservative Era in Canadian Foreign Policy, 1984-93

Nelson Michaud and Kim Richard Nossal

In January 1984, while he was still leader of the Opposition, Brian Mulroney reportedly confided to an adviser that one of the things that he wanted history to remember him for was pursuing a foreign policy that was "distinctive."[1] To date, "history" has been generally cooperative, albeit perhaps not in ways that Mulroney might have been hoping for in January 1984, for the Progressive Conservative government that Mulroney led between 1984 and 1993 indeed tends to be remembered primarily for its most distinctive foreign policy initiative: the negotiation of a free trade agreement with the United States. The distinctiveness of the Canada-United States Free Trade Agreement that came into force on 1 January 1989 cannot be disputed; it was a policy departure of major proportions, abandoning as it did a deep-rooted Canadian political tradition that went back to 1911, when the Conservatives under Robert Borden defeated the Liberal government of Sir Wilfrid Laurier and its proposed free trade agreement with the United States, the Reciprocity Treaty.[2]

Certainly both of the major books on Mulroney's foreign policy that have been published to date – Lawrence Martin's *Pledge of Allegiance* and Marci McDonald's *Yankee Doodle Dandy*[3] – paint the foreign policy of this era as distinctive. However, both authors portray this distinctiveness in unidimensional and largely negative terms: the prime minister purposely set out to alter Canada's foreign relations, particularly with the United States. Both argue that Mulroney had a clear foreign policy agenda that he spent his mandate implementing. For her part, McDonald suggests that Mulroney had what she calls an "American agenda"; and the stated purpose of her book is to try to understand how she and other members of the Canadian media were "manipulated" as the Conservative prime minister "prodded his reluctant citizenry towards an economic vision made in the USA – one that held scant benefit for Canadians."[4] In a similar vein, Martin argues that Mulroney's purpose was no less than the Americanization of Canada. The dustjacket makes clear the essence of his argument: the book is described as the "engrossing account of how the Tories ... brought Canada into line with the United States in almost every respect, from trade to taxes, from foreign policy to film policy ... Martin shows how Canada's destiny was surrendered – was placed squarely and perhaps irrevocably in American hands – by the Tories. With hardly a thought for the integrity of the country they governed, they tossed a century-old tradition of nation-building in favour of 'super relations with the United States.'"

Both books seek to show how Mulroney transformed Canada's foreign relations over these nine years, primarily by signing a free trade agreement with the United States, engaging in blind pro-Americanism on a range of issues, subordinating Canadian interests to those of the United States, and abandoning the traditional tenets of Canadian foreign policy. Mulroney's personal relationships with Ronald Reagan and George Bush, the first two American presidents whose terms of office overlapped with his, were considered particularly important for an understanding of how these changes were brought about. "Pals diplomacy" was the way the personal relations that Mulroney developed with the presidents were characterized. Indeed, both books accuse the prime minister of fawning over Reagan and Bush; in Martin's words, Mulroney engaged in "a degree of sycophancy unholy to Canadian tradition."[5] For example, both authors point to the summit meeting between Mulroney and Reagan in Québec City in March 1985. Both leaders made much of their mutual Irish heritage, and Brian and Mila Mulroney sang *When Irish Eyes Are Smiling* with Ronald and Nancy Reagan, a cloying performance that instantly made the phrase "Shamrock Summit" emblematic in Canadian political discourse for the overly close nature of the Canadian-American relationship during the Conservative era.[6]

Three interrelated assumptions about Canadian foreign policy during the Mulroney period are evident in histories like Martin's and McDonald's. First, there is the assumption that the policies pursued during these nine years reflected a *planned* departure from traditional Canadian foreign policy orientations. Second, both McDonald and Martin assume that causality for the transformations in foreign policy should be most appropriately located with the Conservatives themselves. In their reading, this was the *Conservative transformation of Canada's foreign policy*; neither of them entertain the possibility that causality for the transformation might be found in other factors – that perhaps it might be better characterized as *the transformation of Canadian foreign policy under the Conservatives*. Finally, and most important, they assume that the only foreign policy departure undertaken by the Conservative government worth exploring was the shift in the Canadian-American relationship. Other aspects of Canadian foreign policy in these nine years are either analyzed within the context of Canadian-American relations or are simply not examined at all.

How accurate are these assumptions? It is not at all clear that Canada's engagement in world affairs was, then as now, as unidimensional as McDonald or Martin suggest. While Canadian-American relations necessarily loom large in any period in Canadian history, Canadian governments have always defined foreign policy in more expansive, and indeed often global, terms. Likewise, it is not at all clear that the Mulroney Conservatives came to office with a grand plan for the transformation of Canada and/or its foreign relations.

The purpose of this book is to test these assumptions about Canadian foreign policy during the Conservative era. We do so by subjecting the Mulroney government to a fresh analysis. We begin with an overview of external policy and show not only the degree to which the Mulroney Conservatives arrived in office in September 1984 without a well defined plan for the transformation of foreign relations, but also some suggestive initial evidence of a distinctive foreign policy.

In Chapter 2, Denis Stairs explores how we can best understand the relationship between the changes in Canadian foreign policy evident after 1984 and the election of the Progressive Conservatives. Stairs poses a basic question: "To what extent was the conduct of Canada's foreign policy in the period of Conservative government from 1984 to 1993 a reflection of the political orientation of the Progressive Conservative party and the predilections of its leaders, and to what extent was it a product of insistent imperatives arising from circumstances – some of them changing and some not – at home and abroad? In what measure, in other words, were the Conservatives in office the 'architects' of their foreign policies, creating them (as it were) afresh, and in what measure were they its 'engineers,' installing bridges of standard design over rivers that almost anyone in power would have had to cross?" He concludes that, although the Conservatives embraced a number of shifts in direction, it is more appropriate to conceive of them as engineers than as architects; the "insistent imperatives arising from circumstances" provide the best explanation of the foreign policy changes that we see during the Conservative era.

Guided by Stairs's question, our contributors offer their analyses of a number of different issue areas in Canadian foreign policy between 1984 and 1993: the negotiation of free trade, the decision to move to a continentalized energy policy, environmental diplomacy, the emergence of a maritime policy on the Arctic, and the evolution of defence policy and the transformation of peacekeeping. Three chapters focus on multilateral diplomacy during this period: Mulroney's cooperative stance that allowed the establishment of a summit for la Francophonie; the decision in 1989 to join the Organization of American States; and the prime minister's personal diplomacy at the "mega-conferences" convened by the United Nations in the early 1990s. Canada's policy on apartheid and the pursuit of human rights and good governance are also examined. And because we can also see some differences in the way in which foreign policy was made during the Conservative period, five chapters focus on the policy-making process. To put these fifteen studies into perspective, we begin by locating them within a broad overview of the Conservative era in Canadian foreign policy.

The Conservative Era in Foreign Policy: An Overview

The Conservative era formally began on 17 September 1984, when Mulroney was sworn in as prime minister following the general election of 4 September that had returned 211 Progressive Conservative members of Parliament, the largest majority in Canadian history. It came to an end on 25 October 1993, when the Liberals under Jean Chrétien were returned to power and the Conservatives were reduced to just two seats in the House of Commons. In the intervening nine years, Canada's foreign and defence policies would be marked by a series of important changes.

But in the late summer of 1984 there was little hint of the shift in Canadian foreign policy that lay ahead, for Mulroney came to 24 Sussex Drive without a well developed approach to foreign policy. On the contrary, as Rae Murphy, Robert Chodos, and Nick Auf der Maur put it, bluntly but not inappropriately, his views on international affairs – "to the degree he has ever considered them" – were notable for their "simplicity."[7] In the fifteen months after Mulroney seized the leadership of the Progressive Conservative party from Joe Clark at the leadership convention in June 1983, Mulroney's approach to foreign policy was indeed marked by simplicity.

The Conservatives in Opposition

While leader of the Opposition, Mulroney focused single-mindedly on the deterioration in Canadian-American relations that had occurred since the Liberals, under Pierre Elliott Trudeau, had defeated Clark and the Conservatives in the general election of February 1980. That deterioration had resulted from a number of serious policy disputes between the Liberal government and the Reagan administration and had progressively soured Canadian-American relations over the early 1980s.

Of greatest concern was how the Trudeau government responded to the economic crisis of the 1970s. Canadians, like many others in the developed world, were experiencing the interrelated effects of the emergence of global financial markets with the US decision in 1971 to float its currency, the dismantling of systems of controls on capital flows between national markets, the internationalization of investment, the high unemployment that accompanied the processes involved with the transnational rationalization of production, persistent high inflation, and rising energy prices as a result of crises in the Middle East. When it was returned to office in

February 1980, the Trudeau government's response was to seek essentially national solutions to these various pressures. In particular, it promised throughout 1980 to strengthen the Foreign Investment Review Agency (FIRA), the screening mechanism that had been introduced in 1973 to monitor and regulate foreign investment in Canada. And in October 1980, it introduced the National Energy Program (NEP), a measure designed to achieve energy self-sufficiency, to increase Canadian ownership of the oil and gas sector, and to assert the primacy of the federal government over the provincial governments in regulating resources.

The NEP aroused considerable opposition, both in Canada and in the United States. First, it offended the principles of a new orthodoxy about the economy that was being enunciated in theory by many economists, and embraced in policy both by the British prime minister, Margaret Thatcher, whose Conservatives had swept to power in May 1979, and by the Republicans under Ronald Reagan in the United States following the November 1980 presidential elections. The new neoliberal orthodoxy claimed that the root cause of the economic malaise so evident in the developed world in the 1970s was a misplaced faith in Keynesian theory; rather, the path to economic salvation lay in the embrace of neoliberal economic theory, with its emphasis on zero inflation and opening national economies to international market forces. Just as important, the NEP was seen by many Americans to be directed at the interests of the United States, since the targets of some of its provisions were quite clearly and unambiguously American oil companies. Particularly irritating was the provision that gave the Canadian government a retroactive 25 percent interest in every energy development. And once Reagan reached the White House in January 1981, American protests against the NEP grew increasingly more intense.[8] As Allan Gotlieb, Canada's ambassador to the United States from 1981 to 1989, put it, Canadian-American relations had reached a crisis: Canadians and Americans "were on fast-moving trains headed in opposite directions, one towards more and more interventionism and an expanded role for the state, the other towards deregulation and a shrinking role for government."[9]

These disputes had spillover effects in other areas of the Canadian-American relationship. For example, the US government was not at all sympathetic to complaints from Ottawa that emissions of sulphur dioxide and nitrogen oxide emanating from American sources were being carried by prevailing winds and falling on Canada in the form of precipitation, causing environmental damage. On the contrary, the persistent response of the Reagan administration was that there was no clear relationship between emissions in the United States and the acidification of Ontario lakes or damage to the sugarbush in Québec. Washington contended that more research into acid rain was needed. This prompted the Trudeau government to grow more and more strident in its complaints. Canadian diplomats in the United States gave undiplomatic speeches openly accusing the United States of stalling on the issue. Canadian politicians were even less diplomatic, sometimes openly sneering at the Reagan administration's environmental policies. The Trudeau government eventually was reduced to handing out propaganda to American tourists visiting Canada, urging them to write to their member of Congress to stop American pollution of Canada.[10] Likewise, the Canadian efforts in 1983 to explore the possibility of negotiating a series of sectoral free trade agreements with the United States as a means of countering the increasing protectionism of the United States Congress ended in failure.

Conflict in the Canadian-American relationship over bilateral issues during the Trudeau period was aggravated by deep disagreements over global policy. The early 1980s were marked by a re-intensification of Cold War tensions between the United States and the Soviet Union, and among Ronald Reagan's election themes in 1980 was his promise "to make America Number One again." American global policy during the early Reagan years was aggressively directed towards that goal. On a wide variety of global issues, however, the Trudeau government had marked disagreements with the United States: intervention in the conflicts in Central America, North-South relations, the declaration of martial law in Poland, the United Nations Law of the Sea, the shootdown of Korean Air Lines flight 007 by the Soviet Union, the invasion of Grenada, nuclear strategy, and relations with the Soviet Union in general. Significantly, Trudeau generally made little effort to hide his disdain for Reagan's approach to global affairs; for his part, Reagan and members of his staff had little use for Trudeau's approach to global policy, a difference of opinion that was most clearly seen during the foreign policy initiative that capped his prime ministership, the "peace initiative" of the winter of 1983-84.[11]

To demonstrate opposition to Trudeau's policies in the international realm, Brian Mulroney developed a relatively simple and one-dimensional line in foreign policy: he promised to change both the substance and the tenor of the Canadian-American relationship, to "refurbish" the relationship, as he put it on numerous occasions, by introducing a "new era of civility."[12] A refurbished relationship was crucial, Mulroney argued, for Canadian wealth, for civility was necessary for removing the irritants in the relationship.

Mulroney also promised that a Conservative government would pursue a trade policy that would result in an increase in jobs, but he did not articulate a consistent position on trade. In one speech delivered during the campaign for the Conservative party leadership in 1983, he pledged to raise Canada's share of world trade to 5 percent and bruited the possibility of using counter-trade as the means of doing so.[13] Yet in *Where I Stand,* a book of speeches published to coincide with his leadership bid, Mulroney suggested that free trade was his preferred approach. Noting that "trade is our lifeblood," he asserted that "global protectionism is totally contrary to our interests." Canada "must energetically stand and press for the lowering of barriers to trade ... Government in Canada must see its role as creating with the private sector a greater and freer access to world markets." And he argued that he would make such access "a top priority."[14] This can of course be read in two ways: at face value, it was the standard pitch of those seeking a *multilateral* reduction in impediments to global trade. But given that Canada's "lifeblood," then as now, came from trade with the United States, and given that American protectionism threatened Canada far more than did "global" protectionism, the assertions in *Where I Stand* clearly left the door open to the idea of freer *bilateral* trade with the United States.

As the campaign for the Conservative leadership unfolded, however, Mulroney nuanced his position considerably, eventually rejecting quite explicitly the idea of a bilateral free trade agreement with the United States. "That's why free trade was decided on in an election in 1911," Mulroney told some Thunder Bay delegates to the leadership convention in June 1983. "It affects Canadian sovereignty, and we'll have none of it, not during leadership campaigns, nor at any other times."[15] On another occasion, he told reporters that Canada "could not survive with a policy of unfettered free trade."[16]

But there can be little doubt that Mulroney sought the development of a "special relationship" with the United States. In order to secure this, he promised that a Conservative government would spend more on defence; Canada, he argued, "is a first-class nation" and "first-class means going first class in pay to our men and women who serve this country here and overseas, in training, in weapons, and equipment and deployment capacity. That is the way a Conservative government is going to go – first class in conventional defences."[17] Canada, Mulroney promised, would be less critical of American global policy; it would give the United States "the benefit of the doubt." In short, Canada would be a "better ally, a super ally" of what Mulroney inevitably characterized as Canada's "four traditional allies" – the United States, Britain, France, and Israel (even though Canada has never had an alliance with Israel, Mulroney always added that country to the list of Canada's "traditional allies" in a not very subtle attempt to woo Jewish voters).

Guided by the singular goal of being a "super ally," the foreign policy pronouncements of the Opposition Conservatives consisted largely of agreeing with the United States on global issues. Thus, for example, after Soviet fighters shot down Korean Air Lines flight 007 in the early hours of 1 September 1983, Trudeau characterized the shootdown as an accident.

Mulroney, by contrast, called it an act of cold-blooded murder. When the United States invaded Grenada in October 1983 following a military coup, Conservatives criticized the Trudeau government for refusing to support the action, noting that Washington's failure to consult with the Canadian government prior to the invasion was an indication that Canada had become an "untrustworthy" member of the western hemisphere.[18] Mulroney was also prone to characterize the Soviet Union in largely negative terms: to an international convention of Estonians in Toronto in July 1984, Mulroney roundly denounced the USSR as a "slave" state. He reminded them that another Canadian Conservative, John G. Diefenbaker, prime minister from 1957 to 1963, had criticized the Soviet Union so harshly at the United Nations that the Soviet premier, Nikita Khrushchev, had banged his shoe on his desk in protest; Mulroney promised that he would do no less than Diefenbaker in the cause of eastern Europeans.[19] While Mulroney was merely repeating a hoary but durable Conservative myth (for Diefenbaker was, in fact, at home in Saskatchewan when Khrushchev banged his shoe in protest against a comment made by a Filipino speaker), it nicely reflected the Manichean perspective that the Conservatives had embraced in the run-up to the September 1984 vote.[20]

Mulroney in Power
Once in power, however, Brian Mulroney and the Progressive Conservatives followed a markedly different trajectory in foreign policy than the one that might have been expected given the previous fifteen months in Opposition. Certainly the initial appointments made by the new prime minister to foreign policy positions did not mirror the widespread expectations that he would choose those from the party's right wing (or "Blue Tories") for foreign policy posts; rather, Mulroney's foreign policy appointments were dominated by those in the moderate or progressive wing of the party, or "Red Tories." Joe Clark, who had been unceremoniously dumped as party leader the year before, was appointed the secretary of state for external affairs (as Canada's minister of foreign affairs was termed before 1993); Clark's brief tenure as prime minister in 1979-80 suggested that his foreign policy inclinations were rather less than Reaganesque. Douglas Roche was made ambassador for disarmament. David Macdonald, who had served as a minister in Clark's government, was appointed to oversee famine relief efforts. Flora MacDonald, who had been Clark's External Affairs minister, was made minister of employment and immigration. James Kelleher, another moderate, was appointed as minister of international trade. Monique Vézina was appointed as minister of state for external relations. Roy McMurtry, who had been a Conservative minister in the Ontario government, was sent as high commissioner to London. From Mulroney's large pool of Conservative backbenchers, Thomas

Hockin, an academic whose speciality was in Canadian foreign policy, was chosen to co-chair a special parliamentary committee charged with reviewing Canada's foreign relations; and William Winegard, a former president of the University of Guelph, was the chair of the House of Commons Standing Committee on External Affairs and International Trade. Mulroney also made a number of other appointments that had the effect of consolidating the moderate line in foreign policy. He retained Allan Gotlieb, a senior civil servant, as ambassador in Washington. And in a surprise move, Mulroney asked Stephen Lewis, a former leader of the Ontario New Democratic Party, to be Canada's permanent representative at the United Nations.

The Blue Tories had to content themselves with other portfolios. Sinclair Stevens, who had been the Conservative foreign affairs critic in 1983-84, was appointed as minister of Regional Industrial Expansion, from where he presided over the transformation of FIRA into Investment Canada in late 1984. The national defence portfolio was given to Robert Coates. Pat Crofton, a former navy commander from British Columbia, chaired the Standing Committee on Defence from 1985 to 1988. It is important to note that, within two years, some of the hard-line voices on foreign policy would be gone. Coates was forced to resign in February 1985 for visiting a strip club while inspecting Canadian forces in Germany; Erik Nielsen, the deputy prime minister, became minister of national defence. Stevens was forced to resign over a conflict of interest involving one of his companies.

Changes were also evident in Mulroney's own worldview. By all accounts, he arrived in office with his focus clearly on domestic politics; he was quite happy to leave the handling of foreign affairs to Joe Clark, his former rival. Once in office, however, the prime minister's vision clearly developed; no longer bound by the relative parochialism of a career as a Montreal labour lawyer and president of a Canadian branch plant of an American firm, Mulroney found himself a player on the international stage. And through the years it is evident that he developed a taste for foreign policy and summit meetings.

Canadian-American Relations

In 1984, however, Mulroney's activism on the wider international stage was still in the future. The first item on the Conservative foreign policy agenda was to improve Canada's relationship with the United States. To that end, Mulroney worked hard to establish close personal relationships with both Ronald Reagan and his successor, George Bush. The "Shamrock Summit" in Québec City on St Patrick's Day, 1985, was designed to put in place an institutional mechanism for the regular exchange of views between Canada and the United States at the highest political levels. Throughout the Mulroney period, this regularized summit, usually held in March or April, became a fixed part of the annual prime ministerial and presidential calendars. However, contact was not limited to these formal occasions; it is reported that, while Mulroney was not totally at ease with Reagan at first, soon the phone lines between 24 Sussex Drive and the White House were regularly busy. During the Bush administration, Mulroney would frequently pay Bush informal visits, since both leaders developed a close personal friendship that transcended their political relationship, a friendship that lasted well after both leaders retired from public life. On occasion, the formal summits and the informal get-togethers proved crucial for the evolution of policy decisions during the Conservative era: as Rob Huebert shows, for example, a one-on-one meeting between Mulroney and Reagan allowed the prime minister to put forward an argument about Canadian sovereignty in the Arctic that convinced Reagan to override the objections of his officials and order that an agreement be reached with the Canadians that reflected Mulroney's concerns.

On some issues, however, no amount of goodwill could overcome entrenched conflicts of interest between the two countries. As Heather Smith's chapter shows, the conflict over acid rain persisted well into the Conservative era, and eventually the Mulroney government grew as frustrated as the Liberal government had become – to the point that once again American tourists visiting Canada were confronted with Canadian propaganda reminding them of their country's responsibility for environmental damage in Canada. It is true that the issue of acid rain was "solved" (in the sense that it was removed from the Canadian-American agenda of irritants) during the Mulroney era, but this had more to do with shifts in American politics than with Conservative diplomacy.[21]

While these issues were important, there can be little doubt that Canadian-American relations during the Conservative era were dominated by the issue of trade. Mulroney's change of mind on the issue of a free trade agreement with the United States came after the 1984 election and only after the idea of trying to negotiate a comprehensive free trade agreement was endorsed by a number of key voices in Canada. Among these, arguably the most important was the call by Donald S. Macdonald, the chair of the Royal Commission on the Economic Union and Development Prospects for Canada (established in the dying days of the Trudeau government), for Canadians to take a "leap of faith" and embrace free trade. But, as Brian Tomlin shows in his chapter, the way in which the issue of free trade made it to the agenda demonstrated the fundamental disjuncture between Mulroney's plans in Opposition and the realities that faced him in power. And just as Mulroney's conversion was by no means assured, neither was the actual negotiation of the agreement: as the accounts of the negotiations all make clear, it was a close-run thing.[22] So too was the achievement by Mulroney and the Conservatives of a second majority in the November 1988 elections that smoothed the legislative passage of the agreement. If Canada had had an electoral system more sensitive to the preferences of voters than the first-past-the-post system, the outcome may well have been different.

Moreover, this initiative was quickly to give way to another: the negotiation of a trilateral agreement involving Canada, the United States, and Mexico. The North American Free Trade Agreement of 1993 was a distant descendant of the North American Accord that had originally been proposed by Ronald Reagan during the 1980 presidential election (but which had been dropped because of strong Canadian and Mexican opposition). For the Mulroney government, seeking to trilateralize the United States-Mexican free trade talks had nothing to do with seeking to realize Reagan's vision and everything to do with wanting to protect Canadian interests from the possibility of having the United States and Mexico come to a separate trade deal. Although Mulroney had resigned as leader and the Conservatives had been defeated by the time that all three legislatures had ratified the agreement signed in August 1992, there can be little doubt that the shape of Canadian trade policy in 1993 was as far removed from his protestations in 1983 as could be imagined.

Defence Policy

In power, the Conservatives also distanced themselves from the promises that Mulroney had made to be a "better" ally. While spending on the military was increased in the short term, most of those increases were for commitments undertaken by Liberal governments.[23] Overall, however, defence spending did not increase substantially, for reasons that Norrin Ripsman identifies in Chapter 7. In brief, the Mulroney government was unwilling to make the entirely unpalatable choices that were necessary if a real increase in defence spending was to result: increasing the already ballooning federal deficit, redirecting social spending, and/or increasing taxes. It is true that, for a brief period in 1987, the Conservatives seemed prepared to reverse course: the white paper on defence published that year was underwritten by Cold War assumptions (the Soviet Union being portrayed as seeking global domination) and outlined a range of Canadian commitments to respond to the Soviet threat. However, as Nelson Michaud explains in Chapter 17, the commitments of the 1987 white paper on defence were quickly abandoned.

Likewise, the Mulroney government did not gravitate towards the United States in defence matters as many had expected. The ambiguity in the Conservative position is perhaps best seen in Ottawa's response to the 1985 Strategic Defense Initiative (SDI). SDI, or Star Wars (as it was quickly dubbed by the Democrats), was an American plan to develop a space-based defence shield against ballistic missile attack. On 26 March 1985,

Caspar Weinberger, the US secretary of defense, extended a formal invitation to all American allies to participate in the research program of SDI. The Canadian response was indicative of an ambiguity within the Conservative government concerning strategic matters. While Mulroney himself was clearly in favour of the initiative, particularly the employment possibilities it offered, other parts of the government were hesitant. Opposition to Star Wars emerged not only among the public in general, but also within the ranks of the Conservative backbench. The parliamentary committee charged with reviewing Canadian foreign policy – the Special Joint Committee on Canada's International Relations, co-chaired by Jean-Maurice Simard (a Conservative senator from New Brunswick) and Thomas Hockin (the Conservative MP from London West) – was also asked by the government to offer advice on how to respond to the Star Wars invitation. Throughout the summer of 1985, the committee held public hearings across Canada; everywhere the committee was confronted by opposition to SDI. The committee reached an all-party agreement to recommend that Canada not participate in this scheme. The Mulroney government accepted the committee's advice: on 7 September 1985, it delivered its "polite no" to Washington. The government announced that, while it believed that basic research on SDI was prudent, it had decided not to participate. However, following the spirit of the Special Joint Committee's report recommendations, the Conservative government left a door open: while Canada would not join the SDI program, it did not prevent Canadian firms and institutions from participating if they so wished, therefore making it possible for Canadians to benefit economically from the program.

A similar reversal occurred in the case of the North Atlantic Treaty Organization (NATO). Although at the outset of his mandate Mulroney promised that Canada would "pull its weight within the NATO alliance,"[24] the Conservatives actually ended up doing what the Trudeau government could not bring itself to do in 1968-69 – withdraw Canadian forces from Europe. The rationale for doing this, however, was quite different from the rationale behind the Trudeau government's concerns and much more prosaic: the Conservative government was motivated almost entirely by the prospect of the savings that would accrue to the federal budget through the closure of Canada's European bases and the downsizing of the troop commitment there.[25] Moreover, the thaw in the East-West relations offered Canada a wider margin of manoeuvre to implement its own policy, despite protests from numerous friends and allies, including the United States; western European governments; and, most especially, from the German chancellor, Helmut Kohl, who was facing opposition to conscription within his own country.[26]

The withdrawal from Europe brought a long chapter in Canada's external relations to an end, concretely marking the arrival of what might be considered a post-European and continental orientation for Canada. All governments in Ottawa in the post-1945 period had worked under the explicit assumption that Europe was important for Canadian statecraft; the Mulroney Conservatives, by contrast, were willing to embrace a substantive Canadian withdrawal from Europe. Neither Mulroney nor Clark seemed comfortable in Europe, and they did not devote the kind of time and attention to European affairs that they did to other dossiers.

The Ethiopian Famine and the Reform of Development Assistance

One of the first foreign policy crises faced by the Mulroney government was the famine in Ethiopia, which appeared on the political agenda in October 1984, scarcely a month after the government had been sworn in.[27] As Kim Richard Nossal demonstrates in Chapter 18, the response of the new government to this crisis – creating a special matching fund to which ordinary Canadians could contribute, bringing non-governmental organizations (NGOs) into the process of policy-making, and involving members of Parliament in the process – suggested that the Conservatives were going to take a different approach to the making of foreign policy. It reflected a willingness to try to open up the policy process by establishing what were termed "partnerships" with a broader public. The Ethiopian crisis moved many parliamentarians who had been participants in the process. One in particular, William Winegard, chair of the House of Commons Standing Committee on External Affairs and International Trade, was galvanized to try to reform Canada's development assistance programs. The exploration of official development assistance (ODA) by the Standing Committee on External Affairs and International Trade (SCEAIT) under the leadership of William Winegard led to a 1987 report entitled *For Whose Benefit?*, which was a call for Canadian development assistance programs and policies to be driven first and foremost by development criteria.

While the initial response of the Conservative government – a strategy paper issued in 1988 entitled *Sharing Our Future* – was to implement some of the innovative recommendations advanced by Winegard, only a few survived the massive changes that occurred in the last four years of the Conservative period: Joe Clark, who had worked hard to press the interests of development assistance, was shuffled to constitutional affairs; Margaret Catley-Carlson was replaced as president of CIDA by Marcel Massé; and 1991 saw the beginning of a series of cuts to the CIDA budget that would continue throughout the remainder of the Conservative era (before an even steeper decline once the Liberals took power in 1993).[28] But in the intervening years, David Morrison has argued that the Conservatives – and Joe Clark in particular – brought a marked change in the general approach to North-South relations.[29]

Peacekeeping and Peacemaking
In the years after Lester B. Pearson (Canada's External Affairs minister from 1948 to 1957) won the 1957 Nobel peace prize for his innovative idea of using a United Nations force as a means to resolve the Suez crisis of 1956, peacekeeping became a deeply rooted part of Canadian political culture. After Pearson, no Canadian government was willing to alter that basic commitment to peacekeeping. But, as Manon Tessier and Michel Fortmann demonstrate in Chapter 8, the Canadian approach to peacekeeping experienced a number of changes, particularly during the latter half of the Conservative era. Emblematic of that change was the Mulroney government's decision to withdraw from the long-running UN mission in Cyprus.

The new activism in this area was triggered by Canada's participation in the coalition that used force to evict Iraqi troops from Kuwait in January and February 1991. This represented a significant foreign policy departure by the Conservatives, for it was the first time since the Korean War of 1950-53 that a Canadian government had gone to war. The process by which the Mulroney government committed to the use of force to reverse the August 1990 Iraqi invasion of Kuwait was a slow one, and it involved a fundamental transformation of the mission of the multinational coalition that the Bush administration had organized to oppose the take-over of Kuwait by Iraq. However, it nonetheless reflected the prime minister's enthusiasm about the possibilities of what Bush took to calling the "new world order" ushered in by the unprecedented level of cooperation between the United States and the Soviet Union in the immediate aftermath of the invasion.[30]

The principle that force can and should be used for certain political purposes would also lead Mulroney to approve robust peacekeeping missions in both the former Yugoslavia and in Somalia. In the autumn of 1991, Mulroney was the first Western leader to call for active UN intervention in the growing civil war in Yugoslavia. In December 1992, for example, he told an audience at Harvard University that the UN should impose peace on Bosnia, using force if necessary, and claimed that Canada would heartily support such an operation. Likewise, when he toured Europe in May 1993 just before retiring as prime minister, he expressed the view that force should be used in Yugoslavia "should the courageous peacekeeping attempts by UN forces fail."[31] The Conservatives also joined the American initiative in a forceful rescue mission to Somalia in December 1992, contributing over 1,200 soldiers to the Unified Task Force (UNITAF) put together by the Bush administration. This mission was marred by the torture and murder of a Somali teenager by members of the Canadian Airborne Regiment.[32]

Multilateral Initiatives

Few who followed the evolution of Mulroney's foreign policy positions prior to September 1984 might have expected that he would be a committed multilateralist in his foreign policy. Besides evincing concern with improving the performance of the United Nations and playing an activist role in the Commonwealth, a number of other multilateral initiatives pursued during the Conservative period can be noted. The first involved the personal efforts of the prime minister to remove the stumbling blocks on the road to hosting the same kind of heads-of-government meeting for la Francophonie in Québec City that was hosted in the Commonwealth, a topic explored by Luc Bernier in Chapter 9. Gordon Mace, in Chapter 10, examines the Mulroney government's decision to abandon a long tradition of diffidence towards the Organization of American States (OAS), which had historically been seen as an American-dominated and largely moribund institution that Canada would do well to stay away from. The Conservatives had a different view of the possibilities of the effectiveness of the OAS and joined the organization in 1989.

As noted above, the end of the Cold War had a pronounced impact on Canadian security policy. In fact, as the Cold War waned, the Conservative government became increasingly concerned about the security architecture in the Pacific – or, more properly, the lack thereof. Mirroring efforts by others in the Asia-Pacific area to encourage the institutionalization of security, making it comparable to that developing in Europe with the transformation of the Conference on Security and Cooperation in Europe and NATO's outreach programs, the Conservative government embraced an initiative intended to encourage security dialogue in the North Pacific. Outlined by Joe Clark in July 1990, the North Pacific Cooperative Security Dialogue (NPCSD) envisaged two "tracks" of dialogue: a set of governmental discussions was to be complemented and reinforced by a "second track" of dialogue among non-governmental experts. While the dialogue in the North Pacific was markedly less successful than were the dialogues in other parts of the Asia Pacific (such as the Asian Regional Forum), largely because of American lack of interest, the NPCSD can nonetheless be regarded both as an innovative response to the evolving geostrategic situation in the Asia Pacific at the end of the Cold War and as an illustration of the propensity for multilateral initiatives.[33]

However, it was in the context of the United Nations that Mulroney sought to use personal diplomacy to advance the foreign policy agenda. In Chapter 11 Andrew F. Cooper examines Mulroney's personal involvement in the 1990 World Summit for Children in New York, in the 1992 UN Conference on the Environment and Development (UNCED) in Rio de Janeiro, and in the 1993 Vienna World Conference on Human

Rights. In doing so, he demonstrates how the prime minister's personal initiatives at these meetings helped to shape the international agenda on these issues.

Human Rights and Good Governance

The Conservatives did not come to office in 1984 intending to make the promotion of human rights and good governance one of the central features of Canadian foreign policy. However, as David Black (Chapter 12) and Paul Gecelovsky and Tom Keating (Chapter 13) show, international human rights became a persistent theme over their nine years in office. If its actions on human rights were not as effective as some have claimed, it is important to contrast the Conservative government's approach to that of its predecessor, both bilaterally and multilaterally.

Even though he had promised that a Conservative government would give allies like the United States and Britain the "benefit of the doubt," in fact Mulroney adopted a confrontational approach to those leading the campaign against sanctions – Margaret Thatcher and Ronald Reagan. At the 1985 Commonwealth Heads of Government meeting he joined forces with other leaders against Thatcher; at the Group of Seven (G-7) meeting he found himself pretty much alone. And at the United Nations, Mulroney's commitment to a policy of total sanctions if the South African government did not abandon apartheid evoked an emotional response from other leaders: one delegate told the Canadian ambassador that he never thought he would live to see the day that a Western white leader would stand up against apartheid as Mulroney had done.[34] Moreover, he must have been the only Western leader to express his view that he "understood" why the African National Congress embraced violence as a means to bring apartheid to an end.[35]

If the issue of apartheid were the only example of human rights activism and innovation, then it would be difficult to refer to a "human rights policy." However, one can point to other examples. One measure of the Conservative government's commitment to international human rights was its response to the Beijing massacre of June 1989. Clark took the lead in fashioning the Canadian response, delivering an angry denunciation that even Opposition MPs acknowledged was the harshest statement on human rights ever made by a Canadian government.[36] The Beijing massacre had a profound impact on Hong Kong, which was due to return to Chinese sovereignty in 1997; confidence in the territory sank, and large numbers of Hong Kong people sought to emigrate, with Canada as a prime destination. The events of 4 June 1989 catalyzed the Mulroney government, with the result that it began to pursue an explicit policy of confidence· building in the territory, including intensifying links and organizing an unprecedented five-day visit by Mulroney himself.[37]

By the fall of 1991, the government had explicitly embraced human rights and good governance as a "cornerstone of our foreign policy," as Mulroney put it in October.[38] Moreover, aid conditionality became part of its human rights promotion. Both Mulroney and his new secretary of state for external affairs, Barbara McDougall, who had been appointed to succeed Joe Clark in April 1991, enunciated a new policy that linked aid allocation to human rights and good governance. For his part, Mulroney took his human rights message to the Commonwealth summit in Harare in October and the francophone summit in Paris in November.

Yet another measure of the government's commitment to human rights was its response to the Dili massacre of 12 November 1991, when Indonesian security forces opened fire on mourners at a funeral in the capital of East Timor. As in the case of the Beijing massacre, the Mulroney government followed harsh denunciations of Indonesia with concrete sanctions.[39]

Rethinking State Sovereignty

The explicit embrace of good governance highlights another key change in foreign policy under the Mulroney government: a rethinking of that pillar of the Westphalian international system, the notion of national sovereignty. This is not surprising, for the promotion of good governance implies a willingness to embrace what Deon Geldenhuys has termed "political engagement"[40] – including outright intervention in the internal affairs of sovereign states.

The Canadian response to the outbreak of war in the Balkans illustrated an important new dimension of international relations: more and more conflicts were erupting within countries while wars between countries were declining. How should the international community react to such developments? How can countries intervene in such conflicts when sovereignty is at stake? As Tessier and Fortmann (Chapter 8) demonstrate, the stance taken by the Mulroney government moved Canada from a traditional peacekeeping role to more diverse interventions.

As early as November 1990, Mulroney was arguing for bending the rules of sovereignty in cases of humanitarian need. "The conventions of national sovereignty," he told a meeting of the Conference on Security and Cooperation in Europe, "are becoming too narrow a base from which to resolve the broadening global and regional problems."[41] A year later, he would reiterate his belief in humanitarian intervention: "Some Security Council members have opposed intervention in Yugoslavia, where many innocent people have been dying, on the grounds of national sovereignty. Quite frankly such invocation of the principles of national sovereignty are ... out of date."[42] This theme would continue to be pressed until the end of the Conservative era. In May 1993, McDougall was still arguing that "we have to reconsider the UN's traditional definition of state sovereignty.

I believe that states can no longer argue sovereignty as a licence for internal repression, when the absolutes of that sovereignty shield conflicts that could eventually become international in scope ... National sovereignty should offer no comfort to repressors, and no protection to those guilty of breaches of the common moral codes enshrined in the Universal Declaration of Human Rights."[43]

Canada had enunciated such a position when it joined the Organization of American States (OAS). As Gordon Mace suggests (Chapter 10), part of Canada's traditional reluctance towards joining the OAS was due to its difficulty in negotiating a position between Latin American countries and the United States. In attempting to clearly state its independence from both sides, Canada succeeded, as it had done with NATO, in having the OAS charter include some "Canadian principles." In this case, the principle was that "the protection of democracy" would be a primary Canadian objective.[44] Canada first evoked this type of provision when it wanted to justify intervention in the Haiti crisis.[45]

The Conservative government responded forcefully to what it saw as American infringements on Canadian sovereignty in the Arctic. As Rob Huebert shows in Chapter 6, when the US Coast Guard sent one of its icebreakers, the *Polar Sea*, through the Northwest Passage, the Mulroney government took a number of measures designed to assert Canadian "ownership" of the waters claimed by the United States government as an international strait. Huebert also demonstrates that Mulroney himself managed to take the dispute over Arctic sovereignty off the Canadian-American agenda.

Another manifestation of the changing approach to sovereignty may be found in the Foreign Extraterritorial Measures Act (FEMA). For years Canadian governments had grumbled about the willingness of the United States to extend its jurisdiction extraterritorially as a means of forcing its friends and allies to join with it in sanctioning "enemy" countries such as Cuba. Historically, Ottawa's response to the attempts of the American government to apply such legislation as the Trading with the Enemy Act to those outside the United States was an ad hoc protest to Washington to secure an exemption. The Conservative government was the first to try to turn the tables on Washington's extraterritorial practices by adopting legislation in 1985 that would make it illegal for anyone on Canadian soil – including Americans – to comply with American extraterritorial legislation.

But the Conservative government also embraced a concept of state sovereignty that represented a more fundamental change in traditional Canadian practice. For example, in 1991 the Mulroney government was the first Canadian government to endorse, openly and unambiguously, independence for Ukraine. Never before had a Canadian government encouraged the idea of the disintegration of a federal state. Indeed, so committed had Canadian governments been to the integrity of federal states that, during the Nigerian civil war, Trudeau had been moved to deny the very existence of the breakaway state of Biafra. And a succession of Canadian governments had spent decades denying the importunities of Canadians of Ukrainian origin, who wanted Canada to press for the independence of their homeland. But all this changed when, in the fall of 1991, Mulroney openly supported the move for Ukrainian independence, claiming that Canada would offer their country formal diplomatic recognition if Ukrainians voted to separate.[46]

The Policy-Making Process

While we can see some changes in specific policy issue areas, we can also see shifts in the way in which foreign policy was made during the Conservative era. While a detailed examination of the administration of Canadian external policy between 1984 and 1993 is beyond the scope of this volume, we focus on a number of key features of the policy-making process in this period. J.H. Taylor (Chapter 14), who was the under-secretary of state for external affairs (as the deputy minister of Canada's foreign ministry was known before 1993) between 1985 and 1989, offers a personal memoir on aspects of the foreign policy process during the Conservative period. It was during the Mulroney years that an unprecedented number of women were appointed to senior foreign policy posts, and Claire Turenne Sjolander (Chapter 15) assesses the broader impact of "adding women" to the policy process. Another development during this period was the rise of ethnic groups in the foreign policy process; in Chapter 16 Roy Norton examines how Canadians who had roots in different parts of the world sought to affect Canadian foreign policy towards their homelands. Nelson Michaud (Chapter 17) looks at bureaucratic politics during the Mulroney years, focusing in particular on the making – and unmaking – of the 1987 white paper on defence. And Kim Richard Nossal (Chapter 18) examines Conservative efforts to open up the foreign policy process, introducing new institutional arrangements for receiving, and aggregating, the views of ordinary Canadians on world affairs.

Conclusion

This brief survey of some of the major themes in Canadian foreign policy during the Mulroney era illustrates that there is little evidence to support the assumption, made by both Lawrence Martin and Marci McDonald, that the Conservative government of Brian Mulroney came to power in September 1984 with a clearly formulated foreign policy agenda. On the contrary, it is clear that Mulroney and his team had not given a great deal of thought to foreign policy before the elections; many of the foreign policy positions articulated by Mulroney in his year in Opposition were simplistic and undeveloped. Once in power, however, Mulroney ended up discarding most of those positions. Moreover, it is clear that many of the items that emerged on the Conservative foreign policy agenda between 1984 and 1993 – from the Ethiopian famine in October 1984 and the outbreak of violence in the South African townships in November 1984 to the collapse of the Soviet Union and the outbreak of civil war in Yugoslavia – could not even have been anticipated before the Conservatives came to office.

This overview also suggests that there were numerous changes in Canadian foreign policy during the Conservative era and that these deserve to be analyzed further. The chapters that follow explore a number of key foreign policy areas to determine if, in fact, we can conclude that, rather than simply being a predictable response to transformations in North American trade, Mulroney's foreign policy between 1984 and 1993 did indeed represent a diplomatic departure for Canada in world affairs.

Acknowledgment
We would like to thank Eric Bergbusch for exceedingly helpful comments on an initial draft of this chapter.

Notes
1   L. Ian MacDonald, *Brian Mulroney: The Making of the Prime Minister* (Toronto: McClelland and Stewart, 1984), 298.
2   On the foreign policy aspects of the 1911 elections, see Nelson Michaud, *L'énigme du Sphinx: Regards sur la vie politique d'un nationaliste, 1910-1926* (Québec: Presses de l'Université Laval, 1988), 20-21.
3   Lawrence Martin, *Pledge of Allegiance: The Americanization of Canada in the Mulroney Years* (Toronto: McClelland and Stewart, 1993); Marci McDonald, *Yankee Doodle Dandy: Brian Mulroney and the American Agenda* (Toronto: Stoddart, 1995).
4   McDonald, *Yankee Doodle Dandy*, xv.
5   Martin, *Pledge of Allegiance*, 158.
6   J.L. Granatstein called this "public display of sucking up to Reagan ... the single most demeaning moment in the entire political history of Canada's relations with the United States." See J.L. Granatstein, *Yankee Go Home? Canadians and Anti-Americanism* (Toronto: HarperCollins, 1996), 251.
7   Rae Murphy, Robert Chodos, and Nick Auf der Maur, *Brian Mulroney: The Boy from Baie-Comeau* (Toronto: James Lorimer, 1984), 212.
8   The best account of these tensions is Stephen Clarkson, *Canada and the Reagan Challenge: Crisis and Adjustment, 1981-85*, updated ed. (Toronto: James Lorimer, 1985).
9   Allan Gotlieb, *"I'll Be with You in a Minute, Mr Ambassador": The Education of a Canadian Diplomat in Washington* (Toronto: University of Toronto Press, 1991), 96.
10   Don Munton and Geoffrey Castle, "Reducing Acid Rain, 1980s," in *Canadian Foreign Policy: Selected Cases*, ed. Don Munton and John Kirton (Scarborough: Prentice Hall Canada, 1992), 367-81.
11   Adam Bromke and Kim Richard Nossal, "Tensions in Canada's Foreign Policy," *Foreign Affairs* 62 (Winter 1983-84): 335-53. On American views of Trudeau, see Christina McCall and Stephen Clarkson, *Trudeau and Our Times*, vol. 2: *The Heroic Delusion* (Toronto: McClelland and Stewart, 1994), 372-78. On the peace initiative, see J.L. Granatstein and Robert Bothwell, *Pirouette: Pierre Trudeau and Canadian Foreign Policy* (Toronto: University of Toronto Press, 1990), 363-76.
12   David Taras, "Brian Mulroney's Foreign Policy: Something for Everyone," *The Round Table* 293 (1985): 39.

13 Brian Mulroney, "Canada and the World," mimeo, 10 June 1983, 3-4.

14 Brian Mulroney, *Where I Stand* (Toronto: McClelland and Stewart, 1983), 97.

15 Quoted in Martin, *Pledge of Allegiance*, 44.

16 Quoted in John Herd Thompson and Stephen J. Randall, *Canada and the United States: Ambivalent Allies* (Montreal and Kingston: McGill-Queen's University Press, 1994), 286.

17 Brian Mulroney, "Canada and the World," mimeo, 10 June 1983, 2-3.

18 Canada, Parliament, House of Commons, *Debates*, 25 October 1983.

19 Quoted in Taras, "Mulroney's Foreign Policy," 40.

20 Other parallels between Diefenbaker and Mulroney were used by the Conservatives, as David Black's chapter demonstrates. See also Nelson Michaud, "Canadian Defence Policies: A Framework for Analysis," *British Journal of Canadian Studies* 13, 1 (1998): 112-13.

21 Notably when George Mitchell of Maine, a strong advocate of acid rain controls, became Senate majority leader, replacing Robert Byrd, of the coal-producing state of West Virginia, and when an air-quality agreement was signed with Mexico, which altered opinions in the House of Representatives. See the discussion in Munton and Castle, "Reducing Acid Rain," 376-77.

22 The definitive account is G. Bruce Doern and Brian W. Tomlin, *Faith and Fear: The Free Trade Story* (Toronto: Stoddart, 1991). For insider accounts, see Michael Hart, Bill Dymond, and Colin Robertson, *Decision at Midnight: Inside the Canada-US Free Trade Negotiations* (Vancouver: UBC Press, 1994); Gordon Ritchie, *Wrestling with the Elephant: The Inside Story of the Canada-US Trade Wars* (Toronto: Macfarlane, Walter and Ross, 1997).

23 Michael Tucker, "Canadian Security Policy," in *Canada Among Nations, 1985: The Conservative Agenda*, ed. Maureen Appel Molot and Brian W. Tomlin (Toronto: James Lorimer, 1986).

24 *Ottawa Citizen*, 25 September 1984.

25 Kim Richard Nossal, "Succumbing to the Dumbbell: Canadian Perspectives on NATO in the 1990s," in Barbara McDougall, Kim Richard Nossal, Alex Morrison, and Joseph T. Jockel, *Canada and NATO: The Forgotten Ally?* (Cambridge, MA: Institute for Foreign Policy Analysis, 1992), 17-32; Paul Buteux, "NATO and the Evolution of Canadian Defence and Foreign Policy," in *Canada's International Security Policy*, ed. David Dewitt and David Leyton-Brown (Scarborough: Prentice Hall Canada, 1995), 153-70.

26 Roy Rempel, *Counterweights: The Failure of Canada's German and European Policy, 1955-1995* (Montreal and Kingston: McGill-Queen's University Press, 1996).

27 The best account of the Ethiopian crisis is David R. Morrison, *Aid and Ebb Tide: A History of CIDA and Canadian Development Assistance* (Waterloo, ON: Wilfrid Laurier University Press, 1998), 234-35.

28 Cranford Pratt, "Humane Internationalism and Canadian Development Assistance Policies," in *Canadian International Development Assistance Policies: An Appraisal*, ed. C. Pratt (Montreal and Kingston: McGill-Queen's University Press, 1994).

29 David R. Morrison, "Evaluating Development Assistance, 1987," in *Canadian Foreign Policy: Selected Cases*, ed. Don Munton and John Kirton (Scarborough: Prentice Hall Canada, 1992), 360.

30 Kim Richard Nossal, "Quantum Leaping: the Gulf Debate in Australia and Canada," in *The Gulf War: Critical Perspectives*, ed. Michael McKinley (Sydney: Allen and Unwin, 1994), 48-71; Martin Rudner, "Canada, the Gulf Crisis and Collective Security," in *Canada Among Nations, 1990-91: After the Cold War*, ed. Fen Osler Hampson and Christopher J. Maule (Ottawa: Carleton University Press, 1991); Harald von Riekhoff, "Canada and Collective Security," in *Canada's International Security Policy*, ed. David B. Dewitt and David Leyton-Brown (Scarborough: Prentice Hall Canada, 1995), 240-46.

31 Kim Richard Nossal, *The Politics of Canadian Foreign Policy*, 3rd ed. (Scarborough: Prentice Hall Canada, 1997), 183.

32 David Bercuson, *Significant Incident: Canada's Army, the Airborne, and the Murder in Somalia* (Toronto: McClelland and Stewart, 1996).

33 Andrew F. Cooper, Richard A. Higgott, and Kim Richard Nossal, *Relocating Middle Powers: Australia and Canada in a Changing World Order* (Vancouver: UBC Press, 1993), 154-56.

34 Linda Freeman, *The Ambiguous Champion: Canada and South Africa in the Trudeau and Mulroney Years* (Toronto: University of Toronto Press, 1997), 4.

35   *Globe and Mail*, 31 January 1987; Kim Richard Nossal, *Rain Dancing: Sanctions in Canadian and Australian Foreign Policy* (Toronto: University of Toronto Press, 1994), 96.

36   Nossal, *Rain Dancing*, 172-73; Jeremy Paltiel, "Rude Awakening: Canada and China following Tiananmen," in *Canada Among Nations, 1989: The Challenge of Change*, ed. Maureen Appel Molot and Fen Osler Hampson (Ottawa: Carleton University Press, 1989), 43-58.

37   On Mulroney's Hong Kong policy, see Kim Richard Nossal, "Playing the International Card? The View from Australia, Canada, and the United States," in *Hong Kong's Reunion with China: The Global Dimensions*, ed. Gerard A. Postiglione and James T.H. Tang (Armonk, NY: M.E. Sharpe, 1997), 79-101.

38   *Globe and Mail*, 17 October 1991.

39   Nossal, *Rain Dancing*, 50-51.

40   Deon Geldenhuys, *Foreign Political Engagement: Remaking States in the Post-Cold War World* (London: Macmillan, 1998).

41   Cited in Leonard J. Cohen and Alexander Moens, "Learning the Lessons of UNPROFOR: Peacekeeping in the Former Yugoslavia," *Canadian Foreign Policy* 6 (Winter 1999): 87.

42   Ibid., 86.

43   Cited in Tom Keating and Nicholas Gammer, "The 'New Look' in Canada's Foreign Policy," *International Journal* 48 (Autumn 1993): 727.

44   Canada, Department of External Affairs and International Trade, Press Release 191, 5 October 1993.

45   Nelson Michaud and Louis Bélanger, "La stratégie institutionnelle du Canada: vers une australisation?" *Études internationales* 30, 2 (juin 1999): 383-87.

46   Kim Richard Nossal, "The Politics of Circumspection: Canadian Policy towards the Soviet Union, 1985-1991," *International Journal of Canadian Studies* 9 (Spring 1994): 27-45.

2

Architects or Engineers?
The Conservatives and Foreign Policy

Denis Stairs

The conduct of public policy, foreign policy included, is potentially subject to dramatic change whenever a new government, with a different skipper at the helm and a different political party in the engine room, takes command of the ship of state. Or so we commonly assume. And the assumption is not unreasonable. It lies, after all, at the root of the electoral process and the party system. Each party links itself to values, interests, and orientations that it portrays as distinctive. These, in turn, are thought to have policy significance. This is because they bind the party's members to a pattern of preferences that differentiates them from their adversaries. The net result (in theory, at least) is that the electorate, in deciding who will govern, is presented with meaningful alternatives from which to choose.

In a highly pluralistic political environment, of course, and particularly where a first-past-the-post electoral system prevails, rival parties may have to sacrifice some of the clarity of their respective policy positions in order to attract the support of as large a gathering of diversified interests as possible. Even, however, where the pragmatic search for broadly based electoral approval leads to vacuous political rhetoric and obscures formal policy differences, the presence in the electoral race of competing leadership teams is enough to imply that change will ensue if power is transferred. This is because "idiosyncratic variables" – the quaint appellation that political scientists assign to factors of personality, competence, and character – are also thought to count. They can affect priorities, for example, and hence determine which things are done at all and which are not, which are done first and which are done last, which with enthusiasm and which with reluctance, and so on. They can also affect the *style* of government; that is, the *way* things are done, and the tactical repertoires that leaders deploy in the pursuit of their objectives. Since different styles can have different effects, the style and the substance – the *praxis* and the policy – come to be interrelated. *What* is done depends on *how* it is done. Operational codes matter.

To assume that a change of government will produce a transformation of policy is not to assume that *everything* will be transformed but only that *some* things will. Often, although not always, these are the things that have been kicked up by the political process itself – by the interplay of those who compete with one another for public office and the power that goes with it on the one hand, and the electors who must make the choice and live with the consequences on the other. But whatever the specifics, if no substantial change of policy ever ensued from a change of political leadership, it would not be unreasonable to conclude that the entire game was a sham. It might be significant as a mechanism for determining which names among the already-privileged will dominate the daily news and the daily chatter, which of them will be cited in the history books, and which of them will enjoy a short burst of additional consumption at the public trough. But it would not be significant for anything else. This is part, in fact, of what the Marxists and their offshoots normally *do* conclude. But for those with less radical dispositions, and certainly for those who are inclined to think, in matters of governance, that a little change is a lot, the transfer of power from one party to another is an important event. They expect it to make a difference.

All this seems obvious and sensible enough, and it underlies the way in which politicians argue, journalists report, and citizens debate as they engage with one another on the accessible surfaces of the political process.

On the other hand, in foreign policy particularly (although in other areas, too), *all* governments must deal with what are sometimes called "realities" – conditions at home and abroad that simply cannot be ignored. This may be more true for some powers than for others. We usually assume, for example, that it is more true for the smaller powers than for the greater ones – although that, too, oversimplifies, since the available "freedom of manoeuvre" varies with the issue and the context, and is itself a function of more variables than one. But these qualifying angels, devoted to the fine-tuning of essentially obvious "theory," can happily be left to dance on the head of someone else's pin. For in the present context the essential point is a simple one: What governments do in foreign policy is a function not only of how they think and what they prefer, but also of the conditions they face. That being so, we are often treated (perhaps more often than we like to admit) to similar strokes from different folks.

These observations lead me to the central puzzle that this book seeks to resolve: To what extent was the conduct of Canada's foreign policy in the period of Conservative government from 1984 to 1993 a reflection of the political orientation of the Progressive Conservative party and the predilections of its leaders, and to what extent was it a product of insistent imperatives arising from circumstances – some of them changing and some not – at home and abroad? In what measure, in other words, were the Conservatives in office the "architects" of their foreign policies, creat-ing them (as it were) afresh, and in what measure their "engineers," installing bridges of standard design over rivers that almost anyone in power would have had to cross?

This apparently straightforward puzzle is, however, not so easy to resolve. As we all know very well, we cannot run the same game again under the same conditions but with a different government in place. If we could, we would then be able to inspect the results to determine which of the policy outputs were the same, and which were different, when com-pared with those of the previous round. But this procedure, which lies at the core of experimental science, is impossible here.

The methodological problem is further complicated by the fact that so many of the elements that impinge on foreign policy behaviour are increasingly in motion. Even the ones that are potential sources of behavioural continuity – the things we normally take as "constants," and therefore bury in our *ceteris paribus* assumptions – have been subject to dramatic transformation in the contemporary period. We cannot now rely on geography, for example, to set the same parameters as before (although it certainly sets many of them), if only because technology has put so much of the power of "distance" into decline. Nothing holds still; everything moves.

In addition, we confront here, as elsewhere, the perennial problems associated with descriptive evidence and qualitative analysis. Not all the indicators are in, and we may not agree on how much weight we should give to the ones that are. There may be disputes, as well, about the way in which we categorize events and assign attributes to behaviours. One observer's manifestation of dramatic change is thus another's "more of the same."

In the end, there is no escaping the misery that these complications and others like them create: the "bottom line" is a judgment call, and the judg-ments are always open to dispute. Postmodernists would not have been alone, therefore, in predicting (as they surely would have done had they been asked) that this book would leave the basic issue unresolved. That would have been true even if, in the end, all the authors had appeared to agree, for there would still be room for another cut, another argument, another run at the target. This is not to assert that *any* "cut" will do. Certainly it is not to claim, as some would have it, that all "cuts" are rela-tive, amounting to nothing more than fanciful "constructions" of an inac-cessible reality in the service of power, position, interest, and identity. Evidence, I am determined to insist, is relevant to thought. So are the con-ventions that govern the use of it. But that hardly means that alternative interpretations of what we observe are impossible to devise or that they cannot be given a credible defence. It means only that such alternatives, to be viable, must be grounded not in prejudice and politics alone but in acceptable intellectual procedures.

With these methodological caveats thus firmly declared – unnecessary reminders, one may think, of perils already known well enough – I will risk my own run at the target, keeping in mind that the chapters that follow, all of them by authors far more expert than myself, are where the action really lies and where the interesting answers will be found. I will begin by offering some highly selective and overly generalized observations on, first, the government's management of Canada's relationship with the United States; second, its response to the international security environment at large; third, its reaction to a selection of what I will call, for want of a better term, "residual issues"; and fourth, its handling of certain features of the domestic politics of the policy process. In all this, I will try to leave the explicit "value judgments" to others – although I am sure that *im*plicit ones may be found all over the place. And finally, there being little pattern and less doctrine in what I will unveil, I will conclude without conclusion (or without a satisfying one, at least), finding refuge instead in the thought that imponderables are inevitable, that inconsistencies are as likely to be evident in the behaviours of a single government as are continuities from one government to the next, and that John W. Holmes was right to make so much in his work of the prevalence of paradox in the conduct of foreign affairs.[1]

The American Connection

One of the interesting characteristics of the extant literature on the foreign policy of the Conservative era is how little it focuses on the government's overall foreign policy orientations. Analysts have been hard put to identify in either its behaviour or its rhetoric an underlying set of premises, much less a doctrine, or "vision," of Canada's general role in world affairs. Certainly they have not been successful in identifying a *distinctive* vision – one, that is, that would distinguish the Conservative view from those of their adversaries or even from the ones inherent in the eclectic expectations of the attentive population at large. It is possible, of course, that this is partly due to the fact that few independent observers have seriously tried to do the job. Most of the pertinent literature on the Conservative period has focused on particular issues or issue areas – the negotiation of the Canada-US Free Trade Agreement and the North American Free Trade Agreement (NAFTA), the response to the problem of Apartheid, the attempt to formulate a defence policy under rapidly changing conditions of international security, the reaction to transnational environmental issues, the involvement in Central America, and so on. That this is so may actually be a reflection of certain underlying systemic trends, not least among them being the fact that the broadening – and the domesticating

– of the "foreign policy" agenda has fragmented the academic peanut gallery in much the same way as it has fragmented the official policy community itself. Everyone likes to specialize; no one wants to generalize.

Having said that, it must be recognized also that the official pronouncements of the period did make frequent reference to the attitudes and preferences of the Canadian community as a whole. Deeply embedded ingredients of the Canadian political culture – the persistently prevalent humanisms of the United Church not least among them – were commonly invoked. But these invocations of our higher morality were not attributed, even by Conservatives, to the Conservative party alone (which was just as well, given that spokespersons for other parties constantly invoked them, too). They were ascribed, rather, to the Canadian population at large and to the civilized values that were thought to distinguish the Canadian consensus. It is therefore possible to argue that the principles at issue were not so much a component of the Conservative party platform as an ongoing feature of the national woodwork and, hence, that they served more as a contextual source of continuity than as a uniquely Conservative contribution to the foreign policy process.

To all this, however, there was from the beginning at least one obvious and frequently discussed exception. It had to do with the relationship with the United States, particularly as it bore on the health of the Canadian economy. Early in 1985, David Pollock and Grant Manuge published an article entitled "The Mulroney Doctrine" (joyously subtitled "Business and US Made Respectable"). The "seeds" of that doctrine, they wrote, were "two economic policies ... closer Canada-US economic ties, and greater reliance on foreign investment and the private sector generally."[2] As many others were similarly wont to do, the authors expressed concern that the pursuit of such priorities would lead on the one hand to a continental economic integration that would be inimical to Canada's independence in foreign affairs and, on the other, to a failure to respond appropriately to the real needs of developing countries.

This identification of the prime minister and his government with a market-oriented multinational enterprise (MNE) view of modernity was to be a persistent and central feature of the perceptions of his supporters and critics alike throughout his time in office. The former approved; the latter did not. Either way, the interpretation seemed to be reinforced by circumstantial evidence drawn from Mulroney's personal career with the Iron Ore Company of Canada, a corporation whose basic purpose, typically enough, was to make money by extracting raw materials from the Canadian North and selling them to industrial enterprises south of the border. The assessment was encouraged, as well, by the prime minister's own insistence from the very beginning that one of his leading priorities in foreign affairs was to repair the damage to the Canada-US relationship that had been wrought by his Liberal predecessor. In fulfilment of his commitment, he made a surprisingly ostentatious display of his personal friendship with Ronald Reagan – a display that had to be admired more for its honesty and transparency than for the attention it paid to the require- ments of a contented politics at home.

These perceptions of the government's position were ultimately con- firmed, or so it seemed, by the speed with which it undertook to demolish the remnants of the National Energy Program and by the enthusiasm with which it converted that tentative "keeper of the gate," the Foreign Invest- ment Review Agency, into Investment Canada, an operation whose pur- pose was to attract as much foreign capital to the Canadian economy as it possibly could. The decision soon after to initiate the negotiation of a Canada-US free trade agreement (FTA) seemed, in the end, to say it all.

We hardly need to remind ourselves, perhaps, that this was to say a very great deal. The FTA reversed a long-standing verity of Canadian politics. It was the antithesis of the modern historical traditions of the Conservative party itself. Certainly it was the antithesis of the posture of Conservatives in the Diefenbaker era, some twenty-five years before. Moreover, whether best regarded as a leap of faith or a leap in the dark, it carried enormous long-term risks – economically, culturally, politically, and, from the nation- building point of view, psychologically. In electoral terms, given the state of popular public opinion at the time, it was a gamble, and it was nearly lost. Furthermore, its implications were unlikely to be short-lived. Once the agreement was in place, it was hard to conceive of it ever being reversed, although it was certainly open to being submerged within even larger trading environments. This last was a reality that sophisticated observers recognized from the very beginning, and one that the Liberal party itself – notwithstanding its public promise to turn the clock back, or at least to negotiate dramatic revisions – would shortly have to accommodate.

Given the significance of the stakes, and the momentous implications of the decision to proceed, it might be asserted that here, at least, doctrine was at work and autonomous leadership in play. The only serious impera- tives in Canadian foreign policy derive from the relationship with the United States, and these were now being tackled in near-revolutionary style, from first principles, head on. The rest of the government's per- formances abroad might be interesting, but this was action at the essential core, and, for good or ill (or so it might seem reasonable to assume), it was ideologically driven.

Alas, however, for those who seek to find here a true politics of ideas, the evidence is far too ambiguous to allow for so comforting a conclusion. That the prime minister did everything possible, and with considerable success, to cultivate an amicable personal relationship with President

Ronald Reagan is an incontrovertible fact. But the Foreign Investment Review Agency had been a weak tiger from the start, and it had become a paper tiger by the end of the Liberal regime. Moreover, it can be argued that the dismantling of the National Energy Program had actually begun before the Conservatives came into office, the process having been manifested in a series of small steps that, for political and economic reasons alike, had been forced on their Liberal predecessors almost from the beginning. The Conservatives simply administered a merciful, but enthusiastic, coup de grâce.[3]

And, as Brian W. Tomlin makes clear in Chapter 3, the biggest decision – the decision to opt for Canada-US free trade – was taken only after the winds of economic change had been carefully gauged. By 1985, a bilateral free trade arrangement had been advocated on a number of occasions by the Economic Council of Canada. It had been supported as well by the Senate Committee on Foreign Affairs. It was one of the central recommendations of the Macdonald Commission; indeed, it was the only recommendation that seemed to get serious notice. The commission's findings, moreover, reflected representations that were overwhelmingly supportive of free trade from influential quarters in every part of the country. The free trade option was ultimately endorsed (although not, in every case, with the same degree of enthusiasm) by nine of the ten provinces, and even the hold-out government of Ontario, whose reservations reflected its heavy dependence on American branch plants, was clearly discomfited by cross-pressures. The Canadian Manufacturers' Association, long dedicated to the service of protectionism, discovered, much to its own surprise, that the majority of its members had had a change of heart, and it, too, climbed on the bandwagon. So did the Business Council on National Issues and the Canadian Federation of Independent Business, along with the mainstream think tanks and the orthodox core of the economics profession. The federal bureaucracy (or the parts of it, at least, that mattered) had come largely – although by no means unanimously – to the free trade position. External Affairs had advocated sectoral free trade, if not free trade across the board, even before the Trudeau government had departed from office, and the key players in the determination of foreign economic policy were now happy to take the process one step further. Not *all* of the ducks, perhaps, but certainly most of the influential ones were lined up dutifully in a row, paddling downstream at full speed.[4] In such circumstances, it is always difficult to know who is driving what. The pragmatist likes to put a wet finger to the wind. Would the same course have been selected had the breeze been blowing the other way? Perhaps. But it may be useful here to recall the testimony of John Crosbie. "I don't know," he reports, when Mulroney came to embrace free trade, but his support for the concept was revealed at his so-called Shamrock Summit ... We'd been in office for six months by then, and there had been no discussion in cabinet or in the Conservative caucus about pursuing a free-trade deal with the Americans. As far as any of us knew, Mulroney was still opposed to free trade, as he was during the 1983 Tory leadership campaign. But the [Macdonald Commission] embraced the notion of free trade, and I think probably helped to change Mulroney's thinking.[5]

It may be useful, moreover, to keep in mind the fact that the ultimate source of the pressure lay south of the border and was concentrated in the intensifying protectionism of the American Congress. Canada needed a large market. The "Third Option" strategy of market diversification overseas had failed to produce a viable alternative elsewhere in the world.[6] The United States was thus the only game in town. In the circumstances, security of admission was thought to be essential. To what extent the bilateral initiative that ensued was a product of architecture, and to what extent of engineering, thus remains moot, notwithstanding the unseemly displays of vanity to which we have all recently been exposed by rival claimants, among the Canadian negotiators, for places in the sun.[7] In public affairs, the delusion of agency – the sense of having been "the architect" – is often the biggest price we pay for showing up. The currency is loss of detachment.

Uncertainty in all these matters is cultivated further by the recognition that Ottawa and Washington did not routinely bay in unison on other issues. Perhaps this was because the other issues did not matter very much, and those who subscribe to the view that the real action is *always* the economic action may be drawn to precisely this conclusion. Still, there were significant areas of Canada-US policy disagreement. South Africa was one. Arctic sovereignty was another. Human rights was a third. Acid rain was a fourth. United Nations financing was a fifth. On some dimensions, disarmament was a sixth. Cuba – although perhaps not so insistently as in the Trudeau era – was a seventh.[8] Nicaragua was an eighth.[9] And so on. The degree of continental amiability thus varied with the issue and the circumstances – a phenomenon that was further encouraged by the fact that Washington is not a monolith, and getting along with American presidents is no guarantee of getting along with Congress. Foreign policy is not a single thing. Certainly the Canadian-American relationship is not a single thing. In the face of such diversity – in the presence, inescapably, of what the Canadian scholar-diplomat John W. Holmes used to call "considerations on the one hand and considerations on the other"[10] – the most carefully crafted of general orientations often break down, and reactive adaptations have to be entertained. In this case, the neoliberal economic aspiration did not always apply. Certainly it did not always dominate. To the extent that it was really in play, therefore, it was selectively invoked and pragmatically deployed.

Security

All other things being equal, a somewhat greater display of continuity might be expected in the specialized field of security (where "security" is narrowly defined as defence against external military menace) than in the wide-ranging domain of Canadian-American relations as a whole. If there is a case, after all, for realist compulsions, then it must surely be here. Threats, though disputable, are threats; capabilities, though uncertain, are capabilities; geography, though variably salient, is geography. Taken together, these normally play an important parameter-setting role in calculating what needs to be done. In effect, they narrowly confine the options.

In the Canadian case, however, it can be argued that such causal factors are less influential, if only because the most vital of Canadian security requirements are not ultimately met by Canada alone or even by Canada predominantly; rather, they are guaranteed by the United States and, at a greater distance, by multilateral security arrangements to which Canada makes no more than a marginal, not to say incidental, contribution. In these circumstances, what Canada actually does is a function more of political judgment, and of diplomatic bargaining over the sharing of burdens, than of military necessity.

Within this context, and consistently with their desire to maintain a close working relationship with the United States, the Conservatives arrived at their starting gate with the judgment that the Liberals had been doing much too little, much too late. In a world in which the Soviet Union and its allies were still thought to be a problem, the advantage of Canada's continued participation in the North Atlantic Treaty Organization (NATO) and the North American Aerospace Defence Command (NORAD), as well as in United Nations peacekeeping operations, was taken to be self-evident. The problem was that the Liberals had run down the substantive contributions, and a commitment-capability gap had ensued. Ambitious escalations in defence spending were therefore envisaged, and the security bureaucracy, its appetite whetted by visions of opportunity, moved with brisk enthusiasm to take full advantage of the opening before it. In 1987, through a process detailed by Nelson Michaud in Chapter 17, there issued from the Department of National Defence a white paper, *Challenge and Commitment: A Defence Policy for Canada* – the first such document to appear since 1971.[11] Endorsed by the prime minister as well as by the minister of national defence, it was replete with reminders of the continuation of Soviet menace, and it identified an impressive list of expensive procurements in the offing (nuclear-powered submarines most controversially among them).

Here, too, one might be inclined to conclude that a distinctively Conservative position was at work. Certainly the rhetoric of the white paper, and indeed of the prime minister himself, had moved a long way from the sceptical assessment of Cold War attitudes that had earlier been typical of Pierre Trudeau and his closest foreign policy advisers. The belief that the Cold War itself was a mindlessly futile, wasteful, and dangerous exercise had been at the root of the ill-fated "peace initiative" of Trudeau's final months in office – an attempt, as it were, to contain the influence of pride, passion, and prejudice with help from the voice of reason. For the Conservatives, however, the USSR was still a dark and menacing force. In its presence, the maintenance of stability required not accommodation alone – and certainly not what the prime minister described as "idle dreams" – but accommodation from strength. This demanded in turn a firm and demonstrable commitment to "cooperation with our allies," with whom Canada had a "common history," "shared interests," and a "community of values."[12] Here was reflected a muscular conception of how to deal with international security affairs, a conception governed by the sense that by no means all of humanity, and least of all a humanity in hot pursuit of the hard-nosed rivalries of world affairs, can be trusted to respond in constructive fashion to sweetness and light. That being so, the powder had to be kept dry. It needed also to be made available in plenty.

To repeat, the white paper could be interpreted partly as an attempt by the Department of National Defence to take advantage of the opportunity to promote its procurement ambitions while the buying looked good. But the buying looked good because of the signals that seemed to be coming from the political leadership, and the leadership displayed no initial objection to the grand ambitions to which its own analysis had given rise.

Yet, in the end, the defence white paper died on the order book. This may have been in marginal degree due to the cries of righteous dismay that the paper elicited from vocal members of the peace community and others. The quietly expressed opposition of the American naval establishment to the proposal that Canada acquire nuclear-powered submarines conceivably played a minor role as well – although the rest of the shopping list went down in Washington well enough. But the underlying sources of the government's retreat appear to have been the collapse of the Cold War itself on the one hand and the deepening fiscal crisis in Ottawa on the other. A Conservative might have been expected to hold that a well-armed Canada was both a prudent Canada and a Canada to be respected and reckoned with abroad. But when the pretext (in the guise of the Cold War) became less visible, financial exigencies took over, and the Conservatives in practice moved pretty much in the same direction as their predecessors.

Circumstances won; doctrinal preferences lost. In February 1992 the government decided even to withdraw the last remnants of Canada's on-site military contingents in Europe – thereby completing a process that the Trudeau government had first set in train almost twenty-three years before.[13]

Residuals – or Other Issues
Interestingly, the convergence of the present with the past that was so evident in the defence field was matched by a convergence of the present with the future in other areas. Again, the underlying causes appeared to be rooted more within the international and domestic environments than within the government itself, although here, as elsewhere, the argument can easily be over-stated.

Perhaps the most obvious manifestation of this phenomenon was the government's powerful advocacy of measures in support of human rights abroad (most obviously, but by no means uniquely, in the context of South Africa). This was an advocacy to which the prime minister himself appears to have been genuinely committed.[14] By the end of the Conservatives' time in office, moreover, the commitment – which was certainly consistent with neoliberal values – was being linked to other closely related objectives abroad, including democratization. In the winter of 1992-93, Barbara McDougall, then the secretary of state for external affairs, contributed the lead article for the first issue of the new journal, *Canadian Foreign Policy*.[15] She devoted her discussion to what she described as the "new internationalism." In large measure, no doubt, her preoccupations reflected the growing disillusionment everywhere with the unhappy developments that had so quickly followed the breakdown of the Cold War. There had been a brief display of classical collective security at work in response to the Iraqi invasion of Kuwait, but in general the post-Cold War environment had failed to sustain the rule-oriented optimism with which the new international era had begun. In a surprising number of cases, nation-states were failing, and the conditions in the state of nature to which their inhabitants were then exposed were shown to be very much as Thomas Hobbes had conceived them to be some three and a half centuries before. In too many cases, even where the formal apparatus of government had managed to survive, it seemed to be doing so only by barbarous methods. Ethnic wars, religious wars, nationalist wars – wars, in short, of identity – were breaking out everywhere, and the miseries they generated were broadcast as spectacles for all to see in the comfort of their living rooms every night. Humanists the world over – liberal democrats not least among them – were offended. The agents of globalization, moreover, could see in such phenomena a potential threat to their ambitions. There was thus an increasingly persuasive argument to be made, in extremis, for over-riding local authorities – that is, national governments – in the interest of humanity as a whole. The argument was evident in what McDougall had to say.

In the present context, however, what is particularly intriguing about the observations in her article, as well as in many of her speeches,[16] is the extent to which they presaged the so-called "human security" agenda that was associated with the Liberal government of Jean Chrétien and, in particular with the minister of foreign affairs from 1996 to 2000, Lloyd Axworthy.[17] McDougall's analytical language, together with her policy aspirations, were more cautious, perhaps, and certainly they were less given to eighteenth-century Enlightenment optimism, than were Axworthy's, and there were "downside" warnings in what she had to say. There was a need, for example, to "acknowledge that the sheer rapidity of recent change [had] triggered hostile reactions," and this argued "for prudence before we rush headlong into new policy areas, as well as time for adjustment as new thinking about the linkages between foreign and domestic policies takes hold." If Canadians, moreover, "put other nations under surveillance for the respect they accord human rights and civil liberties," they would have to open their "own country to examination." In any case, the task of engineering remedial political changes in the targeted societies would be far from easy:

> The Yugoslavias and Somalias of this world are daunting challenges. They represent seemingly intractable problems. Ideas put forward to help inevitably fail. The solutions, when and if they come, are as likely to arise from the exhaustion of belligerents as from any shared desire to confront the illogic of civil war in an inter-dependent world. But the difficulty of the problems is no excuse to halt the search for new solutions.[18]

In the face of this sort of analysis, it is hard to avoid the conclusion that McDougall and Axworthy, during their respective periods in office, were responding to a changing international environment in relatively similar fashion. They did so, moreover, within a framework that was established for both of them by certain continuities in the Canadian political culture – continuities to which we now refer in the somewhat tiresome vocabulary of the self-righteous as "Canadian values."[19] The *style* of the enterprise was certainly very different in the two cases, and clearly McDougall was somewhat more dubious than Axworthy about the long-run impact of short-run initiatives. Such hesitations are quite commonly associated with the conservative view of how history works (although they can certainly be associated with other things as well). But the differences in the end seem more tactical than strategic, and they bear mainly on technique. The underlying policy adjustments involved in both cases, therefore, may be usefully interpreted as a "work in progress" – a work that was begun in response to dramatically changing international conditions during the Conservative era and that continues to this day.

All this went in tandem, it hardly needs to be said, with a continuing Canadian commitment to peacekeeping and with the more ambitiously interventionist "second generation" versions of the genre that began to materialize, with escalating frequency, in the post-Cold War period (as in the Balkans and Somalia) explored in more detail by Manon Tessier and Michel Fortmann in Chapter 8. Support for the United Nations remained a central feature of the legitimizing rhetoric of Canadian foreign policy, and Ottawa's advocacies in the cause of UN reform, particularly in relation to the Security Council, echoed the past, just as they are themselves now echoed in the present.[20] The long-standing development assistance target of 0.7 percent of GNP was reaffirmed, even if the time frame had a long-term look that got longer still as time wore on, and even if the guidelines that were supposed to govern the implementation displayed a slightly more commercial flavour under the Conservatives than they had done before. Consistent, moreover, with the performance of governments both before and since, the target was never reached.

The purpose of this recitation is not to argue that no change occurred, or that Conservative ministers, as individuals and as a government, had no impact on policy. This would put the case too starkly by far. It is, however, to suggest that the parameters within which they worked, like the ones that governed the behaviour of those who both preceded and followed them, were relatively narrow, the range of viable choice being much confined by conditions abroad and expectations at home. There was thus more engineering than architecture in the eventual result.

The Policy-Making Process

Given the generality of my purview, this is not the place to ruminate at length on the intricate complexities of the policy-making process and its politics. Many analysts would want to argue, however, that insufficient attention has been paid in what I have said to the power of bureaucracy and the influence of officials. These, their critics sometimes suggest, are the leading conveyors of the dead hand of inertia. By contrast, those who are more charitably inclined tend to portray them as the careful custodians of the "tried-and-true" in the conduct of Canadian policy. A few may even think of them as consistently reliable and authoritative sources of wisely tempered invention and advice. Whatever the case may be, the foreign service professionals are certainly forces in the balance, and their bias tends more to what has worked well before than to high-risk radical departures – a tendency reinforced by their need to satisfy a broad array of sometimes competing players in the bureaucratic game.

But this is a circumstance that *any* government must face, and with which it must make its own accommodation. In the present context, therefore, the feature of the policy process that may be more interesting is the extent to which the Conservatives found it useful to expand the available opportunities for public consultation in the process of developing and legitimizing their policies. To some extent, this reflected the recognition that the boundaries between foreign policy and domestic policy were no longer tightly drawn and that foreign policy, both inside government and out, had become almost everybody's business. In any case, the consultative effort – most of it, but not all of it, conducted through the parliamentary system – was surprisingly extensive, especially in the early years. With a view to stimulating widespread public discussion, a green paper entitled *Competitiveness and Security: Directions for Canada's International Relations* was released in May 1985.[21] A special joint committee of the Senate and House of Commons was established in the following month to review Canada's international relations, and it reported in June 1986 by way of a lengthy document entitled *Independence and Internationalism* (the so-called Hockin-Simard Report).[22] The list of individuals and organized groups from which it received written submissions occupied an appendix of some twenty-seven pages. Six months later, the government produced an eighty-nine-page (English version) formal response.[23] Following proceedings that again involved testimony from a wide array of witnesses drawn from the Canadian Forces (CF), the business sector, non-government organizations (NGOs), the academic community, and others, the Standing Committee on External Affairs and National Defence in February 1986 produced an eighty-one-page report on the renewal of the NORAD Agreement.[24] In May 1987 essentially the same committee generated a similarly detailed report on development assistance under the title *For Whose Benefit?* (the Winegard Report).[25] *Challenge and Commitment*, the ill-fated white paper on defence, was issued in the following month. During the free trade negotiations, elaborate mechanisms were constructed for consultations with the business community on a sector-by-sector basis – an arrangement that persists to this day. Similar procedures were put in place then, as they still are now, for annual encounters of officials with NGOs and others in preparation for the meetings each year of the United Nations Commission for Human Rights. Douglas Roche, Canada's ambassador for disarmament during this period, attempted to advance his agenda with the help of a consultative committee in the field of arms control and disarmament. Environmental groups, too, were increasingly provided with opportunities to have their say. And so on.

By the standards of traditional statecraft, these were highly innovative undertakings. But close examination shows yet again that the initiatives involved were simply part of a longer-term trajectory. The practice of consulting with attentive publics on foreign policy issues had actually begun in a modest way with the Trudeau government in the late 1960s. The intrusions of NGOs even more directly into the processes of Canadian diplomacy were becoming very evident as early as 1972, at the time of the Stockholm Conference on the Environment. Since the departure of the Conservatives from office, moreover, comprehensive reviews of defence and foreign policy have been held once again, and the consultative process has since become even more elaborately institutionalized. While the details have varied to some extent with the government, therefore, and even with the minister, in the final analysis it is hard to avoid the conclusion that the drivers of the consultation phenomenon are ultimately independent of party. They are rooted instead in exogenous factors – the broadening scope of the international agenda, the burgeoning impact of electronic communications, the emergence of a transnational politics of the NGO left to complement that of the MNE right, the development within Canada itself of an increasingly "participatory" democratic culture, and so on. Such forces are systemically interlocked. In the face of them, it seems, Canadian governments of *any* political complexion find it prudent to share their space.

Conclusion

The more specialized research chapters in this volume may seem to some to have the effect of doing my argument in, or at least of bringing it into better balance. Ministers of the Crown, after all, are not merely mechanical robots, responding, as if by rote, to automated sensors. But in the end it is difficult to quarrel with the conclusion of Brian W. Tomlin and Maureen Appel Molot. As they observed in 1985, "to the extent that the new government entered office with a predetermined policy agenda, it was *not* [their emphasis] substantially dissimilar from the agenda the Liberals found themselves with after the turbulent first few years of the 1980s."[26] This initial judgment was confirmed, they thought, by the experience of the ensuing year:

> It is difficult to see in [Mulroney's] positions on South Africa, on superpower relations, or on Canada's ties with either the industrial or developing states anything that is particularly *Conservative* [their emphasis]. To be sure, the new government differs from the Liberals in approach and style, but the Mulroney government's behaviour during 1985 does not portend dramatic change in major aspects of Canadian foreign policy ... When all is said and done, Canada's foreign policy agenda is shaped to a large degree by forces in the external environment, and Canadian policy responses are similarly constrained.[27]

If this assessment, in whole or in part, survives the intricate dissections of the available evidence that are offered in the chapters that follow, then we may confront an even more fundamental question than the one implied by our original agenda. It is a question that George Grant was moved to pose in the wake of the Diefenbaker collapse: Is a distinctively conservative government now possible in Canada at all? Perhaps the country is too pluralistically composed, its culture too liberally inclined, its transnational connections too pervasively enmeshed, for any party save a successful aggregator of diversified interests to survive in federal office or for any foreign policy to win the day save one that adapts itself – prudently, pragmatically, and flexibly – to the passing scene. It is useful to remember, after all, that in other countries in this period – the United Kingdom and the United States notably among them – conservative agendas were both doctrinally driven and hotly pursued, and whatever they produced at home, they certainly produced policies for hawks abroad. Critics in Canada were inclined to put the government of Brian Mulroney in the same camp, and in foreign affairs they pointed to the free trade initiative and the defence white paper as Exhibits One and Two. But on closer inspection the argument is hard to sustain. The Conservatives chose warily and selectively from the neo-conservative agenda, and they defended their choices with arguments that were less philosophical than practical.

In the circumstances, it may seem reasonable to speculate that the alternative, at the federal level at least, would have been politically dysfunctional. If that is the case, then the conclusion may be clear enough after all: Canadians, taken collectively, are "Canadians," and their brokerage politics will out.

Acknowledgments
I would like to thank the Social Sciences and Humanities Research Council of Canada for financial support. The editors of this volume are quite right to draw attention in their Acknowledgments to the profound impact of the council on scholarly inquiry in Canada.

Notes

1 Holmes's fascination with the pervasiveness of contradiction in politics is evident in the title of a book edited by one of the conveners of this conference. See Kim Richard Nossal, ed., *An Acceptance of Paradox: Essays on Canadian Diplomacy in Honour of John W. Holmes* (Toronto: Canadian Institute of International Affairs, 1982).
2 David Pollock and Grant Manuge, "The Mulroney Doctrine," *International Perspectives* (January/February 1985): 5.
3 Tammy Nemeth's excellent chapter (see below) suggests that the dismantling of the NEP was in fact not well under way by the time the Conservatives came to power. My argument is that the Liberals were compelled to backtrack from some of the NEP's pricing and taxation provisions even during its first three years of operation. Still, there can be no doubt that the Liberals were retreating with reluctance, whereas the Conservatives delighted in demolishing the enterprise.
4 Some of these developments are discussed in engaging style by Bruce Doern and Brian W. Tomlin in their *Faith and Fear: The Free Trade Story* (Toronto: Stoddart, 1991), esp. chap. 3.

5 John C. Crosbie, with Geoffrey Stevens, *No Holds Barred: My Life in Politics* (Toronto: McClelland and Stewart, 1997), 307-8.

6 The Third Option was the preferred choice identified in a discussion paper released in the early years of the Trudeau government. It was stimulated by draconian measures that had been introduced by the Nixon administration in August 1971 to deal with a severe trade deficit – measures that suggested that Washington was perfectly prepared to deal very roughly with Canada if this were thought to be in the American economic interest. Taken in the context of the discussion paper as a whole, the option seemed to suggest a strategy that would combine an attempt to diversify Canada's economic activities abroad, together with a renewed emphasis on traditional nation-building policies of various kinds at home. See Mitchell Sharp, "Canada-U.S. Relations: Options for the Future," *International Perspectives*, Special Issue (Autumn 1972).

7 The heaviest of the flurries seems to have been generated by Gordon Ritchie's *Wrestling with the Elephant: The Inside Story of the Canada-U.S. Trade Wars* (Toronto: MacFarlane Walter and Ross, 1997). A sample riposte – although not by any means the most vigorous of the genre – is the one by Canada's former ambassador in Washington. See Allan Gotlieb, "Negotiating the Canada-US Free Trade Agreement," *International Journal* 53 (Summer 1998): 522-38. The feisty assessment of Michael Hart, also on the Canadian negotiating team, adds to the colour. See his "Poor Ritchie's Almanac: Wherein Our Tireless Hero Clinches the Free-trade Deal," *Ottawa Citizen*, 17 October 1997, A19.

8 A full account of Canada's policy on Cuba in the context of its relations with Latin America (and the United States) more generally can be found in John M. Kirk and Peter McKenna, *Canada-Cuba Relations: The Other Good Neighbour Policy* (Gainesville: University Press of Florida, 1997), esp. chap. 5.

9 For the Mulroney government's policies on the Nicaraguan issue and on Latin America as a whole, see James Rochlin, *Discovering the Americas: The Evolution of Canadian Foreign Policy towards Latin America* (Vancouver: UBC Press, 1994), esp. "The Mulroney Years." It is clear that the human rights issue was becoming increasingly salient in this period and was beginning to have a major policy impact.

10 See, for example, the "Introduction" to his *The Better Part of Valour: Essays on Canadian Diplomacy* (Toronto: McClelland and Stewart, 1970), vii.

11 Department of National Defence, *Challenge and Commitment: A Defence Policy for Canada* (Ottawa: National Defence, June 1987).

12 Ibid., 11.

13 For a full account of the withdrawal from Europe, see Roy Rempel, *Counterweights: The Failure of Canada's German and European Policy, 1955-1995* (Montreal and Kingston: McGill-Queen's University Press, 1996).

14 The most frequently cited of Mulroney's commentaries on this issue is probably the one contained in his address on 23 October 1985 to the United Nations General Assembly in New York. See External Affairs Canada, *Statements and Speeches*, 85/14 (Ottawa: Department of External Affairs, 1985). By then the Canadian position (rhetorically, at least) was already well known and firmly established, having been pursued with considerable vigour in the Commonwealth and elsewhere. But his account of his views was, in this case, particularly forceful. "Only one country," he noted, "has established colour as the hallmark of systematic inequality and repression. Only South Africa determines the fundamental human rights of individuals and groups within its society by this heinous method of classification." Such "institutionalized contempt for justice and dignity," he went on, "desecrates international standards of morality and arouses universal revulsion." If there were not "fundamental changes," then Canada was "prepared to invoke total sanctions," and its "relations with South Africa" might even "have to be severed absolutely."

15 "Canada and the New Internationalism," *Canadian Foreign Policy* 1 (Winter 1992/93): 1-6.

16 The following examples, drawn from the External Affairs and International Trade Canada Statement series, are representative: no. 92/14 (delivered to the Cape Town Press Club, 8 April 1992); no. 92/43 (delivered to the Primrose Club of Toronto, 17 September 1992); no. 92/46 (47th Session of the UN General Assembly, 24 September 1992); no. 92/57

(Empire Club of Toronto, 12 November 1992); no. 93/21 (delivered to the International Meeting of Experts on the Establishment of an International Criminal Tribunal, 22 March 1993); and no. 93/36 (Americas Society, New York, 17 May 1993).

17 For an exploration of the Conservative roots of the "human security" agenda, see Jennifer Ross, "Is Canada's Human Security Policy Really the Axworthy Doctrine?" *Canadian Foreign Policy* 8 (Winter 2001): 75-93.

18 "Canada and the New Internationalism," 3-4.

19 "Tiresome" because the phrase implies that no one else has them. That we Canadians are able to indulge such conceits in the way we do, I would argue, derives almost entirely from our unusually fortunate geopolitical and other circumstances. These allow our policy-makers to avoid the more unseemly of the compromises that are so often imposed by security or other requirements on their counterparts in less happily positioned states elsewhere in the world.

20 The flavour of all this – and the extent to which it contained the ingredients of a posture that we associate primarily with Lloyd Axworthy – can be detected in the suggestive account of Andrew F. Cooper. See his *Canadian Foreign Policy: Old Habits and New Directions* (Scarborough: Prentice Hall Allyn and Bacon Canada, 1997), esp. 182 ff.

21 Secretary of State for External Affairs, *Competitiveness and Security: Directions for Canada's International Relations* (Ottawa: Supply and Services Canada, 1985).

22 Special Joint Committee of the Senate and House of Commons, *Independence and Internationalism: Report of The Special Joint Committee on Canada's International Relations* (Ottawa: Queen's Printer, under the authority of the Senate and the Speaker of the House of Commons, 1986).

23 Department of External Affairs, *Canada's International Relations: Response of the Government of Canada to the Report of the Special Joint Committee of the Senate and the House of Commons* (Ottawa: Supply and Services Canada, December 1986).

24 Standing Committee on External Affairs and National Defence, *NORAD 1986: Report of the Standing Committee on External Affairs and National Defence* (Ottawa: House of Commons, February 1986).

25 Standing Committee on External Affairs and International Trade, *For Whose Benefit? Report of the Standing Committee on External Affairs and International Trade on Canada's Official Development Assistance Policies and Programs* (Ottawa: Supply and Services Canada, 1987).

26 Brian W. Tomlin and Maureen Molot, eds., *Canada Among Nations 1984: A Time of Transition* (Toronto: James Lorimer, 1985), 11.

27 Maureen Appel Molot and Brian W. Tomlin, eds., *Canada Among Nations 1985: The Conservative Agenda* (Toronto: James Lorimer, 1986), 3-4. The same theme recurs later in the series. In 1989, for example, they argued again that "the room for Canadian manoeuvrability in the foreign policy realm is limited by Canada's position in the international system. The foreign policy of the Conservative government has, as a result, and despite the expectations raised by the policy reviews, not varied dramatically from that of its Liberal predecessors. It continues to be characterized by the enduring elements of Canadian foreign policy in the postwar era." See Brian W. Tomlin and Maureen Appel Molot, eds., *Canada Among Nations 1988: The Tory Record* (Toronto: James Lorimer, 1989), 8.

Part 2
Policy Issues

3
Leaving the Past Behind: The Free Trade Initiative Assessed

Brian W. Tomlin

In mid-summer of 1985, Brian Mulroney was meeting with senior officials in his office on Parliament Hill. The occasion was a discussion of an advance copy of the report of the Royal Commission on the Economic Union and Development Prospects for Canada, chaired by Donald S. Macdonald, who had been a minister in Pierre Trudeau's Cabinet. The report contained a recommendation for the establishment of a free trade arrangement with the United States. According to those in attendance, Mulroney recognized the opportunity it presented for a bold policy initiative, and he relished the idea of using a former Liberal cabinet minister to give bipartisan legitimacy to the initiative. The volumes of the report arranged on his desk, Mulroney spread his hands over them and told the officials present in his office that summer day that he would use the report to beat Liberal party leader John Turner in the next election.

The decision to negotiate free trade was a fundamental policy shift on the part of the Canadian government, and it was certainly unanticipated at the beginning of the 1980s, even by those at the centre of the policy process. Few would have predicted that within three years Canada would propose sectoral free trade and that, two years later, it would offer to negotiate a comprehensive free trade agreement with the Americans. This decision involved a basic redefinition of Canada's relationship with the United States and represented a fundamental change in policy. In this chapter I want to (1) explain how the issue of Canada's trade relations with the United States made its way to the top of the Mulroney government's decision agenda and (2) demonstrate the need to understand the policy process that led Canada to propose to the United States that the two countries negotiate a bilateral free trade agreement.[1]

To accomplish this, I use a policy model, developed by John Kingdon,[2] that is directed at understanding both agenda-setting and the development of policy alternatives, the two key elements that require explanation here. Kingdon conceives the policy process as consisting of three separate "streams" that, largely independently of one another, flow through and around government: problems, policies, and politics. At certain critical times, these three streams come together, and it is at that juncture that major policy change can occur.

I will examine the process by which particular solutions became joined to particular problems and how this, when combined with favourable political forces, produced free trade. Kingdon argues that this coupling is most likely to occur when policy windows – defined as opportunities to advocate particular proposals – are opened, either by the appearance of compelling problems or by events occurring in the political stream. I begin my analysis with a more complete outline of the model and its elements.

Streams in the Policy Process

How do certain problems surface on the government's policy agenda? and why is a particular policy alternative selected to address a particular problem? For Kingdon, the answer lies in the analysis of the three process streams flowing through the public policy system: streams of problems, policies, and politics.

Problems

It is a fact that governments pay attention to some problems and not others, which obliges us to ask how it is that certain problems capture the attention of important people in and around government and, thereby, secure a place on the governmental agenda.[3] Kingdon argues that objective indicators of the presence of a problem are important but that they require a focusing event to push them onto a governmental agenda.[4] Such an event may arise from the occurrence of a crisis, the creation of a symbol, or the personal experience of a policy-maker. Finally, problem identification is more likely to occur when government officials receive feedback about the inadequacy of existing policies and programs. All of these characteristics may be present, however, and a problem may still not make it on to the government's policy agenda. This is because the policy process consists of more than a stream of problems waiting to be identified; it also includes a stream of policy alternatives that must ultimately be linked to problems.

Policy Proposals

Kingdon argues that ideas about policy alternatives circulate in communities of specialists, both inside and outside government.[5] Advocates for particular proposals or ideas are policy entrepreneurs who are defined by their willingness to invest resources (time, energy, and occasionally money) in order to secure a future return (desired policies, satisfaction from participation, or career rewards). This process of creating alternatives for policy-makers to consider proceeds independently of the process of problem identification. However, viable alternatives must exist before a problem can secure a solid position on the decision agenda. Even in this circumstance, problems and their alternative solutions exist alongside the political stream, which also exerts influence on the policy process.

Politics

In Kingdon's model, developments in the political stream have their most powerful effects on agendas. The stream is composed of elements related to the electoral, partisan, and pressure group considerations of politicians and those who serve them. An important component of the political stream is what Kingdon refers to as the national mood – gleaned from mail, media, and lobbyists, among other sources – which can provide fertile ground for certain ideas. Organized political interests are also important to those in government in so far as they all point in the same direction, thus providing a powerful impetus to move on that course. Turnover and jurisdiction within government are also important in as much as agendas are significantly affected by changing incumbents and by turf battles.

Policy Windows

Much of the time these three streams – problems, policies, and politics – flow through the policy system on largely independent courses. However, the streams come together at critical times, with the result being that a problem is recognized, a solution is developed and available within the policy community, a political change makes the time right for policy change, and potential constraints are not severe. This joining of the streams is most likely to occur when a policy window opens, and policy entrepreneurs play a critical role in what Kingdon calls the "coupling of the streams," which occurs at this time. Typically, a policy window opens because the policy agenda is affected by a change or event in the political stream or by the emergence of a pressing problem that captures the attention of government officials.[6]

This model of agenda setting and policy alternative specification is designed to help us "find pattern and structure in very complicated, fluid, and seemingly unpredictable phenomena."[7] However, it is a highly probabilistic model – one that explicitly leaves room for a residual randomness in the way events will unfold in any particular policy episode. In addition, it is historically contingent: the direction of change depends heavily on initial conditions, and events may develop in different ways depending on how they happen to start. Nevertheless, it provides us with a comprehensive representation of the enduring streams in the policy process and alerts us to the critical ingredients that increase the likelihood of policy change. I will now apply the model to an analysis of how the trade issue rose to the top of the decision agenda and to an analysis of why a Canada-US free trade agreement became the preferred policy alternative for the Mulroney government.[8]

The Evolving Problem Stream

While the decision to negotiate free trade was taken by the Conservative government, this fundamental policy shift originated in the unprecedented conditions of crisis and conflict that marked the early 1980s. The majority Liberal government elected in 1980 had adopted an ambitious national policy agenda designed to enhance the resources and visibility of the federal government. The National Energy Program (NEP) was a central element in this overall strategy, one that had highly negative consequences for foreign investors in the Canadian oil and gas industry. When the government also announced its intention to extend the mandate of the Foreign Investment Review Agency (FIRA) in the regulation of direct foreign investment, the howls of outrage from the American business establishment turned the guns of the Reagan administration on Canada. American plans for retaliatory measures targeted the Canadian Achilles heel of trade dependence on the United States.[9]

This acute conflict, and the sense of vulnerability it created for Canadians and their government, represented a turning point for Canada in its relations with the United States. The United States had overtly threatened the security of access to a market on which Canada was overwhelmingly dependent, with profound implications for employment and investment. This stimulated a reassessment, on the part of both business and government, of the value to Canada of secure and enhanced access to the US market, an assessment that would take place within the context of an economic recession more severe than any experienced since the Great Depression of the 1930s.

The government reassessment was undertaken through a task force, organized initially through the Department of Industry, Trade and Commerce (ITC) but subsequently shifting to the Department of External Affairs (DEA), where it was placed under the direction of Derek Burney, assistant under-secretary for trade and economic relations in External Affairs.[10] This was the first, but would certainly not be the last, time that Burney would be in a position to play a crucial role in the free trade initiative. A concurrent review of the Canada-US relationship was also initiated by External Affairs. As the trade task force conducted its review during 1982, the emerging economic crisis guaranteed that the threat to secure access to the American market for Canada's exports would be defined as the central problem for Canadian trade policy. In consultations with representatives of the Canadian business community and provincial governments, the task force was repeatedly told that the central goal of any trade policy should be to "get the Canada-US relationship right." The US market was fundamentally important to Canadian economic well-being, and preservation of that market required stability in the Canada-US relationship. In particular, the government had to find a means to protect Canadian exporters from the application of US trade remedies, primarily anti-dumping and countervailing duties, to Canadian exports.

The decline in trade that accompanied the recession also made trade policy a central preoccupation for the Reagan administration. However, from Washington's perspective, the problem was the unfair trading practices of its major trading partners, a problem made more serious, or at least visible, by the severity of the recession, which added significantly to protectionist pressures, prompting a greater willingness in the United States to move more aggressively to curb imports. By the time the Mulroney Conservatives came to power in 1984, they faced a mounting tide of US protectionism. There was an increase in the number of investigations of Canadian export practices under the American countervailing duty process as well as the introduction of specific legislation in Congress that would limit Canadian exports to the United States.[11]

For the Conservatives, the problems with trade compounded the problem they faced in the Canadian economy. The minister of finance, Michael Wilson, was convinced by his officials that the economy was in a state of profound malaise, for which there could be no easy cure. In the fall of 1984, Wilson agreed with senior Finance officials that Canada could no longer tax or spend its way out of its economic troubles; instead, the country would have to grow its way out of the problems that beset the economy, and the key to this growth was a significant increase in Canadian trade.

In this way, the Canadian trade policy problem evolved over the first half of the decade, until, by the time the Mulroney government seized the trade issue, the problem was overwhelmingly defined in terms of the threat that US trade remedy action posed to Canadian exports as well as in terms of the need for enhanced and secure Canadian access to the US market. As this problem redefinition occurred, policy entrepreneurs inside and outside government gradually moved the option of comprehensive bilateral free trade onto the menu of policy alternatives that would be presented to the government. I now turn to the story of how ideas about policy alternatives shifted from the 1980 revival of the Third Option – a short-lived effort in the 1970s to promote the restructuring of the Canadian economy and to diversify Canada's foreign economic relations – to bilateral free trade.

Developments in the Policy Stream

The 1982-83 review by the External Affairs task force was an important first step in this shift. It was the crisis in the economy that ensured that

the task force examination of Canada's trade policy would centre on securing access to the US market. And the Canadian business lobby saw to it
that the negotiation of some form of trade liberalization arrangement was
put forward as an option for consideration. Leading advocates included
the Business Council on National Issues (BCNI), made up of major corporations operating in Canada, and the Canadian Manufacturers'
Association (CMA). During 1982 and 1983, the president of BCNI, Thomas
d'Aquino, was active in advocating negotiations for a comprehensive
trade agreement as a means to guarantee access to the US market. Equally
important, however, was the influential CMA's reversal of its long-standing
opposition to free trade with the United States.

In its report,[12] the task force played it absolutely safe and reaffirmed the
centrality of the multilateral GATT (General Agreement on Tariffs and
Trade) system for Canada. Secondarily, however, it also raised the prospect
of pursuing *sectoral* free trade arrangements with the United States as an
additional option for the government to consider. The sectoral option was
not without precedent, since Canada already had three sectoral free trade
agreements with the United States, covering automobiles, defence materials, and agricultural machinery. In fact, in 1981, Canadian embassy officials in Washington, with Ottawa's knowledge, informally discussed
broader sectoral free trade arrangements with officials in the Office of the
US Trade Representative (USTR). This initiative was part of the Canadian
effort to resolve the conflict with the United States over the NEP and FIRA.
It did not proceed, however, because of opposition from within the ITC in
Ottawa, which still carried the trade mandate at that time. Despite these
precedents, free trade was a sensitive political issue in Canada. The pride
of place given by the task force to the GATT undoubtedly eased the task of
the Liberal minister for international trade, Gerald Regan, who received
the report and saw to its acceptance by Cabinet.

Regan was a free trader from Nova Scotia, and it was the sectoral initiative that caught his attention. While stressing the report's reaffirmation of
the GATT with his cautious Cabinet colleagues, Regan persuaded them to
go along with its sectoral option as well, despite the suspicions of the
"nationalist" group in the Liberal Cabinet. With Cabinet endorsement in
hand, Regan turned the report upside down at its presentation at a press
conference in August 1983. Seizing on its most controversial element, he
announced the demise of the Third Option and proclaimed the government's intention to pursue a limited free trade agreement with the United
States. Regan's proclamation did not by any means reflect mainstream
thinking in External Affairs. The concurrent review of the Canada-US relationship that was prepared for the deputy minister for foreign relations
had reaffirmed the basic tenets of the Third Option. That report was over-
taken by events, however. It was the trade policy review that provided the

opening for fundamental change in Canadian-American relations as sectoral free trade negotiations became the preferred option of the Liberal government of Pierre Elliott Trudeau.

The task of implementing the sectoral initiative from the Canadian side fell to Tony Halliday, an experienced trade official in External Affairs. In February 1984, he and his counterparts in USTR were ready to bring Regan and the US trade representative, William Brock, together in Washington where they identified four sectors upon which officials from the two countries could focus. By June, however, little progress had been made in these preliminary discussions, principally because USTR was unable to bring American industries on board. Although Regan and Brock agreed to explore alternative sectors, nothing further was decided on the question of whether and when to begin formal negotiations.

The election of Mulroney and the Conservatives in September 1984 provided an opportunity for advocates of a comprehensive agreement with the United States to promote their idea to a new government. During their first few months in government, the Tories began to sketch the principal dimensions of what would become the Conservative policy agenda. In an economic and fiscal statement presented by Wilson to the House of Commons in November 1984, the government identified its priorities of economic renewal and national reconciliation. Wilson also tabled a policy agenda, setting out a strategy for economic renewal. One element of the strategy was increased and secure access to markets for Canadian exports, especially in the United States. Referring to sectoral free trade, the Finance agenda noted: "This initiative has generated public interest in exploring broadly-based bilateral arrangements with the US."[13]

The Conservatives were still some distance from free trade at this early stage in their mandate, however. The Finance economic renewal statement had not been prepared especially for the Conservatives but was begun in May 1984 while the Liberals still held power. Nor was the concept of "broadly-based bilateral arrangements" cleared through Trade Minister James Kelleher, who was not consulted on the Finance statement. Nevertheless, the autumn of 1984 saw pressures mount for the government to pick up the free trade agenda. Canadian business organizations engaged in a vigorous lobbying effort to shore up support for a comprehensive free trade arrangement, and their position was given serious attention by a government committed to making Canada a better place to do business.[14]

Also circulating in Ottawa at this time was a C.D. Howe Institute study of Canada's trade options, co-authored by Richard Lipsey, one of Canada's most respected economists.[15] Following publication of the study, Lipsey and Wendy Dobson, then head of the C.D. Howe Institute and later associate deputy minister of finance in Ottawa, launched what, for a think tank, was an unprecedented personal lobby to promote the free trade option among key ministers, their staffers, and senior members of the bureaucracy. Their efforts, along with the trade policy studies prepared by the Macdonald Commission, helped to shatter many of the prevailing myths about free trade. In particular, they vigorously argued that, rather than representing a complete break with the Canadian past, the free trade option was quite consistent with Canada's commitment to trade liberalization throughout the postwar era.

Changes in the Political Stream

The importance of politics – particularly the elements of turnover and jurisdiction – in the process that led to the joining of the trade problem and policy streams was apparent even before the election of the Conservatives. The outcome of the 1982-83 trade policy review was fundamentally affected by the major reorganization of ITC, which was undertaken in January 1982 in order to integrate federal industrial and regional development policies. As a result, the trade elements of ITC were split off and integrated into a reorganized Department of External Affairs as a new trade and economic wing reporting to its own minister for international trade. Consequently, in the spring of 1982 the trade policy review was shifted to an External Affairs task force. This shift was important, since the free trade option had less chance of emerging from ITC, with its mandate to protect and nurture Canadian industry. In addition, it created an important role for Derek Burney as manager of the task force.

The fact that the new Conservative government was looking to establish a policy agenda made it particularly receptive to the arguments in favour of a comprehensive free trade agreement. In the event, the first, and very important, act of policy entrepreneurship came from an unlikely source: Donald Macdonald, chairman of the Royal Commission on the Economic Union and Development Prospects for Canada. Established by Trudeau in 1982, the Macdonald Commission was examining Canada-US free trade as part of its study of the Canadian economy. Although the commission had neither completed its studies nor framed its conclusions, Macdonald nevertheless announced in November 1984 that he favoured free trade between Canada and the United States as the principal long-term solution to Canada's economic problems.

Acknowledging that Canadians might be nervous about maintaining their sovereignty in a free trade arrangement with the United States, Macdonald nonetheless argued: "If we do get down to a point where it's going to be a leap of faith, then I think at some point Canadians are going to have to be bold and say, yes, we will do that."[16] Macdonald's call for a "leap of faith" was a big news item in Canada. And because it was bipartisan and seemingly authoritative, his conversion provided important momentum to the free trade option at a critical juncture as the new government was considering its options. This endorsement was followed by a series of government reports and consultations that moved the Mulroney Cabinet ever closer to a final commitment to negotiation.

The first of the reports was the product of a review of trade policy options initiated by Derek Burney in the Department of External Affairs. That review generated sharp conflicts, both in External Affairs and in the Department of Regional Industrial Expansion (DRIE), the successor to the ITC. The conflict resulted from opposition to Burney's determination to put the comprehensive free trade option before the government. From a DRIE perspective, trade liberalization would threaten Canadian industries supported by an average tariff that was roughly double that of their American competition. In External, the opposition centred on traditional concerns over political autonomy. In the end, Burney was forced to override opposition from the most senior administrative levels of his own department, which wanted to suppress the free trade discussion. His task force presented comprehensive free trade as one of the options for Canada in the report prepared for Kelleher. Because the trade minister did not share the reluctance of his senior officials to consider all of the options available to Canada in its relations with the United States, he released the report in January 1985.[17]

This government discussion paper, while acknowledging the importance of multilateral trade liberalization, confirmed the need to seek enhanced and secure access to the US market. To this end, the paper suggested that some form of bilateral trade arrangement should be considered, and it set out the options available to Canada. These were the status quo, sectoral arrangements, a comprehensive trade agreement (the Conservative euphemism for free trade) to remove tariff and non-tariff barriers on substantially all bilateral trade, and a bilateral framework to discuss means to improve and enhance trade relations (a BCNI proposal). Although the paper was careful to avoid identifying a preferred option, it rejected the status quo as inadequate, sectoral arrangements as unattainable, and the BCNI framework as unnecessary.[18] Clearly the government was edging down the path to comprehensive free trade negotiations.

Another policy window was about to open in March 1985 in Québec City at the so-called Shamrock Summit between Mulroney and Reagan, and policy entrepreneurs were ready to take advantage of it. The Shamrock Summit was orchestrated in exquisite detail by Prime Minister's Office (PMO) staffer and Mulroney confidant Fred Doucet. Working closely with Doucet was Derek Burney, who oversaw the drafting of the trade declaration to be issued by the prime minister and the president. Although the declaration contained no explicit statement of bilateral trade policy by either government, it did call for an examination of ways to reduce and eliminate existing barriers to trade. Mulroney and Reagan instructed Kelleher and Brock to report in six months on mechanisms to achieve this end.

Following the summit declaration, Burney's External Affairs task force proceeded to flesh out the free trade option in preparation for the presentation of a recommendation to Cabinet. It continued to encounter considerable opposition to a comprehensive agreement both within External Affairs and other departments. However, it was apparent that Canadian business was now solidly behind the initiative, and this could make all the difference in Cabinet, especially with support from Wilson in Finance. With Canadian business on side, and with the backing of key ministers, Burney was determined to press ahead, despite continued opposition from senior officials.

The politics of the trade issue were right in other respects as well. Free trade was not only congruent with the government's agenda for economic renewal; it also served the Conservative priority of national reconciliation. The western provinces had been deeply disaffected over the NEP, and Mulroney and his minister of energy, Patricia (Pat) Carney, wasted little time in undoing the NEP through the Western Accord. There was also substantial support for free trade in the west, especially Alberta, long a stronghold of Conservative support. Alberta's Conservative premier Peter Lougheed, a strong supporter of the free trade option, was the principal exponent of western grievances, and he held close counsel with Mulroney on the trade issue throughout this period. His support was important in shoring up Mulroney's resolve as the time for decision approached.

Also important was the surprising degree of support for free trade in Québec, home to a substantial number of inefficient Canadian industries that were the least likely to survive the elimination of protective barriers. The province's long-standing opposition to trade liberalization had been an essential element in shaping Canadian trade policy. All that changed, however, with the willingness of the Québec business establishment to support free trade. This support would reinforce Mulroney's strategy to consolidate the Conservative landslide he had achieved in the province in 1984 and, thus, turn the political tables on the Liberals.

Mulroney's path to the free trade decision was also smoothed by the presence of Tory governments in most of the remaining provinces, with the notable exception of Ontario. These premiers were ideologically sympathetic to the pro-market approach of the federal party, and they were deeply concerned about American protectionism. As a result, they were generally positive about negotiating a comprehensive trade agreement for enhanced and secure access to the US market, assuming, of course, that an agreement left untouched such "non-trade" shibboleths as agricultural marketing boards and regional development grants.

A Policy Window

Thus, in the summer of 1985, the streams in the policy process had come together – a problem had been recognized, a solution had been developed and put forward, and a political change had made the time right for policy change. And policy entrepreneurs, both inside and outside government, were ready to take advantage of the policy window that was created by the coupling of these streams. By August, Kelleher was concluding the report on trade relations that he had been directed to prepare following the Shamrock Summit, and he made a preliminary oral presentation to Cabinet's Priorities and Planning Committee at its meeting in Vancouver. Although up to this point in the decision process Cabinet had engaged in no serious comprehensive discussion of the free trade issue, and despite lingering uncertainties on the part of some ministers, the committee moved quickly to confirm the decision the prime minister had already taken to seek comprehensive trade negotiations with the United States.

Shortly after the 5 September 1985 release of the Royal Commission report, to ensure that free trade would be tied to Macdonald, the prime minister indicated, in reply to a question in the House of Commons on 9 September, that the government had decided to pursue "freer" trade with the United States. On 26 September, Mulroney told the Commons that he had telephoned Reagan to ask him to explore with Congress Canada's interest in pursuing negotiations to reduce tariffs and non-tariff barriers between the two countries. This call, and the formal written proposal that followed on 1 October, finally brought to an end four years of policy transformation in Canada.

This reconstruction of events between the decision to undertake a trade policy review in September 1981 and the September 1985 request for negotiations makes it clear that there was nothing inevitable about the Mulroney government's decision to seek free trade with the United States. In its beginnings, the free trade issue was the Liberals' legacy to the Conservative government, for it was they who had placed it on the governmental agenda. That legacy was nurtured and developed by a small, and relatively isolated, group of External Affairs officials led by Derek Burney and supported by key ministers in the Conservative Cabinet who were determined to move the trade issue onto the government's decision agenda. The framing of the problem that needed to be addressed was also critical to the policy process surrounding the issue. The policy papers prepared for ministers by Burney and his External Affairs group focused relentlessly on the trade policy problem of securing access to the US market in the face of growing American protectionism. Canadian business support for free trade was also directed to the need to secure access to their largest market and to escape US trade remedy actions against Canadian exports.

Free trade is more than trade policy, however. It can also serve as an industrial policy to bring about economic restructuring and adjustment. And it was primarily as an industrial policy, loosely defined, that free trade was advocated as the principal long-term solution to Canada's economic problems by the Macdonald Commission. According to the commission's analysis, the source of Canada's economic problems could be found in a manufacturing sector producing at too high a cost for too small a market. Free trade would at once expand the market and remove the protective barriers that insulate inefficient firms from competition. These firms would either adjust, by becoming larger and more competitive, or die. The result would be an increase in total national production. This analysis of industrial policy and its free trade prescription may represent sound economics, but it does not represent sound politics. With fewer but larger firms producing more, there are still likely to be large numbers of disaffected individuals and groups who have been "adjusted" out of jobs and out of business. It is for this reason that protectionist measures – first tariffs, then non-tariff barriers – have enjoyed such popularity with politicians in all countries.

For ministers, the central problem facing Canada was security of access to the country's major market. A comprehensive trade agreement with the United States offered an appealing, if politically sensitive, trade policy solution to the problem. Had the problem been defined primarily in terms of an uncompetitive manufacturing sector, however, then it is likely that a proposal for an industrial policy to subject the economy to a sudden cold shower through free trade would have been viewed as a considerably more risky venture. But these hard economic facts were not laid out for the prime minister because he never received a comprehensive briefing from his senior trade officials on the economics of bilateral free trade.

The way the problem was framed for Mulroney helps explain why this otherwise cautious prime minister would take such a leap of faith. As a trade policy, free trade offered the prospect of secure access to the American market. Although it carried some domestic political risk, the prospect of reducing protectionist harassment in Canada's dominant trade market would make that risk worthwhile. As an industrial policy, however, the removal of barriers to trade offers the potential for market gains but at the risk of potential industry losses. Since the free trade option was framed as a means to achieve secure market access rather than as an equation of gains and losses, it offered a more palatable choice to policy-makers.

This reconstruction of events also makes it clear that the joining of the problem and policy streams alone would have been insufficient to drive this fundamental shift in policy. Change in the political stream was necessary as well. First, of course, was the timing of the failure of the sectoral initiative and the 1984 federal election, which produced Mulroney's majority government. In these circumstances, the significant partisan advantages that free trade offered the Conservatives made the option of comprehensive negotiations attractive. Mulroney was determined to offer a clear alternative to the centralizing, interventionist policies of the Trudeau Liberals and to build a lasting power base for his party. A policy that was market-oriented and had broad appeal in western Canada and Québec served both ends. The summer of 1985 also saw Mulroney and his ministers under fire for a lack of clear direction and purpose. Free trade offered the prospect of immediate partisan advantage to a government in search of a major policy upon which to fix. Finally, when the problem, policy, and politics streams were joined, key policy entrepreneurs took advantage of the policy window (i.e., d'Aquino and Lougheed aligned critical business and political interests, while Burney moved the policy process inexorably towards free trade).

Conclusion

As noted at the outset of this chapter, the decision to negotiate a free trade agreement with the United States was a fundamental policy shift on the part of the government of Canada. It is equally clear, however, that this shift in policy was not the product of a Conservative determination to fashion an agenda of major policy departures. There were significant changes under way in all three of Kingdon's policy streams: the problem was redefined to emphasize the need to ensure secure access to the US market; the range of policy alternatives was expanded incrementally to include comprehensive free trade; and, of course, the electoral, partisan, and interest group dimensions of the political stream had shifted.

In hindsight, it is clear that there was nothing inevitable about the Conservative decision to seek free trade with the United States; rather, it was the product of the alignment of a complex array of conditions in three largely autonomous policy streams – conditions that evolved over a four-year period. Moreover, this alignment simply created windows of opportunity for key policy entrepreneurs who happened to be skilful enough, and lucky enough, to be able to exploit them before they closed. Free trade was not, therefore, a Conservative idea whose time had come; rather, it was a policy that had been thrust onto the agenda through a series of conjunctions of events and that was finally chosen as the result of cold political calculation.

Notes

1 When Mexico requested bilateral free trade negotiations with the United States, Canada overcame its initial reluctance and decided to seek trilateral negotiations to create the North American Free Trade Agreement (NAFTA). See Maxwell A. Cameron and Brian W. Tomlin, *The Making of NAFTA: How the Deal Was Done* (Ithaca: Cornell University Press, 2000).

2 John W. Kingdon, *Agendas, Alternatives and Public Policies* (New York: HarperCollins, 1995). Kingdon's model is a revised version of the "garbage can" model of policy choice, advanced originally in Michael Cohen, James March, and Johan Olsen, "A Garbage Can Model of Organizational Choice," *Administrative Science Quarterly* 17 (March 1972): 1-25. The analytical framework and concepts presented here are drawn from Brian W. Tomlin, "On a Fast-Track to a Ban: the Canadian Policy Process," *Canadian Foreign Policy* 5 (1998): 5-7.

3 On problem definition and agenda setting, see David Rochefort and Roger Cobb, eds., *The Politics of Problem Definition* (Lawrence, KS: University Press of Kansas, 1994); Deborah Stone, "Causal Stories and the Formation of Policy Agendas," *Political Science Quarterly* 104, 2 (1989): 281-300.

4 Kingdon, *Agendas*, 90.

5 On policy communities, see Paul Sabatier and Hank Jenkins-Smith, eds., *Policy Change and Learning* (Boulder, CO: Westview, 1993); Michael Atkinson and William D. Coleman, "Policy Networks, Policy Communities and the Problems of Governance," *Governance* 5, 2 (1992): 154-80; and Peter Haas, "Introduction: Epistemic Communities and International Policy Co-ordination," *International Organization* 46, 1 (1992): 1-35.

6 Michael Howlett, "Predictable and Unpredictable Policy Windows: Institutional and Exogenous Correlates of Canadian Federal Agenda-Setting," *Canadian Journal of Political Science* 31, 3 (1998): 495-524. For a critique of Howlett's analysis, see Stuart Soroka, "Policy Agenda-Setting Theory Revisited: A Critique of Howlett on Downs, Baumgartner and Jones, and Kingdon," *Canadian Journal of Political Science* 32, 4 (1999): 763-72.

7 Kingdon, *Agendas*, 224.

8 The following analysis is drawn from G. Bruce Doern and Brian W. Tomlin, *Faith and Fear: The Free Trade Story* (Toronto: Stoddart, 1991).

9 Stephen Clarkson, *Canada and the Reagan Challenge* (Toronto: James Lorimer, 1982).

10 Michael Hart, Bill Dymond, and Colin Robertson, *Decision at Midnight: Inside the Canada-US Free Trade Negotiations* (Vancouver: UBC Press, 1994).

11 David Leyton-Brown, "Canada-US Relations: Towards a Closer Relationship," in Maureen Appel Molot and Brian W. Tomlin, eds., *Canada Among Nations 1985: The Conservative Agenda* (Toronto: James Lorimer, 1986).

12 Canada, *Canadian Trade Policy for the 1980s: A Discussion Paper* (Ottawa: Department of External Affairs, 1983).

13 Canada, *A New Direction for Canada: An Agenda for Economic Renewal* (Ottawa: Department of Finance, 1984), 33.

14 On the role of the Canadian business community, see Doern and Tomlin, *Faith and Fear*, chap. 3.

15 Richard Lipsey and M. Smith, *Canada's Trade Policy Options* (Toronto: C.D. Howe Institute, 1985).

16 *Globe and Mail*, 19 November 1984.

17 Canada, *How to Secure and Enhance Access to Export Markets* (Ottawa: Department of External Affairs, 1985).

18 David Leyton-Brown, "Canada-US Relations: Towards a Closer Relationship," in Molot and Tomlin, eds., *Canada Among Nations 1985*, 182.

4

Continental Drift: Energy Policy and Canadian-American Relations

Tammy L. Nemeth

The election of the Conservatives in 1984 marked the beginning of an attempt to reconstruct the country along new lines. Where the previous Liberal government under Pierre Elliott Trudeau had created an atmosphere of confrontation within Canada and with its largest trading partner, the United States, the government of Brian Mulroney endeavoured to encourage cooperative federal-provincial relations and to improve Canada's relationship with the Americans. A key example of the difference in the visions of Canada held by both Trudeau and Mulroney, for domestic as well as foreign policy, can be found in each government's energy policy. The Liberal policy, particularly the National Energy Program (NEP), was divisive, bureaucratic, and interventionist; by contrast, Conservative policy was cooperative, mostly unregulated, and non-interventionist.

Although the primary concern and goal of the Conservative energy policy was to unite the country both politically and economically, a welcome side effect was a considerable improvement in Canadian-American relations. In addition, the dramatic difference between the Conservative energy and foreign policy and the previous Liberal policy was that the former realized a continental energy agreement between Canada and the United States, as represented in the energy provisions of the Free Trade Agreement (FTA). As a point of clarification, the meaning of "continental" used here is based on economist Leonard Waverman's definition: "Joint planning of energy production and shipment without regard to borders."[1] This seems to describe accurately the energy provisions of the FTA. Ultimately, however, the most significant aspect of the continental energy agreement, within the context of a departure from previous policy, was its underlying purpose of preventing a future NEP from being implemented without abrogating the current agreement.

This chapter seeks to explain the outcome of a continental energy policy by examining how the independent, or explanatory, variables of economics, ideas, interest groups, and international forces influenced Canada to pursue a continental energy policy with the United States. I will examine the pre-Conservative energy policy, discuss the development of the Progressive Conservative (PC) energy policy, explore the energy provisions of the FTA, and evaluate the four explanatory variables to ascertain why a continental energy policy developed during the Conservative era and how it departs from traditional Canadian policy. I will conclude with a discussion of the implications and legacies of this policy for Canada and Canadian-American relations. Among the questions this chapter aims to answer are: Was this, to use Denis Stairs's formulation, a case of the PCs being "architects" or "engineers"? What were the consequences of a continental energy policy? Why would Canada and the United States agree to limit their independence with respect to energy policy by agreeing to the proportional sharing arrangement? How is a continental energy policy a departure from traditional Canadian foreign policy?

Pre-Conservative Energy Policy

The NEP was created in great secrecy, with little or no consultation with the provinces and industry. It was meant to protect consumers, provide more revenue for the federal government, and expand federal involvement in the oil and gas industry. The contents of the NEP, which were applauded by consumers, managed to upset the producing provinces, the industry, and the United States even more than they had been before.

The primary goal of the NEP was to achieve energy self-sufficiency in Canada by 1990. Energy security was to be achieved by increasing Canadian ownership and participation in the oil and gas industry at the expense of the mostly American-owned multinational corporations (MNCs), by finding new sources of Canadian oil and gas in federally controlled areas, and by increasing the federal share of oil and gas revenues. There were six new taxes introduced, not including income taxes and royalties.[2] However, the NEP was quite similar to the previous Canadian reaction to an oil crisis, except that this time it created an even more complicated regulatory structure.[3] Canadian consumers were to be protected through all of this by receiving priority access to domestic supplies and by benefiting from subsidized domestic prices. But the policy also sought to conserve that supply, with the result that exports of natural gas to the United States were frozen and exports of oil were reduced significantly.[4]

Both the Alberta government and the oil and gas industry were outraged, and both took retaliatory measures; the result was an agreement with Alberta in 1981 regarding revenue sharing. The American reaction was comparably hostile. Initially, the Reagan administration was unsure how to approach the situation, and it oscillated between diplomacy and threats.[5] But continued pressure by Washington led to changes in the NEP in 1982. The remainder of the NEP continued to operate until 1985, when the Conservative government implemented a new energy policy aimed at dismantling it.

Conservative Energy Policy

The NEP had enraged the producing provinces, infuriated the oil and gas industry, and soured the Canadian-American relationship. By 1984 it became clear that change was on its way. Although the Conservatives did not make energy the focus of the 1984 election campaign, energy policy was certainly a priority before, during, and after the election. After Mulroney was elected as leader of the Opposition in the summer of 1983, he appointed Patricia (Pat) Carney as Opposition energy critic. Her task was to develop a Canadian energy policy that would dismantle and replace the NEP.

The process by which the Conservatives made energy policy represented a significant change from that used by the Liberals.[6] Carney looked to industry rather than the bureaucracy for leadership. While in Opposition, she consulted with the provinces and created industry study groups. These groups examined the NEP and proposed alternatives based on the terms of reference supplied by the government. The result was that most of the recommendations made by the study groups were reflected in Conservative energy policy.

The NEP was dismantled through the Atlantic Accord, the Western Accord, and a statement on frontier policy. The Atlantic Accord was based upon an agreement in principle that was negotiated and signed before the 1984 election. It eased the tension between Newfoundland and Ottawa over the control and development of offshore resources.[7] The Western Accord phased out or eliminated all of the NEP taxes and regulations. However, Ottawa retained a force majeure clause that would allow the Canadian government to protect consumers in case of extraordinary fluctuations in world oil prices. The natural gas agreement allowed for buyers and sellers to freely negotiate trade in natural gas and promised to review the National Energy Board's twenty-five-year surplus test. Finally, the frontier policy confirmed that the federal government would not discriminate against foreign investment in the Canadian oil and gas industry. The 25 per cent "back-in," a contentious provision that gave the Crown an automatic 25 percent interest in every development, past or future, on Canada Lands was abolished; but a minimum of 50 percent Canadian ownership of producing wells on Canada Lands was maintained.[8] All of the policies, except for the Atlantic Accord, were rooted in recommendations made by the industry study groups; and with these four policies the NEP was dismantled. The Conservatives were the architects of this policy and they had a clear vision, quite distinct from that of the Liberals, of what Canadian energy policy should embody.

Some authors – including Denis Stairs in Chapter 2 – have suggested that Conservative energy policy was insignificant because the Liberals had already largely gutted the NEP by 1984; in this view, the Conservatives were really just administering changes already set in motion or, as Stairs puts it, delivering a coup de grâce. It can be argued, however, that this depiction is not wholly accurate. The dismantling of the NEP was in fact *not* well advanced by the time the Conservatives took office. The Liberals made adjustments and alterations that were articulated within the 1981 revenue sharing agreement and in the *NEP Update*, but they had no intention of removing the NEP taxes, dismantling the large bureaucratic network they had created to administer it, altering their frontier policy, or coming to an agreement with Newfoundland regarding offshore resources. In short, suggesting that the Conservatives merely administered changes that were already in motion overlooks the actual sequence of events, particularly in light of the extensive work done by the Conservatives while in Opposition to develop a coherent vision and comprehensive policy that was implemented almost in toto when they assumed office.

Where previous governments had increasingly advocated more regulation of, and government involvement within, the oil and gas industry, the Conservatives sought to reduce government interference and to allow market forces to prevail. However, all of these policy changes did not prevent the possibility of another NEP being implemented by a future government. Therefore, the Mulroney government, in a dramatic departure from traditional policy, sought to curtail the ability of future governments to develop comparable discriminatory policies. The method it chose was a continental energy arrangement – the energy chapter in the Canada-US Free Trade Agreement.

FTA Energy Provisions
How exactly did the FTA energy provisions secure deregulation of Canadian and American energy trade? Articles 902 and 903 essentially prevent either country from imposing price controls on oil and natural gas or having a two-tiered pricing system.[9] This means that neither country can export its energy products for a greater price than what it sells them for domestically. One exception to this would be a crisis of national security. According to Article 907, however, national security must refer to armed military conflict rather than the desire of domestic producers to reduce the access of competitively priced imports. This was meant to limit American rather than Canadian producers.

Article 908 reaffirms that the FTA energy chapter is consistent with Canadian and American obligations and commitments in the International Energy Agency (IEA). Through their membership in the IEA, Canada and the United States are committed to share resources in a time of crisis. The inclusion of the controversial proportional sharing clause in Article 904 confirmed this obligation and further limited the potential regulatory actions available to both countries in a crisis situation.[10]

In Article 905 a formal dispute settlement board, or grievance board, was established to help alleviate complaints should one country feel that the other is violating the articles of the agreement.[11] Under the FTA, government incentives for exploration and development could continue.[12] Ownership requirements were addressed in Chapter 16, the investment section of the FTA, particularly in Sections 1602 and 1605.[13] Finally, in an annex to the energy chapter, Canada was allowed to receive Alaskan oil, which had previously been prohibited from export in order to build up the American Strategic Petroleum Reserve. Ultimately, the energy chapter within the FTA served to ensure that discriminatory taxes and regulations could not be implemented by future governments without renegotiating or terminating the agreement. This was a profound alteration of traditional Canadian policy.

Evaluation of Explanatory Variables

Why were both countries so determined to enshrine the deregulatory aspects of energy policy in a bilateral agreement? The idea of a continental energy policy had occasionally been considered by various Canadian governments, but it had never gained widespread acceptance within political circles. After dismantling the controversial NEP the Conservatives decided to take an even greater policy leap by negotiating a free trade agreement with the United States and, with it, the continental energy policy found in Chapter 9 of the agreement. The possible explanations for the Canadian decision to include a continental energy agreement within the FTA, which would constrain future governments from creating another NEP, are economics, ideas, interest groups, and international forces. It is to an examination of which of these four variables, or combination thereof, are most useful in explaining policy outcomes that I now turn.

Economics

The severe recession of the early 1980s "hit the Canadian economy especially hard."[14] The over-regulation of the Canadian oil and gas industry was considered to be a significant contributing factor to the continued recession because it increased costs and inefficiencies for producers and consumers. In Canada, the Mulroney government's position on energy, both before and after the 1984 election, was that energy was to be an "engine of growth" for the Canadian economy.[15] The oil and gas industry sustained thousands of jobs across the country and, in the view of the Mulroney government, had the potential to create thousands more. The additional job growth in the oil and gas industry could be generated if there was increased activity in the oil and gas sector. Increased activity had two potential sources: (1) a decrease in regulation that would provide a stable environment for investment and (2) an increase in the demand for Canadian oil and natural gas that could be accomplished through secure access to the large American market.

Although the economic reasons for desiring deregulation were different for Canada and the United States, respectively, both still aimed to ensure that their deregulatory policies would be secured from future government tampering by enshrining them in a free trade agreement. Canada is an exporting nation and has a large surplus of oil and natural gas; the United States is the world's largest energy consumer and has been a net importer of oil and natural gas since the late 1970s.[16] Historically, Canada's main concern has been to try and secure access to the large US market in order to export its surplus of resources, particularly in a time of depressed prices that began to occur in 1986. Periods of recession normally trigger protectionist actions in the United States, such as the 1972 import restrictions, which would usually attempt to curtail the level of Canadian imports of oil and natural gas. Thus, Canada sought to guarantee the access of oil and natural gas to the American market through the binding mechanism of the FTA, which would prevent future discriminatory import/export regulations being imposed on Canadian energy products. Canada's agreement to the energy provisions within the FTA can be interpreted as an attempt to guarantee the long-term economic stability of oil and natural gas exports to the large American market, with both sides being constrained from imposing protectionist discriminatory taxes and regulations (as they had often done in the past).

Ideas

Both Conservatives in Canada and Republicans in the United States subscribed to the neo-conservative ideas about the economy that were dominant in the 1980s. According to this view, market forces, not governments, should direct the economy; less government control would allow business to operate more efficiently and profitably; and trade liberalization and deregulation were the most appropriate responses to a rising tide of protectionism. Consequently, in the FTA Canada and the United States sought to confirm their commitment to trade liberalization, market prices, and the deregulation of energy resources.[17]

For its part, the Mulroney government introduced changes that reflected these beliefs. Among other policy changes, it dismantled the NEP, removed the natural gas export surplus tests, phased out discriminatory taxes on oil and gas development, and eliminated most oil and gas import and export restrictions. This deregulation was then included in the FTA. As McRae notes, the FTA was "a natural extension of policy for a government committed to allowing the marketplace to allocate resources with a minimum of government intervention." Moreover, creating free trade in energy would make it "impossible for any future government to introduce a policy like the NEP – to the delight of energy producers and to the dismay of energy consumers."[18]

Free market ideas, therefore, not only influenced the deregulation of the Canadian oil and gas industry, but they also motivated Ottawa to extend or include deregulation in the FTA. The agreement is difficult to amend and, thus, would make it troublesome for future governments to stray from the course of trade liberalization and market-oriented energy policies, regardless of pressures brought to bear by politicians or special interests.

Interest Groups

The oil and gas lobby in Canada is quite influential and was directly involved in formulating the energy provisions of the FTA. Many of the companies consulted during the policy-making process were MNCs with headquarters in the United States. These companies were also the most discriminated against between 1980 and 1985 when the NEP was in force, and, therefore, they pushed hard for the Mulroney government to ensure that no future government could enact anything similar to it. Overall, the producers were satisfied with the energy provisions. The western provinces, particularly Alberta, also pressed to ensure market access for oil and natural gas and to preclude the possibility of another NEP; they were quite pleased with the energy provisions, although Ontario was dissatisfied because of the potential costs to its economy in a deregulated crisis situation.[19]

The energy provisions of the FTA essentially guaranteed that market pricing and access would prevail for both countries and that, much to the delight of energy interest groups on both sides of the border, there could not be another NEP unless the agreement was abrogated or the energy provisions renegotiated. What is interesting is the total absence of environmental groups in the formulation of the energy provisions – particularly given the strong influence these groups have on US policy-makers. One might have expected environmental groups to have tried to include some new regulations to govern oil and gas development concerns.

International Forces

The potential threat of OPEC embargoes, and the instability in the Middle East, which affects not only security of supply but also prices, led to the formation of the IEA in 1974. Both Canada and the United States are founding members of the IEA and, thus, are obliged "to impose upon themselves several symbolic and some important material constraints on their behaviour and, at least rhetorically, [to commit] themselves to a co-ordinated and multilateral energy management strategy.

This has made the diplomatic costs of unilateral policies higher than it would otherwise be."[20]

The main purpose of the IEA was to inspire the member countries to plan for emergencies. The IEA has two main provisions. First, in an emergency one IEA member cannot cut off exports to another IEA country. Second, an IEA member can only cut its exports to another member "by the level of the demand restraint it has applied domestically."[21] The proportional sharing clause of the FTA reflected the obligations of both Canada and the United States under the IEA. Perhaps the inclusion of the proportional sharing clause was meant to reaffirm the commitment to IEA principles as well as to limit the regulatory actions available to both countries.

Assessment of Variables

The relentless recession of the early 1980s, coupled with a decade of uncertain oil supply and unstable oil and natural gas prices, prompted the Mulroney governments to look for options that would provide greater economic security. Deregulation was the foremost choice: there was a shared commitment in both Ottawa and Washington to having market rather than protectionist forces prevail, and thus both governments sought a comprehensive bilateral agreement to ensure that the deregulation of the oil and gas industry would be difficult to reverse. The influence of interest groups in Canada was somewhat significant, but not in the way that most would expect, as the oil and gas industry and the producing provinces were asked to participate in the policy-making process rather than left to function as lobbyists. In addition, the vestiges of Canada's NEP and its perceived discrimination against American companies influenced Canadian desires to limit the ability of future governments to implement another NEP. Through their membership in the IEA, Canada and the United States are committed to share resources in a time of crisis. The inclusion of the proportional sharing clause confirms this obligation and further limits the potential regulatory actions available to both countries in a crisis situation.

Although economics, ideas, interest groups, and international forces combined to influence the Mulroney government to embark upon a continental energy policy, economics and ideas are the strongest explanations for this outcome. The overriding concern for the Conservatives during this period was the rejuvenation of the economy, and there was a pervasive belief that the oil and gas industry could be used as an "engine of growth" for this purpose. The way to increase the activity of the industry, which would, in turn, create employment across the country and bolster the economy, was to remove the many regulations that had prevented it from operating efficiently and increase the level of exports without fear of

American protectionism. The former was accomplished through deregulation and the latter was achieved through the securing of deregulatory policies within the energy provisions of the FTA.

Canadian policies towards deregulation of the oil and gas industry, and the solidification of that deregulation in the FTA, were determined largely by economics, but they were also determined by the idea that market forces should prevail if the operation of the economy is to be successful. In the case of energy policy, ideas took precedence over interest-based explanations because many, though not all, Conservatives subscribed to the ideology that market forces should be left to guide the economy; therefore, less government regulation and intervention would allow the oil and gas industry to operate efficiently and profitably. Armed with these neo-conservative ideas, the Conservative government did not need to be strongly influenced by the oil and gas industry lobby with respect to deregulation because their beliefs were essentially the same. The Canadian government was so devoted to these ideas that it chose to minimize the concerns of consumer-based Ontario to the benefit of producer-based Alberta.

The Conservatives chose to depart from previous energy and foreign policy and to formulate a continental energy policy because they believed that restrictive regulations concerning oil and natural gas policy harmed the economy and were fundamentally at odds with the neo-conservative ideology of less government intervention in the market. The energy provisions of the FTA, which are essentially based upon the Western Accord, provide for less federal involvement in the oil and gas industry, prevent future governments from imposing harsh regulations that would interfere with market forces, and stand as evidence that, with regard to government policy in the Mulroney years, the Conservatives were architects rather than engineers. In the end, Canada was led to deregulate its oil and gas industry and sought to secure that deregulation in a bilateral agreement due to the overriding influence of economic concerns and ideological forces.

Conclusion

The consequences of Mulroney's continental energy policy are many, and they demonstrate a dramatic departure from traditional Canadian trade and foreign policy. Since the FTA's energy provisions affect both Canada and the United States, it is useful to discuss their implications for both countries. Unless the energy provisions of the FTA are renegotiated or the entire agreement is abrogated, Canadian and American governments are committed to freer trade in oil and natural gas and are limited in their policy options. This is particularly significant in the case of Canada because it represents a conscious effort by the Conservatives to constrain future governments from implementing another NEP. Neither country can impose price controls on oil and natural gas, establish a two-tiered pricing system, or impose import or export charges without levying the same amount on domestic consumers. Both countries may continue to provide government incentives for oil and gas exploration and development, but investors must be treated fairly in both countries. Regulatory changes in one country that also affect the other country must be discussed by both before being implemented. This is meant to discourage discriminatory regulations. Canada gains access to Alaskan oil, which is not allowed to be exported to any other country. Both countries limit the regulatory actions available to them through the proportional sharing arrangement so that neither country can arbitrarily cut off exports to the other in a time of crisis or conservation. The reduction must maintain the same proportion of export to supply as was averaged over the previous thirty-six months. Since Canada exports more oil and natural gas to the United States than it imports from it, this provision is often considered to be more favourable for the latter than to the former.

Debate surrounding the energy provisions in the FTA is usually centred upon the proportional sharing clause and the import and export pricing restrictions because they do limit Canadian policy options. Why would Canada agree to measures that compromise its independence? Energy crises are uncommon, whereas more general fluctuations in the market are not. It was prudent for the government to secure guaranteed access to the large American market even if it entailed the remote possibility that Canada's independence would be constrained in a time of crisis. Through their membership in the IEA, Canada and the United States are committed to share resources in a time of crisis. The inclusion of the proportional sharing clause confirms this obligation and further limits the potential regulatory actions available to both countries during a crisis situation.

Canada's entry into a continental energy agreement with the United States was a departure from traditional Canadian energy policy, and it benefited both countries equally, albeit in different ways. The Mulroney Conservatives were inspired by the neo-conservative ideas that privileged trade liberalization and the free flow of market forces. Never before had a Canadian government sought to curtail its policy choices with respect to the precious resource of oil and gas. Yet the Conservatives were willing to limit Canada's freedom to manoeuvre in order to ensure that the deregulation of trade and of both the Canadian and American oil and natural gas industry would be difficult to alter. They firmly believed that such action would improve the economy and that the market, not the government, should be the regulator of the resource. Since Canada exports more oil and natural gas than it imports or consumes,[22] and since oil crises do not happen often and do not last long, Canada's agreement to the energy provisions of the FTA can be interpreted as an attempt to guarantee economic stability through ensuring that Canada's oil and natural gas exports have long-term access to the large American market. As for the United States, it would have access to Canadian resources and not have to be so dependent upon OPEC oil.

Notes

1 Leonard Waverman, "Reluctant Bride: Canadian-American Energy Relations," in *The Energy Question: An International Failure of Policy*, vol. 2: *North America*, ed. Edward W. Erickson and Leonard Waverman (Toronto: University of Toronto Press, 1974), 217.

2 Canada, Department of Energy, Mines and Resources (DEMR), *The National Energy Program* (Ottawa: Supply and Services Canada, 1980).

3 Edward A. Carmichael, *Energy and the Canada-US Free Trade Agreement* (Toronto: C.D. Howe Institute, 1988), 7.

4 Robert N. McRae, "Canadian Energy Development," *Current History* 87, 527 (March 1988): 117.

5 Stephen Clarkson, *Canada and the Reagan Challenge*, updated ed. (Toronto: McClelland and Stewart, 1985), 71-81.

6 Tammy Nemeth, "Pat Carney and the Dismantling of the National Energy Program," *Past Imperfect* 7 (1998): 87-123.

7 DEMR, *The Atlantic Accord* (Ottawa: Supply and Services Canada, 1985), 2-11.

8 DEMR, *The Western Accord* (Ottawa: Supply and Services Canada, 1985), 2-4; DEMR, *Agreement on Natural Gas Markets and Prices* (Ottawa: Supply and Services Canada, 1985), 1-5; and DEMR, *Canada's Energy Frontiers* (Ottawa: Supply and Services Canada, 1985), 5-19.

9 Richard G. Lipsey and Robert C. York, *Evaluating the Free Trade Deal* (Toronto: C.D. Howe Institute, 1988), 51.

10 Carmichael, *Energy and the Canada-US FTA*, 9. For example, if exports to the United States totalled 20 percent of Canada's total supply, and Canada decided to conserve its resources by reducing its supply, then it would have to continue exporting to the United States at a level of 20 percent of the supply. Thus if Canada had 100 barrels of oil and exported twenty of them, and then reduced the supply to fifty barrels, then the export level to the United States would have to be ten barrels.

11 Ibid. Carmichael notes that simply because there is a mechanism for consultation does not mean that the decisions will always be favourable to the complaining country. However, Canada is in a stronger negotiating position because the dispute settlement would take place at the Cabinet level.

12 Canada, Department of External Affairs, *The Canada-US Free Trade Agreement* (Ottawa: Supply and Services Canada, 1988), 147.

13 Ibid., 233-37.

14 Bruce Doern and Brian W. Tomlin, *Faith and Fear: The Free Trade Story* (Toronto: Stoddart, 1991), 19.

15 Canada, Natural Resources Canada, document EP 5000-2-2, memorandum, "Prince Albert Caucus, Progressive Conservative Agenda for Government, Policy Area: Energy," 5 July 1984. On PC policy after September 1984, see the 8 November 1984 economic statement presented by the minister of finance, Michael Wilson (Canada, Department of Finance, *Economic Fiscal Statement 8 November 1984* [Ottawa: Supply and Services Canada, 1984], 11-12).

16 United States, Department of Energy, *US Energy Policy* (Washington: Department of Energy, 1988), 140.

17 Bruce W. Wilkinson, "Trade Liberalization, the Market Ideology, and Morality: Have We a Sustainable System?" in Ricardo Grinspun and Maxwell A. Cameron eds., *Political Economy of North American Free Trade* (Montreal and Kingston: McGill-Queen's University Press, 1993), 27. When referring to the ideology of trade liberalization and market integration in North America, Wilkinson states that the Canada-US FTA "stress[es] the importance of

market forces and market objectives in such an ideology." See also John Herd Thompson and Stephen J. Randall, *Canada and the United States: Ambivalent Allies* (Montreal and Kingston: McGill-Queen's University Press, 1994), 274, 277.

18 McRae, "Canadian Energy Development," 118.
19 Ibid., 119.
20 Glen Toner and Gregg Legare, "Canadian Energy Security: The State of Canada's Emergency Preparedness System," *Canadian Public Administration* 33 (Spring 1989): 69.
21 Ibid., 89.
22 Industry Canada, *Strategis*, Trade Data Online, "Canadian Imports-Specific Products-HS 270900," http://strategis.ic.gc.ca/cgi-bin/wow.wow.codeCountrySelectionPage. Canada receives most of its crude petroleum imports from Norway at 34 percent. See also "US Imports-Specific Products-HS 270900," http: //strategis.ic.gc.ca/cgi-bin/wow.wow.code CountrySelectionPage. Canada usually averages between 12 percent and 14 percent of total US imports, with most US imports coming from Saudi Arabia.

5
Shades of Grey in Canada's Greening during the Mulroney Era
Heather A. Smith

During the Conservative era, the environment moved from a relatively marginal dimension of Canadian foreign policy to an issue that, according to Robert Boardman, achieved the status and flavour of high politics.[1] Especially after the fall of the Berlin Wall, environmental degradation captured the attention of government leaders, including the Canadian prime minister: Brian Mulroney's rhetoric captured the essence of the movement towards international greening as he advocated a new global environmental ethic.

The promotion of an environmental vision may lead one to assume that, in the case of international environmental politics, Canada was an architect, to draw on the metaphor used by Denis Stairs. Such a conclusion would, however, be hasty and simplistic. Following Stairs's argument, I find that Canada's international environmental policy was more engineering than architecture, for the Mulroney government's policies were shaped largely by the external environment – understood both figuratively and literally. This said, Canada, through its multilateral activities, did often function as part of a team of architects; however, Canadian representatives on those teams were not politicians but the bureaucrats whose technical expertise contributed to the building of international environmental regimes.

I begin by describing the place of the environment on the Mulroney government's agenda as exemplified by the 1986 report of the Special Joint Committee on Canada's International Relations, chaired by Thomas Hockin and Jean-Maurice Simard. I also discuss the international "greening" that occurred in the late 1980s. The second section turns to a specific set of environmental issues: acid rain, ozone depletion, and climate change. The third section identifies some patterns across these three atmospheric issues. While the issues vary in many ways – including the number of actors involved, the degree of scientific consensus on the issue, the place of the issue on the policy cycle when addressed by the Mulroney government, the sense of urgency associated with the issue, and the role of the provinces – it is nonetheless possible to draw some conclusions about whether the Mulroney Conservatives were architects or engineers in this area. While I suggest that there is evidence to support both characterizations, I ultimately argue that, in the international environmental arena, the Mulroney government functioned more as engineers than as architects.

Environmental Issues during the Mulroney Era: An Overview

The marginal importance of environmental issues early in the Mulroney era can perhaps best be seen in the report of the 1986 Special Joint Committee on Canada's International Relations, *Independence and Internationalism.*[2] The Hockin-Simard report is a reflection of the times. East-West concerns are on the top of the agenda, followed by international trade and competitiveness. Relative to other issues on the foreign policy agenda in 1986, environmental issues seem to have little significance. This is consistent with the general tendency at the time to marginalize environmental issues and place them in the realm of low politics. Practically, the limited treatment of environmental issues is explained in part by the division of labour within the bureaucracy, as we will see below. Finally, the document is a reflection of the fact that environmental issues tend to rise on the international agenda during relatively relaxed times, such as during the detente period.

This foreign policy document precedes the broader international shift of environmental awareness. The greening of international relations in the 1980s is often associated with a number of events. The discovery of the ozone hole fostered a sense of global environmental vulnerability. The 1987 publication of *Our Common Future*,[3] the report of the World Commission on Environment and Development, popularized the term "sustainable development" – a concept much more palatable to government leaders than were previous environmental concepts (e.g., "no-growth"). Sustainable development was based on a philosophy that recognized the interconnectedness between the environment and development. The following year was the hottest year on record to that point, and it was marked by a sense of crisis about the potential implications of global warming. Nineteen eighty-eight also saw the term sustainable development used in the Toronto Group of Seven (G-7) Summit communiqué, arguably setting the groundwork for the 1989 "Green Summit" in Paris.[4] Finally, the fall of the Berlin Wall fundamentally reconfigured the international system, providing the opportunity for states to turn their attention to issues otherwise subsumed by Cold War tensions.

That the place of the environment changed, or at least appeared to change, in the late 1980s does not mean that environmental issues had previously been irrelevant. The Mulroney government was engaged in environmental issues on a variety of fronts. It inherited bilateral Canada-US issues such as acid rain and the management of Pacific salmon. Environmental issues in the early 1980s were also integral to the Canada-European Community relationship, in particular to the 1983 EC ban on the import of baby seal skins. By the mid-1980s Canadian scientists were also beginning to note the decline of the Atlantic cod stocks, the implications of which would become all too obvious with the closure of the cod fisheries in 1992.[5] The Mulroney government also inherited the ozone issue, which will be discussed in the next section.

The breadth of environmental issues addressed by the Mulroney government is best expressed in the 1990 Green Plan.[6] The plan was a response to the fall of the Berlin Wall, to international greening, and to the rise of environmental awareness among the Canadian public. It was also a tribute to the tenacity of the minister of the environment, Lucien Bouchard, who had to fight to get the document through Cabinet. The plan outlined a set of principles designed to guide Canadian environmental policy. These principles included: respect for nature, the need to meet environmental goals in ways that promote economic prosperity and make use of market forces, the efficient use of resources, shared responsibility with the provinces and global neighbours, federal leadership, and informed decision-making.[7] The federal government committed three billion dollars over five years.

While the principles outlined in the Green Plan may be dismissed as mere rhetoric, they do represent an attempt to address the tension between economic prosperity and environmental protection – a tension that informs all of the issues addressed here. The Green Plan also offers a useful catalogue of activities undertaken by the Mulroney government. The issues covered in the Green Plan ranged from the reduction of pollution in the Great Lakes to sustainable fisheries to climate change. The fight against environmental degradation has had, and continues to have, many front lines.

Three Cases: Acid Rain, Ozone Depletion, and Climate Change

In assessing the efforts of the Mulroney government to combat acid rain, ozone depletion, and climate change, one should not, as noted in the introduction, expect consistency. However, the three cases provide a sense of the multiple forces affecting Canadian international environmental policy during the Mulroney era and offer us a means by which to address whether the government functioned as architects or engineers.

Acid Rain[8]

Acid rain was a source of considerable friction between the Canadian and American governments, at least until Mulroney's arrival on the scene. Under

Mulroney the Canadian government functioned in a relatively conciliatory fashion while, at the same time, trying to use multilateral fora to impress upon the United States the need to address the transboundary issue. The acid rain story, however, predates 1984.

As a result of observations in the Muskoka Lakes in Ontario, the issue of acid rain came to the attention of the Canadian public in 1979; although, as is the case with all the issues here, what was new to the public was not new to the scientific community. Recognizing the transboundary source of the problem, the federal government quickly initiated a series of meetings with the Americans. The United States was reluctant to negotiate because American officials were not convinced that acid rain was an issue: their science did not warrant action.

While acid rain became a public issue in 1979, multilateral efforts to address the issue date back to 1977, when Canada allied with Norway and Sweden to develop an international agreement on sulphur dioxide emissions reductions. In 1979 the Convention on Long-Range Transboundary Air Pollution was signed. As a result of opposition from Britain, the United States, and Germany, the convention did not have any binding commitments regarding the reduction of sulphur dioxide emissions, the primary cause of acid rain. The negotiation of this convention did not put acid rain on the American agenda, and so the Canadian government pushed for joint action. A Memorandum of Intent (MOI) between Canada and the United States was signed in 1980, committing the two countries to begin negotiating an acid rain accord in one year. However, the incoming Reagan administration refused to be bound by this agreement. In response to this stalemate, the Canadian government under Pierre Elliott Trudeau engaged in an aggressive round of public diplomacy, returned to the international arena, and looked to the provinces, who were dragging their heels in terms of domestic control programs.

Internationally, the federal government turned to its Nordic allies for support. In March 1984, the minister of environment, Charles Caccia, hosted a meeting between Canada and nine other countries, which resulted in the establishment of the "30 Percent Club." Don Munton and Geoffrey Castle describe this club as "a group of western developed states committed to reducing [sulphur dioxide] emissions within their own territories by at least 30%."[9] The 30 Percent Club, designed to put pressure on the United States, might have embarrassed American observers but did not change the views of the Reagan administration.[10] The Trudeau government tried to negotiate a deal with the provinces, but a control program was not established until after the election of the Conservatives in 1984.

The Mulroney government was determined to have friendly relations with the Americans on all fronts, and this included acid rain. In the face of American unwillingness to accept the scientific evidence of acidification, the Canadian government kept active internationally and attempted to broker a deal at home. After difficult negotiations with the provinces, the Canada Acid Rain Control Program was enacted in February 1985, although Nova Scotia and New Brunswick did not sign on until 1987. In the seven easternmost provinces, this agreement's target was to reduce sulphur dioxide emissions to 50 percent of their 1980 levels by 1994. On the international front, Canada signed the Helsinki Protocol on Sulphur Dioxide, with the hope of pressuring the United States to take action. The United States did not sign the Helsinki Protocol. Bilaterally, and consistent with the new "cooperative era,"[11] the Mulroney government adopted less aggressive tactics in dealing with the United States. After the Shamrock Summit in March 1985, special envoys were appointed; however, while they agreed that acid rain was a serious issue, they did not recommend emissions reductions.[12] The envoy process achieved nothing positive. On the contrary, according to Doern, the report was seen by Canadian media "as evidence of Canadian delay and lack of influence in US political circles."[13] Munton and Castle argue that it was a face-saving gesture representative of a softer line taken by the Mulroney government.[14] Top level contacts between Mulroney and Reagan were also used as a means by which to express Canadian concern about acid rain, but these too were viewed as shallow gestures.

Ultimately, Canada and the United States did make a deal on acid rain. In 1991 the Canada-US Air Quality Agreement was signed. For the first time Canada established a national cap on sulphur dioxide reductions. The agreement also extended the timetable set in the 1985 federal-provincial agreement, with the deadline for the reductions being moved from 1994 to 2000. The reason for this extension may be difficulties with emissions reductions and/or an attempt to ensure symmetry with the United States. The key reason that the Air Quality Agreement was signed will not be found in Canadian diplomacy. The efforts of the Mulroney government had little effect on the American perspective, and the softening of the line with the Reagan administration did little to pressure the Americans; rather, US willingness to sign the agreement can be traced to changes in American domestic politics, in particular the election of George Bush, the change in leadership in the Senate, and the impact of the signing of an air quality agreement with Mexico.[15]

Ozone Depletion

One of the few real success stories in international environmental cooperation can be found in the efforts to combat ozone depletion. In 1987 the Montreal Protocol on Substances that Deplete the Ozone Layer was signed by representatives of twenty-four nations, plus the Commission of the European Communities.[16] Since that time the protocol has been ratified by 165 countries and amendments to it have tightened original restrictions.

In Canada and other developed states chlorofluorocarbons (CFCs) were phased out by January 1996, and in 1997 global CFC production was 88 percent below the 1,260 kilotonnes recorded in 1988.[17]

The ozone story, like acid rain and climate change, began before the election of the Mulroney government. In the early 1970s scientists expressed concern about the relationship between CFCs and ozone depletion. Initially, given industry scepticism about the science, there was little state activity. However, in 1978 the United States banned CFCs in non-essential aerosols. Canada, as a result of in-house scientific evidence, announced its intention to control ozone-depleting substances in 1976, with regulations becoming law in 1979 and being implemented in 1980.[18]

International negotiations to control CFCs began in 1982, and in 1983 the Toronto Group was formed. Initially, the group, named after the city in which it first met, included Canada, Norway, Sweden, and Switzerland.[19] The United States joined later that year. This group advocated a ban on non-essential CFCs in aerosols, an easy position to adopt given that they had all already taken that action at home. This group functioned as a coalition in the negotiations that eventually resulted in the Vienna Convention of 1985.

The Vienna Convention for the Protection of the Ozone Layer did not include a control program, and there were three reasons for this: (1) industry remained sceptical about the science and thus opposed regulation; (2) the United States was unwilling to lead on the issue, given the anti-regulatory philosophy of the Reagan government; and (3) the Toronto Group position clashed with the European Community, which had 45 percent of the CFC market.[20] The division between the Toronto Group and the European Community was based on the latter's advocacy of a cap on production and the former's advocacy of a cap on use. In spite of the relative stalemate, the participants in the Vienna negotiations did agree to negotiate a protocol within two years. Significantly, 1985 was also the year that the ozone hole was discovered. Arguably, this functioned as a catalyst, forcing state leaders to recognize the imperative of coming to some consensus on CFC regulation.

In the period before the Montreal Protocol negotiations there was a series of meetings, sponsored by the United Nations Environment Program, to discuss scientific issues and regulatory options. At one of these meetings, which took place in 1986 in Leesburg, Virginia, the Canadian government made a significant contribution to the process.[21] At this meeting the work of two Canadians, who were focusing on control options regarding CFCs, offered a compromise between the Toronto Group and the European Community.[22]

It has been argued that Montreal was selected as the site for the final set of negotiations because of Canada's leadership to that date.[23] During the

Montreal Protocol negotiations Canada continued to function under the umbrella of the Toronto Group. This said, the Canadian delegation was viewed as significant enough to be included in a series of closed-door meetings with nine other delegations. At these meetings, Mostafa Tolba, head of the United Nations Environment Program, tried to broker a deal between the Toronto Group and the European Community.[24] Richard Benedick also notes that Canadian and American scientific and economic assessments helped break the stalemate over the timing of reductions.[25] Finally, Canada proposed an industrial rationalization clause that "permitted [an] extra production allowance to be used on behalf of smaller producer countries."[26] In so far as Canada produced a mere 2 percent of CFCs, this clause served Canadian interests. The Montreal Protocol established staggered reductions of CFCs, which amounted to approximately 50 percent of 1986 levels. In the face of new scientific evidence, the timetable was moved up at subsequent meetings. The Canadian response was rapid: in 1989 Environment Canada issued regulations restricting ozone-depleting substances.[27]

Climate Change[28]

Climate change is an issue upon which Canada adopted a position of rhetorical leadership. Practically speaking, this period of leadership lasted about a year, beginning in June 1988, when a conference entitled Our Changing Atmosphere: Implications for Global Security was held in Toronto. Held in the middle of the hottest summer on record,[29] the Toronto Conference was co-sponsored by the Canadian government, the United Nations Environment Program (UNEP), and the World Meteorological Organization (WMO). At this meeting the Mulroney government promoted the adoption of a law of the atmosphere, an idea that originated in the Atmospheric Environment Service (AES) of the Department of Environment (DOE). In 1986, Tom McMillan had spoken before the Brundtland Commission and offered to hold a conference on an aspect of global environmental change. Consultations quickly followed, with AES as the lead agency. During the consultations Howard Ferguson, an assistant deputy minister in the DOE, floated the idea of a law of the atmosphere, which was adopted and promoted by the minister. The essence of the idea was to take a holistic approach to environmental issues that recognized and reaffirmed the linkages between major atmospheric issues.[30]

The forum for the articulation of this idea was the June 1988 Toronto Conference, which is often cited as the beginning of international political efforts on climate change.[31] Typically, it is noted for its emissions-reductions target. Less well known is its inclusion of a reference to a law of the atmosphere, which emerged in the conference statement as a call for a comprehensive global convention and which was promoted by both Mulroney and McMillan. In an attempt to capture the momentum from the Toronto Conference, and perhaps in an attempt to take advantage of the media attention, Mulroney proposed a follow-up meeting to consider the necessary and rapid development of a law of the atmosphere.

The follow-up meeting of legal and policy experts was held in Ottawa in February 1989. Although the final communiqué included a reference to the law of the atmosphere, essentially, the concept died at that meeting. Statements from subsequent conferences on climate change focus on a framework convention and/or on a protocol specific to climate change as opposed to the umbrella convention envisioned by proponents of the law of the atmosphere. Moreover, US participation was deemed necessary because the United States was the largest emitter of carbon dioxide (CO_2), and the law of the atmosphere did not have American backing.

Canada continued to participate in the numerous meetings that led up to the beginning of the negotiations of the Framework Convention on Climate Change (FCCC) in early 1991. During this time Canada's claims of leadership were tempered. The movement away from rhetorical leadership can be explained by federal interdepartmental competition, which saw Energy, Mines and Resources Canada claim the right to develop domestic policy, thus countering both the ecological zeal of Environment Canada and the intransigence of the provincial governments. The federal government was constitutionally obliged to consult the provinces on this matter of natural resources, but provincial governments were (and continue to be) reluctant to adopt what are perceived to be economically costly emissions reductions strategies. Given these constraints, Canada adopted a commitment to limit CO_2 emissions and other greenhouse gases not covered under the Montreal Protocol to 1990 levels by the year 2000.[32] The December 1990 Green Plan outlined a comprehensive commitment that included CO_2 and other gases such as methane, nitrous oxide, and ozone. Such a commitment, in the view of policy-makers, allowed the Canadian government the flexibility to deal with the gases that could be most readily reduced. This position placed Canada ahead of the United States, which was seen as an international laggard; but it also separated Ottawa from the EC, which was calling for a CO_2-only convention.

During the negotiations of the Framework Convention on Climate Change, Canada's self-described role was that of facilitator. Government officials shunned aggressive behaviour and worked to try to narrow the divisions between the United States and the European Community. For Canada the middle road was the comprehensive stabilization commitment – a commitment that it saw the United States potentially moving towards in the latter part of the negotiations and that it felt the Europeans would also accept. Although this commitment was reasonable to the

Canadian negotiators, the EC coalition was suspicious, widely assuming that Canada was simply working on behalf of the United States.

The 1992 United Nations Conference on the Environment and Development (UNCED) was held hostage by George Bush. He threatened to not attend the conference, thus putting in jeopardy the integrity of the FCCC. The United States was the largest producer of CO_2, and, without a US commitment, the framework convention would be meaningless. Mulroney, interestingly, went to UNCED promoting the Biodiversity Treaty, which was also to be signed. In contrast to the United States, which refused to sign the agreement because of perceived impacts on the American pharmaceutical industry, Mulroney was seen as a champion of the treaty. He was not, however, viewed as a champion of the climate change convention, although Canada did sign and quickly ratify the FCCC. Shortly after the UNCED meeting the federal government, in tandem with the provinces, initiated the process of implementing the FCCC, which called for a voluntary stabilization of greenhouse gases at 1990 levels by 2000.

Engineers or Architects? Analyzing the Three Cases
My analysis suggests that there is considerable evidence to support the argument that, in the international environmental arena, Canada's activities were largely engineering in nature. External forces and domestic concerns shaped the Mulroney government's behaviour, and the bridges that were built were constructed in such a way that any government might have built them, regardless of political orientation. One of the central external factors that functioned as a catalyst was the recognition of ecological dependence. This recognition necessitated Canadian action as it was clear that none of the issues under examination could be resolved unilaterally. In the case of acid rain, this dependence was especially obvious as the bulk of acidic precipitation came from south of the Canadian border. Ozone depletion and climate change clearly indicated global ecological vulnerability. One may argue that this was a case of interdependence; however, at the heart of global environmental issues is a dependence on other states and peoples to take action to reduce environmental degradation.

Ecological dependence and the global/regional nature of environmental issues compelled the Mulroney government to turn to multilateral fora. In the case of acid rain and ozone, Canada was committed to multilateral endeavours prior to the election of the Mulroney government. This commitment created the expectation that Canada would participate in multilateral construction of environmental regimes.

Where ecological dependence and prior international commitments moved Canada to take action, there was a significant exogenous factor that constrained the government's behaviour and functioned to define the parameters of Canada's policy: the United States. Environmental activism was tempered by economic dependence on the United States, and more broadly, Canadian activism was shaped by the dominant neoliberalism of the period. Canada is economically intertwined with the United States, and this was reflected in our policy development. In the case of ozone, Canada timed its phase-out mechanisms to parallel those adopted by the United States, thus ensuring a level playing field between the two states.[33] The extension of the deadline for the Canadian reduction of sulphur dioxide in the 1991 Air Quality Agreement was yet another example of the government trying to ensure that its environmental initiatives would not put Canada at an economic disadvantage vis-à-vis its largest trading partner. More broadly, we can see how concern for economic initiatives takes precedence over environmental integrity as the Mulroney government, attempting to ensure a friendly relationship with the United States, and with its eye to free trade negotiations, softened its position on acid rain.

One could argue that Canada's behaviour in terms of the United States was merely pragmatic. Indeed it was. But the behaviour was also evidence of Canadian support of the American vision. Central to Canadian environmental policy initiatives (such as the Green Plan) that were developed during the Mulroney era was the promotion of market mechanisms as a means of addressing environmental degradation; although it was an approach that was by no means unique to that era. The Green Plan also called for meeting environmental goals in ways that promote economic prosperity. Throughout this period, the Mulroney government promoted a new global environmental ethic, but it also took several actions that suggested that, ultimately, it saw economic growth as more important than the environment. For example, directly after an assertive speech at the 1988 Toronto Conference, Mulroney announced further subsidies to the Hibernia project. Green Plan money allocated in 1990 was cut in the following budget. And Canada was, at the time of the Green Plan, the second highest per capita emitter of CO_2 (even though Canadians are responsible for only 2 percent of the world's CO_2 emissions). Likewise, at the same time that Mulroney was championing the Biodiversity Convention at Rio, the Atlantic cod fisheries were closed as a result of overfishing.

However, to focus solely on the engineering metaphor portrays Canada and the Mulroney government as simply puppets of the system. This perspective denies the ability of state leaders and bureaucrats to make a difference in international fora. As this chapter makes clear, there was some architectural design taking place in the three cases studies, for in all three cases Canada often functioned as a technical or entrepreneurial leader. Drawing on the work of Andrew F. Cooper one may argue that, in the case of climate change, Canada functioned both as a catalyst and as a facilitator. A catalyst seeks "the generation of political energy around a particular issue"; a facilitator "entails the planning, convening and hosting of meetings, setting priorities for future activity and drawing up rhetorical declarations and manifestos."[34] The cases explored in this chapter are rich with examples of meetings that were initiated and hosted by Canadians. Recall the Toronto Group in the ozone negotiations and the fact that Montreal hosted the final negotiations on a protocol to restrict CFCs. The climate change case offers us the 1988 Toronto Conference and the subsequent Ottawa meeting that addressed the Canadian idea of a law of the atmosphere. Canada's role as a facilitator in the acid rain case preceded the election of the Mulroney government. That Canada did not act as a facilitator with regard to attempts to reduce acid rain may be indicative of the Mulroney government's retreat from a confrontational style and its move to quiet bilateral chats.

Why did Canada act as a facilitator? The answer lies in the technical expertise housed within Environment Canada and, especially, the Atmospheric Environment Service. Behind the scenes, individuals such as Jim Bruce and Tom Brydges worked on acid rain. Likewise, it was the work of two Canadians that helped broker the deal in Leesburg, Virginia, when the ozone negotiations seemed to be at a stalemate: Kenneth Hare and Jim Bruce, both of whom had a long history of international environmental service, played pivotal roles in propelling Canada into the climate change limelight. And the Atmospheric Environment Service was the catalyst behind Canada's promotion of the Law of the Atmosphere. Simply put, Canada had extensive functional expertise with atmospheric issues. People like Bruce, Brydges, Hare, and countless others functioned internationally as architects, usually in tandem with other bureaucrats, whose technical expertise enabled Canada to participate in designing international environmental regimes.

Conclusion

The cases of acid rain, ozone depletion, and climate change support Denis Stairs's observation that environmental policy during the Mulroney era was more a matter of engineering than of architecture. Canada responded to a new environmental crisis (i.e., climate change), while at the same time continuing to participate in ongoing negotiations on acid rain and ozone depletion. It is likely that, had a different government been in power, it would have shown at least a similar level of concern for the environment.

Does this make the political party in power irrelevant to an understanding of policy outcomes? The answer must be an emphatic no. Despite the tension between ecological and economic dependence, the Mulroney government did try to promote an ecological vision, even if that vision was wrapped in neoliberal ideology. The Mulroney government supported science, produced the Green Plan, and actively engaged in issues such as climate change. There were choices involved, as there always are.

To put the Conservative choices into perspective, it is instructive to note that the Liberal government of Jean Chrétien, elected in 1993, slashed funding to the Department of Environment and saw environmental issues as fundamental challenges to economic competitiveness. Environmental integrity was lost in the shuffle, and this suggests that an engineer's perspective quickly becomes a structural perspective that absolves governments of any responsibility, enabling them to simply cite the constraints of circumstance. To recognize that in the 1980s and early 1990s Canada was – and could still be – an architect means that one can impose some accountability on government; it also holds out the hope that a new environmental ethic might not only be promoted, but also implemented.

Acknowledgments
The author gratefully acknowledges the insightful contributions of David Black, Don Munton, Claire Turenne Sjolander, and Dan Wingham in the preparation of this chapter.

Notes

1 Robert Boardman, "The Multilateral Dimension: Canada in the International System," in *Canadian Environmental Policy: Ecosystems, Politics and Process*, ed. Robert Boardman (Toronto: Oxford University Press, 1992), 233.
2 Canada, Special Joint Committee of the Senate and the House of Commons on Canada's International Relations, *Independence and Internationalism* (Ottawa: Supply and Services Canada, 1986).
3 World Commission on Environment and Development, *Our Common Future* (New York: Oxford University Press, 1987).
4 Canada, Office of the Prime Minister, Notes for an Address by the Right Honourable Brian Mulroney, Prime Minister of Canada, at the International Environment Bureau Award, Washington, DC, 2 May 1989.
5 Greenpeace, *Canadian Atlantic Fisheries Collapse*, (http: //www.greenpeace.org/~comms/ cbio/cancod.html.), 1999, 3.
6 Canada, *Canada's Green Plan for a Healthy Environment* (Ottawa: Supply and Services Canada, 1990).
7 Heather A. Smith, "A New International Environmental Order? An Assessment of the Impact of the Global Warming Epistemic Community," (PhD diss. Kingston, Queen's University, 1993), 139-40.
8 This section draws heavily upon the work of Don Munton and Geoffrey Castle, and the essential argument is theirs. See Don Munton and Geoffrey Castle, "The Continental Dimension: Canada and the United States," in *Canadian Environmental Policy: Ecosystems, Politics and Process*, ed. Robert Boardman (Toronto: Oxford University Press, 1992); and "Reducing Acid Rain, 1980s," in *Canadian Foreign Policy: Selected Cases*, ed. Don Munton and John Kirton (Scarborough: Prentice-Hall Canada, 1992).
9 Munton and Castle, "Continental Dimension," 218.
10 Edward A. Parson with Rodney Dobell, Adam Fenech, Don Munton, and Heather Smith, "Leading While Keeping in Step: Management of Global Atmospheric Issues in Canada," in *Learning to Manage Global Environmental Risks: A Comparative History of Social Responses to Climate Change, Ozone Depletion and Acid Rain*, ed. William C. Clark, Jill Jager, Josee van Eijndhoven, and Nancy M. Dickson (Cambridge, MA: MIT Press, 2001), 17.
11 Munton and Castle, "Continental Dimension," 218.
12 Ibid., 219.

13 G. Bruce Doern, *Green Diplomacy: How Environmental Decisions Are Made* (Toronto: C.D. Howe Institute, 1993), 42.
14 Munton and Castle, "Continental Dimension," 219.
15 On these changes, see Munton and Castle, "Reducing Acid Rain, 1980s," 376-77.
16 Richard Elliott Benedick, *Ozone Diplomacy: New Directions in Safeguarding the Planet* (Cambridge, MA: Harvard University Press, 1991), 99.
17 *National Environmental Indicator Series*, "Stratospheric Ozone Depletion: Issue Context," (http://www3.ec.gc.ca/~ind/English/Ozone/Bulletin/st_iss_e.cfm).
18 Parson et al., "Leading While Keeping in Step," 22; Ian H. Rowlands, *The Politics of Global Atmospheric Change* (Manchester: Manchester University Press, 1995), 104.
19 Benedick, *Ozone Diplomacy*, 42.
20 Doern, *Green Diplomacy*, 52.
21 Ibid., 53.
22 Ian H. Rowlands, "The International Politics of Global Environmental Change," in *Global Environmental Change and International Relations*, ed. Ian Rowlands and Malory Greene (London: Macmillan, 1992), 24.
23 Parson et al., "Leading While Keeping in Step."
24 Benedick, *Ozone Diplomacy*, 85.
25 Ibid., 88.
26 Ibid., 81.
27 Parson et al., "Leading While Keeping in Step," 25.
28 Much of this section is drawn from Douglas Macdonald and Heather Smith, "Promises Made, Promise Broken: Questioning Canada's Commitments to Climate Change," *International Journal* 55 (Winter 1999-2000): 107-24.
29 The record was surpassed in 1998. See Canada, Environment Canada, *Media Advisory*, "1998 – The Warmest Year on Record," http: //www.ec.gc.ca/press/1998_m_e.html, January 1999.
30 Howard Ferguson, *Draft – World Conference on the Changing Atmosphere – Highlights of the Planning Process* (Toronto: Atmospheric Environment Service, 1988), 2.
31 Matthew Paterson, *Global Warming and Global Politics* (London: Routledge, 1996), 33.
32 Canada, *Canada's Green Plan*, 100.
33 Parson et al., "Leading While Keeping in Step," 50.
34 Andrew F. Cooper, "Niche Diplomacy: A Conceptual Overview," in *Niche Diplomacy: Middle Powers after the Cold War*, ed. Andrew F. Cooper (New York: St Martin's Press, 1997), 9.

6
A Northern Foreign Policy: The Politics of Ad Hocery
Rob Huebert

Early in the Conservative government's first term, the United States Coast Guard icebreaker *Polar Sea* transited the Northwest Passage and precipitated a crisis in Canadian-American relations. Evidence suggests that the Americans did not make the transit to assert their claims regarding the status of the passage but simply because of operational requirements. Whatever the motivation, the voyage resulted in a major re-evaluation of Canadian Arctic policies. This chapter explores how these policies evolved during the Conservative era. In particular, I address the degree to which the new Conservative government had a clear plan for Canada's Arctic waters and the degree to which it was simply responding to events in an ad hoc fashion. On 10 September, Joe Clark, the secretary of state for external affairs, announced six policy initiatives that formed the basis of government action for the remainder of the decade and that constituted what might be thought of as a northern foreign policy. These initiatives provided for the establishment of a legal Canadian claim to these waters and to their protection under Canadian law; they also elaborated a framework for the conduct of Canadian-American relations in the Arctic. However, while these initiatives appear to indicate a comprehensive policy approach to the Arctic, I argue that they were really the result of a hurried government effort to create the appearance of action.

The Polar Sea Transit

In August 1985, the *Polar Sea* sailed through the Northwest Passage. The immediate catalyst for the voyage was the simple fact that the US Coast Guard had too many requirements and too few icebreakers. Its fleet was small, aging, and heavily tasked. In 1985, the Americans had five icebreakers, only two of which had been built since 1954.[1] The *Northwind*, which normally runs supplies to the American airbase at Thule in Greenland, was found to be unfit to operate following its annual maintenance inspection. In its place, the decision was made to send the *Polar Sea*, based in Seattle, to Thule. Although it was possible to send the *Polar Sea* through the Panama Canal on the eastward portion of the voyage, there would be insufficient time for it to return via the canal to the western Arctic to complete its normal western missions off the coast of Alaska.[2] It was decided to send it home via the Northwest Passage.

Once this decision had been made, the US Coast Guard contacted the US State Department and the Canadian Coast Guard. The planned voyage was approved, and, on 21 May 1985, the Canadian desk sent a cable to the US embassy in Ottawa requesting that it notify Canada. In the demarche, the United States emphasized the practical nature of the voyage, pointing out its operational rationale. It also invited Canadian participation in order to undertake mutual research. However, the demarche also acknowledged the different positions that the two countries held regarding the status of the Northwest Passage.[3]

The Canadian response came on 11 June 1985. It claimed that the passage fell within Canadian internal waters; however, it welcomed the American offer to proceed with the voyage on a cooperative basis.[4] Nowhere did it ask the United States to request any form of permission for the upcoming voyage. The voyage was deemed to be acceptable in principle with only the details regarding pollution control to be worked out. The State Department responded on 24 June; it welcomed Canada's "positive response" to the "invitation" for Canadian participation on the voyage, and it stated that consultations between the US Coast Guard and the Canadian Coast Guard had already begun. The note ended by re-stating that "the United States considers that this transit, and the preparations for it, in no way prejudices the juridical position of either side regarding the Northwest Passage, and it understands that the Government of Canada shares that view."[5]

At this point, officials at the US State Department believed that the issue had been resolved.[6] However, Canada's position began to shift. On 31 July, the day before the voyage was due to begin, Ottawa issued a demarche to the United States with a much less accommodating tone: the government agreed with the American position that the voyage did not prejudice the legal position of either state; however, it then expressly granted Canada's consent for the voyage – consent that the United States had never requested.[7]

The voyage was relatively uneventful except for the media attention it created and the protests of some Canadian groups, such as the Council for Canadians, which strongly opposed it.[8] Likewise, editorial opinion tended to be critical of the government's lack of action, particularly during the voyage through the Canadian section of the passage.[9] Because of this public outcry, the government decided that it had to be seen to be defending Canadian interests. As a result, in August 1985, the Privy Council Office (PCO) was given the task of coordinating an immediate reaction to the voyage.[10] PCO officials contacted various government departments and asked them to prepare a list of current projects that could be publicly presented as a means of sovereignty protection and to classify their actions into three broad categories: (1) measures directly relevant to Canada's Arctic waters claims, (2) measures of a practical character that indirectly enhanced Canada's claims, and (3) measures of symbolic value. Once this review had been completed, recommendations were presented to the Cabinet's Priorities and Planning Committee, which met in Vancouver from 21 to 23 August.[11] Although the minutes of the meeting remain classified, Clark had earlier told reporters that the option of taking the issue of Canadian claims of sovereignty over the Arctic waters to the International Court of Justice (ICJ) was being considered, although no decision had yet been made.[12]

The Mulroney Government's Response

Clark publicly announced the government's decisions on 10 September 1985. They included the following: the immediate adoption of an order-in-council establishing straight baselines around the Arctic archipelago as of 1 January 1986; a Canadian Laws Offshore Application Act; talks with the United States on cooperation in Arctic waters, "on the basis of full respect for Canadian sovereignty"; an increase of surveillance over-flights of Arctic waters by Canadian Forces aircraft; increased Canadian naval activity in the eastern Arctic in 1986; the withdrawal of the 1970 reservation to Canada's acceptance of the compulsory jurisdiction of the ICJ; and construction of a large icebreaker capable of polar operations.[13]

Straight Baselines

Canada had first used straight baselines in 1964, under the Territorial Sea and Fishing Zone Act.[14] The intent was to allow the government to claim a fishing zone and territorial sea following the negotiations at the UN Conferences on the Law of the Sea – UNCLOS I in 1958 and UNCLOS II in 1960. However, it was not until 1967 that the first set of regulations was adopted to actually implement the fishing regulations within the zone; and even then these regulations established baselines only on the east and west coasts.[15]

The decision to draw straight baselines in the Canadian Arctic can be traced to the voyages of the *Manhattan* in 1969 and 1970. Following the first *Manhattan* voyage, the government of Pierre Elliott Trudeau explored three broad policy alternatives, one of which was to enclose the entire Arctic archipelago by drawing straight baselines. Eventually, the government decided to focus on measures other than the declaration of baselines because it was believed that international law was not sufficiently developed at that time to support such a move.[16]

However, by 1985, the assessment of how straight baselines would be viewed under international law had changed, and External Affairs officials urged the government to adopt this measure for the Arctic.[17] There was little opposition to this suggestion, and since much of the actual determination of where the baselines would be located had already been completed, all that remained was the decision to declare their existence. For a government eager for policies that could be immediately implemented, this policy was easy to accept. The baselines were declared to be established on 10 September 1985 and came into effect on 1 January 1986.[18]

Canadian Laws Offshore Application Act

Of the six policy initiatives selected by Clark, the inclusion of the Canadian Laws Offshore Application Act was perhaps the one least readily related to the protection of Arctic sovereignty, since it was intended to respond to issues quite different from those raised by perceived intrusions into Arctic waters. The main catalyst for it was the development of offshore oil drilling platforms in the Arctic beyond the twelve-mile territorial sea. Although the Law of the Sea negotiations of the early 1980s were leaning in the direction of giving states some level of jurisdiction over offshore resources beyond their territorial sea, it was not clear whether the Canadian legal system adequately covered offshore activity beyond the twelve-mile limit. A review in 1984 had determined that, due to the lack of a specific government policy, there was little consistency in how Canada enforced its laws in this area.[19] The Canadian Laws Offshore Application Act was therefore designed to provide police enforcement agencies with appropriate legislation.

According to Canadian officials, the measure was conceived as a means of protecting Canadian sovereignty only after the voyage of the *Polar Sea* had occurred. The purpose of the bill's inclusion on Clark's policy list, therefore, can be seen as a means of increasing the number of initiatives being announced. However, it took two attempts to get this bill through, and it was not passed until December 1990. By then, so much time had gone by that the government no longer felt obligated to justify it as a means of sovereignty enforcement. (The act was eventually repealed in 1996, on passage of the Ocean Act, which established a twenty-four-nautical-mile contiguous zone within which Canadian laws are enforced and that was more in keeping with international law.)

Increased Aerial and Naval Activities

The increased northern patrol flights and planning for naval activity were to be implemented by the Canadian Forces. However, this announcement was not much more than a "re-packaging" of existing policies. Both the northern patrol flights (NORPATS) and the northern deployment of naval vessels (NORPLOY) had their origins in the early 1970s. The main impact of the *Polar Sea* voyage was to raise the profile of both programs and, in the case of the NORPLOYs, to reinstate it.

As was the case for the Canadian Laws Offshore Application Act, the genesis of long-range northern aircraft patrols can be traced to the early 1970s and to the discovery of oil in the North. It was widely believed that a northern "presence" was required to protect Canadian interests, and overflights were seen as a relatively easy way of doing this. At the same time, the *Manhattan* voyages of 1969 and 1970 served to underline the reality of challenges to Canadian claims.[20]

One of the first steps taken by the government in response to the *Polar Sea* voyage was to order the overflight of the American icebreaker by both CP-140 Aurora and CP-121 Tracker aircraft; between them, the aircraft flew twelve patrols.[21] But it can be argued that Clark's inclusion of a promise to increase Arctic surveillance flights in the North was, to a large degree, simply a reiteration of existing trends. Eight Arctic flights occurred in 1980, increasing to twenty-two in 1990. Significantly, there were fourteen flights in 1984, seventeen in 1985, but no further increases until 1988, when nineteen flights occurred.[22] So while an increase did ensue, it was only part of an existing trend and took place over a period of three years.

Two years after the 10 September policy announcement, an attempt was made to increase the number of aircraft available to undertake the over-flights. The 1987 defence white paper listed "at least six additional long-range patrol aircraft" as a means of maintaining proper surveillance over the North.[23] However, in the budget of 27 April 1989, the purchase of the additional aircraft was cancelled, and all twenty-nine CP-121 Tracker air-craft were to be retired by 1992.[24] In their place, three Arcturus aircraft (simplified versions of the Aurora) were purchased. However, since these aircraft were not outfitted with the full array of surveillance equipment as were the Aurora aircraft, their primary use has been in the field of train-ing. Thus, the Arcturus purchase added to overflight capabilities only in so far as it freed up Auroras from training missions.

The decision to send naval vessels into the eastern Arctic was not so much a new decision as a resumption of an old activity. Canadian naval forces had last entered Arctic waters in 1982, but they had been visiting this area since at least 1971.[25] Exercises in the North are difficult for the navy mainly due to the hull damage that can be caused by ice. Only two types of vessels can operate safely and freely in Arctic waters: icebreakers and nuclear-powered submarines. All other vessels are confined to opera-tions in southern Arctic waters for a short time in August, when ice con-ditions permit.[26] The Canadian navy had no nuclear submarines, and its one icebreaker had been transferred to the Coast Guard in 1958.[27] Thus, naval deployment has been possible only for short periods of time and has been of limited use.

NORPLOY began in 1971.[28] These deployments generally occurred annually from 1971 to 1979 and were usually carried out by replenishment vessels. The purposes of the voyages included port visits to isolated communities, civilian and defence research, and sovereignty enforcement. The deployments became irregular after 1979 and no longer included the larger naval vessels. The light auxiliary tender *Cormorant*, which was commissioned in 1978,[29] and the Canadian Forces Auxiliary Vessel *Quest* were deployed when the northern deployments resumed in 1982. Thus, the deployments of both the *Cormorant* and the *Quest* in 1988 and 1989, respectively, suggest that they were considered a normal component of fleet exercises.[30] And the fact that such exercises had also taken place in 1982 suggests that the decision to include them in the September 10 announcement was, at best, the resumption of an old policy.

Withdrawal of the 1970 ICJ Reservation

Following the voyages of the *Manhattan* in 1969 and 1970, Canada passed the Arctic Waters Pollution Prevention Act (AWPPA), which created a 100-mile-wide pollution protection zone beyond Canada's Arctic archipelago. However, the Trudeau government feared that this legislation would be unable to withstand a challenge to the International Court of Justice. The pollution protection zone was an innovation in international law: nothing in customary law or in UNCLOS I or UNCLOS II gave a country the right to legislate pollution protection in areas beyond its territorial sea. As a result, in 1970 the government decided that it would not allow the newly enacted AWPPA to be challenged in the ICJ. The Trudeau government's reservation specified that Canada would not accept the compulsory jurisdiction of the court on "disputes arising out of or concerning jurisdiction or rights claimed or exercised by Canada in respect of the conservation, management or exploitation of the living resources of the sea, or in respect of the preservation or control of pollution or contamination of the marine environment in marine areas adjacent to the coast of Canada."[31]

However, between 1973 and 1982, two developments in international law completely changed this situation. First, Canadian negotiators at UNCLOS III had successfully pushed for the inclusion of Article 234 – the so-called "ice-covered areas article" – in the new Law of the Sea. Second, UNCLOS III had embraced Exclusive Economic Zones (EEZ). Both provided international support for the AWPPA and decreased the likelihood of an adverse ruling against Canada.

Ottawa's decision to lift the reservation to the ICJ was made at one of the PCO/External Affairs meetings held in late summer of 1985, when External Affairs officials argued that international law had developed to the point that it would support the AWPPA. But it is important to note that the decision to drop the ICJ reservation could have been taken by Canada any time after the development of the EEZ and the acceptance of Article 234 at the Law of the Sea negotiations. It is telling that Canadian officials did not do so until required to act for the political reasons created by the voyage of the American icebreaker.

Construction of a Polar 8 Icebreaker

Of the six policies contained in the 10 September announcement, the proposed construction of an icebreaker capable of polar operations was the one most heavily debated within the government.[32] With estimates running from $230 million to over $600 million, it would have been the most expensive of the six policies had it been implemented. However, after an extended period of indecision concerning the selection of the builder, the project was first suspended and then cancelled outright.

The idea of building a polar icebreaker was first bruited in the early 1970s. Like the case of the ICJ reservation withdrawal and the declaration of straight baselines around the Arctic, the two driving forces in the early stages of the icebreaker proposal were the voyages of the *Manhattan* and the possibility of resource development in the North.[33] However, no action was taken until the mid-1970s when Cabinet approved funding for the design phase of a "class 7" icebreaker.[34] But the government then spent the next ten years vacillating and revising its requirements.[35] It was not until July 1984 that a decision was finally reached concerning which propulsion system to use;[36] however, soon afterwards the project team was instructed to hold off sending a proposal regarding the commencement of construction until "there [was] a significant demand for the ship as an escort for the year round transport of hydrocarbons in the Arctic by freighter."[37] In short, by 1985, no firm decision had been made.

Of all the September 1985 initiatives, the proposal to commit to the building of a class 8 icebreaker – or Polar 8, as it was known – provoked the fiercest debate. The Department of National Defence in particular was worried that the costs of the vessel would very quickly exceed the estimates of $350 to $500 million, and it feared that such a large expenditure could result in cutbacks in the naval modernization program then being planned.[38] Defence officials were also concerned that the project would result in a vessel that was unable to respond to the threat of submarine intruders in the North.[39]

The acquisition process was marked by numerous delays. Several companies bid to build the icebreaker, and the Mulroney government then struck a commission to select among the three main proposals. However, even after the commission reported, the government delayed until the spring of 1987. In the end, it was decided to award the contract to

Versatile's Vancouver yards.[40] Problems continued to plague the project once this decision had been made. Versatile experienced financial problems, and the designers determined that they had been overly optimistic in their initial estimates. In May 1988, it was reported that the design team had encountered difficulties with the propulsion unit of the vessel.[41] In late summer, sources close to the design unit of the project informed the media that, if a diesel electric propulsion system was to remain, then the ship would cost an additional $70 to $80 million.[42]

The design team completed its work by fall 1988. The design cost was over the $350 million ceiling, but Coast Guard officials would not say by how much. However, an industry source stated that the estimated cost had skyrocketed to $527 million.[43] Recognizing that Cabinet was unlikely to accept such a large increase, the Coast Guard agreed to pay Versatile and the design consortium an extra $1.5 million to prepare a new estimate based on a different and cheaper propulsion system. However, the new estimate was still substantially over budget. And then Versatile's shipyards were put up for sale in December 1988.[44]

All of these problems proved to be too much for the project. Initially, there was no specific decision to put the project on hold. But the minuscule funding given to the project in the April 1989 budget had the effect of doing exactly that. The project was given only $1.6 million, $1.5 million of which had already been earmarked for the redesign of the propulsion system.[45] Finally, on 19 February 1990, the Polar 8 project was cancelled. In his budget speech, Michael Wilson, the minister of finance, cited the increase in costs of the icebreaker program – its price had climbed to $680 million[46] – as one of the main reasons for the cancellation. Wilson also claimed that changes in the international environment, highlighted by the US-Canada Arctic Cooperation Agreement (discussed below), decreased the necessity of the project.[47]

The icebreaker was the only September 1985 initiative that came with a high price tag relating to new spending. Some of the other initiatives had continuing costs. The northern overflights and northern naval activity were not cheap, but they were already established in the Department of National Defence budgets. The costs associated with the four other policy initiatives were related only to the work hours required to develop them. The icebreaker was priced at anywhere between $230 million to $680 million, and this was only with regard to expenses associated with the building of the vessel. Once built, it would have to be operated and supplied, thus requiring an additional yearly expenditure.

Negotiations with the United States

The decision to negotiate directly with the United States was the only one, among the six policy initiatives, that was made specifically as a result of the 1985 voyage. The primary goal was to reach an agreement with the Americans that would recognize Canadian claims to Arctic waters. Failing that, the Canadian government wanted to gain some "control" over transits made by American vessels, both government and commercial.[48] In exchange, Canada would provide assurances for the passage of American vessels – assurances that would meet their security and commercial concerns.[49]

There were two distinct phases to the discussions. Initially, the negotiations were conducted by bureaucrats. Most of their efforts to reach an agreement could be characterized as relatively low-level and informal, consisting mainly of meetings and telephone calls between officials in the State Department and External Affairs. The second phase emerged when the leaders of the two countries determined that negotiations were proceeding too slowly and decided that political pressure had to be injected into the process. In order to accomplish this, special envoys were appointed to report directly to the political leadership of the two states.

The initial negotiating positions of the two states were based on the Law of the Sea Convention.[50] External Affairs officials claimed that, under Article 234, Canada had the right to establish control over the Northwest Passage. They cited the ice-covered areas article, which bestows special rights to a coastal state that has an ice-covered EEZ. Canadian officials argued that this gave them the right to control navigation over the passage in order to protect the marine environment. American officials responded by citing Article 236, the sovereignty immunity clause. State Department officials argued that, since the *Polar Sea* was a state-owned vessel, it was exempted from any laws that Canada may have passed to control navigation in order to protect the marine environment. In short, a government vessel did not need to meet any standards and, therefore, did not need to seek permission.

Having failed to make their case on the basis of the Law of the Sea Convention, Canadian officials focused their efforts on reaching a negotiated agreement with the Americans. The Canadians first attempted to reach a comprehensive agreement under which the United States, for its part, would recognize Canadian sovereignty over the passage, while Canada, for its part, would allow American transit in the area. Various drafts of different agreements were circulated, and, as time progressed, this tended to complicate the agreement. However, it became apparent that American officials would not recognize Canadian claims to the passage.[51]

As the discussions became deadlocked, the personal intervention of Reagan and Mulroney revitalized the process. The factors that had the greatest positive impact on the negotiation were the three summit meetings (1985, 1986, and 1987) between the two leaders. The Shamrock Summit in Québec City in 1985 had taken place before the voyage of the *Polar Sea*. But this summit was important because it established good working and personal relationships. At the 1986 summit held in Washington, one of the major issues of discussion was the need to resolve the problems created by the voyage.[52] According to several US officials, Mulroney was concerned that the *Polar Sea* problem would hinder other United States-Canada issues, particularly the free trade talks. Reagan appeared to be sensitive to the Canadian position on the voyage. Mulroney then successfully persuaded Reagan to elevate the level of negotiations by appointing special negotiators in an attempt to facilitate a solution. Edward Derwinski was selected for the American side and Derek Burney for the Canadian side. Both men had worked together before and enjoyed the confidence of their political leaders.

This change in approach was strenuously objected to by both the American Coast Guard and the US Department of Defense (DoD), among others. However, the objections of these departments were overcome by shifting the focus of the tentative agreement from one that covered all vessels to one that included only icebreakers. It was also moved along by the personal intervention of Mulroney during the April 1987 summit. Meeting in the prime minister's office, Mulroney showed Reagan a globe that included the normal ice cover in order to make his point that the Northwest Passage was indeed "unique." Afterwards, Reagan promised Mulroney that the United States would not do anything in the Arctic "without your consent." He told his officials that he wanted "something more for the prime minister" in his address to Parliament, and this resulted in the insertion into his speech of a last-minute paragraph on the need to resolve the Arctic sovereignty question.[53] Following the summit, the final stages of the drafting of the agreement went smoothly. The final draft of the agreement was ready for Cabinet approval by October and was formally signed by Clark and US Secretary of State George Shultz on 11 January 1988.

The Arctic Cooperation Agreement is short and simple. In the first two articles, both governments agree to cooperate in the Arctic and agree to "not adversely affect the unique environment of the region and the well-being of its inhabitants." The third and fourth articles are the most significant. The third states that "the Government of the United States pledges that all navigation by US icebreakers within waters claimed by Canada to be internal will be undertaken with the consent of the Government of Canada." The fourth clause states that nothing in the agreement will affect the respective legal position of either state.[54] It is generally regarded by officials of both governments as a practical, albeit limited, agreement. The Mulroney government was criticized for having failed to achieve outright American recognition of Canadian sovereignty over the passage.[55] However, it did succeed in resolving the specific problem of the transit of American icebreakers. During the Mulroney government's remaining time in office, the agreement was activated three times – in 1988, 1989, and 1990.

There is some debate as to the significance of the agreement. Some analysts have suggested that it served as an important means of managing a significant irritant in Canadian-American relations. Furthermore, since the two governments had such differing positions, the fact that any agreement was reached is important for maintaining good relations.[56] There is no question that the process of reaching agreement was important. There are also significant lessons to be learned regarding the importance of relationships between leaders. Clearly, the warm friendship between Mulroney and Reagan was a contributing factor in their reaching an agreement. However, in and of itself, the Arctic Cooperation Agreement is limited and narrowly defined.[57] Nevertheless, it eliminated the possibility of a recurrence of the problems created by the 1985 voyage. Because only icebreakers or nuclear-powered submarines are capable of traversing the Northwest Passage, and because commercial vessels, even if they are ice-strengthened, require the assistance of at least one icebreaker, the agreement effectively included all surface vessels that might wish to use the passage. The limiting aspect of the agreement is the fact that it does not deal with submarines. American officials, and particularly officials from DoD, had been adamant that the issue of submarine passage remain outside the scope of the negotiations.[58]

A Northern Foreign Policy

The September 1985 statement was the result of the Mulroney government's need to be seen as responding to the voyage of the *Polar Sea*. As such, it is only to be expected that the policies chosen would appear as an ad hoc combination of old and new. However, in the period following the voyage, the six policies were soon to be entrenched as the core component of Canadian northern foreign policy. Indeed, a full chapter of the parliamentary review of foreign policy conducted by the Conservative government was devoted to the issue of a "northern foreign policy." The Special Joint Committee on Canada's International Relations, chaired by Thomas Hockin and Jean-Maurice Simard, examined three areas: (1) general issues of concern in the north, (2) the question of sovereignty, and (3) defence questions.[59] The Hockin-Simard report made nine policy recommendations, ranging from such issues as the fur trade to Aboriginal self-government to new submarines. While the committee did not highlight a specific northern maritime policy, most of its recommendation regarding the question of sovereignty did focus on maritime issues.

Significantly, the report had a strong effect on government policy.[60] When Clark presented his response in the House of Commons, he specifically noted the importance that the committee had placed on the "northern dimension of Canadian foreign policy."[61] The government's reply to the policy recommendations of the Hockin-Simard report included a general policy position statement on northern foreign policy.[62] The impact of the *Polar Sea* voyage was clearly evident in the report. And the government's response to Hockin-Simard sought to entrench what it called a "comprehensive northern foreign policy." According to the government, such a policy would have four dominant themes: (1) affirming Canadian sovereignty, (2) modernizing Canada's northern defences, (3) preparing for commercial use of the Northwest Passage, and (4) promoting enhanced circumpolar cooperation.[63] Moreover, a year later Clark gave a speech in Tromso, Norway, explaining how these four themes were to be implemented.[64]

The principal elements of the affirmation of Canadian sovereignty were based on the 10 September policy statement and included: talks with the United States over the status of the Northwest Passage, the building of the Polar 8 icebreaker, and the passage of the Canadian Laws Offshore Application Act. An additional component to the affirmation of Canadian sovereignty, which had not been a part of the September 10 speech, was the recognition of the importance of the Inuit to Canadian claims. The second theme, the modernization of Canadian Arctic defence, focused primarily on developing means of effectively monitoring the North, both in the air and under the ice. Such means included an increase in the northern sovereignty patrol flights and increased naval activity. Beyond the policy statement of 10 September, the government also pledged itself to upgrading the northern early warning system through the installation of a North Warning System. The possibility of replacing the Oberon submarines with a class that could operate under the ice was also mentioned. The third policy theme, the preparation of the Northwest Passage for commercial use, concerned the protection of the environment and the building of the Polar 8 class icebreaker. Vague references to "develop[ing] the necessary infrastructure and operational capabilities" were made but were not elaborated upon.[65] In essence, the construction of the Polar 8 was the core program.

It is clear that the six initiatives here discussed were seen as part of the core component of Canadian northern policy, particularly of its maritime Arctic policy. Thus, what amounted to a crisis-management policy reaction to a single event in the summer of 1985 resulted in the entrenchment of a northern maritime policy.

Conclusion

This analysis shows how a single event – the voyage of the *Polar Sea* – galvanized the Mulroney government into creating a northern maritime policy. While the September 10 statement ostensibly deals with Arctic sovereignty, what it did, in fact, was create a northern maritime policy. Moreover, the creation of this policy occurred within a crisis environment: the six policies of which it consists were an ad hoc collection of initiatives that, for the most part, were being developed for other reasons. Nevertheless, they came to form the main component of Canada's northern maritime policy.

The six policies had various degrees of success. The declaration of straight baselines and the withdrawal of the ICJ reservation could have been enacted earlier than 1985. Both were feasible by 1982, when the UNCLOS III was completed. Conversely, by attempting to define the Canadian Laws Offshore Application Act as a sovereignty-protection measure, the government may have delayed passage of the bill. Increased sovereignty overflights and northern naval deployments were efforts to pad the September 10 announcement – for both were already being conducted. The two policies that had the greatest potential to alter Canadian Arctic maritime policy involved the decision to build the Polar 8 class icebreaker and the negotiations with the United States over transit in the Northwest Passage.

Had the icebreaker project not been cancelled, Canada could have had the most powerful icebreaker in the world. Almost all of the Canadian Arctic waters would have become navigable for Canada during much of the year, thereby giving Canada a physical presence in all of its northern waters. This stands in stark contrast to the current ability of the Canadian Coast Guard. Such an icebreaker would have had enormous practical and symbolic value for Canada's claims over its northern waters. However, in the face of the tremendous pressures on the budget caused by the federal deficit, it is easy to understand why it was not built. Nevertheless, it is still instructive to observe that the *Polar Sea*'s voyage came close to providing enough impetus for the successful completion of the Polar 8.

The 1988 Arctic Cooperation Agreement between Canada and the United States is limited. Nevertheless, the American agreement to seek "consent" for the passage of its icebreakers was an important gain for Canada. The agreement effectively means that the only state to openly challenge Canadian claims to its northern waters – the United States – has agreed to limit the right of transit of its surface vessels in the Northwest Passage. While the agreement specifies only government icebreakers, it is difficult to imagine any commercial vessel, even those that are ice-strengthened, being able to traverse the passage without icebreaker assistance. Thus, de facto, the agreement controls any possible attempt of an American commercial vessel to transit the passage, since it would require the escort of either a Canadian icebreaker or, conceivably, an American icebreaker.

Of course, the fact that nuclear-powered submarines were not mentioned in the agreement leaves open the possibility of a future crisis between Canada and the United States. As noted earlier, American submarines do occasionally use the passage, though the frequency is a closely guarded secret.[66] Were an American submarine, while in the Northwest Passage, forced to the surface as the result of an accident or mechanical problem, it is possible that the Canadian government of the day would find itself repeating the same process that occurred in 1970 following the voyage of the *Manhattan*, and in 1985 following the voyage of the *Polar Sea*. That government would probably find itself creating its Arctic maritime policy within a crisis environment similar to that within which the Mulroney government created its maritime policy.

Notes

Portions of this chapter appeared as "Polar Vision or Tunnel Vision? The Making of Canadian Arctic Water Policy," *Marine Policy* 19, 4 (July 1995): 343-64, reprinted with permission from Elsevier Science.

1 United States Department of Transportation, US Coast Guard, *United States Polar Icebreakers Requirements Study*, Interagency Report July 1984, pp. 2-4 to 2-8; also "Revised Memorandum of Agreement between the Department of the Navy and the Department of the Treasury on the Operation of Icebreakers," 22 July 1965.
2 For details of the decision to send the *Polar Sea*, see Rob Huebert, "Polar Vision or Tunnel Vision? The Making of Canadian Arctic Water Policy," *Marine Policy* 19 (July 1995): 343-64.
3 United States, Department of State, 85 State Telegram 151842 (172114Z May 85); 85 Ottawa telegram 03785 (211810Z May 85).
4 Canada, Department of External Affairs, Canadian Embassy, Washington, Note No. 331, 11 June 1985.
5 United States, Department of State, American Embassy at Ottawa Note No. 222, 24 June 1985.
6 Interviews with State Department officials, Washington, April 1990.
7 Canada, Department of External Affairs, Legal Affairs, "Memorandum for: the Secretary of State for External Affairs: Subject – Voyage of the U.S. Coast Guard Icebreaker *Polar Sea*," 30 July 1985.
8 "Arctic 'Incursion' Protest Planned," *Globe and Mail*, 6 August 1985; and Ken MacQueen with Andrew Nikiforuk, "The New Race For the North," *Maclean's*, 19 August 1985.
9 "For the Defence of Sovereignty," *Globe and Mail*, 2 August 1985; Kevin Doyle, "Our Precious North," *Maclean's* 19 August 1985. Comparable views can be found in other Canadian newspapers.
10 Interview with External Affairs official, Canadian Embassy, Washington, 1990.
11 "Ottawa Experts Split Over Claim to Arctic Seas," *Toronto Star*, 12 August 1985.
12 Secretary of State Joe Clark, press scrum, Uplands Airport, 2 August 1985.
13 Canada, Department of External Affairs, *Statements and Speeches*, 85/7, "Policy on Canadian Sovereignty," Joe Clark, House of Commons, Ottawa, 10 September 1985.
14 Territorial Sea and Fishing Zone Act, R.S.C. 1964., c. 22.
15 J. Bruce McKinnon, "Arctic Baselines: A Litre Usque Ad Litus," *Canadian Bar Review* 66 (December 1987): 795.
16 John Kirton and Don Munton, "The Manhattan Voyages and their Aftermath," in *Politics of the Northwest Passage*, ed. Franklyn Griffiths (Montreal, Kingston: McGill-Queen's University Press, 1987), 73, 82.
17 Interview with External Affairs official, Canadian Embassy, Washington, April 1990.
18 Territorial Sea Geographical Coordinates (Area 7) Order, SOR/85-872, 10 September 1985: *Canada Gazette*, Part 2, vol. 119, no. 20.

19 J.J.M. Coutu (chief superintendent, assistant director, criminal investigation, Royal Canadian Mounted Police) to Philippe Kirsch (director, legal operations division, External Affairs), 25 May 1984.

20 Canada, Department of National Defence, "CP 140 Aurora Northern Patrols," *Backgrounder*, April 1989.

21 Department of National Defence, Mission Report Arctic Surveillance, 4 August 1985, 5 August 1985; 6 August 1985; National Defence Headquarters, Telex – Monitoring USCG *Polar Sea*, 1201hrs, 12 August 1985.

22 Bob Fowler, then assistant deputy minister (policy) DND, reported that there had been twenty flights in 1986. See House of Commons, Standing Committee on External Affairs and National Defence, *Proceedings*, 28 January 1987, 14. However, in a letter dated 9 September 1992, the minister of national defence indicated to the author that there had been only seventeen flights.

23 Department of National Defence, *Challenge and Commitment: A Defence Policy for Canada* (Ottawa: Supply and Services Canada, June 1987), 57.

24 Paul Koring, "Tory Defence Promises Wiped Out," *Globe and Mail*, 28 April 1989; Koring, "Defence of Arctic Left to Allies by Budget Cuts," *Globe and Mail*, 28 April 1989; and Canadian Institute for International Peace and Security, *The Guide to Canadian Policies on Arms Control, Disarmament, Defence and Conflict Resolution* (Ottawa: CIIPS, 1989), 123.

25 Fred Crickard, "The Role of Maritime Strategy in Ocean Development and Management," in *Canadian Ocean Law and Policy*, ed. David VanderZwaag (Toronto: Butterworths, 1992), 533.

26 For problems of naval operations in the Arctic, see the testimony of Rear Admiral N.D. Brodeur, Deputy Chief of the Defence Staff, in Senate, Standing Senate Committee on Foreign Affairs, *Proceedings of the Subcommittee on National Defence*, 9 March 1982, 23: 29-30.

27 The 7,100-tonne *Labrador* was transferred when it was decided that the navy would no longer be responsible for icebreaking duties. See Kim Richard Nossal, "Polar Icebreakers: The Politics of Inertia," in Griffiths, *Politics of the Northwest Passage*, 220-21.

28 Department of National Defence, *Defence 1971* (Ottawa: Information Canada, 1972), 40.

29 Department of National Defence, *Defence 1978* (Ottawa: Supply and Services Canada, 1979), 38.

30 Crickard, "Maritime Strategy"; and Lieutenant Commander Malcolm Palmer, "NORPLOY 89," *Canada's Navy Annual* 5 (1990/91): 20-23.

31 "Documentation Concerning Canadian Legislation on Arctic Pollution and Territorial Sea and Fishing Zones," *International Legal Material* 9 (1970): 599.

32 Interviews with External Affairs officials, Halifax, June 1990; Canadian Embassy, Washington, April 1990.

33 For discussion of Canadian icebreaker acquisition, see Nossal, "Polar Icebreakers," 217. A Transport Canada document makes it clear that the prospects of resource development in the north and the voyage of the *Manhattan* were the two factors that ignited consideration of building a large (Polar 7 or larger) icebreaker. Transport Canada, *Discussion Paper: Polar Icebreaker Program*, No. TC 31-80, 27 October 1980, 3; House of Commons, Standing Committee on Indian Affairs and Northern Development, *Minutes of Evidence and Proceedings* 25 (15 June 1971), 25: 5-6.

34 The Canadian government assigns different classes to icebreakers on the basis of their capacity to make their way through ice of different thickness. The Canadian Coast Guard's largest icebreaker, the *Louis St Laurent*, was a class 4.

35 Nossal, "Polar Icebreakers," 228-31.

36 Carey French, "3 Firms to Seek Job of Building Icebreaker," *Globe and Mail*, 9 July 1984.

37 Fisher, "Experts Get Cracking on Super Icebreaker Plans," *Globe and Mail*, 7 August 1985.

38 Confidential interviews with Canadian officials.

39 Carey French, "Commitment to Super-Icebreaker Not Popular With Naval Planner," *Globe and Mail*, 3 October 1986.

40 House of Commons, *Debates*, 2 March 1987, 3723.

41 "Ice Ship Defects Outlined," *Calgary Herald*, 10 May 1988; and "Propulsion System for Polar 8 is Guaranteed, Bouchard Says," *Montreal Gazette*, 11 May 1988.

42 "Icebreaker's Cost Climbing: Coast Guard," *Montreal Gazette*, 14 July 1988.

43 Paul Koring, "Bouchard Delays Plans for Polar 8 as Cost Rises," *Globe and Mail*, 8 May 1989.
44 Ken Romain, "Polar 8 Delay Leaves Shipyard Short of Work," *Globe and Mail*, 15 May 1989.
45 Koring, "Bouchard Delays Plans."
46 Ken MacQueen, "Ottawa's Paper Ship: A Massive Waste of Time, Talent and Money," *Montreal Gazette*, 22 February 1990.
47 See Deborah Wilson, "Axing of the Polar 8 Seen as a Cruel Blow But BC Shipbuilder Plans to Stay Open," *Globe and Mail*, 22 February 1990, B22; Paul Koring, "Polar 8 Founders on Shoals of Tory Cuts," *Globe and Mail*, 20 February 1990.
48 Interview with External Affairs official, Canadian Embassy, Washington, April, 1990.
49 Christopher Kirkey, "Smoothing Troubled Waters: The 1988 Canada-United States Arctic Co-operation Agreement," *International Journal* 50 (1995): 405-8.
50 The following account is based on interviews conducted in April 1990 with an External Affairs official, Canadian Embassy, Washington; a United States Coast Guard official; and other confidential interviews.
51 Several American officials made it clear that while the State Department had been willing to compromise, the US Navy refused to bend because it was concerned about the precedent that would be created if Canada were to be granted full sovereignty.
52 Interview with former National Security Council (NSC) official, Washington, April 1990.
53 Interviews with former NSC official, Washington, April 1990; and External Affairs official, Ottawa, April 1993. See also Kirkey, "Smoothing Troubled Waters," 412-13; Ross Howard, "De Facto Control of Non-Arms Shipping Won in Northern Passage, Officials Say," *Globe and Mail*, 8 December 1987; and United States, State Department, "President's Visit to Canada," *Bulletin* (June 1987): 7. Reagan also added personal comments on the issue of acid rain.
54 "Agreement between the Government of Canada and the Government of the United States of America on Arctic Cooperation," signed in Ottawa, 11 January 1988.
55 "U.S. Rejects Canada's Claim to Sovereignty in Arctic Treaty," *Ottawa Citizen*, 12 January 1988.
56 Kirkey, "Smoothing Troubled Waters," 422-26.
57 Donald Rothwell, "The Canadian-US Northwest Passage Dispute: A Reassessment," *Cornell International Law Journal* 26 (Spring 1993): 345-46.
58 Confidential interviews with Canadian and American officials.
59 Special Joint Committee of the Senate and of the House of Commons on Canada's International Relations, *Independence and Internationalism* (Ottawa, June 1986), 127-35.
60 Department of External Affairs, *Canada's International Relations: Response of the Government of Canada to the Report of the Special Joint Committee of the Senate and of the House of Commons* (Ottawa, December 1986).
61 House of Commons, *Debates*, 4 December 1986, 1763-5.
62 *Canada's International Relations*, 31-33; 85-87.
63 Ibid.
64 Department of External Affairs, *Statement*, 87/72, speech by Clark to the Norway-Canada Conference on Circumpolar Issues, Tromso, Norway, 9 December 1987.
65 Canada, Department of External Affairs, *Statements and Speeches*, 85/7, "Policy on Canadian Sovereignty," Joe Clark, House of Commons, Ottawa, 10 September 1985.
66 In late 1999, Inuit hunters sighted a submarine in Cumberland Sound off Baffin Island. An Aurora aircraft was dispatched but no submarine was found.

7

Big Eyes and Empty Pockets: The Two Phases of Conservative Defence Policy

Norrin M. Ripsman

Canadian defence policy under the Mulroney government can be divided into two distinct phases. The first phase ended with the white paper published by the minister of national defence, Perrin Beatty, in 1987. Although there are many who see the white paper as a significant departure from previous Canadian defence policies and as a reflection of the philosophies of both Mulroney and the Conservative party, I will argue that, except in its unprecedented use of Cold War rhetoric, it was in fact a logical outgrowth of the policies pursued by the Liberal government of Pierre Elliott Trudeau in the early 1980s. The Mulroney government reaffirmed Canada's commitment to both the North Atlantic Treaty Organization (NATO) and North American Aerospace Defence Command (NORAD); it promised to increase defence spending to modernize Canada's conventional coastal, anti-submarine warfare (ASW) and air defences; and it restructured the Canadian commitment to Europe. While these priorities were at odds with Trudeau's 1971 defence white paper, they were consistent with the Trudeau government's later recognition of the growing importance of conventional weapons in NATO's war-fighting doctrine and also the need for Canada, rather than the United States, to meet coastal and air defence requirements to maintain Canadian sovereignty. Thus, to paraphrase Denis Stairs, the white paper was less a reflection of the political orientation of the Conservative party than it was a product of insistent imperatives arising from circumstances. It did, nonetheless, constitute a significant change in the Canadian-American security relationship as part of Mulroney's broader efforts to extend the Canadian-American partnership.

The second phase, however, represented a considerable retrenchment of Canadian defence commitments and, therefore, constituted a radical departure from the past. By mid-1992, pressure to reduce the budgetary deficit, public opposition to defence spending, and the sweeping changes in the Soviet Union and eastern Europe compelled the Conservatives to change policies in midstream. The two ministers of finance during this period, Michael Wilson and Don Mazankowski, cancelled the controversial purchase of twelve nuclear-propelled submarines, scaled back the modernization of conventional forces, and, most significantly, announced the withdrawal of the Canadian commitment to West Germany – the hallmark of Canadian defence policy throughout the Cold War. These dramatic changes – which were, once again, inspired by domestic and international circumstances rather than party philosophy – conspired both to reduce Canadian influence in the NATO alliance and to irritate Canadian-American security relations.

Big Eyes: The Defence White Paper of 1987

During Mulroney's first government, the Conservatives sought to expand the Canadian role in NATO and North American defences. As the Department of External Affairs indicated in its response to a 1986 report on foreign policy by a special joint committee of the Senate and the House of Commons, these measures were necessary to reaffirm and deepen Canada's political and military alignment with the United States, to increase Canadian influence within NATO, and to safeguard Canadian sovereignty.[1]

The definitive statement of the government's defence policy was the ambitious 1987 defence white paper published by Perrin Beatty, which Nelson Michaud (Chapter 17) identifies as a considerable departure from previous defence policies. Cast in stark Cold War rhetoric, this document recognized that political tensions and the Soviet Union's military build-up over the previous fifteen years meant that "the great hopes of the early 1970s have not been realized" and that "the early promise of détente was exaggerated." The white paper called for "a more sober approach to international relations and the needs of security policy."[2] Surprisingly, the document did not address the beginnings of the revolution introduced by Mikhail Gorbachev in the Soviet Union or the promising Reykjavik summit when assessing the international threat situation; instead, it asserted that "the new Soviet leadership continues to view the World as divided into two antagonistic camps. There is every reason to believe that its long-term aims continue to include the dissolution of NATO, the neutralization of non-communist Europe and the weakening of the West as a whole ... it continues to seek to translate military power into gain."[3]

It identified five primary goals for Canadian defence policy within such a menacing international environment: strategic deterrence, conventional defence, protecting Canadian sovereignty, peacekeeping, and arms control. The document further recognized that Canada's defence budget was insufficient to meet its growing defence commitments. Consequently, Canadian defence policy was suffering from an increasing "commitment-capability gap." The document argued:

The truth ... is that much of the equipment of most elements of the Canadian Forces is in an advanced state of obsolescence or is already obsolete. Modernization programs have not kept pace with obsolescence. The maritime forces have too few operational vessels ... The land forces have severe equipment shortages and too few combat-ready soldiers ... The air forces suffer from a serious shortage of air transport [and] maritime patrol aircraft. They lack sufficient numbers of modern weapons for the CF-18.[4]

To redress this commitment-capability gap, the Conservative government committed itself to an annual increase in defence spending of no less than 2 percent above inflation for a period of fifteen years. Increasing defence expenditures would finance a host of new weapon procurements, including: six Aurora long-range patrol aircraft to participate in ASW operations; six additional helicopter-bearing patrol frigates for ASW operations in Atlantic and Pacific waters; a new ship-borne helicopter to replace the aging Sea King; mine countermeasures vessels; array-towing vessels for underwater surveillance; between ten and twelve nuclear-powered attack submarines to assist in ASW operations, especially in the Arctic, where diesel submarines are incapable of sustained operation under the ice; and fixed sonar systems for submarine detection in the Arctic region. Furthermore, the document called for the modernization and upgrading of Canada's existing medium-range Tracker aircraft fleet, coastal radar installations, and airfields in the north. These acquisitions and modernization plans would complement improvements to the NORAD air defence network that had already been agreed to at the March 1985 Shamrock Summit between Ronald Reagan and Brian Mulroney. This network was known as the North American Air Defence Modernization Program (ADMP), and it included the construction of a North Warning System.[5] It also complemented efforts to modernize the Tribal class of destroyers, begun in June 1985. As well, Canada would participate in research on American air defence systems, such as space-based radar, in conjunction with the Air Defense Initiative (ADI), despite domestic concerns that this effort might eventually lead to Canadian participation in the Strategic Defense Initiative (SDI).[6]

The white paper also announced a modernization program for the reserves. This program would entail more frequent training for the supplementary reserve, reactivation of university training programs for reserve officers, higher pay and benefits for reserve personnel, and an increase in total reserve force strength to 90,000. Moreover, as part of a "total force concept," the distinction between reserve forces and regular forces would be reduced. Both regular and reserve personnel would increasingly serve together in military units in all Canadian defence theatres. In addition, the naval reserve was assigned wartime control of shipping and maritime coastal defence.

Finally, the white paper announced a major reorganization of the Canadian force structure in Europe. To make the Canadian commitment to NATO more effective, the government cancelled the 1967 Canadian pledge to respond to a threat to Norway with a Canadian Air Sea Transportable (CAST) Brigade Group. This decision was taken due to the difficulties of transporting, deploying, and resupplying the Canadian-based CAST Brigade to Norway in a timely manner, especially if opposed; instead, this brigade (the 5 GBC) and its air support were reallocated to Germany to augment the understaffed and undersupported main Canadian force on the central front in southern Germany, which would be brought up to divisional strength. The effectiveness of this contingent would be further enhanced by the acquisition of new battle tanks, pre-positioned equipment and supplies, and additional airlift capability.

As Manon Tessier and Michel Fortmann make clear in Chapter 8, peacekeeping was not high on the Conservative agenda during its first term, and the white paper paid little attention to peacekeeping capabilities. It did identify peacekeeping as one of the primary missions for the Canadian Forces (CF), but no effort was made either to augment the pool of up to 2,000 personnel that could participate in such operations or to provide them with state-of-the-art equipment. This is hardly surprising, though, given the white paper's Cold War focus.

Taken out of context, Beatty's expansive defence program might appear to have been a distinctive expression of Conservative philosophy and a radical departure from the past. After all, the previous defence white paper, issued by the Trudeau government in 1971, had reached rather different conclusions. In 1971, the Liberal government had concluded that the presence of nuclear weapons and the onset of détente made conventional war between NATO and the Warsaw Pact unlikely. Moreover, since the countries of western Europe had completed their recovery from the Second World War, they could now, in a nuclear age, mount whatever conventional forces were necessary to prevent war in Europe without a sizeable Canadian commitment. Hence the Liberals reduced defence spending and cut new weapons procurements. Furthermore, they displayed less enthusiasm for NATO and less interest in NORAD, which they believed was no longer necessary since the Soviet Union had developed a credible intercontinental ballistic missile (ICBM) program to supplant its bombers as the primary delivery vehicles for nuclear warheads.[7]

On the whole, however, the Conservative defence policy did not represent a significant political departure from previous defence policies. Prior to the 1971 white paper, commitments to NATO and NORAD had been considered foremost national security priorities throughout the Cold War.[8] Even after the 1969 defence review and the 1971 white paper, NATO continued to play a central role in Canadian defence planning in the 1970s. Thus by the 1975 NATO summit, Trudeau had changed his tune completely, committing himself to "the concept of collective security, Canada's support for NATO, and Canada's pledge to maintain a NATO force level which is accepted by our allies as being adequate in size and effective in character."[9] Consequently, in the mid-to-late 1970s, the Trudeau government had initiated a modest force modernization effort that included the purchase of new main battle tanks, long-range patrol aircraft, anti-submarine aircraft, and fighter aircraft.[10] Moreover, because of the Soviet arms build-up throughout the 1970s, the development of new Soviet bomber and missile technology, and the Soviet invasion of Afghanistan, even the Trudeau government realized the need for a strong NATO and a functioning NORAD as a means of deterring Soviet adventurism and coaxing the Warsaw Pact to the arms control bargaining table.[11] Indeed, in late 1982, after bilateral study of neglected continental air defences, the government agreed to revamp Canadian surveillance and air defence capabilities in response to proposals in the US Air Defense Master Plan. Even more surprisingly, after having committed his government to a freeze on weapons delivery systems in the 1970s, in 1982 Trudeau allowed the United States to test cruise missiles over Alberta.[12] And, under growing allied criticism that the CF were incapable of meeting their alliance commitments, the Liberals increased the defence budget over their final years in office from under $6 billion in 1981 to a projected $9.5 billion for 1985.[13] Consequently, Trudeau's last term in office coincided with new Canadian weapons purchases (including 138 American F-18s). "By the early 1980s," Michel Rossignol observes, "the NATO and NORAD commitments had recouped much of their original importance."[14]

Thus, the 1987 white paper – and the initial Conservative approach to security policy in general – was a logical extension of the Liberal program of the 1980s rather than a sea change in policy. It continued to reflect the parlous security environment of the mid-1980s and the inadequacy of the existing CF structure. If it differed in tone from Liberal rhetoric, casting itself in stark Cold War terms, it did not differ markedly in substance. Indeed, the only fundamental innovation was the controversial plan to purchase nuclear-powered submarines. It can hardly be considered, therefore, a "diplomatic departure."

While the overall Conservative defence and security agenda does not represent a significant change from previous policy, its tone and its approach to the United States on defence issues were unique. The Trudeau government had pursued a fiercely independent policy towards Washington, particularly in matters of international security and national defence, to the point of irritating bilateral relations. Under Trudeau,

Canada sought an independent role within the North American alliance. Early on, Canadian and American security policies clashed over the Vietnam War and the 1971 defence white paper.[15] Canadian independence was further manifested in the 1973 nuclear alert, when Canada refused to support American policy and would not allow Canadian personnel to participate in crisis-related operations at NORAD.[16] In the early 1980s, Trudeau required industrial offsets for Canadian military purchases from the United States and elsewhere; in order for Canada to issue a purchase order from a foreign company, the company had to agree to invest in and/ or purchase parts and raw materials from Canada.[17] This economic nationalist approach to defence procurement rubbed against the free-market sensibilities of the Reagan administration. Finally, Trudeau's 1983-84 "peace initiative" – undertaken without prior consultation in Washington – further alienated the United States. His multi-country "farewell" tour promoting a new superpower détente provoked the ire of cold warriors in the United States, who were enraged that Trudeau would place Canada equidistantly between the United States and the Soviet Union rather than firmly within the Western camp.[18]

By contrast, Mulroney sought a much more cooperative relationship with the United States. Certainly, revitalizing NORAD and Canadian coastal ASW capabilities was bound to please the Reagan administration, with its strategic emphasis on defence. Reaffirming the commitment to NATO forces in Europe was an even more direct way of securing Washington's favour. American political and military leaders had always viewed the Canadian commitment to NATO as of greater importance than its participation in NORAD. The former was an important symbol for the smaller European NATO members; the latter could be replaced by American personnel and equipment.[19] Finally, by framing Canadian defence policies in terms of the rhetoric of the Cold War and deterrence, and by proffering complete support for Reagan's two-track diplomacy, the Conservatives were providing considerable moral and political support for the Reagan military build-up.

Despite these efforts to deepen the Canada-US security partnership and to demonstrate Canada's utility as a loyal American ally, on several matters the defence white paper pursued an independent Canadian line, perhaps to demonstrate to both domestic and international observers that close relations with the United States would not threaten the distinct Canadian identity.[20] The first of these was the strategic defense initiative (SDI). Caspar Weinberger, the US secretary of defense, invited Canada to participate in the research and development of the proposed space-based system for detecting and intercepting nuclear missiles; in September 1985, Mulroney declined, although the government permitted Canadian companies and research institutions to be associated with the research effort if they wished. The government's polite refusal stemmed from widespread Canadian opposition to the program – which many believed was precluded by the 1972 ABM (anti-ballistic missile) Treaty and could destabilize mutual assured destruction – as well as the government's own appraisal that Canadian participation was unlikely to yield a significant research or investment payoff.[21]

A second area of independence in the Conservative white paper concerned efforts to safeguard Canadian sovereignty. While ostensibly the development of coastal defences, ASW capability, and air defences was intended to ward off a potential Soviet attack, a significant purpose of these endeavours was to prevent American incursions against Canadian sovereignty. Given that the defence of North American airspace and coastal waters was an essential component of American national defence, it would have been incumbent upon the American military establishment to perform these duties if Canada declined. Canadian participation in continental defence, therefore, gave.Canada some control over American decisions affecting the defence of Canada.[22] For this reason, Mulroney insisted on contributing $760 million – fully 40 percent of the price tag – for the expensive North Warning System (NWS) rather than allowing the Americans to foot the bill and run the show.[23] Moreover, in light of the Canadian-American dispute over the Northwest Passage, maintaining Canadian patrols in the region would serve to reinforce the claim that these are internal Canadian waters rather than an international waterway. Indeed, as Rob Huebert demonstrates in Chapter 6, early in its mandate asserting claims to the Canadian Arctic became a high priority for the Mulroney government. Thus, while American leaders might have preferred it if they could have taken care of continental air and coastal defences, leaving Canada to concentrate the bulk of its defence contribution in Europe, they had to accept both Canadian participation and influence in North American defence.

A particular manifestation of sovereignty requirements and the conflict of priorities they engendered between Canada and the United States was the white paper's nuclear-powered submarine program. The American military objected to this purchase on the grounds that these submarines constituted an inefficient use of scarce Canadian defence resources. Furthermore, they did not take kindly to the prospects of the CF interfering with the underwater transit of their own nuclear submarines through Arctic waters.[24] The Conservatives, however, maintained that it would be impossible for Canada to monitor its coastal waters for Soviet submarine activity without them. Thus, either Canada had to purchase nuclear-propelled submarines or the task of Canadian Arctic defence would have to be surrendered to the US Navy. There were, therefore, certain limits to Mulroney's defence and security courtship of the United States.

Empty Pockets: The Erosion of the Conservative White Paper

Cast as it was in Cold War terms after the final thaw had already begun, the 1987 Conservative blueprint for defence was rapidly undercut by world events, budgetary pressures, and declining domestic interest in defence spending. Moreover, as Michaud shows in Chapter 17, within this complex policy environment, the main proponents of the white paper's expansive proposals lost control of policy. At the core of all these changes was the profound political metamorphosis under way in the Soviet Union under Gorbachev. At the Reykjavik summit of October 1986 – almost a year before the defence white paper – Gorbachev demonstrated his willingness to reverse the Brezhnev military build-up that had inspired the more aggressive Canadian defence programs of the 1980s. Indeed, by mid-1987, the United States and the Soviet Union were on the verge of reaching agreement on an Intermediate-Range Nuclear Forces (INF) Treaty, which would eliminate all Soviet SS-20, SS-4, and SS-5 missiles from Europe, together with NATO's Pershing II missiles and ground-launched cruise missiles in the European theatre. This development was followed by the dramatic political events of 1989, which signalled an end to Soviet domination of eastern Europe. By 1990, NATO and the Warsaw Pact had initialled the Conventional Forces in Europe (CFE) agreement, drastically reducing the numbers of conventional forces deployed in Europe and, more important, eliminating the Warsaw Pact's overwhelming conventional forces superiority on the continent. The superpowers were also close to reaching a Strategic Arms Reduction Talks (START) Treaty to reduce each side's stockpiles of ICBMs. Clearly, the Soviet Union and its allies no longer posed the formidable threat that had prompted the defence build-up envisaged by Beatty's white paper.

This fundamental shift in the international security environment coincided with intense pressure to reduce the Canadian budgetary deficit. In fiscal year 1989, the Canadian budget deficit was expected to reach $39.4 billion.[25] By the end of 1990, the federal debt had swelled to $380 billion.[26] For a business-oriented government, this state of affairs was intolerable. Thus, in January 1989, Mulroney announced that reducing the federal deficit had become the government's top priority, and, in a Cabinet shuffle designed to tackle deficit reduction, he replaced Defence Minister Beatty with Bill McKnight.[27] Clearly, the level of defence spending that Beatty had envisaged would come under increasing pressure from the minister of finance, Michael Wilson.

In this tumultuous policy environment, domestic opinion weighed in to further constrain the Conservative government. Initially, the government's critics focused primarily on the proposed nuclear submarine purchases, which environmentalists, peace activists, and many in the public at large saw as unnecessary, expensive, overly militaristic, and a potential violation of the Non-Proliferation Treaty.[28] After most Canadians had concluded that the Cold War was over, their dissatisfaction grew to encompass the whole of the Conservative defence modernization plan. It was natural, therefore, for newspapers, business leaders, and the public at large to encourage the government to reduce the deficit by cutting defence spending.[29]

While proponents of the white paper's plans were prompted by these pressures into a rearguard action to defend as many of the white paper programs as possible, including the commitment to NATO and modernization programs already announced,[30] in time, the entire 1987 program would be scaled back. Aerospace and maritime defence programs – including the nuclear submarines, the six Aurora long-range patrol aircraft, the Tracker aircraft upgrade, surveillance systems, and additional CF-18 purchases – were the first to go, casualties of the 1989 federal budget, which cut $2.74 billion from the defence budget over a five-year period.[31] In 1990, McKnight made it clear that, since deficit reduction continued to be the government's overriding priority, he would be unable to provide the annual funding increase necessary to maintain the CF at their existing strength.[32] Sure enough, further defence cuts announced as part of the 1991 defence budget threatened the viability of the newly revamped commitment to NATO and European security. Accordingly, in 1992, the new minister of finance, Don Mazankowski, and yet another defence minister, Marcel Masse, announced that, since "the Soviet Union has ceased to exist and the conventional military threat in Europe has all but disappeared," the government would withdraw all Canadian forces from Europe and close Canadian bases in Germany in 1994; instead, 1,100 of the 6,600 strong force plus two CF-18 squadrons would be stationed in Canada "ready to answer any call."[33] The last vestiges of the 1987 white paper had been gutted.

These defence cuts, of course, had nothing to do with the political orientation of the Conservative party. Ironically, while the Conservatives came to power in the mid-1980s intent on rebuilding the CF and strengthening Canada's contribution to the NATO alliance, their lasting impact was quite the reverse. Not only did they pare military spending to the bone, but they also cancelled the alliance commitment that had served as the pillar of Canadian defence and security policy for decades. That, in and of itself, was no catastrophe; if the policy had truly outlived its usefulness, then it would be mere sentimentalism to cling to it. The real problem was that the government cancelled its commitments without a clear blueprint for Canadian security needs in the post-Cold War era. If the existing direction of Canadian defence and security policies was no longer appropriate, then the government might have drafted a new white paper – as many academics and other defence commentators demanded – to identify defence priorities in the new international environment and to construct the policies to meet them;[34] instead, Wilson, Mazankowski,

McKnight, and Masse merely reacted to budgetary pressures without creating a post-Cold War Canadian vision. As a result, Paul Buteux could charge that "[a] military engagement with Europe that had begun in the light of a clear strategic assessment of Canada's security needs ended under the pressure of budgetary exigencies."[35]

The post-Cold War defence retrenchment also took its toll on the close and cooperative security relationship that Mulroney had tried to cultivate with the United States. To be sure, his government continued to talk the talk of a good ally: policy statements stressed the continued commitment to NATO, NORAD, and continental defence. Moreover, when called upon to support American military activities abroad, Mulroney readily obliged. During the 1989 invasion of Panama, the prime minister announced that Canada regretted the use of force but strongly supported Bush's actions.[36] A year later, Ottawa responded to Bush's request for Canadian support in the Persian Gulf (to compel Saddam Hussein to withdraw from Kuwait) with two destroyers, a supply ship, a squadron of CF-18 fighter planes, and a field hospital.[37] In both cases, the Mulroney government opened itself up to considerable domestic criticism from Canadians who did not want their government supporting Washington's wars.

While these gestures of support were doubtless appreciated, Canada's credibility as an effective and reliable ally was nonetheless damaged by the post-Cold War defence cuts. "Unfortunately," as John Halstead noted, "the deeds of Canada's defence policy did not match the words of Canada's foreign policy."[38] Canadian defence cuts diminished Canada's value as an ally to the United States, which, together with the European NATO members, made its displeasure quite clear.[39] As a result, two of the primary political goals of the 1987 defence white paper – increasing Canadian influence in NATO and strengthening the Canada-US security partnership – were placed in jeopardy by the successive defence budget cuts.

Conclusion: The Legacy of Mulroney's Defence Policies

Less by design or party ideology than by the relentless pressure of circumstances, the Mulroney government's legacy in the defence and security area was one of retrenchment, cuts, and unfulfilled promises. While the Conservatives saw themselves in the 1980s as saviours of the badly neglected CF, their approach to security affairs did not differ markedly from the policies followed by Trudeau in his final years; nor could their rebuilding plan endure the sweeping changes in eastern Europe and budgetary pressures at home. Furthermore, while Mulroney's approach to Canadian-American relations in the context of security and continental defence represented a significant departure from Trudeau's indifferent and often conflictual style, it, too, was swept away by the empty pockets and shifting priorities of the post-Cold War era.

The Mulroney experience illustrates the extraordinary difficulty of formulating appropriate defence and security policies in a rapidly changing external environment. Perhaps, had the Conservatives been quicker to grasp the implications of the embryonic Gorbachev revolution and the Reykjavik summit, they could have toned down the 1987 white paper, de-emphasizing the Cold War missile detection and ASW capabilities in favour of a more general and more limited CF modernization. A more modest program of this nature, not justified as a counter to an implacable Soviet menace, might have been easier to maintain as the Warsaw Pact crumbled; instead, as the raison d'être of the defence white paper evaporated, so did the political will to implement it. It is much easier, though, to plan with the benefit of hindsight. To the Mulroney government's credit, it displayed admirable flexibility, as the rationale for its defence build-up evaporated in the late 1980s, rather than wedding itself to dated programs. Nonetheless, its legacy could have been of more enduring value if, instead of merely cancelling programs in the pipeline, it had initiated a new proactive post-Cold War defence white paper to equip the CF for the new global security context. In other words, employing Denis Stairs's terminology, the Conservative contribution to Canadian defence policy would have been more enduring had the Conservatives acted as proactive architects rather than as reactive engineers.

Notes

A French version of this chapter was published in *Études internationales* 31: 2 (June 2000).

1 Canada, Department of External Affairs, *Canada's International Relations: Response of the Government of Canada to the Report of the Special Joint Committee of the Senate and the House of Commons* (Ottawa: Supply and Services Canada, 1986), 12, 27-30.
2 Canada, Department of National Defence, *Challenge and Commitment: A Defence Policy for Canada* (Ottawa: Supply and Services Canada, 1987), 2.
3 Ibid., 15. By contrast, External Affairs did consider recent Soviet policies to be "positive developments." See *Canada's International Relations*, 6.
4 Canada, *Challenge and Commitment*, 43.
5 In addition to the NWS (a radar surveillance network stretching from Alaska, across the Canadian Arctic, down to Labrador, and supplemented by over-the-horizon backscatter radars along the east and west coasts), the ADMP involved upgrading airfields in Yellowknife, Inuvik, Rankin Inlet, Kuujjuaq, and Iqaluit (to serve as Forward Operating Locations for interceptors) as well as additional airfields to serve as bases for NORAD's Airborne Warning and Control System (AWACS) aircraft. See Joel J. Sokolsky, "The Bilateral Defence Relationship with the United States," in *Canada's International Security Policy*, ed. David B. Dewitt and David Leyton-Brown (Scarborough, ON: Prentice-Hall, 1995), 177-78; and M.J. Tucker, "Canadian Security Policy," in *Canada Among Nations, 1985: The Conservative Agenda*, ed. Maureen Appel Molot and Brian W. Tomlin (Toronto: Lorimer, 1986), 70-71.
6 Michel Rossignol, *Canadian Defence Policy* (Ottawa: Research Branch of the Library of Parliament, 1988), 25-29; and Sokolsky, "Bilateral Defence Relationship," 178-79.
7 Canada, Department of National Defence, *Defence in the 70s* (Ottawa: Information Canada, 1971). See also J.L. Granatstein and Robert Bothwell, *Pirouette: Pierre Trudeau and*

Canadian Foreign Policy (Toronto: University of Toronto Press, 1990), 3-35; and Ann Denholm Crosby, *Dilemmas in Defence Decision-Making: Constructing Canada's Role in NORAD, 1958-96* (London: Macmillan, 1998), 67.

8 D.W. Middlemiss and J. Sokolsky, *Canadian Defence: Decisions and Determinants* (Toronto: Harcourt Brace Jovanovich, 1989), 18-30. On the Canadian commitment to NATO, see Tom Keating and Larry Pratt, *Canada, NATO and the Bomb: The Western Alliance in Crisis* (Edmonton: Hurtig, 1988), 15-48.

9 Quoted in Granatstein and Bothwell, *Pirouette*, 254.

10 Middlemiss and Sokolsky conclude that Trudeau's defence review had only a minimal impact. See Middlemiss and Sokolsky, *Canadian Defence*, 39-41.

11 For example, Granatstein and Bothwell, *Pirouette*, 260. Reviewing Mulroney's first year in office, M.J. Tucker cautioned that "it would be a mistake to see Canada's new-found concern for a strengthened military presence in the [NATO] alliance as a post-Trudeau phenomenon." See Tucker, "Canadian Security Policy," 72.

12 "Canada to Allow U.S. to Test Cruise Missiles," *New York Times*, 11 April 1982, 5; David Cox, "The Cruise Testing Agreement," *International Perspectives* (July-August 1983): 3-5.

13 "Canada Aims to Beef Up Its 'Stop Gap' Policy on Defence," *Financial Times (London)*, 15 November 1984; and "NATO Chiefs Ask Canada for More Troops," *Financial Times* (London), 25 February 1982.

14 Rossignol, *Canadian Defence Policy*, 12; See also Middlemiss and Sokolsky, *Canadian Defence*, 37-45.

15 On differences over Vietnam, see J.L.Granatstein and Norman Hillmer, *For Better or For Worse: Canada and the United States to the 1990s* (Toronto: Copp Clark Pitman, 1991), 253-55; Douglas A. Ross, *In the Interests of Peace* (Toronto: University of Toronto Press, 1984).

16 David J. Angell, "NORAD and Binational Nuclear Alert: Consultation and Decision Making in the Integrated Command," *Defense Analysis* 4 (June 1988): 129-46.

17 When Canada placed orders with McDonnell-Douglas for the CF-18 fighter planes, for example, the American firm agreed to offsets totalling 126.3 percent of the purchase price. See R.B. Byers, "Canadian Defence and Defence Procurement: Implications for Economic Policy," in *Selected Problems in Formulating Foreign Economic Policy*, ed. Denis Stairs and Gilbert R. Winham (Toronto: University of Toronto Press, 1985), 184; and Sokolsky, "The Bilateral Defence Relationship," 180-81.

18 The response in Washington was so universally negative that even the ordinarily pro-Canadian Lawrence Eagleberger suggested that Trudeau's proposals "resembled nothing so much as those of a leftist high on pot." See Granatstein and Bothwell, *Pirouette*, 365-72; Patrick Gossage, *Close to the Charisma: My Years between the Press and Pierre Elliott Trudeau* (Toronto: McClelland and Stewart, 1986), 253-63.

19 Sokolosky, "Bilateral Defence Relationship," 176.

20 Granatstein and Hillmer, *For Better or For Worse*, 297.

21 Joel Sokolsky, "Changing Strategies, Technologies and Organization: The Continuing Debate on NORAD and the Strategic Defense Initiative," *Canadian Journal of Political Science* 19 (December 1986): 751-74; and Boris Castel, "Ballistic Missile Defense, Arms Control and the Implications for Canada," in *The U.S.-Canada Security Relationship: The Politics, Strategy and Technology of Defense*, ed. David G. Haglund and Joel J. Sokolsky (Boulder, CO: Westview, 1989), 205-13.

22 Joseph Jockel, *No Boundaries Upstairs: Canada, the United States and the Origins of North American Defence* (Vancouver: UBC Press, 1987).

23 Granatstein and Hillmer, *For Better or For Worse*, 295-96.

24 Joel Sokolsky, "Parting of the Waves? The Strategy and Politics of the SSN Decision," in Haglund and Sokolsky, *U.S.-Canada Security Relationship*, 275, 279-83; John Honderich, *Arctic Imperative: Is Canada Losing the North?* (Toronto: University of Toronto Press, 1987), 132-33; and David Buchan, "Fortress Canada Toughens Up," *Financial Times* (London), 5 August 1987, who noted that Washington "would prefer Canada to build more surface escorts for transatlantic convoy duties, and not to try to play in the big league of nuclear-powered submarines."

25 Maureen Farrow and William B.P. Robson, "The Long Road Back to Balance: Federal Fiscal Policy Following the April 1989 Budget," *Fiscal Policy Monitor* 2 (July 1989): 1-16; Larry Welsh, "Raise Taxes to Cut Deficit, Group Says: C.D. Howe Institute Urges Tough Action in Spring Budget," *Toronto Star*, 22 February 1989.

26 Shawn McCarthy, "Spend Less, Lower Deficit, Ottawa Told," *Toronto Star*, 18 December 1990.

27 "Mulroney Shifts Cabinet, Takes Aim at Deficit," *Reuters News Service*, 31 January 1989.

28 Fen Osler Hampson, "Call to Arms: Canadian National Security Policy," in *Canada Among Nations, 1987: A World of Conflict*, ed. Maureen Appel Molot and Brian W. Tomlin (Toronto: Lorimer, 1988), 75-79.

29 Indeed, in a February 1990 public opinion poll, an overwhelming majority of Canadians polled felt the government should reduce the deficit by cutting military spending. "Military Spending Cuts Favored by 71% in Poll," *Toronto Star*, 5 February 1990. Pollsters attributed this result to the end of the Cold War.

30 Tim Harper, "Ottawa Remains Committed to Buying Nuclear Submarines," *Toronto Star*, 5 April 1989; Carol Goar, "Canada Maintaining Role in NATO Despite East Bloc Reforms, PM Says," *Toronto Star*, 22 November 1989. In fact, as late as 1990, McKnight was trying to maintain some of the white paper's modernization program with the incredible claim that "the capability of the USSR strategic forces has not lessened." Quoted in Joel J. Sokolsky, "The Future of North American Defence Co-operation," *International Journal* 46 (Winter 1990-91): 27.

31 In addition, Wilson announced imminent military base closings and the cancellation of planned tank purchases. See Rosemary Speirs, "Leak Forces Wilson to Table Tough Budget Early: No Nuclear Submarines, And Your Taxes Will Go Up," *Toronto Star*, 27 April 1989; and Dan W. Middlemiss, "Canadian Defence Policy: An Uncertain Transition," in *Canada Among Nations, 1989: The Challenge of Change*, ed. Maureen Appel Molot and Fen Osler Hampson (Ottawa: Carleton University Press, 1990), 123-24.

32 Tim Harper, "Deficit Will Force Defence Cuts, Minister Warns," *Toronto Star*, 17 October 1990.

33 Fred Langan, "Canada's Budget Brings Home NATO Troops," *Christian Science Monitor*, 28 February 1992; Tim Harper, "'Political Voice' In Europe Feared Lost," *Toronto Star*, 27 February 1992.

34 Middlemiss, "Canadian Defence Policy," 124; and Harriet W. Critchley, "Does Canada Have a Defence Policy?" *Canadian Defence Quarterly* 19 (Autumn 1989): 13-15.

35 Paul Buteux, "NATO and the Evolution of Canadian Defence and Foreign Policy," in Dewitt and Leyton-Brown, *Canada's International Security Policy*, 153. The government did initiate a defence review in 1989. Nonetheless, it was repeatedly delayed as a result of external events and did not make a coherent policy statement on Canadian defence needs in the new era.

36 Edison Stewart, "'Thug' of Panama Deserves It: PM," *Toronto Star*, 20 December 1989.

37 Martin Rudner, "Canada, the Gulf Crisis and Collective Security," in *Canada Among Nations, 1990-91: After the Cold War*, ed. Fen Osler Hampson and Christopher J. Maule (Ottawa: Carleton University Press, 1991), 241-80. Canada subsequently supplied troops for the UN peacekeeping force on the Kuwaiti-Iraqi border.

38 John Halstead, "A New Order in Europe: Evolving Security Systems," in Hampson and Maule, *After the Cold War*, 161.

39 Jeff Sallot, "Allies Let Fly at Canada Over Pullout," *Globe and Mail*, 9 April 1992, A7; John Hay, "Canadian Defence Policy Is a Muddle of Wishful Thinking," *Ottawa Citizen*, 2 March 1992; Andrew Cohen, "Security and NATO," in *Canada Among Nations, 1992-93: Global Jeopardy*, ed. Christopher J. Maule and Fen Osler Hampson (Ottawa: Carleton University Press, 1993), 252-53.

8
The Conservative Approach to International Peacekeeping

Manon Tessier and Michel Fortmann

In 1984, *Globe and Mail* columnist Jeffrey Simpson issued a challenge to observers of Canadian politics: "Just for fun, take five or 10 seconds and ask yourself what policies separate Brian Mulroney's Conservatives from John Turner's Liberals. If you come up with something substantial, you will have performed a miracle of political insight. If you can't think of anything, join the crowd."[1] In 1986, two academics added grist to the mill of this comparison when they came up with one of the first negative assessments of the Conservatives' foreign policy: "All problems identified by the previous Liberal regime preoccupied the Tories. So did the security issues, although the Mulroney government assumed a lower profile on international security questions than did its predecessor. To be sure, the new government differs from the Liberals in approach and style, but the Mulroney government's behaviour during 1985 does not portend dramatic change in major aspects of Canadian foreign policy."[2]

These two quotes suggest that, at first glance, Conservative policies in the area of international security were not particularly original, at least not during the Mulroney government's first year. But is this also true of peacekeeping, an area in which improvisation and a posteriori reaction are the order of the day for all middle-power governments, and especially for Canadian governments, which take immense pride in their involvement in peacekeeping? And can the same conclusions be made for the Conservative government's entire peacekeeping record over its two terms of office? This is a complex question requiring two initial observations.

The first relates to domestic policy. Peacekeeping activity is so firmly rooted in the collective Canadian "psyche" that it is almost impossible to imagine an elected government openly opposing or fundamentally questioning the importance of peacekeeping in the country's foreign policy. This unconditional support is fuelled by more than just a feeling of pride, a vocation, or accumulated expertise. It is a sort of founding myth that the collective Canadian imagination feeds on and that refers to the societal values of tolerance, respect, and mediation. Within this logic, peacekeeping is custom-made for Canadians, and opposition to it is tantamount to a rejection of "Canadian values." Any challenges to the myth run the risk of being politically unpopular and inviting criticism from the activist base and public opinion.

The governments of John G. Diefenbaker and Pierre Elliott Trudeau are eloquent proof of the strength of the internationalist theme of peacekeeping.[3] These two prime ministers were not known to be overly enthusiastic about peacekeeping; however, faced with these political realities, they supported the UN peacekeeping missions that were created during their terms of office. The fact that peacekeeping had officially sunk to the last place among Canadian defence priorities in 1971 did not prevent the Trudeau government from agreeing to participate in four new peace missions during his term of office.

Thus, even in a political climate of reticence and caution with regard to peacekeeping, it appears that no government in Ottawa can easily evade what is widely seen as its responsibility for international peacekeeping. So strong is this reality that the central question of this chapter can already be answered in the negative: "No, the Conservatives would not be able to go against the weight of tradition and refuse to pursue an active peacekeeping policy."

Second, we need to explore Canadian peacekeeping policy by analyzing it within its international context. This helps to clarify things considerably, especially for the period between 1988 and 1993, since the Mulroney government had the privilege of occupying a ringside seat at the very moment when international peacekeeping was being affected by profound changes. Despite the importance of events in the early 1990s, however, Canadian peacekeeping should not be seen as merely echoing international events. Canadian policy was not simply a passive response to UN demands. In fact, policy was influenced by two focal points – on the one hand, domestic political culture and, more specifically, the traditional attachment of Canadians to the internationalism of Lester B. Pearson – and, on the other, international pressures related to peacekeeping and conflict resolution. From this perspective, it was expected that the first term of the Mulroney government would reflect the continuity of Canadian policy and, therefore, modest but active support for peacekeeping. In other words, the influence of political culture would be crucial during this period. However, the second term would be characterized by a fundamental transformation of the context and practice of peacekeeping, and this, in turn, would call into question Canadian policy and how it was perceived by public opinion.

The Mulroney Government's First Term, 1984-88

The first four years of Conservative government coincided with the end of a ten-year period (1978-88) during which the United Nations did not create any new peacekeeping missions. Canada's disillusionment over peacekeeping during this period[4] was intensified by the multilateralism crisis being experienced by the United Nations itself. The newly elected Conservative government initiated the debate over peacekeeping in its green paper on the directions of foreign policy in Canada, which included the following question: "Do Canadians agree that we should encourage a return to the practice of UN sponsorship of peacekeeping operations, and devote additional Canadian resources to the enterprise – despite the frustrations involved?"[5] Thus, the very beginning of the first Conservative mandate was characterized by typically Canadian vacillation as the government attempted to establish a delicate balance between tradition, obligation, and realism. Of course, the exercise was rather symbolic, for it was obvious that it would be politically impossible for a Canadian government to abandon peacekeeping. Indeed, the support of Canadian political elites and public opinion were clearly expressed in the conclusions of the parliamentary report released in the summer of 1986. It recommended:

- that the government consider making significantly greater use of the reserve forces for peacekeeping service, either individually or experimentally in small units;
- that Canada continue to make its peacekeeping expertise available to the armed forces of other countries;
- that the government continue to support training seminars on peacekeeping that are hosted at Canadian universities and to assist the International Peace Academy;
- that the best approach to invitations to become involved in peacekeeping operations is for Canada to apply its criteria on a case-by-case basis, while maintaining its preference for operations under United Nations auspices.[6]

These recommendations were explicitly accepted in December 1986.[7] The question posed by the green paper received the following official response: "Canada will continue to favour operations under United Nations auspices."[8] In the spring of 1987, the white paper on defence followed suit and specified that, "as a responsible member of the world community and an active and committed member of the United Nations, Canada has a respected record of peacekeeping service ... Canada also plays a vital role in preventing a major rift between our alliance partners by maintaining peacekeeping forces in Cyprus. In all these instances, the use of our armed forces for peacekeeping or truce supervision ... serves our national interest as well as the broader community."[9]

Despite this support in principle, the dilemma between tradition and scepticism was very much present in Conservative policy, particularly in relation to the UN mission in Cyprus, as the Conservative government, like the Liberals before them, tried unsuccessfully to find a solution to funding problems. This was reflected in the 1986 report, which bluntly stated: "It is time for other countries to consider taking Canada's place."[10] However, once again, compliance with international obligations and habit took precedence over disillusion and the temptation to withdraw from this mission. The government deplored this fact but hesitated to take action: "Unless such countries come forward, the committee concludes that a continuing Canadian contribution to the United Nations peacekeeping force in Cyprus helps to prevent fighting on the island."[11]

To conclude, the Mulroney government's policy on peacekeeping during this first term did not differ markedly from that of the Liberals. This is not in the least surprising because peacekeepers generally do not require much in the way of resources. As was already stated in the introduction to this chapter, the international context has a considerable influence on Canadian peacekeeping policy. From this perspective, the lack of dynamism on the part of the United Nations during the 1980s was perfectly suited to Ottawa's cautious, sceptical internationalism during this period.

The figures in this regard are significant: when the Conservatives were elected, there were 740 Canadian soldiers involved in four different missions: the UN Force in Cyprus (UNFICYP), the UN Disengagement Observer Force (UNDOF) in the Golan Heights, the UN Truce Supervision Organization (UNTSO) in Palestine, and the UN Military Observer Group India-Pakistan (UNMOGIP). These four missions were all "first-generation" missions,[12] requiring little equipment and money. The 1985 decision to participate within the Multinational Force and Observers (MFO) in the Middle East increased the number of Canadian soldiers involved in missions to approximately 900. These figures were maintained until the last year of Mulroney's first term: by 1988, Canada was deploying approximately 960 armed forces personnel on missions around the world, including five Canadians in the United Nations Good Offices Mission in Afghanistan and Pakistan (UNGOMAP) that was established to supervise the withdrawal of Soviet troops from Afghanistan.

The United Nations' peacekeeping inertia also had consequences for the development of Canadian defence and foreign policy. The theme of peacekeeping was still present in official documents published during the first term (as tradition required), but it was regularly replaced with issues related to North American Aerospace Defence Command (NORAD), arms control, or protection of sovereignty in the Arctic. For example, only four out of the 121 recommendations contained in the Canadian government's response to the 1986 Special Joint Committee of the Senate and the House of Commons related to peacekeeping. For its part, the 1987 white paper on defence made virtually no mention of peacekeeping, with only one out of eighty-nine pages being devoted to the issue.

The MFO: An Original or Traditional Decision?

In this regard, Canada's participation in the MFO was probably the only major decision made in the area of peacekeeping during Mulroney's first term. The initiative is all the more interesting as a subject of analysis since the MFO was not a new mission, having been created in 1982; and, by agreeing to participate, the Conservatives disregarded "the wariness that kept Canada out of the MFO at the time of its inception."[13] Indeed, Canada had supported the Camp David Accords, which were the source of this mission, but not the mission itself because of "concern over non-UN sponsorship, a recognition that an American-directed initiative could create political difficulties in other Canadian external ventures, a belief that it would rekindle the Arab perception of a pro-Israeli bias, jeopardizing economic gains, and a recognition that Canadian participation was unnecessary given the extent of confirmed West European involvement."[14]

The Conservatives therefore stood out clearly from the previous government, all the more so because the contribution was not merely symbolic. As Martin Shadwick recalled: "The new commitment, involving 136 Canadian military personnel and nine CH-135 Twin Huey tactical transport helicopters, is the largest in-theatre commitment of Canadian military aircraft to a peacekeeping operation since the early days of the first United Nations Emergency Force."[15] In addition, participation in the MFO required modifications to Canadian military equipment so that the helicopter fleet could be adapted to extreme desert conditions. The mission was also important because it created "an experienced cadre of personnel in a whole new area of expertise."[16]

Finally, the Conservative decision to participate in the MFO is significant for one other reason. It was a decision of "engineers," to use Denis Stairs's analogy in the introduction to this book. This decision committed future governments because it laid the foundations of a Middle East peacekeeping policy that still prevails today. But did this decision represent a real change in the Canadian position? It appears rather that the decision to participate in the MFO was still typical of Canada's fundamentally favourable attitude towards peacekeeping. In fact, the Conservative government had responded to an official request by the Israeli and Egyptian governments to replace the contingent whose mandate was coming to an end. Moreover, the mission had been shown to be useful in the regional peace process. As well, despite its particularities, this mission was still a classic first-generation mission. For all these reasons, to decline this offer to participate, while several other Canadian allies were doing so, would have been viewed negatively. Thus, it would be difficult to see the MFO as an exception in the first mandate of the Mulroney government, which, essentially, continued to be characterized by the tradition of participation in peacekeeping.

International Peacekeeping: The First Signs of Change

The final months of Mulroney's first mandate were characterized by an upsurge of multilateralism impelled by renewed dynamism within the UN Security Council. In 1988 and 1989 – that is, after ten years of inactivity in the area of peacekeeping – the UN authorized the creation of four new missions. This had an immediate effect on Canadian peacekeeping practices: in 1988-89, the number of Canadian soldiers serving on peacekeeping missions abroad increased from 960 to 1,250 due to participation in the United Nations Iran-Iraq Military Observer Group (UNIIMOG) and the United Nations Transition Assistance Group in Namibia (UNTAG). Canada provided 525 and 237 soldiers, respectively, to these missions. It also deployed some 170 armed forces personnel to the United Nations Observer Group in Central America (ONUCA, after the Spanish, Grupo de Observadores de las Naciones Unidas en Centroamérica), as well as eight civilian monitors to the International Support and Verification Mission and the UN Observer Mission to Verify the Electoral Process in Nicaragua (ONU-VEN), two bodies set up to complete the work of ONUCA. The United Nations Angola Verification Mission (UNAVEM) was also created during this period, but Canada was not invited to participate.

Not only soldiers were called upon to participate in these missions. For the first time, Royal Canadian Mounted Police officers, recruited through a call for volunteers, participated in a UN mission in Namibia, which was followed by many others. Elections Canada officers was also involved: between 1984 and 1989, they participated in seventeen electoral missions. From January 1990 to February 1993, this number rose to 116.[17] The increase in numbers had a direct effect on costs: by 1989, peacekeeping commitments were in excess of forty million dollars.[18]

In spite of a decade marked by many disillusions, these facts underline that Canada remained a strong supporter of multilateralism. Moreover, the government continued to have high hopes for the United Nations and viewed its new efforts at conflict management in a good light. The fact that the international context was less tense also explains Canadian enthusiasm for participating in the new missions launched by the United Nations in the late 1980s. The latter were not constraining and had all the characteristics of traditional missions. They certainly put additional pressure on the military resources of the Canadian Forces (CF), but, at the time, this was not an insurmountable obstacle.

Transformation of Peacekeeping, 1990-93

Although the peacekeeping missions undertaken during the last two years of the decade could still be considered as traditional, this was not true of those started from 1990 onwards. Described as second-generation missions, they involved forceful interventions in ongoing conflict situations, whether interstate conflicts (e.g., Iraq's invasion of Kuwait in 1990) or civil wars (e.g., the civil war in Yugoslavia that began in 1991). Obviously, the norms and practices of traditional peacekeeping no longer applied. Moreover, the UN peacekeepers had more diversified tasks, ranging from humanitarian aid to disarmament and including election monitoring, the maintenance of public order, and the reconstruction of societies affected by war.

Despite this, Canada also embraced the wave of internationalist enthusiasm that swept the international community at the beginning of the 1990s. After all, was this not the ideal time, as the world was freeing itself from the straitjacket of the Cold War, to build a new international order? Moreover, the coalition's victory over Iraq strongly underlined that the international community could once again act in a coherent and effective manner. From this point of view, it is not surprising that Canada would want to join this movement.

The Mulroney government's initial reactions to the new peacekeeping challenges were, therefore, enthusiastic. Speaking at Stanford University on 29 September 1991, Mulroney affirmed that Canada was aware of the changes that were taking place in the area of peacekeeping and was favourable to the idea of "re-thinking the limits of national sovereignty in a world where problems respect no borders."[19] A few days prior to that speech, the secretary of state for external affairs, Barbara McDougall, had told the United Nations General Assembly: "We must not allow the principle of non-intervention to impede an effective international response ... the concept of sovereignty must respect higher principles, including the need to preserve human life from wanton destruction."[20]

At the end of the year, McDougall clearly announced the government's intentions:

> Through the framework of the UN, Canada will continue, indeed even expand, its peacekeeping efforts. The Western Sahara, Cambodia, Yugoslavia, and perhaps again the Middle East are all areas of conflict where Canadian expertise will likely be required. The UN's vocation is evolving from peacekeeping to peacemaking and even – as we see in Cambodia – into quite intrusive nation-building. The international

community, urged on by Canada and others, is increasingly assuming such functions as electoral supervision, refugee protection and even the development of democratic institutions – actions that were once considered to fall under the exclusive purview of national governments.[21]

True to its word, in the fall of 1991, Canada requested that a meeting of the Security Council be convened to discuss the situation in the Balkans. Furthermore, Canadian diplomats put pressure on the United Nations to act as quickly as possible. In the spring of 1992, Canada immediately joined the UN mission in Croatia. In March 1992, the Department of National Defence (DND) announced that 1,200 Canadian peacekeepers would participate in UNPROFOR (United Nations Protection Force) for an initial period of one year. Finally, in April 1992, the Canadian government promised that 750 Canadian soldiers would participate in UNOSOM (United Nations Operation in Somalia), and an airborne battalion was subsequently sent to Somalia.[22]

This new enthusiasm reflected more than the changes taking place on the international scene. Nor was the Conservative government's idealism the result of a late conversion to Pearsonian internationalism; rather, Mulroney played this card for fairly transparent political reasons. On the one hand, peacekeeping still enjoyed popularity among the Canadian public. Indeed, a majority of Canadians considered this task to be the main mission of their armed forces,[23] and the end of the Cold War accentuated this trend. Surveys carried out between 1990 and 1992 confirmed, moreover, that peacekeeping was given priority over all other CF missions.[24] Thus the popularity of the CF increased considerably around 1990. As Martin Shadwick noted: "In 1990-1992, Canadians heard more about their armed forces and saw more evidence of the professionalism of their armed forces, than at any time since the early 1950s. Indeed, the only way in which the CF could have garnered additional media attention would have been if one of our search and rescue aircraft had spotted Elvis Presley waving from a life raft."[25] Thus the period opened up with a wave of enthusiasm as the United Nations declared its determination to intervene more actively in an increasingly dangerous world. In spite of their wish to benefit from a peace dividend after the Cold War, a majority of Canadians, shocked by the violence in the former Yugoslavia, offered their support for a strong Canadian presence in Bosnia. In fact, they showed more activism than ever before. According to a Gallup poll taken in September 1992, 64 percent of Canadians said that they would accept CF personnel in Yugoslavia using their weapons to enforce peace; only 26 percent opposed such use.[26]

It is therefore logical that the Mulroney government would want to take advantage of this new wave of popular enthusiasm for peacekeeping, all the more so because, at the end of its second term, the Conservative government's popularity was falling, particularly in relation to domestic policy matters. As a *Globe and Mail* journalist pointed out: "Frustrated by the slow pace of constitutional reform and the failure of the economy to rebound as quickly as anticipated, Mr. Mulroney has turned away from domestic issues in his public remarks ... to focus on global issues of peace and security."[27] A parallel can certainly be drawn between Conservative activism in the area of peacekeeping in the early 1990s and Trudeau's famous initiative in favour of disarmament. Indeed, these two acts clearly reflected the political opportunism of governments on their last legs.

It should also be noted that Canadian military leaders had their own reasons for enthusiastically embracing peacekeeping as the priority mission of the CF. Given the end of the Cold War and subsequent political pressures to reduce military spending, National Defence officials were well aware that peacekeeping was "the sole military role that had any public support."[28]

For all these reasons, the intensification of Canadian involvement in peacekeeping from 1991 to 1993 was impressive. For example, while the CF had participated in nineteen multilateral peacekeeping missions in the thirty-nine years between 1947 and 1986, Ottawa contributed armed forces personnel and equipment to eighteen missions (sixteen UN and two non-UN missions) in the five years from 1988 to 1993.[29] In the 1980s, there were an average of 1,600 members of military personnel involved in peacekeeping operations, compared with 4,000, or 10 percent of the UN forces, in 1992. In budgetary terms, the fourteen operations in which Canada participated between 1945 and 1980 created only $266 million in additional expenses, that is, 0.4 percent of the total national defence budget, or $7.6 million per year.[30] In contrast, from 1991 to 1995, the total costs assumed by DND for peacekeeping increased to nearly three billion dollars. Thus, the cost of Canadian participation during this period was evaluated at $200 million per year.[31] The scope of the effort undertaken by the CF within the framework of new peacekeeping missions can be seen in Table 8.1.

The Withdrawal from Cyprus: A Short-lived Burst of Pragmatism

The principal consequence of this enthusiasm was the exhaustion of military resources, which reached a critical level in 1993. In 1992-93, Canada deployed 4,300 Canadian soldiers throughout the world, and the government's supplementary budget estimates added $83.3 million to UN peacekeeping operations.[32] In fact, in 1992-93 it cost Canada approximately $175 million to fulfil its peacekeeping obligations; that is, there was an increase of 100 percent over the preceding year. The Conservatives, who had relied on "tradition" since 1984, now had to deal with the pressure

Table 8.1

Canadian participation in peacekeeping missions, 1991-95

International mission	CF members
Gulf crisis	500
UN Observers for the Verification of Elections in Haiti (ONUVEH)	11
UN Iraq-Kuwait Observer Mission (UNIKOM)	301
UN Mission for the Referendum in the Western Sahara (MINURSO)	740
UN Angola Verification Mission (UNAVEM II)	15
UN Observer Mission in El Salvador (ONUSAL)	2
UN Advance Mission in Cambodia (UNAMIC)	103
UN Transitional Authority in Cambodia (UNTAC)	214
UN Protection Force (UNPROFOR)	2,008
UN Operations in Mozambique (ONUMOZ)	15
UN Operations in Somalia (ONUSOM)	5
Unified Task Force (UNITAF/Somalia)	1,260
UN Observer Mission Uganda-Rwanda (UNOMUR)	2
UN Assistance Mission in Rwanda (UNAMIR)	2

put on limited military resources by these peacekeeping obligations. It was time to make decisions, and Cyprus became a choice target. Although it had defended the mission during its previous term, the Conservative government changed its tune. Officials began issuing public warnings that Canada might not be in a position to participate in every UN mission, particularly if it resulted in the institutionalization of "permanent peace-keepers," as in Cyprus. Ottawa grew increasingly blunt about the longevity of the Cyprus mission. As one official put it: "After 28 years, we felt we had done our bit and we could perhaps use our resources more effectively elsewhere."[33]

The decision to withdraw from Cyprus killed two birds with one stone, allowing Canada to both cut costs that were not reimbursed by the United Nations and reduce the number of peacekeepers in service to 575. However, the withdrawal from Cyprus (as well as the recall of NATO troops stationed in Germany, which was decided during the same period) provided only temporary relief from the pressures associated with international peacekeeping. In other words, even though the withdrawal from Cyprus gave the government some breathing space, the structural conditions – the overuse of military resources for peacekeeping purposes – remained.

A Public Plagued by Doubts

Faced with these realities, the Conservative discourse based on the Canadian tradition of peacekeeping changed only slowly; wishful thinking still prevailed in 1991 and 1992. In September 1991, Mulroney was still pledging to audiences that Canada would "fulfil its obligations." However, as Alex Morrison put it: "Some might note that such an undertaking could be viewed as ironic, made as it was less than two weeks after the minister of national defence had announced sweeping reductions in the strength and capabilities of the Canadian armed forces."[34] The end of the Cold War rendered the Conservative government's white paper on defence obsolete, and, therefore, in 1992 it published a short policy statement on defence in which it acknowledged the phenomenon of increasing solicitation for peacekeeping missions. Because of the particularity of the post-Cold War conflicts, which involve both peacekeeping and peace enforcement, the Conservatives admitted that they were unable to predict the eventual needs of certain missions. Faced with this dilemma, Ottawa chose to maintain forces for traditional-type missions and new missions: "Our past successes have not been due to a specialization in the requirements of peacekeeping tasks, but to the general purpose nature of our forces, which are highly trained, adequately equipped, well-commanded, disciplined, professional and prepared for the hardship of conflict."[35] This excerpt is typical of the Conservative government's difficult and slow adjustment to reality, which would soon catch up with it.

By the time Canada's monument to peacekeeping was unveiled in Ottawa in October 1992, many critical voices were beginning to make themselves heard. Some commentators, such as Desmond Morton, pointed to the fact that peace enforcement is inherently dangerous;[36] this was also underscored by General Lewis MacKenzie, who strongly criticized the poor showing of the United Nations in the Bosnian quagmire. Canadian peacekeeping forces in the field appeared to be utterly vulnerable and powerless to stop violence. But the public debate would increasingly focus upon the resource constraints experienced by Canada, which faced a threefold increase in its peacekeeping activities in 1992 and 1993.

Thus, on the occasion of the UN secretary-general's visit to Ottawa in May 1992, Mulroney lashed out against countries that were in arrears to the world organization, noting that Canada had been one of only fourteen countries that had paid peacekeeping dues in full. Also, in September of that year, McDougall criticized the UN Security Council for its intention to charge Canada additional costs related to the Yugoslavian crisis. In McDougall's view, Canada could not work miracles. Canadian commitment to peacekeeping forces had increased from 2,000 to 4,300 troops in a short period, and Canada could not be expected to do more.[37] In November 1992, General John de Chastelain, the chief of defence staff, announced that the CF would not be able to participate in any more missions, or even maintain the same level of commitment, without additional resources.[38]

The serious problems brought to light by the operations carried out in Somalia and ex-Yugoslavia caused the Canadian public, for the first time in decades, to have some fundamental doubts about the UN interventions. Within the context of these bloody confrontations, in which, most of the time, the peacekeepers are either unable to accomplish their mission or become victims themselves, peacekeeping is no longer seen as a miraculous panacea. The scandal that accompanied the failure of the Somalia mission dealt a final blow to public perception of peacekeepers by bringing the discipline problems within the armed forces into sharp focus. The Canadian peacekeepers' image of excellence was tarnished as a result of the tragic incidents of March 1993. The Commission of Inquiry into Somalia underscored the fact that, if Canadians wanted their country to continue to play a peacekeeping role, then they could no longer go everywhere and respond to every request made by the United Nations. Consequently, questions flew from all sides: Under what conditions should a mission be refused? On what criteria should a mission be accepted? With what funds should the equipment needed by the Canadian peacekeepers be purchased? Should Canada specialize in specific niches (telecommunications, training, etc.)? Should Canada limit itself to traditional missions? Should reservists be involved to relieve the ground forces?

The Conservatives were caught off guard by all these questions. They did not have an adequate white paper or discussion paper. All they had was the UN secretary-general's *Agenda for Peace*, which was out of date one year after it was written. In 1994, therefore, the government entrusted the Standing Senate Committee on Foreign Affairs and the Standing Committee on National Defence and Veterans with the task of studying the upheavals in international peacekeeping. The fact that, in the space of a few months, two committees were asked to tackle the same subject was evidence of the Conservative government's sense of urgency and its desire to find a solution to peacekeeping problems.

Unfortunately for the Conservatives, they were unable to receive the answers that they were so keen on hearing. A decrease in popularity; a new leader; an election campaign; and, finally, a crushing defeat at the polls prevented them from reaping the fruit of the efforts undertaken in 1993 to examine this issue – efforts that led to a major national debate and a review of Canada's foreign and defence policy. Although the Conservatives can be criticized for not having reacted quickly enough to the pressures of second-generation missions, they nevertheless were responsible for setting in motion the in-depth review of Canadian peacekeeping, the effects of which continue to be evident today.

Conclusion

What should we conclude from this analysis? Have we succeeded in meeting Jeffrey Simpson's challenge, introduced at the beginning of this chapter? That is, did the Conservatives distinguish themselves from their Liberal predecessors in the area of peacekeeping? Given our basic premise that the Canadian government, regardless of its political allegiance, will remain faithful to the sacrosanct principle of peacekeeping, we did not expect to find a fundamental break between the Liberal and the Conservative approach to peacekeeping. As demonstrated during Mulroney's second term, the pressures of the international context combined with domestic pressures have slowly but surely changed collective Canadian attitudes.

Traditionalism dominated during the first term because there was no external pressure to challenge it. The rapid succession of upheavals within international peacekeeping and the doubts of Canadian public opinion during the second term led to a change in attitudes. This change did not call into question Canada's deep commitment to peacekeeping, but it was strong enough to make the nation want to learn from past mistakes and to be realistic about its own limits. These new attitudes coloured the great national debate in 1993, which was unique in Canada's fifty-year history of peacekeeping. For all these reasons, the record of the Conservatives in peacekeeping is one of tradition (re: behaviour) and re-examination (re: motivations and attitudes). However, while the implications of a third Conservative term for peacekeeping practices can only be imagined, what is certain is that the road to pragmatism after 1993 was paved under the Conservative regime.

Notes

A French version of this chapter was published in *Études internationales* 31: 2 (juin 2000).

1 *Globe and Mail*, 20 June 1984.
2 Maureen Appel Molot and Brian W. Tomlin, "The Conservative Agenda," *Canada Among Nations, 1985: The Conservative Agenda* (Toronto: James Lorimer, 1986), 3-4; see also David Taras, "Brian Mulroney's Foreign Policy: Something for Everyone," *The Round Table* 293 (1985): 35-46.
3 For an overview, see Guy Gosselin, "Le Canada et les Nations Unies," in *De Mackenzie King à Pierre Trudeau: quarante ans de diplomatie canadienne*, ed. Paul Painchaud (Québec: Les Presses de l'Université Laval, 1989), 167-92; Michel Fortmann, "Le Canada et le maintien de la paix," in *Regards sur le système de défense du Canada*, ed. André Donneur and Jean Pariseau (Toulouse: Presses de l'Institut d'études politiques de Toulouse, 1989), 105-35.
4 Disillusionment was provoked by problems encountered by the International Control Commission in Vietnam, by the powerlessness of the United Nations during the 1964 financial crisis, by the less-than-honourable withdrawal of UN Emergency Force II in 1967, and by the quagmire of the Cyprus mission.
5 Canada, Secretary of State for External Affairs, *Competitiveness and Security: Directions for Canada's International Relations* (Ottawa: Supply and Services Canada, 1985), 41.
6 Canada, Parliament, Special Joint Committee on Canada's International Relations, *Independence and Internationalism: Report of the Special Joint Committee on Canada's International Relations* (Ottawa: Supply and Services Canada, 1986), 59-61.
7 Canada, *Canada's International Relations: Response of the Government of Canada to the Report of the Special Joint Committee of the Senate and the House of Commons* (Ottawa: Supply and Services Canada, 1986).
8 Ibid., 51.

9   Department of National Defence, *Challenge and Commitment: A Defence Policy for Canada* (Ottawa: Supply and Services Canada, June 1987), 24-25.

10   *Independence and Internationalism*, 59.

11   Ibid.

12   With the exception of the Congo mission in the early 1960s, peacekeeping missions prior to 1988 are usually considered "first-generation," characterized by a small number of lightly armed soldiers with a straightforward mandate (such as border surveillance). Again with the exception of the Congo, missions were impartial and the consent of the parties was obtained prior to deployment.

13   M.R. Dabros, "The Multinational Force and Observers: A New Experience in Peacekeeping for Canada," *Canadian Defence Quarterly* 16 (October 1986): 35.

14   David Dewitt and John Kirton, *Canada as a Principal Power: A Study in Foreign Policy and International Relations* (Toronto: John Wiley, 1983), 398.

15   R.B. Byers and Michael Slack, *The Canadian Strategic Review 1985-86* (Toronto: Canadian Institute of Strategic Studies, 1988), 175.

16   Dabros, "Multinational Force," 35.

17   Figures taken from Henry Wiseman, "United Nations Peacekeeping and Canadian Policy: A Reassessment," *Canadian Foreign Policy* 1 (Autumn 1993): 147.

18   Figures from *The Guide to Canadian Policies on Arms Control, Disarmament, Defence and Conflict Resolution 1989* (Ottawa: Canadian Institute for International Peace and Security, 1989), 152.

19   Office of the Prime Minister, "Notes for an Address by Prime Minister Brian Mulroney on the Occasion of the Centennial Anniversary Convocation," Stanford University, 29 September 1991.

20   Quoted in Tom Keating and Nicholas Gammer, "The 'New Look' in Canada's Foreign Policy," *International Journal* 48 (Autumn 1993): 725.

21   Canada, Department of External Affairs and International Trade, "Notes for a Speech by the Honourable Barbara McDougall, Secretary of State for External Affairs," Toronto, 10 December 1991.

22   Andrew F. Cooper, *Canadian Foreign Policy: Old Habits and New Directions* (Scarborough: Prentice Hall Allyn and Bacon Canada, 1997), 184.

23   Decima Research, *Reports to the Department of National Defence*, Studies No. 2136 (December 1986), No. 2672 (November 1987), No. 2846 (March 1988), and No. 3726 (February 1989).

24   Longwoods Research Group, *Report to the Department of National Defence*, LC2136 (November/December 1990); Centre de recherche sur l'opinion publique (CROP), *The Canadian Armed Forces: Perceptions and Attitudes of Canadians*, (Report No. 92411), November 1992.

25   Quoted in Joseph Jockel, *The Canadian Forces: Hard Choices, Soft Power* (Toronto: Canadian Institute for Strategic Studies, 1999), 30.

26   *The Gallup Report: Majority Support U.N. Intervention in Former Yugoslavia* (Toronto: Gallup Canada, 26 October 1992); interviews conducted 10-14 September 1992.

27   Jeff Sallot, "PM Taking Foreign Approach," *Globe and Mail*, 26 May 1992, quoted in Cooper, *Canadian Foreign Policy*, 185.

28   Canada, Parliament, Special Joint Committee of the Senate and the House of Commons on Canada's Defence Policy, *Minutes of Proceedings and Evidence*, 19 April 1999, 2: 9.

29   Alex Morrison, "Canada and Peacekeeping: A Time for Reanalysis," in *Canada's International Security Policy*, ed. David Dewitt and David Leyton-Brown (Scarborough: Prentice Hall Canada, 1995), 217.

30   Albert Legault, "Canada's Contribution to Peacekeeping Operations," in *International Peacekeeping in the Eighties: Global Outlook and Canadian Priorities*, ed. John Sigler (Ottawa: Carleton University Press, 1982), 17-28.

31   Albert Legault, "Le maintien de la paix: Les leçons tirées par le gouvernement du Canada," in *Les Politiques nationales en matière de maintien de la paix*, ed. Josiane Tercinet, Grenoble Cahiers du CEDSI no. 21 (Centre d'études de défense et de sécurité internationales, Université Pierre Mendès France, October 1998), 79-95.

32 Figures from *Canadian Annual Review of Politics and Public Affairs, 1992* (Toronto: University of Toronto Press, 1993), 95-96.
33 Quoted in ibid., 94-95.
34 Morrison, "Canada and Peacekeeping," 212-13.
35 National Defence, *Canadian Defence Policy* (Ottawa: April 1992), 34.
36 *Toronto Star*, 23 August 1992.
37 *Ottawa Citizen*, 25 September 1992.
38 *Ottawa Citizen*, 6 November 1992.

9
Mulroney's International "Beau Risque": The Golden Age of Québec's Foreign Policy

Luc Bernier

The development of Québec's foreign policy after the Quiet Revolution in the 1960s is usually explained by a number of interrelated developments. First, it is often argued that the rapid modernization drive of the 1960s – the Quiet Revolution – opened a window of opportunity for international activities that had not even been imagined up to that point. A second explanation is Charles de Gaulle, the president of France, whose personal interventions helped accelerate the development of Québec's foreign policy. Third, it is often argued that the hostility of the federal government in Ottawa helped the development of a distinct external profile for Québec, since so much provincial time and energy was spent on reacting to federal pressures. Fourth, the nature of Québec's foreign relations can be explained by the need of the provincial government to develop relations with the United States, its most important economic partner, but its inability to duplicate the type of relationship it had established with France. Not only did the openness and diffuseness of the American political system make it difficult to generate the focus established with the centralized French state, but Québec's integration into the North American economy made policy coordination difficult, if not impossible.[1]

To this list, Claude Morin, who was at the centre of the development of Québec's international activity, adds one further element. He calls this residual factor "la présence de circonstances favorables"; that is, timing and chance.[2] This chapter follows Morin's insights and argues that the Progressive Conservative government of Brian Mulroney constituted an important "favourable circumstance" for Québec's foreign policy. After sixteen years of Liberal government under Pierre Elliott Trudeau, the international extension of Mulroney's domestic "beau risque"[3] made it possible for the provinces to have a greater role on the international stage, and Québec took advantage of this possibility. In some areas of foreign policy, one might conclude that the departures during the Conservative era were rather limited, as some other chapters in this book argue. In this case, however, after the continuous and stubborn opposition of the Trudeau era, the Mulroney government represented an important time of change. On both la Francophonie and free trade – the two essential issues in Québec international activities – tremendous progress was achieved while Mulroney was prime minister. Indeed, it can be argued that, given the retrenchment of Québec's international relations by the Parti Québécois (PQ) government of Lucien Bouchard in the 1990s,[4] the Mulroney era can be considered the golden age of Québec foreign policy.

Windows of Opportunity: The Quiet Revolution and Its Aftermath

Québec's foreign policy originated in the process of political modernization that took place during the 1960s.[5] The Quiet Revolution included an ideological element that saw the provincial state as the instrument of "liberation" for the French-Canadian nation; a transfer of power and authority to the state, or province-building;[6] and a confrontation with the traditional élites that had controlled Québec's society until then – the Roman Catholic Church over health and education matters, the English bourgeoisie over economic matters, and the federal government over political matters.[7] The fight with the Church over education and health lasted only a few years: by 1965, the Ministry of Education had been created, and by 1971 Medicare was fully developed. The rise of a Francophone bourgeoisie ended the debate about the control of Québec's economy at the beginning of the 1980s, and globalization made it obsolete. Québec's modernization also conflicted with the federal government, challenging the federal state's legitimacy.[8] The redistribution of powers between Ottawa and Québec that has been at the heart of the Canadian constitutional turmoil for the past decades also poisoned Québec international activities in the mid-1960s.

Three events launched Québec's foreign policy: the establishment of a provincial "délégation générale" in Paris in 1961, the formulation of a doctrine by Paul Gérin-Lajoie in 1965, and the signing of the first two "ententes," concerning education, with the French government. Although a commercial office already existed in New York City, the government wanted to initiate its new network of delegations in Paris. The choice of Paris for a first delegation was made easier by the fact that the French government was more than helpful.[9] Québec opened its delegation in Paris in 1961 to the almost complete indifference of the federal government because the Progressive Conservatives under John Diefenbaker had almost no interest in, and less understanding of, what was happening in Québec.[10]

Paul Gérin-Lajoie, the minister of education, also played a crucial role in the development of Québec's international relations by formulating a "doctrine" to justify provincial international activities. This doctrine was enunciated in two speeches, one to the diplomatic corps in Montréal on

12 April 1965, the other to French, Belgian, and Swiss university professors on 22 April 1965. For the first time, an important minister asserted, in front of foreign representatives, Québec's desire to engage in international activities without the consent or supervision of the Canadian government. Gérin-Lajoie argued that Québec would increase its activities internationally, just as it was doing domestically. He suggested a reversal of the traditional policy process. Claiming that the division of powers was no longer satisfactory, at least for Québec, and noting that the Statute of Westminster gave no indication that only the federal government should take care of international affairs, Gérin-Lajoie indicated that Québec would involve itself in any area of policy that it was responsible for implementing. This speech sought to establish the principle of the international extension of Québec's domestic powers – "le prolongement externe des compétences internes."[11]

The Gérin-Lajoie "doctrine" illustrates the initial fragility and anarchical nature of Québec's policy, being, as it was, the product of a Quiet Revolution that had not been carefully planned and that had only limited popular support. It became the official policy of the government more by accident than due to a lengthy formulation and coordination process. Gérin-Lajoie gave his speech while Jean Lesage was abroad on vacation, and when, upon his return, Lesage was asked by journalists what he thought of Gérin-Lajoie's statement, it was clear that he did not know what his minister of education had said.[12] Nevertheless Lesage approved, surprising his civil servants, who had become used to the premier's denials whenever his ministers had not first cleared their public appearances with him. So what was to become an important part of Québec's state-building was proclaimed official policy because Lesage was in a good mood when he landed at the Québec City airport.

It should also be noted that these two speeches were to remain the only official policy documents until a 1991 policy paper on international affairs was issued by Québec – *Québec and Interdependence: Global Horizons.* This paper defined two major poles for Québec's international activities: the Americas and Europe, with the emphasis being on "Québec's partners of choice," the United States and France.[13] (Another document on international relations had been drafted in 1984-85 shortly before the Liberals replaced the PQ, but it was never implemented.)

Thus, until 1991, if we exclude Gérin-Lajoie's speeches, policy implementation was achieved without or before policy formulation. This might explain why Christopher Malone, writing in 1973, concluded that Québec's foreign policy demonstrated only limited rationality and continuity. On the contrary, Malone argued that it was marked by a lack of planning, the absence of coordination, and high turnover among key personnel.[14] Poulin and Trudeau came to similar conclusions a decade later, noting that the Québec delegations had no strategic plan and no objectives to fulfil, particularly in the United States; the only real planning was done with regard to France-Québec relations.[15]

If the formulation of policy was not clear until late in the process, the organizational aspects also took some time to develop. From 1960 onwards, there were frequent organizational transformations, since the government was, in essence, learning foreign policy-making while doing it.[16] Nevertheless, the result was that Québec developed the most sophisticated provincial bureaucracy in Canada with regard to international relations.[17] Until 1989, international affairs was one of the responsibilities of the Department of Intergovernmental Relations, and it was split between external trade and international relations.

In Québec, decisions about reorganization have had more to do with the personalities in Cabinet than with organizational logic. In 1982, René Lévesque created the Ministry for External Trade to satisfy one of his ministers, Bernard Landry (who was to become leader of the PQ and premier of the province in 2001). This created a conflict with the intergovernmental affairs minister, Jacques-Yvan Morin, who had been trying to redefine his ministry in terms of external trade.[18] In 1988, the Ministry of International Affairs was created (ministère des Affaires internationales, or MAI), resulting in the merger of the ministère des Relations internationales (MRI) and the external trade ministry. The new ministry was not only to coordinate, but also to lead Québec's foreign policy implementation.[19]

The process was thus completed in 1988 while Mulroney was in power in Ottawa. That year, introducing the bill creating the MAI, Liberal minister Paul Gobeil said that he was continuing what had been done since 1960 and that he was improving the coherence of Québec's foreign policy.[20] He stressed that nobody had ever contested the idea developed by Gérin-Lajoie regarding the international extension of domestic jurisdictions. He even said that Canada's foreign policy benefited from Québec's international activities because the latter made the former more balanced. Gobeil argued that Québec's international role had gained legitimacy and was seen as necessary. He gave three examples: first, Québec was a member of the Agence de coopération culturelle et technique; second, on 8 November 1984, Mulroney recognized publicly the legitimacy of the relations between Québec and France; and third, an agreement had been signed between Ottawa and Québec that made it possible for the premier of Québec to attend the conferences of the heads of government of la Francophonie. These improvements in international policy were made possible by a transformation of federal-provincial relations.

Federal-Provincial Relations and Foreign Policy
Federal-provincial relations and international relations have been intertwined in Québec since the early 1960s. International relations were used

for federal-provincial purposes, and they were always a source of difficulty for foreign policy formulation and implementation. But Québec's foreign policy further developed between 1968 and 1984, despite Trudeau's fierce opposition.

During this period, relations between Ottawa and Québec can reasonably be described as bellicose. As Québec's international activities developed in the late 1960s, the federal government decided to react: in 1968, it published a white paper, *Federalism and International Relations*.[21] This paper argued that only the federal government was empowered to act on behalf of Canada in international affairs; that is, only the federal government could negotiate and conclude treaties, be a member of international organizations, and accredit and receive diplomatic representatives. Devolving Canadian sovereignty into the hands of "provincial, linguistic, and cultural interests," the white paper argued, "would lead to the disintegration of the Canadian federation."

However, despite the assertions of the 1968 white paper, there was some confusion regarding the question of whether the provinces could engage in international activities. The British North America Act, 1867, was unclear about which level of government was responsible for foreign policy. The Constitution Act, 1982, which Québec refused to sign, also left equivocal the question of the competence of the provinces in the area of foreign affairs.[22] The British tradition demands that one consider other relevant documents besides the British North America Act, 1867: the Statute of Westminster, 1931; the Colonial Laws Validity Act, 1865; and the various acts admitting new provinces to the federal union. From colonial times comes the British "Foreign Agency Act," which made it possible for six Canadian provinces to open offices in London and in former colonies such as Hong Kong (where eight of them have had offices).

In the Labour Convention case, 1937, the Judicial Committee of the Privy Council held that "the distribution of legislative powers between the Dominion and the provinces [regarding treaty implementation] is based on classes of subjects; and as a treaty deals with a particular class of subjects so will the legislative power of performing it be ascertained."[23] As one analysis later noted: "The decision was an attempt to deal with the dilemma arising from jurisdictional authority over the processes of *formation* and *performance* of international treaty obligations ... The safeguarding of provincial autonomy inherent in the Judicial Committee's ruling ... limits the federal government's ability to guarantee the performance of treaty obligations with other countries when matters under provincial jurisdiction are involved."[24] For many analysts, this case results in the greatest limitation on federal treaty powers within such constitutional systems.[25] Since 1937, neither the provincial government nor the federal government has dared to ask the Supreme Court to clarify which level of government is constitutionally responsible for foreign policy. One of the results of this is the very limited number of Québec laws framing Québec's international activities. These include the laws that create the delegations, the law that creates the *Office franco-québécois de la Jeunesse,* and the successive laws pertaining to the ministère des Affaires internationales.

Québec developed its foreign policy because the government in Québec City felt that its interests were not being properly represented by the federal government.[26] In a confidential analysis prepared in December 1990, the MAI concluded that the federal government's network of 125 embassies and consulates around the world had tremendous difficulties in attempting to represent and explain Québec's specific interests because its natural tendency was to speak for English Canada. Nonetheless, according to several Québec civil servants, relations between the Canadian missions and the Québec delegations were far better during the Mulroney era than during the Trudeau era.

However, it is important to recognize that opposition in Ottawa to the development of Québec's foreign policy was not limited to Trudeau. There was also hostility from the Department of External Affairs (DEA) (as the Department of Foreign Affairs and International Trade was then known). DEA's hostility is understandable for three overlapping reasons.[27] The first reason is historical: in Québec's international activities DEA officials were witnessing a process that, merely a generation earlier, they themselves had undergone with the imperial government in London. From 1909, when External Affairs was created, to the 1940s, when Canada's foreign policy reached its maturity, the Canadian government struggled to develop an autonomous diplomatic presence. In the view of some Ottawa mandarins, history was repeating itself: Québec was doing the same thing during the 1960s.

The second reason for the hostility of External Affairs to the development of Québec's foreign policy was cultural. During the 1960s, French-Canadians were, for the first time, being appointed to senior positions in the DEA – only to be told by Québec that they were not properly representing the province. In the 1960s, these French-Canadians, who were emerging at the top of the hierarchy at External Affairs, were not willing to be challenged by the only French-speaking province.[28] They had paid a price to be where they were. When compared with their English-Canadian counterparts, a consistently higher percentage of French-Canadian foreign service officers have held two or more university degrees. At all levels of the hierarchy, French-Canadians had more education than did English Canadians.[29] And these French-Canadians were working in English. Even in a department in which fluency in different languages was very useful, English-Canadians were not required to have a minimal understanding of French.[30] For Marcel Cadieux, who became under-secretary of state for external affairs in 1964, "the pretensions of the Québec government to independent jurisdiction in international affairs [was] considered abhorrent, if not treasonable."[31] For officials like Cadieux, the Québec government's international activities were undermining a position that had been laboriously and painfully achieved.

The third reason for DEA's hostility was bureaucratic. During the late 1960s, External Affairs increasingly had to share leadership over international affairs with other federal departments, such as the Department of National Defence and the Department of Industry, Trade and Commerce – even though a former External Affairs official, Lester B. Pearson, was the prime minister. DEA officials worried that the department was in danger of having its role as the central manager of Canadian foreign policy disappear and, thus, saw the efforts by Québec to control provincial foreign policy as a further challenge to its primacy.

Federal-provincial relations initially lent an aura to international relations it would not otherwise have had; the link with federal-provincial relations also kept international relations at the centre of the government's agenda. But, from the federal perspective, the link maintained the idea that foreign policy was not being developed for its own sake. The development of Québec's foreign policy can be explained, in part, by the confrontation between the federal government and the Québec government. Certainly the importance given to federal-provincial relations explains the difficulties in formulating Québec's foreign policy and the difficulties in establishing provincial priorities. Throughout his sixteen years in power, Trudeau and his government remained deeply hostile to provincial activities abroad; it is no coincidence that the only major expansion of provincial international activity – the establishment of a Québec delegation in Mexico – was negotiated in 1979 during the nine months that Joe Clark was prime minister. In short, Québec's participation in the Francophone summit of 1985 had more to do with Trudeau's retirement than with any of the diplomatic efforts made during his sixteen years as prime minister.[32] It also had a great deal to do with the support of France.

Québec, France, and "la Francophonie": From de Gaulle to Mitterrand

While the innovations introduced by Mulroney were important for the development of Québec's foreign policy, it can be argued that nothing would have been possible without the intervention of de Gaulle, who wanted Québec to become an international actor. He remains the single most important actor in the development of Québec's foreign policy.[33] Without de Gaulle, Québec's foreign policy would have been limited to the commercial aspects handled by the Ministry of Industry and Trade and to the debt operations of the Department of Finance. Without de Gaulle, as Morin himself has conceded, the international element of Québec's accelerated modernization would have been dull and probably sterile.[34] De Gaulle's followers in the French administration made it possible for him to push forward his preoccupations vis-à-vis Québec (even though many in the French government did not share his enthusiasm for Québec's evolution). This opportunity was unique. Nothing had prepared Québec for it, and nothing comparable has happened since.

These relations with France have been maintained. Indeed, de Gaulle's government initiated a policy that has made it possible for Québec to establish itself internationally. Québec's eventual participation in la Francophonie, which consolidated its place in international relations, was made possible by the support of the French government.[35] And it was mostly French government interest that helped Québec's foreign affairs develop so quickly during the early days of the Quiet Revolution. However, on the Québec side, everything had to be improvised. France was offering Québec more than it could handle, particularly after de Gaulle's visit in 1967.[36]

Long after de Gaulle's retirement, however, French support for Québec remained strong. In November 1977, René Lévesque went to Paris where he was received as a head of state. He was made a grand officer of the Légion d'honneur, and senior French officials indicated their support for Québec. For example, proposing a toast, the president of the National Assembly, Edgar Faure, praised Québec's effort "to rid itself of colonization."[37] The French president, Valéry Giscard d'Estaing, reiterated that French policy was based on the formula of "non-ingérence, non-indifférence" (non-interference, non-indifference – a formula used since then by French officials). However, unlike de Gaulle, Giscard d'Estaing, Raymond Barre, and Alain Peyrefitte decided to wait until Québécois had decided the matter before announcing that they were in favour of Québec's sovereignty. In 1990, the French government indicated that it would not intervene in the constitutional choice to be made by "what was still a Canadian province." Paris adopted a "wait and see" attitude.[38]

De Gaulle's patronage was also essential for Québec's ability to engage in multilateral diplomacy. In February 1968, Québec participated in the conference of education ministers held in Libreville, Gabon. This was the beginning of Québec's involvement in la Francophonie. Although Paris "advised Gabon and other countries that they could have direct relations with Québec in matters of education,"[39] Québec and Ottawa had frequent clashes over education ministers' conferences that were held in French-speaking Africa: first in Gabon, later in Zaire, then in Niger. How French diplomats explained the subtleties of the Canadian constitution in Gabon and/or Niger probably differed considerably from the official federal

Canadian line. With regard to the Niger conference, the French government put that country in an impossible situation vis-à-vis Ottawa by forcing it to invite Québec without inviting Ottawa.[40] After two summits in
Niamey, in 1969 and 1970, respectively, Québec became a "participating
government" in the Cultural and Technical Cooperation Agency (Agence
de coopération culturelle et technique, or ACCT). Considering Ottawa's
opposition, this would not have been possible without France's support.[41]
The ACCT was to develop multilateral cooperation in the fields of education, training, culture, science, and technical-vocational skills.

The establishment of the ACCT was an important step, but it lacked the
legitimacy and the high profile of summit diplomacy involving heads of
government. Nonetheless, for the first time Québec was a participating
government in a multilateral agency. Moreover, the lack of legitimacy was
eventually solved. After years of delay caused by the inability of the various governments to agree on Québec's form of participation, the first summit of la Francophonie finally took place in February 1986, following the
1985 negotiation of an understanding between the Canadian and Québec
governments regarding the nature of Québec's participation. It was agreed
that Québec would be able to participate fully on issues of cooperation
and development, act in concert with Ottawa on economic issues (after
appropriate consultation), and be an "interested observer" on political
issues.[42] Moreover, the French government lent its support to the
Canadian agreement. François Mitterrand, widely perceived to be a friend
of Mulroney, took a very different line than had de Gaulle on the Québec
issue.[43] The Paris summit was followed by a second one in Québec City,
and others have followed since.

Free Trade with the United States
The United States was (and remains) the primary market for Québec's
exports and the main source of its foreign investment. At the end of the
Mulroney era, Québec exported roughly 40 percent of its Gross Domestic
Product (GDP), of which 75 percent went to the United States. In 1993,
Québec's exports jumped 19.8 percent to $32.6 billion, 79.4 percent of
which were destined for the United States.[44] Just as the Mulroney
Conservatives saw the free trade agreement as essential for Canadian inter-
ests, so too did Québec, especially its business community.

And just as Ottawa deemed the Canadian-American relationship important to Canada, so too did Québec City deem it important to Québec.
However, as Ivo Duchacek has pointed out, compared to its intimate emotional, cultural, and political links with France, "Québec's second unpro-
claimed, or tacit, special relationship ... with its only foreign neighbor, the
United States ... is a non-sentimental, dominantly pragmatic, and commercial relationship."[45]

Clearly the government of Québec needed to maintain and develop this second relationship. However, its relationship with France could not simply be duplicated vis-à-vis the United States. As much as the French state is centralized and unified, the American state is permeable and decentralized. The separation of powers makes it difficult to know exactly on whom the Québec government should spend its very scarce resources. What is even more striking is the limited interest of the Québec government in the American political system.[46] And the reverse is also true: Québec is a topic of interest for only a very small group of American specialists.[47]

In the United States, Québec has to secure its "non-sentimental, pragmatic and commercial relationship" in economic and political circles. Unlike its relationship with France, many elements of Québec's relationship with the United States are not the business of the state. Business relations and other transborder exchanges between Québec and the United States are achieved without state intervention. Nonetheless, public relations and monitoring efforts on the part of the Québec state continue to be seen as necessary. For example, Québec's language laws, although eased over the years, have been criticized in the United States. The US Department of State's 1994 annual report on civil rights in 193 countries had a paragraph on language rights in Québec, prompting the minister, John Ciaccia, to denounce the report as inaccurate.[48]

The separation of powers and the numerous American political actors outside the executive branch also posed a problem for Québec. What were initially domestic problems became foreign relations issues. For example, surplus electricity in Québec led Hydro-Québec to search for clients in the United States, but American environmentalists began to demonstrate an interest in the issue due to the lobbying efforts of the Cree. Similarly, acid rain, caused by pollution in the US Midwest, created problems for Québec forests. The Québec government's resources for developing its relationship with the United States have always been limited.

Conclusion: Assessing the Mulroney Era

I have argued that Québec's foreign policy development was largely improvised. It was also reactive, and it had a very limited legal base. Timing and good fortune were crucial: having Mulroney in power made things easier. In 1960, the government of Québec had no ministry in charge of international relations; its only foreign service officers were six Ministry of Industry and Trade civil servants based in New York. Three decades later, when the Berlin Wall came down, the same government was, in a matter of weeks, ready to send a delegation to eastern Europe. What had happened? The Québec government was prepared for international relations in the 1990s not because it had carefully planned to be, but because the world had changed. The end of the Cold War shifted international priorities towards economics, and this global shift gave a post-facto rationality to Québec's building process. The Chrétien government has moved back to the more hostile stance that characterized the Trudeau era. For Québec, the Mulroney government period will remain the golden age of foreign policy.

From their exhaustive literature review, Bélanger et al. conclude that Québec wanted to be active internationally. Québec accorded cultural and educational importance to France, and economic importance to the United States. Other than its relationship with France and the United States, it is difficult to perceive anything that could be characterized as Québec foreign policy. As Bélanger et al. point out, when we move further away from its French and American relationships, we enter microanalyses and it becomes impossible to find any coherence in Québec's international activities.[49] Québec's foreign policy is certainly not based on a "geopolitical paradigm"[50] but, rather, is the result of the domestic policies of the Quiet Revolution. In other words, what is important is to catch up with developments elsewhere in North America and/or Europe. Specifics were always left to be decided later. As Roland Parenteau wrote in connection with another part of the Québec state system, policy instruments were created in order to implement policies that were to be written years later.[51]

W.L. Mackenzie King once said that Canada has too much geography and too little history. Québec's foreign policy is quite the opposite; instead of being afflicted by geography, it has been plagued by history. The architects of Québec's "window on the world" attempted to build a bridge over the Atlantic but forgot that New York City is only a few hours' drive from Montréal. Québec's initial international breakthroughs in the 1960s were with the French-speaking world; during the 1980s this area was also important, for, with Mulroney in power, it became possible for Québec to participate fully in la Francophonie. The attention given to the United States increased in the second half of the 1970s but, except for trade, has remained limited.[52] However, Québec has not invested enough in its relations with Washington, and it has invested too much in its relations with Paris.[53]

Over the years, the globalization of the economy made it essential to secure markets for goods and services that are produced in Québec and to maintain access to financial markets. Again, Mulroney's political will to defend and implement free trade was a significant factor here. The cultural survival of the only viable French-speaking community in North America has also been secured through international activities.[54] In foreign policy, as in other policy domains, to have interests is not sufficient for the development of policy. Governments have to take advantage of opportunities, and the Québec government benefited from those few occasions when the Conservatives were in power in Ottawa: the delegation in Paris was opened under Diefenbaker, the delegation in Mexico was opened under Joe Clark. Although Mulroney will never be as important for Québec's foreign policy as was de Gaulle, it is nonetheless difficult to envisage what would have happened without him. Presumably, some of the consolidation in Québec would have been achieved, for, after the Macdonald Commission, free trade deals would have been difficult for any government to avoid. Over the nine years that Mulroney was prime minister, Québec became a full participant in la Francophonie and was involved in free trade agreements. Catalonia, Scotland, and other non-central European governments have developed international relations, but none have done so to the same degree as has Québec. What makes Québec's international activities different is their institutional nature, particularly with regard to France. And this institutional status was achieved because Mulroney gave Québec the opportunity to take a "beau risque."

Notes

This chapter is drawn not only from earlier research published in Luc Bernier, *De Paris à Washington: la politique internationale du Québec* (Sainte-Foy: Presses de l'Université du Québec, 1996), but also from interviews conducted in 1998-99. The author gladly acknowledges the help of Nelson Michaud and Kim Richard Nossal on a preliminary version of this chapter.

1 For a systematic examination of Québec foreign policy, see Louis Bélanger, Jean-Philippe Thérien, and Guy Gosselin, "Les relations internationales du Québec: efforts de définition d'un nouvel objet d'étude," *Revue québécoise de science politique* 23 (1993): 143-70. For other studies, see the special issue of *Études internationales* 8, 2 (juin 1977); Jacques Brossard, *L'Accession à la souveraineté et le cas du Québec* (Montreal: Presses de l'Université de Montréal, 1976); R.B. Byers and David Leyton-Brown, "The Strategic and Economic Implications for the United States of a Sovereign Québec," *Canadian Public Policy* 6 (1980): 74-90; Louise Beaudoin and Jacques Vallée, "La reconnaissance internationale d'un Québec souverain," in *Répliques aux détracteurs de la souveraineté du Québec*, ed. Alain G. Gagnon and François Rocher (Montreal: VLB, 1992), 181-205. On the consequences of Québec's foreign policy, see Gordon Mace and Guy Gosselin, "La politique internationale après l'échec du lac Meech," in *Le Québec et la restructuration du Canada 1980-1992*, ed. Louis Balthazar, Guy Laforest, and Vincent Lemieux (Sillery: Septentrion, 1991), 217-43; and Commission sur l'avenir politique et constitutionnel du Québec (the Bélanger-Campeau Commission), *Éléments d'analyse économique*, working paper no. 1 (1991).

2 Morin was the deputy minister of intergovernmental and international affairs in the 1960s, and he was the minister between 1976 and 1981. His book, *L'Art de l'impossible* (Montreal: Boréal, 1987), has been viewed as one of the most important documents written on the topic. See J.L. Granatstein and Robert Bothwell, *Pirouette: Pierre Trudeau and Canadian Foreign Policy* (Toronto: University of Toronto Press, 1990), chap. 5; Louis Balthazar, "L'émancipation internationale d'un État fédéré (1960-1990)," in *Bilan québécois du fédéralisme canadien*, ed. François Rocher (Montreal: VLB, 1992), 152-79.

3 René Lévesque, asked by a reporter whether it was risky to accept Mulroney's invitation to discuss constitutional matters, replied that there was a risk but that it was a promising risk ("un beau risque").

4 After becoming Québec premier, Bouchard moved to close most of Québec's offices around the world and also separated international relations from trade. Bouchard had been Mulroney's ambassador to Paris before leaving the Conservatives to found the Bloc Québécois.

5   Confidential interview, March 1994; see also Claude Morin, *Les choses comme elles étaient* (Montreal: Boréal, 1994), chap. 9.
6   Marsha Chandler and William M. Chandler, *Public Policy and Provincial Politics* (Toronto: McGraw-Hill, Ryerson, 1979), 8; see also Robert Young, Philippe Faucher, and André Blais, "The Concept of Province-Building," *Canadian Journal of Political Science* 17 (1984): 783-818.
7   This description draws partly on Kenneth McRoberts, *Québec: Social Change and Political Crisis* (Toronto: McClelland and Stewart, 1988), but mostly from Guy Lachapelle et al., *The Québec Democracy: Structures, Processes and Policies* (Toronto: McGraw-Hill Ryerson, 1993), chap. 4.
8   Hubert Guindon, "The Modernization of Québec and the Legitimacy of the Canadian State," in *Modernization and the Canadian State*, ed. Daniel Glenday, Hubert Guindon, and Allan Torowetz (Toronto: Macmillan, 1978), 212-46.
9   In 1967, de Gaulle received Johnson, Lesage's successor, with even more fanfare than he had received Prime Minister Lester B. Pearson in 1964. See Shiro Noda "Relations internationales du Québec de 1970 à 1980: Comparaison des gouvernements Bourassa et Lévesque," (PhD diss., Université de Montréal, 1988), 43.
10 Christopher Malone, "La politique québécoise en matière de relations internationales: changement et continuité (1960-1972)" (Thèse de maîtrise, Université d'Ottawa, 1974), 258-59.
11 Although he did not use these words then, in 1967 Gérin-Lajoie used the phrase "prolongement sur le plan externe" during the debate about the creation of the ministère des Affaires intergouvernementales. See Québec, Assemblée nationale, *Journal des débats*, 2 sess., 28 leg., 13 avril 1967, 2176.
12 Morin, *L'Art de l'impossible*, 30-31; see also confidential interview, March 1994.
13 Gouvernement du Québec, ministère des Affaires internationales, *Québec and Interdependence: Global Horizons, Elements of an International Affairs Policy* (Québec: Éditeur officiel, 1991).
14 Malone, "La politique québécoise en matière de relations internationales," 310-12.
15 François Poulin and Guy Trudeau, "Les conditions de la productivité des délégations du Québec à l'étranger," École nationale d'administration publique, Québec, October 1982, 20.
16 Confidential interviews, 1994.
17 Nossal, *Politics of Canadian Foreign Policy*, 265-66.
18 Graham Fraser, *PQ: René Lévesque and the Parti Québécois in Power* (Toronto: Macmillan, 1984), 326.
19 Luc Bernier, "La planification stratégique au gouvernement du Québec," *Management international* 3 (1998): 15-24. In January 1994, history repeated itself: in the Cabinet shuffle that followed the replacement of Premier Robert Bourassa with Daniel Johnson Jr., the minister of culture was awarded control over the "Francophonie" branch of the department. Once it returned to power, the Parti Québécois reintegrated this branch within the ministère des Affaires internationales. But not for long: following another Cabinet shuffle, the Ministry of Immigration and Cultural Communities was merged with the MAI. Most of those interviewed for this project agreed that there was no synergy to this merger. In 1996, as in 1982, trade and international relations were divided, and all but six offices around the world were closed.
20 Paul Gobeil, ministre des Affaires internationales, "Intervention à l'Assemblée nationale à l'occasion du débat en deuxième lecture sur le projet de loi 42," ministère des Affaires internationales, 26 octobre 1988, 18.
21 Canada, Secretary of State for External Affairs, *Federalism and International Relations* (Ottawa: Queen's Printer, 1968).
22 Nossal, *Politics of Canadian Foreign Policy*, 258-59.
23 Ibid., 260.
24 Dwight Herperger, *Distribution of Powers and Functions in Federal Systems* (Ottawa: Supply and Services Canada, 1991), 27.

25 Curiously, Gérin-Lajoie did not refer to the Labour Conventions case in his 1965 speech but, rather, to an 1883 case, *Hodge* v. *Regina*, 1883, 9, Appeal Cases 117.

26 Renaud Dehousse, *Fédéralisme et relations internationales: une réflexion comparative* (Brussels: Bruylant, 1991). Canada's ambassador to the United States, Derek Burney, gave a good example of this at a conference in Washington in October 1992 when he quoted a controversial report by the Royal Bank of Canada that predicted disaster if voters rejected the Charlottetown constitutional accords and Québec moved toward sovereignty.

27 The following draws from R. Barry Farrell, *The Making of Canadian Foreign Policy* (Scarborough: Prentice Hall Canada, 1969), chap. 3.

28 Morin, *L'Art de l'impossible*, 45-46.

29 Farrell, *Canadian Foreign Policy*, 97-98, 117.

30 Granatstein and Bothwell, *Pirouette*, 122.

31 Ibid., 123; see also Morin, *L'Art de l'impossible*.

32 Morin, *L'Art de l'impossible*, 453.

33 Confidential interview, February 1994.

34 Claude Morin, review of Dale Thompson, *"Vive le Québec libre!"* (Toronto: Deneau Publishers, 1988) in *Recherches sociographiques* 30 (1989): 113.

35 Thérien, Bélanger, and Gosselin, "An Expanding Foreign Policy," 265.

36 Confidential interview, January 1994; see also Morin, *L'Art de l'impossible*, 83.

37 Fraser, *PQ*, 126.

38 Louis-Bernard Robitaille, "Le 'Vive le Québec libre' de de Gaulle n'avait rien d'improvisé," *La Presse*, 13 novembre 1994, A-1; in 1979 Mitterrand declared that France would help an independent Québec join the United Nations. See Robitaille, "La question du Québec: les Français ont d'autres chats à fouetter," *La Presse*, 12 novembre 1994, A-1.

39 Granatstein and Bothwell, *Pirouette*, 409, note 55.

40 Morin, *L'Art de l'impossible*; Granatstein and Bothwell, *Pirouette*, 410.

41 Morin, *L'Art de l'impossible*, 222.

42 Thérien, Bélanger, and Gosselin, "An Expanding Foreign Policy," 267.

43 Lucien Bouchard, *À visage découvert* (Montréal: Boréal, 1992); Christian Rioux, "La France pleure Tonton," *Le Devoir*, 9 janvier 1996, A-1, A-8; and "Mitterrand et le Québec," *Le Devoir*, 11 janvier 1996, A-1.

44 Maurice Jannard, "Exportations québécoises: premier surplus en 1993," *La Presse*, 8 juin 1994, D-1.

45 Ivo D. Duchacek, *The Territorial Dimension of Politics within, among and across Nations* (Boulder: Westview Press, 1986), 270.

46 Jean-François Lisée, *In the Eye of the Eagle* (Toronto: HarperCollins, 1990), 178.

47 On the US government's interest in Canada, see Joseph T. Jockel, "Canada-U.S. Relations in the Bush Era," *Canadian-American Public Policy* 1 (1990).

48 Marie Tison, "Au Québec, les minorités 'connaissent des difficultés,' s'inquiète Washington," *Le Devoir*, 3 février 1994, A-2; Normand Delisle, "Ciaccia dénonce un rapport de Washington," *La Presse*, 5 février 1994, A-17.

49 Bélanger, "Les relations internationales du Québec."

50 Paul Painchaud, "L'État du Québec et le système international," in *L'État du Québec en devenir*, ed. Gérard Bergeron and Réjean Pelletier (Montréal: Boréal, 1980), 351-70.

51 Roland Parenteau, "Les sociétés d'État au Québec: autonomie ou intégration," mimeo, 8 mai 1980.

52 Elliot J. Feldman and Lily Gardner Feldman, "Québec's Internationalization of North American Federalism," in *Perforated Sovereignties and International Relations*, ed. Ivo D. Duchacek, Daniel Latouche, and Garth Stevenson (New York: Greenwood, 1988), 69; see also confidential interviews with civil servants, Ottawa, and Québec City.

53 Confidential interview, February 1994.

54 Luc Bernier, "The Foreign Economic Policy of a Sub-National State: the Case of Québec," in Duchacek, *Perforated Sovereignties*, 125-39.

10

Explaining Canada's Decision to Join the OAS: An Interpretation

Gordon Mace

On 4 October 1989, the Canadian government decided that the country should become a full-fledged hemispheric actor by seeking membership in the Organization of American States (OAS); on 13 November 1989, Canada signed the OAS Charter, thus becoming the thirty-third member of the organization; that decision became effective on 8 January 1990, when the Mulroney government formally ratified the charter.[1] This happened some eighteen years after the government of Pierre Elliott Trudeau, in the aftermath of the foreign policy review, sought and obtained permanent observer status in February 1972. The decision to join the OAS came as a surprise, at least to observers from outside the decision-making apparatus, mostly because of the limited character of the consultation process and also because of the manner in which the decision was made public. (Possible membership in the OAS was mentioned for the first time by the prime minister himself while vacationing with the US president, George Bush, at Kennebunkport, Maine, in August 1989.)

Given the circumstances, it is therefore understandable that analyses in the months following the announcement expressed both puzzlement concerning the significance of the decision and scepticism concerning the usefulness of the move. Some saw "little reason or necessity"[2] for Canada to join the OAS at that time. Peter McKenna, for his part, wrote that if the decision did represent "a notable departure from past Canadian governments" then it did not signify "a fundamental shift in foreign policy" or "a dramatic reorientation of Canada's overall policy approach toward the hemisphere."[3]

As to the significance of the move, an initial examination of the decision could lead to the conclusion that membership in the OAS should not be considered a diplomatic departure since Canada, after all, already had permanent observer status. Moving from observer status to full membership status could, therefore, be seen as merely a continuation of past policy or as an addition to the process of rapprochement that had started twenty years previously.

But if we accept the assumption that the decision to seek permanent observer status in 1972 was, in fact, a way of refusing or eschewing full participation in the inter-American system, then the 1989 decision takes on a completely different meaning. I suggest that this is exactly the case. Canada's policy regarding the inter-American system was designed during the Second World War, when, in April 1940, O.D. Skelton, then under-secretary of state for external affairs, wrote the following in answer to a query on the government's position concerning the Pan-American Union: the "one general statement that might perhaps be made is that we refrain carefully from becoming involved in any political commitments."[4]

This policy of not becoming politically involved in inter-American affairs continued to shape Canada's relations with the Americas for the five decades following Skelton's statement. Indeed, until the end of the 1980s, Ottawa was notably absent from major inter-American discussions or negotiations, and the emphasis was put on trade, investment, and foreign assistance when it came to Canadian-Latin American and Canadian-Caribbean relations. Consequently, the decision to have Canada become a full member of the OAS has to be seen as a very significant diplomatic departure as well as a fundamental change of policy.

This observation having been made, there remains the central question of why the federal government took this decision and at this precise moment in time. I attempt to answer this question, and I do so by means of a two-step process. First, I revisit the reasons put forward by the Canadian government for not becoming a member of the OAS prior to 1989. If these reasons were no longer valid in 1989, then this would, in large part, explain the decision taken in the fall of that year. If, on the contrary, the historical reasons for not joining the OAS were still valid at the end of the 1980s, then I would need to look elsewhere to find an explanation for the change in policy. Since I believe that the latter is the case, I pursue this line of reasoning further and show that the change in Canadian policy on the OAS is explained by two clusters of factors: (1) the changes taking place in the world and, particularly, in the world economy at that time, and (2) the particular dynamics in the Americas during the second half of the 1980s.

The Rationale for Not Joining Prior to 1989

Over the years, various arguments for not joining the OAS had been put forward by analysts and policy-makers alike. Some said that Canada was politically and culturally closer to Europe and the Commonwealth and that expanded participation in the inter-American system could be considered by some of our allies as a manifestation of isolationism or even as a threat to Canada's commitment to the Atlantic community. Others were worried about the cost of membership in an organization still overly dominated by the United States. Still others were concerned that opting for a multilateral channel could endanger the benefits resulting from the pursuit of bilateral relations with the major countries in the region. They also had in mind the potential security implications of OAS membership in the advent that participation in the OAS would also imply becoming a member of the Rio Treaty, which would result in obligations for Canada.[5]

The official reasons invoked by successive governments in Ottawa are more or less summarized in the Canadian foreign policy papers published in 1970. From the federal government's point of view, the three main reasons for not joining the OAS were (1) the fear of creating tensions in Canada-US relations, (2) the cost of membership, and (3) the obligations arising from the Charter and (eventually) the Rio Treaty. In the latter case, these could relate to the application of political and economic sanctions against other countries as a result of a two-thirds vote by member countries.[6] But the two fundamental arguments for not joining the OAS – whether stated or not – were the first two.

Canadian membership in the OAS would put the government in a position where, in the event of a conflict, it would have to side either with the United States or with Latin American governments. Taking either side would naturally have consequences, since opposing the United States might bring retaliation on Canadian-US bilateral issues, whereas antagonizing Latin American governments could endanger the economic benefits that Canada hoped to gain by joining the OAS. And joining the OAS would bring limited results since it would imply becoming a member of an inefficient organization – inefficient both in terms of its internal functioning (as the OAS was almost always in need of administrative and budgetary reforms) and in terms of its legitimacy (as many believed that the organization was too much under the influence of the United States).

Were these arguments still valid at the end of the 1980s when the Mulroney government was pondering whether to join the OAS? With regard to the first traditional reason for staying out of the OAS (i.e., not wanting to jeopardize Canada-US/Canada-Latin American relations), it is true that the second half of the 1980s was a period characterized by a relatively high level of harmony in US-Latin American relations. Indeed, an outside observer could have been led to believe that the conflicts and acrimony of the past had been forgotten. From the point of view of Washington at least, the move towards political and economic liberalization in Latin America throughout the 1980s promised an era of unprecedented convergence in inter-American affairs. At the time, the speeches of the main US policy-makers were filled with terms such as "convergence of values," "window of opportunity," and "turning point,"[7] which may have led others, including the Canadian government, to believe that the Americas were indeed entering a new era of cooperation and community-building.

Moreover, among high-ranking Canadian decision-makers, and certainly in the mind of the Conservative prime minister, there was a clear perception that Canada-US relations had now reached a degree of harmony unheard of during the Trudeau government. This could lead one to believe that serious foreign policy conflicts between Canada and the United States, particularly in the hemisphere, were now unthinkable. This perception was naturally made all the stronger by the smooth personal relationship that the prime minister had managed to develop with both US president Ronald Reagan and his successor George Bush.[8]

Nevertheless, when perceptions are set aside and the situation as it stood in 1988 or 1989 is examined closely, one finds that there were no concrete indications that inter-American relations had changed dramatically. This was demonstrated by the US military intervention in Grenada in October 1983 and in Panama in December 1989. Objective examination of the situation could only lead to the conclusion that Canada, upon becoming a full member of the inter-American system, would still be confronted with the risk of having to side either with the United States or with Latin America should a serious crisis develop in hemispheric affairs.

This has not yet happened because the 1990s were singularly free from major crises in inter-American relations. Canadian government support for the US invasion of Panama in 1989 could have eliminated the benefits of joining the OAS in terms of Canadian-Latin American relations. But the US military action was seen as somewhat different from past American military interventions in the region because Washington had managed to convince its neighbours that Panamanian president Manuel Noriega was engaging in drug-related activities, thereby giving a certain legitimacy to the intervention. On the other hand, Canadian opposition to the Helms-Burton legislation of March 1996 could have seriously clouded Canadian-US relations. But the fact that the legislation was really a result of partisan politics in Washington and that it essentially targeted US allies in the industrialized world transformed what was initially an inter-American issue into something much larger.

With regard to the second traditional argument made against Canada joining the OAS (i.e., its inefficiency and lack of legitimacy), here again one finds no concrete evidence in the second half of the 1980s that the organization's situation had changed in any significant manner. Still weakened by important budgetary and administrative problems, the OAS had also failed, in the eyes of most outside analysts, to be an effective instrument in the region's conflict management system.[9] As for the promotion of democracy and human rights, the only measure adopted by the OAS was the 1985 Cartagena Protocol.[10] All the other measures and instruments concerning the new role of the OAS in the field of democracy and human rights would only appear after 1990; that is, after Canada's entry into the organization.

Finally, with regard to legitimacy, if the events of the 1980s demonstrated one thing, it was that the governments of Latin America no longer viewed the OAS as a significant agency and/or forum for finding solutions to their problems. The establishment of the Latin American Economic System (SELA) to deal with the economic problems of the region, the creation of the Contadora Group to help find solutions to the crises in Central America, the formation of the Cartagena Group to deal with the foreign debt crisis, and the formation of the Rio Group (which became the main Latin American multilateral forum within which to discuss the problems affecting member countries) were all manifestations of increasing Latin American disillusionment with the OAS.

Consequently, the basic rationale that was traditionally used to argue against joining the OAS was still valid in the second half of the 1980s. The two central arguments against membership in the OAS had been neither weakened nor eliminated by any new development. And so the explanation for Canada's decision to join the OAS must lie elsewhere. I believe that the 1989 decision to join the OAS can be explained by two groups of factors. The first group relates to Canada's relationship to the world at large (i.e., the evolution of Canadian commercial and investment relations and the organization of the world after the Cold War); the second group relates to the particular dynamics within the Americas after the Conservatives came to power in 1984. The determinants here are the Canada-US Free Trade Agreement (FTA); the Mexico-US free trade discussions, which would lead to the North American Free Trade Agreement (NAFTA); and the changes in the political and economic landscapes in Latin America and the Caribbean.

Canada and the World at Large: Foreign Economic Relations

Given that more than one-third of Canada's gross domestic product (GDP) is generated by exports, economic relations with the outside world have always been of strategic importance to it. As early as the end of the 1960s it was felt that trade and investment relations were too concentrated with the United States and that this could become a serious threat to Canada's independence.[11] One of the objectives of the 1972 Third Option strategy consisted, therefore, of using foreign policy instruments to support the diversification of Canada's external relations in order to strengthen Canadian sovereignty.[12]

What did the Mulroney government see at the end of the 1980s when it was examining Canadian trade and investment relations with the outside world during that decade? Figures 10.1 and 10.2 summarize the situation. The graph in Figure 10.1 shows the annual proportion of Canadian foreign investment by major world regions from 1980 to 1990. What the

Figure 10.1

Proportion of Canadian direct foreign investments according to world regions by year, 1980-90 (%)

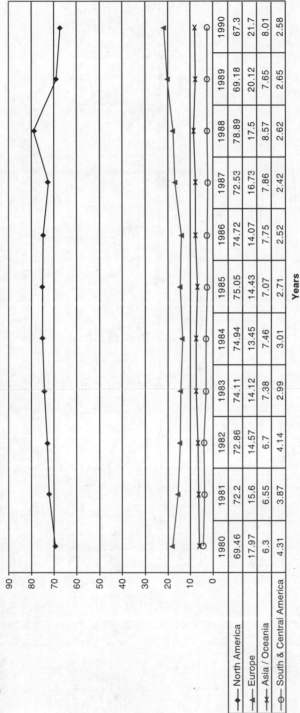

	1980	1981	1982	1983	1984	1985	1986	1987	1988	1989	1990
North America	69.46	72.2	72.86	74.11	74.94	75.05	74.72	72.53	78.89	69.18	67.3
Europe	17.97	15.6	14.57	14.12	13.45	14.43	14.07	16.73	17.5	20.12	21.7
Asia / Oceania	6.3	6.55	6.7	7.38	7.46	7.07	7.75	7.86	8.57	7.65	8.01
South & Central America	4.31	3.87	4.14	2.99	3.01	2.71	2.52	2.42	2.62	2.65	2.58

Years

Source: Statistique Canada, *Bilan des investissements internationaux du Canada, données historiques 1926-1992*, catalogue 67-202 (Ottawa: Ministère de l'Industrie, des Sciences et de la Technologie, 1993).

Note: The regions are made up of the following: North America includes the United States, Bahamas, Bermudas, Dutch West Indies, Mexico, and other North American countries. Europe includes the European Union, Switzerland, Austria, Norway, and other European countries. Asia-Oceania includes Singapore, Australia, Indonesia, Hong Kong, Japan, Taiwan, Malaysia, South Korea, other countries in the Pacific, the Middle East, India, and other countries in Asia.

Figure 10.2

Proportion of Canadian exports according to world regions by year, 1980-90 (%)

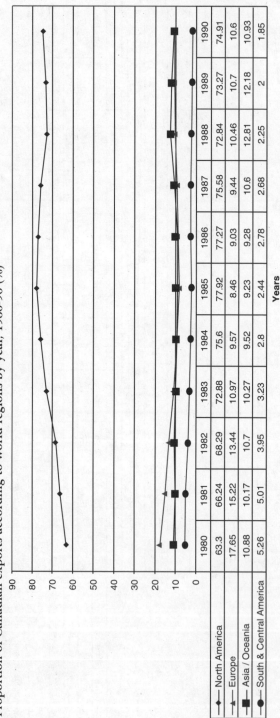

	1980	1981	1982	1983	1984	1985	1986	1987	1988	1989	1990
North America	63.3	66.24	68.29	72.88	75.6	77.92	77.27	75.58	72.84	73.27	74.91
Europe	17.65	15.22	13.44	10.97	9.57	8.46	9.03	9.44	10.46	10.7	10.6
Asia / Oceania	10.88	10.17	10.7	10.27	9.52	9.23	9.28	10.6	12.81	12.18	10.93
South & Central America	5.26	5.01	3.95	3.23	2.8	2.44	2.78	2.68	2.25	2	1.85

Years

Sources: For 1980-81, Statistique Canada, *Exportations, commerce de marchandises, 1982*, catalogue 65-202 annual (Ottawa: Ministère des Approvisionnements et Services Canada, 1983). For 1982-83, Statistique Canada, *Exportations, commerce de marchandises, 1984*, catalogue 65-202 annual (Ottawa: Ministère des Approvisionnements et Services Canada, 1985). For 1984-93, Statistique Canada, *Exportations, commerce de marchandises, 1993*, catalogue 65-202 annual (Ottawa: Ministère de l'Industrie, des Sciences et de la Technologie, 1994).

Note: The regions are made up of the following countries: North America includes Greenland, St-Pierre and Miquelon, and the United States. Europe includes European Union, Gibraltar, Malta, Austria, Finland, Norway, Switzerland, and other European countries. The South and Central American region also includes the West Indies.

data reveal, first and foremost, is not only the extreme concentration of Canadian direct foreign investment in North America (which means, essentially, the United States), but also the fact that the level of concentration was almost exactly the same at the start of the decade as it was at the end of the decade (69.46 percent in 1980, 78.89 percent in 1988, and 69.18 per cent in 1989). The rest of the world was way behind, and the curves remained almost the same throughout the 1980s for every other region except Europe, where the curve began to rise in 1986. However, the percentage in 1988 was more or less the same as it was in 1980.

The basic significance of both types of data was that external trade and foreign direct investment diversification had not achieved the level that had been hoped for when the Third Option strategy was launched seventeen years before. On the contrary, what the figures showed fundamentally was that Canada's economic dependence on the United States had increased significantly – to the point where Canada's situation had now become one of "extreme vulnerability."[13] Furthermore, as we will discuss next, this evolution of Canada's economic relations with the outside world was occurring precisely at the time when the reorganization of that world, in the aftermath of the Cold War, was marked by several real and perceived threats to a country like Canada.

The World after the Cold War

If the end of the Cold War is generally associated with the fall of the Berlin Wall in 1989, then one could say that the whole second half of the 1980s was characterized by events that signalled the shape of things to come. For Canada, among the various threats associated with the remodelling of the world, two stood out. The first one was the very real menace arising from the uncertainties characterizing the orientations of US trade policy and, more particularly, the increasing US economic protectionism. The second one was the concern that, after the Cold War, the world would be reorganized according to major economic blocs.

As regards US trade policy, the first years of the Reagan presidency had already witnessed a change in attitude on the part of the US Congress, which had started to express doubts concerning the usefulness of multilateralism. The new attitude of both Congress and the administration concerning trade matters would be made more concrete with the Trade and Tariff Act, 1984, which, among other things, would introduce bilateralism as a viable foreign trade policy option for Washington.[14] The significance of this aspect of the Trade Act was that it revealed to American trade partners that Washington was now ready to consider preferential free trade zones as an alternative to multilateral trade negotiations. The signing of a free trade agreement with Israel the following year would only serve to make this point more strongly.

In addition to the introduction of the bilateral option, the mid-1980s also revealed how protectionism was creeping into US trade policy formulation. The US government was asserting more and more firmly that it considered the practices of many of its commercial partners, notably Japan and the members of the European Union, to be unfair and detrimental to US interests. Themes such as "reciprocity," "equitable trade," and "strategic trade" all became parts of the regular discourse on US trade policy,[15] culminating in the adoption of the Omnibus Trade and Competitiveness Act, 1988. A major component of this legislation was a significant reinforcement of Section 301 of the Trade Act, 1974, by which more power was given to agencies such as the United States Trade Representative (USTR). The latter was given a mandate to identify, among other things, foreign markets in which unfair trade practices were detrimental to US businesses. The USTR had the authority to use bilateral negotiations (or unilateral actions) to force foreign governments to eliminate these practices and, thereby, to open their markets to US exports.[16]

This dramatic shift towards increasing protectionism in US trade policy and behaviour since the mid-1980s had significant implications for the major US trading partners. It definitely created a climate of uncertainty and extreme anxiety for a country like Canada. The United States, after all, was Canada's most important market, and Canadian dependence on that market had been increasing constantly since 1980. It is true that the Canadian government was seldom the main target of US retaliatory trade measures, but it could very well find itself in the crossfire of trade measures and counter-measures between the United States and Japan or the European Union, the Mulroney-Reagan personal friendship notwithstanding. The "Nixon shocks" of August 1971 had occurred without any prior consultation or warning to the Canadian authorities, and Washington did initially put Canada on the same footing as anybody else. There was absolutely no indication that things would be different this time round.

Besides the threatening horizon that was being created as a result of Washington's increasingly protectionist trade policy, other elements of uncertainty concerning the organization of the post-Cold War world were also starting to appear. Of concern to countries such as Canada and the larger Latin American countries was the increasing perception that the post-Cold War world would be structured and dominated by three major economic blocs.

This perception initially appeared as a result of two important occurrences, both of which signalled a leap forward in the integration of Europe. First, the Single European Act was adopted in Luxembourg in December 1985. Its purpose was to reinforce the political integration of western Europe by increasing the role of European Parliament in the European Community's legislative process and by replacing the practice of unanimity with qualified majority voting in the Council of Ministers. Second, in June of the same year, the EC published a white paper announcing the creation of a single market. Both events marked what many came to be see as "a dramatic new phase in Europe's economic and political transformation."[17] For countries such as the United States and Canada, for whom Europe was an important economic partner, the reinforcement of European integration was perceived as a potentially threatening development because it could put foreign enterprises at a significant disadvantage within the huge European market.

The fears about the emergence of a "Fortress Europe," together with the difficulties of the 1986 multilateral trade negotiations in Montevideo, started to feed a perception that the international system was coming to a major turning point. The perception that the Cold War structure would soon be replaced by a world architecture dominated by "triads," "economic blocs," and "trade blocs" appeared increasingly in the literature produced by economists and political scientists in the late 1980s and early 1990s.[18] But the political actors of the time had already incorporated these beliefs and perceptions in their foreign policy calculus of the second half of the 1980s. In Canada's case, however, these factors did not have an immediate and direct bearing on the Canadian government's decision to apply for membership in the OAS; rather, they served as important contextual elements in the overall rationale leading to the decision to join the OAS. The assumption is that they had a very strong impact on the sequence of events that characterized the political and economic dynamics in the Americas in the late 1980s as well as on Canada's role in these developments.

The Impact of Regional Dynamics in the Americas

It is not only the events that took place in the Americas in the second half of the 1980s that are important, but also the sequence of these events. Among the determinants to be examined, the Canada-US Free Trade Agreement must certainly be singled out as the most central element in the causal chain leading to the Canadian decision to join the OAS.

The FTA

The growing concentration of Canadian exports to the US market, the manifestations of increasing US protectionism, and the possibility of emerging trade blocs (particularly in Europe) all combined to create what was probably the most powerful incentive for the Mulroney government to seek a free trade agreement with the United States. The Canadian decision was made public in September 1985, and the negotiations, which started in May 1986, lasted nineteen months; the agreement entered into force on 1 January 1989.[19]

If the "government's reasons for action were clear,"[20] the significance of the trade agreement was not immediately evident and would take some time to sort out. The prime minister himself painted a very positive picture of the agreement, both during the 1988 federal elections and afterwards,[21] saying that it would secure the US market for Canadian exports as well as act as a kind of testing ground for Canadian businesses, which, increasingly, would have to compete within the new environment of globalization. Canadian opponents to the FTA saw it as an attack on the Canadian state, even on the whole fabric of Canadian society.[22]

Without examining in detail the pros and cons of the arguments put forward by both sides concerning the possible impact of the FTA on Canadian society or on the multilateral trading system, what is certain is that the Canadian decision to enter into a free trade agreement with the United States was a dramatic reversal of policy that, for over 100 years, had refused continentalism. What was involved here was more than simply trade matters as the FTA also dealt with trade in services, investment, business travel, and economic policy.[23] As one source put it, "In many ways, it changed the relationship between government and society in North America, particularly in Canada."[24]

Whatever the possible domestic consequences of the FTA on Canadian society,[25] the Canadian decision to seek a free trade agreement with the United States was seen from the outside as a defensive move whose main effect was to lock Canada's economic future to that of the United States.[26] In a period during which the idea of trading blocs was given more and more attention, the Canadian government's initiation of negotiations leading to a free trade agreement with the United States was, in fact, a signal to the outside world that Canada was choosing to become a member of one of the trade blocs.[27]

Consequently, the fundamental significance of the FTA for Canada was that it constituted a strategic diplomatic departure and a pivotal foreign policy decision that would certainly change its relations with the Americas and, quite possibly, with the rest of the world. The FTA did not imply that the Canadian government would be concentrating most of its foreign policy in the Americas; but it did imply that certain pretensions were being abandoned.[28] The FTA signalled clearly that Canada was no longer a "principal power," if it had ever been one, and that it might not even be a "big-league player"[29] anymore, in spite of the rhetoric of "soft power" and "human security" used by the Liberal government in the mid-1990s. The deliberate linking of the Canadian economy with that of the United States in a clearly asymmetrical relationship also undermined the premise of the Third Option strategy; namely, that diversifying Canada's political and economic relations by establishing closer relations with other industrialized regions of the world would decrease its dependence on the United

States. The FTA was simply a manifestation of the failure of this strategy, indicating, as it did, that diversification was becoming more and more difficult if not impossible.

Mexican-US Discussions on Free Trade

At almost the same time as the FTA was coming into force, Canadian policy-makers were receiving indications that the new Mexican administration of President Carlos Salinas de Gortari was also thinking of discussing free trade matters with the United States. Using more or less the same calculus that had guided Canadian foreign policy since the mid-1980s, the new Mexican government was arriving at the same conclusions concerning the orientations of the world economy and their impact on Mexico.

Salinas came to power with a bold and precise agenda for economic liberalization in Mexico. He also had an open mind concerning foreign economic relations in general, and Mexican-US economic relations in particular. An invitation to president-elect George Bush's home in Houston in late 1988 had helped to establish a sound basis for dialogue between the two new administrations, and discussions on trade matters had started early in 1989. It is not clear what kind of opening was made during these discussions and how far down the road Salinas had gone towards a free trade agreement with the United States, but the Understanding Regarding Trade and Investment Facilitation Talks, which was reached in October 1989, committed the two governments to enter "proactive negotiations" in order to deal with issues such as "intellectual property, services and investment."[30] Salinas finally made the decision to seek a free trade agreement with the United States in February 1990 after a trip to Europe convinced him that that region could not play a significant role in Mexico's strategy for diversifying its external relations. This decision was officially made public in June 1990 in Washington.

The Mulroney government understood the significance of a possible US-Mexico free trade agreement only too well. While the FTA was locking the Canadian economy ever more closely into a strongly asymmetrical relationship with the US economy, and while Canada was choosing the North American bloc, thereby reducing its claims to be a big-league player, a possible free trade agreement between Washington and Mexico would simply multiply the negative effects of the 1988 Canadian decision by limiting foreign policy manoeuvrability. It would mean a "hub-and-spoke" type of arrangement for the management of North American affairs, within which the "hub" (i.e., the United States) could assure its supremacy by playing the "spokes" (i.e., Canada and Mexico) against each other. Being a "spoke" was certainly not what the Canadian government had in mind when it had decided to make the hemisphere "our home."[31]

Consequently, one of the central elements of Canadian foreign policy in 1989 was to try to eliminate the possibility of a hub-and-spoke type of arrangement for the management of North American relations and, eventually, for hemispheric affairs. The Canadian reaction took two forms. In the first case, the government of Canada became a "less than eager participant"[32] in the negotiations that led to the North American Free Trade Agreement (NAFTA) of 1 January 1994. Given the place and role of the anti-continentalist sentiment in Canadian history, it is understandable that Ottawa was reluctant to become part of an arrangement that some see as being not only – or not at all – about freeing trade,[33] but, rather, about much broader elements of governance and the harmonization of policies in North America.[34] That the Canadian government felt itself compelled to follow such a policy course says much about its perceived lack of room to manoeuvre. In the second case, the government of Canada decided to join the OAS in the hope of reinforcing multilateral institutions and their role in the management of hemispheric affairs.

Political and Economic Liberalization in Latin America

The third important determinant of the Canadian decision to seek membership in the OAS was the dramatic transformation that had taken place throughout Latin America and the Caribbean during the 1980s. Although some of these changes could be observed at the end of the 1970s, notably in Peru, Chile, and Bolivia, the major impetus for significant policy reorientations was the combined effect of the 1981 world economic recession and the 1982 Latin American external debt crisis.

In addition to being at the source of major economic disruptions in the region for most of the decade,[35] the world recession and the debt crisis also generated what can be called a psychological shock for many of the Latin American and Caribbean elite. Things could not continue as they had in the 1960s and 1970s. The governments of the region had to make fundamental changes in the economic policies they had followed up to then, and they had to shed the political practices of the past. Otherwise, the rest of the world – and, most important, the industrialized countries – would lose interest and turn their backs on the region. This attitude was reinforced as the image of a Fortress Europe became more prominent, and a fear spread that the development funds that traditionally went to Latin America and the Caribbean would start to be diverted to the former Communist states of eastern Europe.

The combination of these factors engendered what some have called an "acute fear of marginalization,"[36] which, along with other domestic factors, became a major driving force behind the significant political and economic reorientations that characterized the whole region throughout the 1980s. At the end of that decade, liberal democracy had triumphed in

Latin America and the Caribbean as most countries were then under democratic rule, and the situation of civil and political rights had not been so good since the early 1970s.[37] Although the situation was still far from perfect, there was no denying that it had improved, at least in comparison with the 1970s. Significant changes had also occurred almost everywhere as countries such as Chile, Peru, and others led the way in replacing the old "industrialization-by-import-substitution" model with privatization, deregulation, and "open regionalism."[38]

The significance of these changes for Canada was that the government in Ottawa could now establish closer and more diversified relations with Latin American and Caribbean countries, with greater support from many sectors of Canadian society. The spread of democratic rule in the region convinced many social and community interest groups in Canada – groups that had traditionally opposed relations with Latin American and Caribbean dictatorships – that it was now legitimate to seek closer links with countries south of the Rio Grande. The federal government also used the move towards economic liberalization to try to convince Canadian businesses that economic opportunities now existed for them in Latin America and the Carribean. Without being the most significant determinant in the decision that was taken, the changes in the political and economic landscape in the Americas outside the United States were nevertheless important because they gave the government some assurance that there would be no domestic opposition to stronger Canadian involvement in inter-American affairs.

Conclusion

Why did the Canadian government decide in 1989 to involve Canada in the regional system of the Americas by officially becoming a member of the OAS when only four years earlier the region was in no way a foreign policy priority for it?[39] The process leading to the final decision may well have been influenced by domestic factors such as the personal inclination of the secretary of state for external affairs (because of the role he played in the efforts to bring an end to the crisis in Central America), bureaucrats (particularly those responsible for Latin American affairs at External Affairs), or even the desires of local constituencies and/or the economic hopes of the business community.

But my central argument is that the explanation for the 1989 decision lies with events occurring outside Canada during the second half of the 1980s. I have tried to show that there are basically two parts to this explanation. With regard to the first, the evidence of increasing Canadian dependence on the United States at a time when US trade policy was becoming more and more protectionist and the threat of emerging economic blocs in Europe and in Asia combined to create the almost irresistible incentive for the Canadian proposal of a free trade agreement with the United States. With regard to the second, once the FTA had been signed, another set of events occurred in the Americas. At the same time that the FTA was anchoring Canada more and more to North America, the imminence of discussions pertaining to a free trade agreement between Mexico and the United States brought forward what Andrew F. Cooper terms "fears of entrapment"[40] due to the hub-and-spoke type of arrangement that would result from the two trade agreements. It is at this time that a second policy direction came about – one that Denis Stairs has referred to as one of the essential strategic premises of Canadian policy: "Wherever possible, diversify."[41]

As applied to the Americas, diversification could only mean stronger Canadian involvement in hemispheric affairs. And this was rendered politically feasible and potentially economically rewarding by the moves towards democratization and economic liberalization that had occurred throughout the region during the 1980s. But how to convince Latin American governments, who had frequently been sceptical about Canada's real interest in the region, that the Canadian authorities were now serious in their intention to become significantly involved in the regional system of the Americas. The announcement of a new Canadian foreign policy for Latin America was interesting[42] but, by itself, insufficient because such policies normally contain only measures for the future. What was needed was a concrete and immediate manifestation of Ottawa's political will, and membership in the OAS perfectly suited that purpose.

To paraphrase Hillmer and Granatstein, with the FTA, NAFTA, and Canadian membership in the OAS, the Mulroney government made more sweeping changes to Canada's relations with the Americas than had any other government.[43] Contrary to what has often been argued, this realignment in favour of the hemisphere did not have that much to do with domestic factors, commercial considerations, or even economic determinism;[44] rather, it had to do, at a quite fundamental level, with Canadian sovereignty.

Acknowledgments

A French version of this chapter was published in *Études internationales* 31, 2 (juin 2000). I would like to thank Valérie Bisson for her help in gathering and assembling information on commercial and investment flows. Thanks also to Louis Bélanger, David Haglund, Manon Tessier, and Jean-Philippe Thérien for very useful comments on previous drafts. Finally, many thanks to Maureen Magee for linguistic revisions, to Élise Lapalme for typing the manuscript, and to the Social Sciences and Humanities Research Council of Canada and the Fonds FCAR for financial support.

Notes

1 Canada, Office of the Prime Minister, "Notes for an Address by the Right Honourable Brian Mulroney," 27 October 1989, San José, Costa Rica; External Affairs and International Trade Canada, "Notes for Remarks by the Right Honourable Joe Clark, P.C., M.P., Secretary of State for External Affairs, at the Meeting of the General Assembly of the Organization of American States, Washington, 13 November 1989."

2 Peter McKenna, "Canada Joins the OAS: Anatomy of a Decision," in *America and the Americas*, ed. Jacques Zylberberg and François Demers (Québec: Presses de l'Université Laval, 1992), 254; see also Stephen J. Randall, "Think Twice before Joining the OAS," *Globe and Mail*, 26 October 1989, A7; Jeffrey Simpson, "The Folly of Joining the OAS," *Globe and Mail*, 4 October 1989, A6; and Allan Gotlieb, "Arguments against Joining the OAS from a Tired Old Refrain," *Globe and Mail*, 23 October 1989, A6.

3 McKenna, "Canada Joins the OAS," 254 and 263.

4 Cited in J.C.M. Ogelsby, *Gringos from the Far North: Essays in the History of Canadian-Latin American Relations, 1866-1968* (Toronto: Macmillan Canada, 1976), 50.

5 Peter McKenna, *Canada and the OAS* (Ottawa: Carleton University Press, 1995), chap. 5; see also James J. Guy, "Canada Joins the OAS: A New Dynamic in the Inter-American System," *Revista Interamericana de Bibliographia* 39 (1989): 503-6; and David MacKenzie, "'The World's Greatest Joiner': Canada and the Organization of American States," *British Journal of Canadian Studies* 6 (1991): 209-15.

6 Canada, *Foreign Policy for Canadians: Latin American Booklet* (Ottawa: Queen's Printer, 1970), 22-24.

7 For example, Gordon Mace, "The Origins, Nature, and Scope of the Hemispheric Project," in *The Americas in Transition: The Contours of Regionalism*, ed. Gordon Mace, Louis Bélanger et al. (Boulder, CO: Lynne Rienner, 1999), 30-31.

8 Andrew Cohen has written that Mulroney "says he was Ronald Reagan's closest confidant in high diplomatic circles, and that he understood him better than others." See "Mulroney Boasted of Close Ties with Reagan: Book," *Globe and Mail*, 1 October 1999, A11.

9 David Mares, "Looking for Godot? Can Multilateralism Work in Latin America This Time?" in *Multilateralism and Regional Security*, ed. Michel Fortmann, S. Neil MacFarlane, and Stéphane Roussel (Clementsport, NS: Canadian Peacekeeping Press, 1997), 92.

10 The Protocol was a charter amendment by which the OAS articulated more explicitly a commitment "toward the promotion and strengthening of representative democracy." See Guy Gosselin and Jean-Philippe Thérien, "The Organization of American States and Hemispheric Regionalism," in Mace et al., *Americas in Transition*, 178-79; see also Richard J. Bloomfield, "Making the Western Hemisphere Safe for Democracy? The OAS Defense-of-Democracy Regime," *Washington Quarterly* 17 (1994): 157-69.

11 J.L. Granatstein and Robert Bothwell, *Pirouette: Pierre Elliott Trudeau and Canadian Foreign Policy* (Toronto: University of Toronto Press, 1990), chap. 2; see also Ian Lumsden, ed., *Close the 49th Parallel etc.* (Toronto: University of Toronto Press, 1970).

12 The government's position was made public in a semi-official document. See Mitchell Sharp, "Canada-US Relations: Options for the Future," *International Perspectives* (Autumn 1972). For analyses of the strategy, see Harald von Riekhoff, "The Third Option in Canadian Foreign Policy," in *Canada's Foreign Policy: Analysis and Trends*, ed. Brian Tomlin (Toronto: Methuen, 1978), 87-109; and Gordon Mace and Gérard Hervouet, "Canada's Third Option: A Complete Failure?" *Canadian Public Policy/Analyse de politiques* 15 (1989): 387-404.

13 Kim Richard Nossal, *The Politics of Canadian Foreign Policy*, 3rd ed. (Scarborough, ON: Prentice-Hall Canada, 1997), 30.

14 Stephen L. Lande and Craig VanGrasstek, *The Trade and Tariff Act of 1984: Trade Policy in the Reagan Administration* (Lexington, MA: Lexington Books, 1986). On US protectionism, see Michael Hart with Bill Dymond and Colin Robertson, *Decision at Midnight: Inside the Canada-US Free-Trade Negotiations* (Vancouver: UBC Press, 1994), chap. 3.

15 Among the vast literature on the subject, see Stanley D. Nollen and Dennis P. Quinn, "Free Trade, Fair Trade: Strategic Trade and Protectionism in the US Congress, 1987-88," *International Organization* 48 (1994): 491-525; William R. Cline, *Reciprocity: A New*

Approach to World Trade Policy? (Washington, DC: Institute for International Economics, 1982); and Pierre Martin, "The Politics of International Structural Change: Aggressive Reciprocity in American Trade Policy," in *Political Economy and the Changing Global Order*, ed. Richard Stubbs and Geoffrey R.D. Underhill (Toronto: McClelland and Stewart, 1994), 439-52.

16 Judith H. Bello and Alan F. Holmer, "The Heart of the 1988 Trade Act: A Legislative History of Amendments to Section 301," *Stanford Journal of International Law* 25, 1 (Autumn 1988): 1-44; Jagdish N. Bhagwati and Hugh T. Patrick, eds., *Aggressive Unilateralism: America's 301 Trade Policy and the World Trading System* (Ann Arbor: University of Michigan Press, 1990).

17 Charles Pentland, "Europe 1992 and the Canadian Response," in *Canada Among Nations, 1990-91: After the Cold War*, ed. Fen Osler Hampson and Christopher J. Maule (Ottawa: Carleton University Press, 1991), 132.

18 A sample of some titles would include Richard S. Belous and Rebecca S. Hartley, eds., *The Growth of Regional Trading Blocs in the Global Economy* (Washington: National Planning Association, 1990); Lester Thurow, *Head to Head: The Coming Economic Battle among Japan, Europe and America* (New York: Warner Books, 1992); Diana Brand, "Regional Bloc Formation and World trade," *Intereconomics* 27, 6 (November/December 1992): 274-81; Susan Strange, "Are Trade Blocs Emerging Now?" paper presented at the 15th World Congress of the International Political Science Association, Buenos Aires, August 1991; and Frans Buelens, "The Creation of Regional Blocs in the World Economy," *Intereconomics* 27, 3 (May/June 1992): 124-32.

19 A chronology of the process can be found in Hart, Dymond, and Robertson, *Decision at Midnight*, 417-22.

20 Norman J. Hillmer and J.L. Granatstein, *Empire to Umpire: Canada and the World to the 1990s* (Toronto: Copp, Clark, Longman, 1994), 335.

21 For example, Elaine Plourde, *Déterminants de la réorientation de la politique commerciale canadienne dans le libre-échange avec les États-Unis: 1984-1988* (MA thesis, Université Laval, 1999).

22 André C. Drainville, "Social Movements in the Americas: Regionalism from Below," in Mace et al., *Americas in Transition*, 221-23.

23 Hart, Dymond, and Robertson, *Decision at Midnight*, 390; and Hillmer and Granatstein, *Empire to Umpire*, 336-40.

24 Hart, Dymond, and Robertson, *Decision at Midnight*, 390.

25 See, among others, Craig Ip, "The Borderless World," *Globe and Mail*, 6 July 1996, D1, D5; and Heather Scofield, "Canada Pushed on Several Fronts toward Integration with the US," *Globe and Mail*, 4 June 1999, A2.

26 Andrew Wyatt-Walter, "Regionalism, Globalization, and World Economic Order," in *Regionalism in World Politics*, ed. Louise Fawcett and Andrew Hurrell (Oxford: Oxford University Press, 1995), 85; and Hurrell, "Regionalism in the Americas," in ibid., 269.

27 John Whalley, "Regional Trade Arrangements in North America: CUSTA and NAFTA," in *New Dimensions in Regional Integration*, ed. Jaime de Melo and Arvind Panagariya (Cambridge: Cambridge University Press, 1993), 369-70.

28 In this regard, a parallel can be made, up to a point, between the Canadian decision to seek a free trade agreement with the United States and the Argentinian decision to propose an integration treaty with Brazil in 1985-86. While other considerations existed, it was clear that the integration treaty with Brazil meant that Argentina had definitively abandoned its pretension of becoming the leader of South America both in the region and in dealings with the outside world.

29 Fen Osler Hampson, Michael Hart, and Martin Rudner, eds., *Canada Among Nations, 1999: A Big League Player?* (Don Mills, ON: Oxford University Press, 1999).

30 Federick W. Mayer, *Interpreting NAFTA: The Science and Art of Political Analysis* (New York: Columbia University Press, 1998), 38.

31 Canada, Department of External Affairs and International Trade, "Notes for Remarks at the Meeting of the Council of the Organization of American States," Joe Clark, secretary of state for external affairs, 13 November 1989, 1.

32 Donald Barry, "The Road to NAFTA," in *Toward a North American Community? Canada, the United States and Mexico*, ed. Donald Barry, Mark O. Dickerson, and James D. Gaisford (Boulder: Westview Press, 1995), 10.

33 For example, Sidney Weintraub, "US-Mexico Free Trade: Implications for the United States," in *Assessments of the NAFTA: North American Free Trade Agreement*, ed. Ambler H. Moss Jr. (Coral Gables, FLA: North-South Center Press, 1993), 93; and W. Andrew Axline, "Conclusion: External Forces, State Strategies, and Regionalism in the Americas," in *Foreign Policy and Regionalism in the Americas*, ed. Gordon Mace and Jean-Philippe Thérien (Boulder: Lynne Rienner, 1996), 200.

34 Gilbert R. Winham and Heather A. Grant, "NAFTA: An Overview," in Barry, Dickerson, and Gaisford, *Toward a North American Community*, 15-31.

35 See, among the vast literature on the subject, Miguel S. Wionczek and Luciano Tomassini, eds., *Politics and Economics of External Debt Crisis: The Latin American Experience* (Boulder: Westview Press, 1985); and Peter Nunnenkamp, *The International Debt Crisis* (Brighton: Wheatsheaf, 1986).

36 Andrew Hurrell, "Regionalism in the Americas," in *Latin America in a New World*, ed. Abraham F. Lowenthal and Gregory F. Treverton (Boulder, CO: Westview Press, 1994), 170.

37 Gordon Mace, Guy Gosselin, and Louis Bélanger, "Regional Cooperative Security in the Americas: The Case of Democratic Institutions," in Fortmann, MacFarlane, and Roussel, *Multilateralism and Regional Security*, 126-27.

38 Economic Commission for Latin America and the Caribbean, *Open Regionalism in Latin America and the Caribbean* (Santiago: United Nations Publications, 1994).

39 The 1985 green paper on Canada's international relations, for example, contained only three lines on the OAS seeking Canadians' opinions on the idea of membership. There was little more than one page dealing with Latin America and the Caribbean, and the main point of interest for the government seemed to be the Central American crisis. See Secretary of State for External Affairs, *Competitiveness and Security: Directions for Canada's International Relations* (Ottawa: Supply and Services Canada, 1985).

40 Andrew F. Cooper, *Canadian Foreign Policy: Old Habits and New Directions* (Scarborough: Prentice Hall, Allyn and Bacon, 1997), 252.

41 Denis Stairs, "Change in the Management of Canada-US Relations in the Post-War Era," in Barry, Dickerson, and Gaisford, *Toward a North American Community*, 56.

42 The document was never made public, but the main elements are found in Edgar J. Dosman, "Canada and Latin America: The New Look," *International Journal* 47, 3 (1992): 529-54.

43 Hillmer and Granatstein, *Empire to Umpire*, 342. They apply the idea to Canada's relations with the United States.

44 Examined in David G. Haglund, "Grand Strategy – Or Merely a Geopolitical Free-for-all? Regionalism, Internationalism, and Defence Policy at the End of 'Canada's Century,'" in Hampson, Hart, and Rudner, *Canada Among Nations, 1999*, esp. 186-90.

11
Good Global Governance or Political Opportunism? Mulroney and UN Social Conferences
Andrew F. Cooper

The Mulroney years are often remembered as a time of retreat from deeply ingrained political habits.[1] In international affairs, it is commonly assumed that, during this period, there was a sharp erosion of multilateralism (long considered to be the pillar of Canadian foreign policy). The Conservatives were said to privilege bilateral relations with the United States or plurilateral connections in the Group of Seven (G-7). In domestic affairs, the Mulroney government is most often connected with the weakening of Canada's social fabric. Ideologically, the Mulroney government has been closely identified with the neo-liberalism that was dominant in the 1980s and early 1990s.[2] As Stephen McBride and John Shields put it: "The Mulroney government's policies were driven by an ideological predisposition for neo-liberal economics, free trade, minimal state involvement in the economy and social policy retrenchment."[3]

An examination of the Mulroney government's role at the United Nations "mega-conferences" of the early 1990s – the 1990 World Summit for Children in New York, the 1992 UN Conference on the Environment and Development (UNCED) in Rio de Janeiro, and the 1993 Vienna World Conference on Human Rights – suggests conclusions about the Conservative record that are quite at odds with the traditional criticism. Indeed, the Mulroney government has begun to receive a ripple of kudos for its performance at these conferences, particularly for its embrace of good global governance. Although still maintaining that there were flaws in the overall Conservative record, some commentators have argued that the Mulroney government decisively and constructively caught the moment that was offered by these mega-conferences.[4] The Mulroney government's performance is increasingly being re-interpreted not as a decisive break with traditional Canadian approaches to multilateral diplomacy but, rather, as an adaptive form of Conservative activism.

Judgments about Mulroney and international social conferences tend to be made on the basis of the prime minister's performance at UNCED.

While offering some valuable insight, UNCED alone is not enough to enable one to arrive at a balanced assessment. A good part of the puzzle concerning the connection between UN-based multilateralism and Mulroney's style of political leadership hinges on whether Mulroney's participation in UNCED was an aberration or part of a distinctive pattern. On the one hand, it is clear that Canada's leadership styles at each of these major conferences differed markedly. Yet, under the Conservatives, the Canadian approach at these conferences was consistent. Mulroney's performance at the September 1990 World Summit for Children in New York exhibited a good deal of the activist character that would be seen at Rio, albeit with very little of the detailed preparation or attendant positive publicity. At the 1993 Vienna conference Mulroney was less assertive, but his government nonetheless extended the interactive and integrative process between state officials and non-governmental organizations (NGOs) built up at Rio.

All of these conferences must be seen not only as an attempt at external problem-solving, but also as a pragmatic/opportunistic response to internal political imperatives. The hallmark of the Mulroney government's approach to these mega-conferences was not just how well its activist stance was playing in the international arena, but also how well its diplomacy was playing at home. From this perspective, the embrace of activism (whether through a robust or low-key style of leadership) had all the attributes of a compensatory form of activity – one designed to deflect or distract attention from other issues. For all of its positive features, Mulroney's diplomacy at the UN social conferences was marked by illusion and manipulation.

What stands out about Mulroney's approach to international social conferences is the priority given to tactics over strategy. Although bursts of leadership offered by the Conservatives suggested an element of commitment (both in terms of the international order and policy reform), there was also a high degree of convenience attached to this approach. Here the skill set displayed by Mulroney as prime minister and politician has to be more fully appreciated. Two facets are particularly salient for understanding how Mulroney was able to develop (and have magnified in retrospect) his reputation as a diplomatic player at the UN social conferences. The first was his ability to take chances, or at least calculated risks, when presented with an opportunity. The second was his ability to delegate responsibility and leave the details to his ministers and officials. This did not mean that Mulroney abandoned centre stage with regard to these activities. On the contrary, for him, a good deal of the attraction of the UN conferences lay in the opportunities they offered for personal diplomacy.

Re-assessing Mulroney's Leadership Style
Mulroney is commonly portrayed as a classic brokerage type of politician – someone both willing and able to accommodate opposing interests.[5]

There are numerous examples of his eagerness to exploit his capability as a transactional agent. Internationally, Mulroney threw himself into the role of mediator on General Agreement on Tariffs and Trade (GATT)/agricultural issues as well as on the issue of apartheid in South Africa. Domestically, Mulroney was no less a master of the charm offensive – as the issue of the South Moresby national park shows.[6] These characteristics do not, in themselves, distinguish Mulroney from a good many other prime ministers (going back to Mackenzie King). The difference was more in the gusto (or hubris) with which he threw himself into these endeavours.

The image of a broker is buttressed by a number of other traits. Mulroney was often portrayed as having little interest in the "interplay of ideas."[7] Conrad Black, an entrepreneur of ideas in his own right, conveys the concern of more ideologically driven conservatives about the shallowness and inconsistency of Mulroney's intellectual toolkit. In Black's words, "the Pollyanna flippancy ... of [Mulroney's] positions disconcerted his friends, including me ... His knowledge of how to get ahead was geometrically greater than any notion he had of what to do when he reached his destinations."[8] What Mulroney possessed was not only the ambition but the acumen of a professional deal-maker. As one of Mulroney's senior cabinet members put it: "Remember Mulroney was one of the most skilled labor lawyers in Canada before he came to office. He looks at problems one at a time and also looks to one solution at a time ... He is not the type to add them all together to make sense out of the whole thing."[9]

What this orthodox perspective on Mulroney misses is his impulse to gamble on issues of even the highest sensitivity and importance. Mulroney broke the cautious, incremental mould associated with many other Canadian leaders. Whereas the implementation of a transactional approach needs an enormous amount of self-discipline, Mulroney's character as leader was marked by a great degree of risk-taking. As a senior official commented: "Mulroney is not the most focused politician ... Once in a while, he would declare that one issue – say, the deficit – was the priority issue for the government. That would hold for a while, or until another issue that caught his attention came around."[10]

This gambler instinct did not prevent Mulroney from becoming absorbed by particular issues for a concerted period of time. Within the foreign policy context, the case of the free trade agreement is an obvious illustration of this. But what stands out is the way that his gambler instinct created even more unevenness within the decision-making process. Mulroney's willingness to "roll the dice" tended to create the impression that he was an opportunist and a manipulator, even though his risk-taking allowed him to move out in front of issues in an unconventional manner. As Bruce Doern and Brian Tomlin describe the "leap of faith" on free trade: "It was the prime minister alone who ultimately decided that the risks of pursuing the free trade initiative were worth the political candle."[11]

The International/Domestic Interplay of Mulroney's Summit Diplomacy

Brian Mulroney's performance as a summit diplomat has long been a subject of controversy. In large part, this was because he was such an "avid summiteer."[12] Mulroney put much of his own stamp on foreign policy. His strengths were well exhibited in these forums: his ability to connect with a wide variety of other political leaders (Mikhail Gorbachev and Bob Hawke as well as Ronald Reagan and George Bush), his enthusiasm and flexibility in kick-starting the summit of la Francophonie, and his capacity for mediation.

Of course, these forums also allowed Mulroney to exhibit his weaknesses. The mirror-image of his enthusiasm was his status-seeking. His impulse to mediate was often interpreted as uncalled for intrusion or as an indication of a "busybody" streak. His capacity for building connections was seen by many as a propensity for self-indulgence. The main criticism, often made in the context of Canada-US relations, was that Mulroney placed his own personal gratification ahead of the national interest. The style of these meetings accentuated this perception in that the coziness of many of these forums – the March 1985 "Shamrock Summit" in Québec City comes immediately to mind – set a tone that many observers found unpalatable. The backlash against Mulroney increased in tandem with the push for a renewed special relationship with the United States through the free trade agreement (FTA) negotiations. Critics pointed to Mulroney's willingness "to do anything to get a deal."[13]

What is most interesting about Mulroney's role in the UN social conferences is the way that his performance both elaborates and shades these basic impressions. Mulroney's role at the September 1990 World Summit for Children in New York demonstrates both his diplomatic agility and the constraint imposed by the nexus between the international and the domestic. Pushed by growing public interest in the issue of children's rights, Mulroney took the opportunity to play a personal and prominent role as the co-chair of the New York Summit. In keeping with the traditional Canadian habit of multilateral diplomacy, the prime minister emphasized the usefulness of this gathering as a catalyst, claiming that "the summit has the potential to put children's issue on the top of the international agenda." The summit was also seen as a facilitator for further technical/specialist work on the part of public officials. As Mulroney stated: "Summits do what nothing else can do. Put leaders face to face with each other and raise public awareness of issues. There is nothing like [that] for galvanizing a bureaucracy."[14]

Mulroney's lead role at this summit was nonetheless overshadowed by criticism at home, which focused on his propensity to subordinate commitment to convenience. A common argument had it that, given the condition of children in Canada, Mulroney was hardly well positioned to press for children's welfare at the global level. As an editorial in the *Globe and Mail* put it, the prime minister should lead by example: "Brian Mulroney can show leadership at the summit by pledging money to fight disease and hunger at home, a shameful item of unfinished business that Canadian activists who have travelled to New York for the meeting will not let him (or other delegates) forget."[15] Thus, Mulroney's international activism went only so far in winning kudos. While it might well serve the international reputation of Canada and, by extension, its leaders, it also served to intensify the process of domestic scrutiny.

In some respects the context of the Rio conference was little different from that of the Children's Summit. On the international front, as Heather Smith notes in Chapter 5, the Mulroney government had been active in moving the agenda ahead on matters relating to the ozone layer and climate change. Most notably, the Conservative government had played host to a number of conferences designed to stimulate international activity on atmospheric pollution. Begun in tandem with the activities of the World Commission on Environment and Development, this work was highlighted by a conference on the ozone layer in Montréal in September 1987. Despite such activity, however, the Mulroney government received little praise at home for its environmental policy. On the contrary, environmental activists remained highly critical of the government's claims to leadership in the international domain when its record on the domestic front left so much to be desired. They regularly pointed to the inconsistencies between the government's international activity and its unwillingness to address domestic environmental issues. As one "green" activist said bluntly: "Our international reputation as environmental advocates far exceeds our accomplishments at home."[16]

Against this background of cynicism, one must ask why Mulroney received such a different and increasingly positive response for his actions at the Rio UNCED conference. One explanation points to style rather than substance. The increased access offered to NGOs during the Rio process succeeded in getting many (although by no means all) of the environmental activists "on side," and this provided the prime minister's performance with a degree of credibility.[17]

Another explanation hinges on the technical management of Mulroney's image. As at least one commentator suggests, an array of "spin doctors" worked hard to present Mulroney and his officials in a positive light: "More than 30 pages of the 100-page Rio strategy memo that the federal bureaucrats forwarded to Cabinet dealt with communication objectives.

And of the more than 100 official Canadian delegates well over a third (42 by one count) were with the Prime Minister's Office. A good deal of these PMO staffers were detailed to inundate the media with press releases and arranged interviews."[18]

Still, to be effective, this elaborate exercise in signalling had to have something positive to communicate – something in the form of a message from the prime minister. In this regard, Mulroney's willingness and ability to gamble was decisive. He seized the opportunity presented first by George Bush's indecisiveness about whether he was going to attend the summit and subsequently by the US president's obstinate insistence on "timetables and tables" at the Rio convention itself. A series of high-profile gestures highlighted Canada's (and Mulroney's) good international environmental citizenship: on 27 March 1992 Ottawa announced that Mulroney would attend the Rio Summit, and it issued a package of Canadian initiatives designed to boost the "green" image of Mulroney and the Canadian delegation. Closer to the summit, Mulroney made a major speech establishing a five-point agenda for UNCED and defining a Canadian yardstick for success. This was quickly followed by a press conference on 12 June that indicated some progress on these points. As a climax to these efforts, immediately upon his arrival in Rio, Mulroney moved to have Canada become the first country to sign the Convention on Biological Diversity. All of these gestures were political events designed to grab the attention not just of political insiders, but also of the media and the general public.

In the case of Rio, the risks of Mulroney's tendency to take gambles were reduced in several ways. The prime minister looked carefully before he leaped, and he had talked extensively to Bush about strategy and tactics. Furthermore, Canada did not stand alone in departing from the United States on environmental issues; other G-7 countries (particularly Germany and Britain) were also at odds with the Americans.[19] And, notwithstanding Mulroney's show of commitment with regard to working towards the ratification of the convention, the Canadian delegation to the Rio Summit made it clear that it had a number of reservations on such issues as patent protection.

Despite these caveats, however, it is undeniable that Mulroney's initiatives played well back home. The activism created the impression that Canada was prepared to distance itself from the American position on many of the conference's key issues. Moreover, this impression was reinforced by the decisiveness with which Mulroney acted. His decision to sign and ratify the biodiversity convention came only twenty-four hours after Bush announced that he would not sign it. Moreover, Mulroney used the opportunity to make a broader political point: "We don't subcontract our rights and obligations to the United States in any way."[20]

This sense of triumph was interpreted in the media almost exclusively as the individual success of the prime minister. Soon after the announcement that Mulroney would be going to Rio, *Ottawa Citizen* columnist John Hay opined that the Earth Summit "runs a fair-to-middling chance of being a foul-tempered failure. What a good thing, therefore, that Brian Mulroney will be there."[21] On the conclusion of the summit, the *Toronto Star* ran an editorial that acknowledged (somewhat grudgingly) Mulroney's diplomatic success: "His environmental record at home is nothing to boast about. But Brian Mulroney deserves full credit for his performance at the Earth summit in Rio de Janeiro ... [He] emerged as a progressive leader willing to do Canada's part."[22]

Delegating Authority to Ministers

Leadership involves more than just direct participation at the prime ministerial level; it also involves being responsible for those other ministers who are actually at the helm. As Kim Richard Nossal puts it: "While prime ministers tend to be the central figures in the development of many aspects of Canada's foreign policy – determining what the priorities will be, shaping the administration, policy-making at the summit – they do not engage in the foreign policy process alone. They are assisted by, and must deal with, other ministers in cabinet, including those whose portfolios touch on the wide-ranging issues in foreign affairs."[23]

One of most interesting aspects of the puzzle about Canada's role in the UN social conferences concerns how the delegation of ministerial responsibility fits into Mulroney's general pattern of governance. Given his extensive business background, it is tempting to see Mulroney as either a chief operating officer or as a chief executive officer. As shown in the evolution of policy towards the UN social conferences, however, this style allowed for an enormous range of executive outcomes. At one end of the continuum, his style of leadership allowed a high degree of centralization of authority among the Prime Minister's Office (PMO) and the Privy Council Office (PCO) and specific key advisers. Most significantly, in the run-up to the Rio conference, Derek Burney took on a vital role in the agenda-setting process. As Mulroney's former chief of staff and lead official on the FTA negotiations, Burney not only had the confidence of, but direct access to, the prime minister. As Canada's ambassador to the United States, Burney also served as the central conduit between Ottawa and Washington on climate change and other sensitive issues.

At the other end of the continuum, a tremendous amount of overlap can be found in the delegation of authority with respect to the Rio negotiations. To some degree, this fragmentation came about because of the ongoing turf war at the bureaucratic level between External Affairs and Environment Canada, which goes back to the Stockholm conference of

1972.[24] Nonetheless, the dispersion of authority was much more complicated than this historical divide would imply. Although the UNCED task
force was run by an official from External Affairs, a special advisor to the
secretary of state for external affairs was also appointed, and the alternative head of the Canadian delegation was the executive director of the
National Secretariat for UNCED at Environment Canada. Adding to the
mix was the appointment of a special advisor on international affairs to
the minister of the environment along with the prime minister's personal
representative to UNCED.

Amidst this clutter, key ministers could still use the Rio Summit process
to do some running of their own. As the minister of fisheries and oceans,
John Crosbie served as an effective message carrier for Canada's evolving
public information campaign on conservation, particularly with respect
to high seas fishing. As environment minister, Jean Charest proved well
able to handle a sharp learning curve. While he was not the sort of strong
mission-oriented environmental minister that Lucien Bouchard had been
prior to his departure from federal politics, neither was he exclusively a
status participant.[25] Getting a good press and a positive media spin were
major concerns for Charest. While he was far more willing to try to avoid
confrontation than was Bouchard, he was just as tenacious with regard to
pushing the environmental dossier. As the head of the Canadian delegation, it was Charest, not Mulroney, who handled day-to-day procedural
matters and the application of strategy. Charest's success as a communica-
tor and handler of the Canadian delegation may be judged by the fact that
Mulroney asked him to continue to hold his large morning delegation
meetings even after the prime minister had arrived. In terms of substantive diplomatic engagement, Charest was one of fifteen ministers included in the intensive negotiations over the wording of the final text.

This relative autonomy did not mean that Mulroney and the PMO did
not leave their thumbprints all over the Rio Summit dossier. To a large
extent, these thumbprints did not have to be applied very hard. The mere
fact that "the Boss" was going to Rio was enough to mobilize the bureaucracy, unlocking problems and resolving turf differences. And if problems
remained, then the thumbprints were applied more forcefully. On the
issue of clutter in the Canadian delegation, for example, the main casual-
ty was Monique Landry, the minister of state for external relations, who
had responsibility for the Canadian International Development Agency
(CIDA). Although CIDA had moved to emphasize the theme of international sustainability, the PMO told Landry the day before she was to leave
that she was not going to Rio.

It must be asked again whether Rio was an exceptional case. Certainly
the pattern of delegated authority for Canadian participation at the 1993
Vienna Human Rights Conference seems very different. On the question

of clutter, the Canadian preparations for this summit exhibited a good deal more coherence at the bureaucratic level. There continued to be a degree of fragmentation, with a federal-provincial committee chaired by an official from the Department of Multicultural Affairs. However, a much greater sense of bureaucratic coherence was achieved when External Affairs and International Trade Canada (EAITC) assumed the "lead" position on this dossier. The interdepartmental consultations were coordinated through a committee chaired by an External Affairs official, the director-general of international organizations. Anne Park, of EAITC, took on the responsibility not only of heading the Canadian delegation throughout the preparatory process of the negotiations on the conference, but also of chairing the UN grouping (the Western European and Others Group). EAITC's lead position, therefore, allowed for both domestic continuity and international status.

What was lacking at Vienna was the sense of focus applied by the short but intense burst of prime ministerial and ministerial attention. Somewhat paradoxically, this lack of high-level attention enhanced the sense of bureaucratic coherence on routine matters. The deficit was in the lack of political leverage to seize the moment of the Vienna conference in a more dramatic fashion. EAITC officials kept trying to get the secretary of state for external affairs engaged in the process, to publicize the Vienna conference before the House of Commons Standing Committee on External Affairs and International Trade, to discuss the dossier at the Cabinet Committee on Foreign and Defence Policy, to put out a position paper on Canada's priorities, and to help break some of the deadlocks mounting up in the negotiating process. But these efforts appear to have fallen on deaf ears.

In contrast to the activist role played by Jean Charest at the Rio Summit, Barbara McDougall was a rather passive and distracted observer during the Vienna negotiating process. Why there was such a difference in participation level invites some speculation. At an organizational level, it is clear that there was not only a greater concentration of authority in the PMO/PCO, but also a higher degree of unevenness of approach in the latter stages of Mulroney's government. As his popularity among Canadians slid dramatically, Mulroney showed an increased willingness to take some high-profile initiatives – as witnessed most notably on peacekeeping/humanitarian interventions. This left little space for innovation at the ministerial level.

Exacerbating this condition were McDougall's difficulties in handling the transition to the post-Cold War era. McDougall's reputation suffered during her time as minister of External Affairs. She was often portrayed as being uncomfortable in the position,[26] and she was perceived as having made a number of errors of judgment (e.g., during the August 1991 coup in the Soviet Union she had said that Canada could do business with the junta). In policy terms, McDougall did not seem interested in the widening "social" agenda in international relations. She showed no sense of personal engagement with either the Rio or the Vienna process. While her absence at Rio was understandable given the clutter in the Canadian delegation, her suggestion that the expectations of the UNCED summit were too high indicates a sense of caution at odds with the exuberance displayed by Mulroney and Charest.[27] McDougall's lack of interest in the Vienna dossier is even more surprising given her experience with issues such as the situation of refugee women. Indeed, at least one foreign policy insider described her as a caretaker minister: "Barbara is not interested in External Affairs. She's basically biding her time. She has no intuition into it, she has no particular experience. She's been totally marginalized by the PMO and Mulroney, who wants to use foreign affairs as a way to rehabilitate himself with the Canadian people."[28]

In addition, the timing of the Vienna conference – 14-25 June 1993 – ensured that the politicians would be distracted. In the spring of 1993, Mulroney, widely regarded in Canada as a leader who had gone well beyond his shelf-life, had announced his retirement from politics. The Vienna conference occurred in the midst of the convention to pick a replacement as prime minister and leader of the Conservative party. McDougall herself was deeply involved in the struggle for succession, first as an aspirant to the leadership and then as a player in the struggle between Kim Campbell and Jean Charest. Her decision not to attend Vienna came in the midst of this leadership campaign.

Conclusion: Assessing the Conservative Approach to the UN Social Conferences

This examination of the Canadian role at UN social conferences suggests that we need to revise our assessment of the Conservative government's overall performance in international affairs. Far from turning away from activist multilateral diplomacy, Canada during the Mulroney era remained a substantial player in defining and framing the agenda for the post-Cold War global order. High-profile gestures, such as the move to have Canada become the first country to sign the Convention on Biological Diversity, were symbolically important. In an attempt to strengthen the message that Canada was a leader rather than a follower on environmental issues, the Mulroney government's approach to UNCED was linked to the evolution of a coherent domestic strategy on sustainable development.

The merits of these types of initiative are somewhat devalued, however, by the fact that they were relatively risk- and cost-free. The willingness to go out ahead of the Bush administration on the biological diversity issue was not accompanied by concerted pressure on the Americans to sign the convention. And, for all of its declaratory statements with respect to its commitment in working towards the ratification and implementation of the convention, Canada made it clear that it had a number of reservations on matters such as patent protection. Likewise, the proposed externalization of the Green Plan was not accompanied by major initiatives on issues such as technology transfer.

A similar sort of tension emerged at the 1993 Human Rights conference. As at Rio, the main Canadian initiatives at Vienna were externally oriented. For example, the Mulroney government strongly supported extending the "grave breach" provisions of the Geneva convention to include acts of sexual violence against women, defining them as falling under "inhumane treatment," "general suffering," or acts causing serious injury to body or health. Conversely, however, the Conservatives demonstrated a great reluctance to extend this universal principle to domestic policy – most notably with regard to having gender persecution taken into consideration with respect to refugee claims.[29]

In short, for all of its various expressions of robust and credible multilateralism, the Mulroney government's performance at UN social conferences exuded a strong odour of opportunism. Tactically astute, Mulroney's diplomatic approach became involved in a very complex two-level game. Internationally, this approach represented an elaborate exercise in image-building (or image-repairing). The primary objective was to send a signal that Canada remained a good international citizen, willing to, and capable of, promoting a reformist agenda and the extension of rules-based regimes. Domestically, the central aim was to restore the credibility of the Mulroney government with respect to social policy. In both dimensions of the game, the approach was part of an ongoing Conservative attempt to show that the FTA had not impaired Canada's autonomy in other areas of world affairs.

If there is no agreement about whether the Mulroney government's performance at the UN mega-conferences of the early 1990s was more the result of political convenience than a serious policy commitment, it cannot be denied that the Conservatives contributed to the changing nature of global governance. As the international social agenda became more complicated, the priorities and personality of the prime minister were central to the form, scope, and intensity of the Canadian diplomatic response. When, for a variety of reasons, Mulroney decided to focus on UNCED, the machinery of government swung into action. Central agencies became involved, selective ministers were given space to operate, the bureaucracy was mobilized to try to deliver as best it could, and innovative practices with respect to governmental/non-governmental cooperation were tried out. With Mulroney preoccupied with other foreign policy activities and on his way out of office, the Canadian contribution to the 1993 Vienna conference was almost left on auto-pilot. Without the intervention of the prime minister, the level of activity was not enough to lift the performance of Canadian diplomacy to the level reached at UNCED. Mulroney's instinct to gamble on high-profile initiatives, an instinct that was so evident in Rio, was simply absent in Vienna.

Notes

1 See Andrew F. Cooper, *Canadian Foreign Policy: Old Habits and New Directions* (Scarborough, ON: Prentice Hall Canada, 1997), chaps. 1-2.
2 Robert W. Cox, "Global Restructuring: Making Sense of a Changing International Political Economy," in *Political Economy and the Changing Global Order*, ed. Richard Stubbs and Geoffrey R.D. Underhill (Toronto: McClelland and Stewart, 1994), 49; Stephen Gill, "Theorizing the Interregnum: Double Movement and Global Politics in the 1990s," in *International Political Economy: Understanding Global Disorder*, ed. Bjorn Hettne (Halifax, NS: Fernwood, 1995), 72.
3 Stephen McBride and John Shields, *Dismantling a Nation: The Transition to Corporate Rule in Canada*, 2nd ed. (Halifax, NS: Fernwood, 1997), 12.
4 Elizabeth May, "A Non-Tory Misses Brian Mulroney," *Globe and Mail*, 22 June 1998, A17.
5 Peter Aucoin, "Organizational Change in the Machinery of Canadian Government: From Rational Management to Brokerage Politics," *Canadian Journal of Political Science* 19, 1 (1986): 3-27.
6 Elizabeth May, *Paradise Won: The Struggle for South Moresby* (Toronto: McClelland and Stewart, 1990), 178-79, 232.
7 Aucoin, "Organizational Change."
8 Conrad Black, *A Life in Progress*, quoted in Michael Bliss, *Right Honourable Men: The Descent of Canadian Politics from Macdonald to Mulroney* (Toronto: HarperCollins, 1994), 284n.
9 Cited in Donald J. Savoie, *Thatcher, Reagan, Mulroney: In Search of A New Bureaucracy* (Toronto: University of Toronto Press, 1994), 272.
10 Ibid., 272.
11 G. Bruce Doern and Brian W. Tomlin, *Faith and Fear: The Free Trade Story* (Toronto: Stoddart, 1991), 272.
12 John Kirton, "Managing Global Conflict: Canada and International Summitry," in *Canada Among Nations, 1987: A World of Conflict*, ed. Maureen Appel Molot and Brian Tomlin (Toronto: James Lorimer, 1988), 33.
13 Stephen Clarkson, "Disjunctions: Free Trade and the Paradox of Canadian Development," in *The New Era of Global Competition: State Policy and Market Power*, ed. Daniel Drache and Meric S. Gertler (Montreal/Kingston: McGill-Queen's University Press, 1991), 116.
14 Quoted in Paul Lewis, "World Leaders Gather for Summit Meeting on Children," *New York Times*, 30 September 1990.
15 "A Better Start for the World's Children," *Globe and Mail*, 29 September 1990.
16 David McRobert, "On Global Warming, Canada Is Full of Hot Air," *Globe and Mail*, 18 February 1991; Robert Boardman, ed., *Canadian Environmental Policy: Ecosystems, Politics, and Process* (Toronto: Oxford University Press, 1992).
17 Andrew Fenton Cooper and J-Stefan Fritz, "Bringing the NGOs In: UNCED and Canada's Environmental Policy," *International Journal* 47, 4 (1992): 796-817.
18 Rick Boychuk, "Descending from the Earth Summit," *Canadian Forum*, October 1992, 35.
19 Paul Lewis, "U.N. Opens Environment Talks: Europe Spurs U.S. to Act Urgently," *New York Times*, 3 March 1992.
20 Quoted in James Rusk, "Mulroney Signs Ecopact," *Globe and Mail*, 12 June 1992.
21 "Earth Summit May Prove Embarrassing," *Ottawa Citizen*, 13 April 1992.
22 *Toronto Star*, 15 June 1992.
23 Kim Richard Nossal, *The Politics of Canadian Foreign Policy*, 3rd ed. (Scarborough, ON: Prentice Hall Canada, 1997), 219.

24 F.H. Kelman, "Stockholm in Retrospect," *International Journal* 28 (Winter 1972-73): 28-49.
25 On this typology see Donald J. Savoie, *The Politics of Public Spending in Canada* (Toronto: University of Toronto Press, 1990), 190-91.
26 Olivia Ward, "McDougall's U.N. Debut Awkward," *Toronto Star,* 26 September 1991.
27 "You're Right, Barbara, Stay Home," *Canadian Dimension,* April-May 1992, 33.
28 Linda Hossie, "New Generation Sees Aggressive Role for Canada," *Globe and Mail,* 18 October 1991.
29 For a review of some of these tensions, see Kathleen E. Mahoney, "Human Rights and Canada's Foreign Policy," *International Journal* 47, 3 (Summer 1992): 567-88.

12

How Exceptional? Reassessing the Mulroney Government's Anti-Apartheid "Crusade"

David R. Black

It has come to be widely accepted that the Conservative government of Brian Mulroney played an exceptional leadership role in the international campaign to promote fundamental political change in apartheid South Africa.[1] There are typically two variants of this argument. The first is the mainstream view, associated with participants in the policy-making process at the time as well as most popular press and some scholarly accounts. In this view, Canada's policy towards South Africa and the wider southern African region during the Mulroney period was an outstanding example of international activism – Canada at its enlightened best.[2] Indeed, the Mulroney government's southern Africa policy cast a long, rose-coloured shadow, helping to shape subsequent policy approaches and departures.[3]

The second is a more critical view, associated with those in the anti-apartheid movement as well as many southern Africanist scholars. It concedes that there was indeed an "exceptional moment" in Canadian policy towards the region: during 1985 and 1986, Ottawa departed from long-standing practice to impose limited economic sanctions against South Africa, sharply differing with its most important allies. This dramatic departure was driven principally by the convictions of the prime minister himself, supported by a small circle of political appointees (though, in this view, considerably less enthusiastically by Joe Clark, his External Affairs minister). It was also strongly facilitated by the crisis of capitalism in South Africa at the time.[4] By 1987, however, the politics of "sanctions fatigue" had set in; Canada's activism towards South Africa had essentially "run out of steam," and the government had retreated to a more characteristically limited and compromised policy based on the pursuit of "soft options."[5]

It is clear that the Mulroney government's South Africa policy, particularly in its early years, departed sharply from previous Canadian policy. Indeed, the Mulroney government remained among the front rank of

Western states in its anti-apartheid activities throughout the pivotal 1985-90 period (preceding South Africa's transition to majority rule). The simple fact of a change of government in Ottawa in September 1984 facilitated a policy shift. Moreover, unprecedented time, energy, and resources were devoted to South Africa, belying its apparently marginal place among Canada's core economic and strategic concerns. Finally, the new cohort of foreign policy leaders, led by the prime minister, took the South African issue more seriously, in a more consistent manner, and with a more urgent tone than had any of its predecessors. In these senses then, both party and personality made a difference to policy, reinforced by the Conservatives' sense of their historical role, beginning with John Diefenbaker, in launching South Africa's journey into the diplomatic wilderness with its 1961 departure from the Commonwealth.[6]

However, when this policy departure is examined comparatively, it looks much less exceptional than it has typically been portrayed. While Canada remained *among* the front rank of Western governments in its opposition to apartheid, it was frequently behind several of them on specific aspects of policy and generally orchestrated its efforts on a collective basis; that is, in conjunction with other "leading" states. Moreover, while the government's policy represented a clear departure from previous South African policies, its activist response on this issue was broadly similar (in both character and limitations) to other diplomatic initiatives before and since. In other words, notwithstanding the strong personal engagement of key political actors on this issue, Bernard Wood is probably not far off the mark in arguing that "it is ... quite possible that under the circumstances of 1984 and subsequent years, a Trudeau government or any other Canadian government would have come to adopt similar approaches."[7] The basic parameters of Ottawa's policy were largely shaped by domestic and, especially, international imperatives. In Denis Stairs's terms, there was, in the end, more engineering than architecture in this policy departure, although it doubtless felt quite different to those involved. To support this argument, I will review four key dimensions of Canadian policy towards South(ern) Africa in the 1985-90 period and then examine why the myth of Canadian exceptionalism on southern Africa has been so widespread and resilient.

Canadian Policy in Practice

Canada's policies towards southern Africa encompassed four key elements: (1) sanctions, (2) diplomatic activity in support of change, (3) aid to "victims and opponents of apartheid" inside South Africa and to its vulnerable neighbours in the Southern African Development Coordination Conference (SADCC),[8] and (4) security assistance to Mozambique in response to South Africa's ruthless destabilization campaign.

Sanctions

As resistance and repression in South Africa grew, and as Pretoria's campaign to destabilize its neighbours mounted, the traditional liberal argument (favoured by both Western interests and the English-speaking business elite in South Africa) that unfettered commercial relations would erode apartheid rapidly lost credibility. The transnational anti-apartheid movement, along with the African National Congress (ANC) in exile, was increasingly successful in portraying sanctions as *the* crucial test of a country's anti-apartheid commitment. It was on this issue that the Mulroney government's departure from past Canadian practice was most dramatic, while its subsequent failure to fulfil the expectations it had fuelled regarding sanctions was primarily responsible for the criticism it endured towards the end of the 1980s.

Historically, successive Canadian governments had consistently resisted calls for economic sanctions, in southern Africa and elsewhere, except on the basis of a mandatory UN Security Council resolution. Clarence Redekop identified five traditional arguments in support of this position. First, the health of the Canadian economy was trade-dependent. Second, the government wished to avoid precedents that could fuel calls for sanctions on other issues; only a UN Security Council mandate could avoid problems of "moral selectivity." Third, the benefits of sanctions were thought to be minimal and ephemeral at best. Fourth, sanctions were ineffective in bringing about political change, especially if imposed unilaterally or by a small group of states. And fifth, sanctions were "unenforceable."[9] Adherence to this position wavered in the case of South Africa in the wake of the Soweto uprising in 1976 and the imposition of a mandatory arms embargo by the UN Security Council in 1977. In December of 1977 the secretary of state for external affairs, Don Jamieson, announced a limited set of punitive economic measures. However, they were so minimal as to be "negligible" in effect.[10] Thus, if the government's conventional wisdom on sanctions had wavered, it remained effectively unmoved.

Under Mulroney, this traditional opposition to economic sanctions was swept aside. With the South African townships in revolt and the white capitalist elite anxious and restive, Ottawa launched an in-depth policy review in early 1985. In July, Clark announced a mild sanctions package that built on the 1977 measures, followed by a succession of additional measures in conjunction with Commonwealth decisions. The basic configuration of Canada's sanctions was largely set with the adoption of the steps recommended by the August 1986 Commonwealth "mini-summit," at which Mulroney and five other Commonwealth leaders broke definitively with the British prime minister, Margaret Thatcher. At that time, Mulroney and his collaborators endorsed a package of sanctions that included a ban on imports of South African agricultural products, uranium, coal, iron, and steel. Thereafter, additional measures amounted to minor tinkering, such as tightening the ban on government contracts with majority-owned South African companies or extending the ban on sales of high technology items to private-sector end users.[11]

The high point of the Conservative government's sanctions policy was in fact rhetorical – Mulroney's speech to the UN General Assembly on 23 October 1985. After condemning the apartheid regime in eloquent terms, he stated: "My government has said to Canadians that if there are not fundamental changes in South Africa, we are prepared to invoke total sanctions against that country and its repressive regime. If there is no progress in dismantling apartheid, Canada's relations with South Africa may have to be severed absolutely."[12]

Renate Pratt argues that this threat was not an "eccentric self-indulgence"; rather, as she demonstrates, it was reiterated before and after by both Mulroney and Clark and, thus, represented "a clear statement of policy."[13] Precisely why this marker was laid down has been a matter of some speculation and will be discussed further in the next section. In effect, however, it became the standard to which the Mulroney government was subsequently held by much of the anti-apartheid community in Canada as well as by Opposition politicians and sections of the press. There were doubtless many officials in External Affairs who came to rue the day this statement was uttered.

The various measures adopted by Canada are summarized in Table 12. 1. They were never more than partial. Several, such as the bans on new bank loans, on the export of petroleum, and on the promotion of tourism to South Africa, were voluntary.[14] Renate Pratt and others argue persuasively that the sanctions were often "minimized, at times softened, reinterpreted and inadequately implemented," particularly by External Affairs;[15] certainly there were times when they were interpreted narrowly and permissively. They generally avoided any measures that could impose specific losses of corporate profitability or employment in Canada, even temporarily.[16]

Because Canadian sanctions were partial and often narrowly interpreted, they left the government open to periodic embarrassments. Most conspicuously, in the run-up to the February 1989 Harare meeting of the Commonwealth Committee of Foreign Ministers on Southern Africa, which Clark chaired, the government was twice stung. First, it had to deal with the publication of embarrassing trade figures showing a 68 percent jump in imports from South Africa and a 44 percent jump in exports for the first eleven months of 1988. While these increases came mainly because of the rising *value* of goods traded as opposed to their volume, which was declining overall,[17] such nuances were lost in the ensuing controversy. Even more discomfiting was the revelation that the government had approved a $600 million loan by the Bank of Nova Scotia to MINORCO,

Table 12.1

Canadian action on South Africa

Trade-related	Financial investment	Sporting contacts	Other actions
I – No Canadian government promotion of trade with South Africa.	I – Abrogated double taxation agreement.	I – Canada's policy governs all sporting contacts between Canada and South Africa. This applies to sport contacts between Canadians and South Africans at professional and amateur levels and in individual and team sports, no matter where these contacts occur (i.e, in Canada, in South Africa, or in a third country).	I – Assistance to victims of Apartheid ($7.8 million in 1988/89). Major areas include: education and skills training for disadvantaged South Africans in South Africa or Canada; legal and humanitarian aid to political detainees and their families; assistance for small-scale community projects involving Canadian and local NGOs; labour education; and assistance to refugees in neighbouring countries via multilateral agencies.
II – IMPORTS Mandatory bans on: a) all agricultural products b) uranium c) coal d) iron products e) steel products f) arms from South Africa.	II – Ban on new corporate investments in South Africa. III – Voluntary ban on new bank loans (both public and private sectors) to South Africa. IV – Capped trade credits to South Africa and requested Canadian banks to make loan rescheduling terms as short as possible.	II – Visas denied to individuals travelling on South African passports seeking to enter Canada to participate in any sporting event or activity. III – Sport associations required to suspend members who participate in sports events in South Africa.	II – $1 million Canadian Action Plan to counteract South African propaganda and censorship.
III – EXPORTS Mandatory bans on: a) all arms and munitions of war b) all high technology and other sensitive equipment, such as computers.	V – Established a code of conduct for Canadian businesses in South Africa.		

▼ *Table 12.1*

Trade-related	Financial investment	Sporting contacts	Other actions
Voluntary ban on: petroleum and petroleum products. IV – OTHER a) voluntary ban on Krugerrands b) ban on air links with South Africa c) discontinued export market development grants for South African market d) discontinued insurance to Canadian exporters to South Africa (provided by the Export Development Corporation) e) voluntary ban on tourism promotion to South Africa f) terminated Canadian contracts, grants, and sales to South African majority-owned companies g) ended toll-processing of Namibian uranium		IV – Sport associations required to deny invitations, to protest, or to withdraw from competitions in third countries involving South Africa. V – Sport associations required to pressure their international federation to suspend members who participate in sport events in South Africa. VI – Sport associations' compliance with government policy on sporting contacts tied to government funding.	III – $1.6 million Dialogue Fund to promote dialogue about a non-racial future (a portion of these funds was committed to projects outlined in the Canadian Action Plan because censorship was an impediment to dialogue). IV – Security assistance to the Front Line States towards the protection of infrastructure projects (i.e., fuel, clothes, spare parts, communications equipment, food, and balances of payments support (over $4 million committed to date). V – Trebling of funding for Canada's global Military Training Assistance Program between 1988 and 1990, a substantial proportion of which went towards training of military personnel from the Front Line States.

h) terminated Canadian government procurement of South African goods and services (limited exception for CIDA and Canadian Embassy activities in southern Africa).

VI – Ending the issuance of visitors' visas by Canadian Embassy in Pretoria and requiring all South African visitors to Canada to apply in person for a visa outside South Africa.

VII – Restrictions on contact between officials of the two governments.

VIII – Cancellation of non-resident accreditation to Canada of South African diplomats (in particular science, labour, mining, and agriculture attachés).

IX – Maintain an Anti-Apartheid Register for Canadians to publicly demonstrate their opposition to apartheid.

a South African-controlled company based in Luxembourg that was bidding for control of British mining giant Consolidated Gold Fields. Approval was justified on the narrow interpretive grounds that, since the deal was formally between the Bank of Nova Scotia's London branch and a Luxembourg-based company, it was beyond the jurisdictional reach of Canada's voluntary ban on new bank loans. Both controversies served to underscore the gap between Canada's partial sanctions and Mulroney's earlier threat to sever relations with South Africa "absolutely." They led to charges of "backsliding" and a "major policy retreat" on sanctions.[18]

Assessing the validity of these charges depends at least partly on how one interprets the purpose of the original threat of comprehensive sanctions discussed in the next section. What should in fairness be said is that neither Mulroney nor Clark ever wavered in their support for the utility and effectiveness of sanctions. In a 28 September 1989 speech to the Council on Foreign Relations in New York, for example, Clark asserted: "Our position has been that sanctions are necessary to convince the South African regime that change is necessary," and "we can state without equivocation that *sanctions have worked*."[19] Over the course of the 1985-90 period, moreover, Canadian exports to South Africa stagnated, constituting 0.13 percent of Canadian exports in 1985 and 0.12 percent in 1990, while imports from South Africa declined significantly, from 0.2 percent to 0.1 percent. The dollar value of imports fluctuated significantly but declined in absolute terms from CAD$227,734 in 1985 to CAD$205,959 in 1989. The biggest single drop occurred between 1986 and 1987, reflecting the adoption of the measures agreed to at the mini-summit of 1986, when Canada dropped from the fourteenth to the nineteenth largest importer of South African goods.[20] All told, then, Canadian sanctions implied some real (albeit minor and diffuse) cost to the South African economy as well as some opportunity cost for Canadian companies.

Comparatively, however, while Canada was among the front rank of Western contributors to the sanctions "wave" of the mid-1980s, it was certainly not at its forefront. Its policy was essentially equivalent to that of Australia, which imposed the same Commonwealth measures. It was slightly behind that of the United States Congress, whose October 1986 Comprehensive Anti-Apartheid Act marginally exceeded Canadian sanctions in terms of scope and enforceability, and substantially exceeded them in terms of impact. It was significantly less extensive than that of the Nordic countries, which, with the exception of Iceland, imposed comprehensive merchandise trade bans between December 1986 and July 1987. And this leaves aside entirely non-Western states such as India, which imposed a comprehensive (albeit leaky) trade embargo in 1946. In short, notwithstanding Ottawa's high profile threats of comprehensive sanctions, its policy, in practice, was hardly exceptional.

Diplomacy

Canada's sanctions policy was closely linked with its diplomatic efforts to build a broadly based coalition to put pressure on the apartheid regime. The government's strategy was based on the obvious fact that, on its own, or even among a small group of small and middle-sized states, Canadian sanctions would have limited impact. However, if it could persuade countries like Britain, the United States, and West Germany to adopt new sanctions – even partial ones – then the impact would be substantial. Coincidentally, a more broadly based sanctioning coalition would minimize Canadian risk and exposure. It is in this context, I would argue, that the government's threat to "sever relations absolutely" should be understood. While there were some in government who were sympathetic to comprehensive sanctions (rumoured to include, at times, the prime minister himself), the logic of this position was probably designed primarily to lay down a marker against which to mobilize movement on sanctions across a wide front as well as to galvanize bureaucrats in Ottawa for a significant policy departure.[21] There was arguably little chance that Canada would move unilaterally to fulfil this threat, notwithstanding the clear implication that it was willing to do so.

In the *multilateral* context, the United Nations had, for decades, been very active on the issue of apartheid and the related issue of independence for Namibia,[22] and the new Canadian ambassador to the United Nations, Stephen Lewis, injected fresh energy and visibility into Canada's work on these agenda items. However, the two forums within which Canadian multilateral efforts were concentrated were the Commonwealth and the Group of Seven (G-7); and, of the two, the former was much more preoccupying for Canadian policy-makers. The "modern" (post-decolonization) Commonwealth has long held a prominent place in Canadian foreign policy, despite its limited economic and strategic implications for this country, not least because Canada is undeniably important within it. Moreover, like Trudeau before him, Clark was a "Commonwealth convert" and brought some of the zeal of the converted to his engagement with the association. As with earlier instances of intense Canadian activity over southern Africa (e.g., regarding Rhodesia's Unilateral Declaration of Independence in 1965 and the renewal of British arms sales to South Africa in 1971), it is almost inconceivable that Canada would have become so deeply engaged with South Africa during the 1980s in the absence of the Commonwealth connection.

The Commonwealth's work on South Africa in the 1985-90 period can be divided into two phases, pivoting around the October 1987 Commonwealth Heads of Government Meeting (CHOGM) in Vancouver. In the first phase, Mulroney and his government played a central role in a concerted effort to manoeuvre Britain into supporting a partial sanctions package that, given the importance of British-South African trade and investment links, would have had real clout. In anticipation of the 1985 CHOGM in Nassau, Mulroney dispatched Bernard Wood, then director of the North-South Institute, to consult with the leaders of key southern African member-states. At Nassau itself, Mulroney and Rajiv Gandhi of India played key mediation roles with Thatcher, facilitating agreement on a mild package of economic "measures" (so termed in deference to Britain's outspoken opposition to economic *sanctions*) and, more important, on the creation of a Commonwealth eminent persons group (EPG) to encourage a process of dialogue between the South African government and the "true repre-sentatives" of the black majority, the aim being the dismantling of apartheid.[23] Most observers were pessimistic about the EPG's chances of success. However, a successful outcome would obviously be welcome, while a failure would reinforce the case for additional sanctions pressure, perhaps inducing Britain to support an expanded package and creating a "snowball effect" vis-à-vis the European Community and the United States.[24]

The EPG mission was ultimately stymied by Pretoria, but the group made a compelling case for additional sanctions pressure. This set the stage for the Commonwealth mini-summit of August 1986 in London, at which seven heads of government considered how to respond to the EPG report. It became clear that Mulroney was collaborating with the secretary-general of the Commonwealth, Sonny Ramphal, and heads of government from Australia, India, Zambia, and Zimbabwe in an effort to win Thatcher's support for partial sanctions. The proposed sanctions package was there-fore designed to be easily implemented by Britain and South Africa's other major Western economic partners. However, no amount of strategic con-centration could turn Thatcher. She defied the consensus among the rest of the group, which proceeded to recommend a set of new sanctions with-out British support, as noted in the previous section.

For the remainder of the decade, the "Commonwealth minus Britain" sought to maintain a common front on South Africa, while Thatcher attempted to discredit the majority position in her characteristically sanctimonious manner. In the course of this unfolding drama, she and Mulroney had a number of sharp exchanges, including what Stephen Lewis termed an "electric moment" at the 1987 Vancouver CHOGM when Mulroney dramatically challenged her stand on South Africa.[25]

In the second phase of Commonwealth activity from the Vancouver CHOGM onwards, the South African issue was taken up by the Commonwealth Committee of Foreign Ministers on Southern Africa (CFMSA) – a Canadian proposal that Clark chaired until his departure from the External Affairs portfolio in 1991. Accompanying this diplomat-ic departure was a shift in the primary locus of responsibility for Canadian policy, with Clark taking over from Mulroney.

Clark's approach to South Africa was manifestly less flamboyant and more cautious than Mulroney's, though arguably no less personally dedicated. Certainly, both he and the Southern Africa Task Force in External Affairs spent what many elsewhere in the department regarded as an inordinate amount of time and effort on this issue, especially as they took primary responsibility (with the Commonwealth Secretariat) for organizing the work of the CFMSA over the course of its four meetings between Vancouver and the Kuala Lumpur CHOGM of 1989.[26] Nevertheless, the CFMSA process was often troubled for Clark and for Canada. By this time, the limited international sanctions "wave" of the mid-1980s had lost momentum. This placed the various members of the Commonwealth in difficult positions. Britain – the only member-state with economic clout vis-à-vis South Africa – was now firmly dug in on its anti-sanctions stance; and South Africa's "Front Line" neighbours, which were among the most vocal sanctions advocates, had understandably decided that they could not impose sanctions themselves.[27] Canada, Australia, and New Zealand were therefore left as the only states that could impose even marginally effective new "Commonwealth" sanctions. This they were reluctant to do. Thus, while the CFMSA process commissioned several studies focusing on the effects of sanctions and ways they could be "widened, deepened, and intensified," with particular emphasis on financial sanctions, it did not result in the adoption of any substantial new sanctions measures. In the meantime, Clark and his officials attempted to use the meetings to focus more attention on "reaching into South Africa to aid the victims and opponents of Apartheid, to promote dialogue, and counteract South African censorship and propaganda."[28] As laudable as these goals were, when combined with the government's retreat from the threat of comprehensive sanctions and the highly publicized embarrassments at Harare noted above, they fed critics' charges of sanctions "backsliding" and the abandonment of Canadian leadership.[29] Nevertheless, the CFMSA process as a whole did succeed in maintaining a high level North-South focus on the need for sanctions pressure at a time when there was clearly some effort to discredit such measures internationally. It also helped to stimulate some positive and creative developments on other fronts, as we will see below.

Overall, Canada's Commonwealth diplomacy with regard to South Africa was pivotal to the organization's overall effort, but that effort was ultimately limited in effects and effectiveness. Moreover, Ottawa's effort was always carefully orchestrated with several other sources of Commonwealth leadership, notably Australia, India, Zambia, Zimbabwe, and the Commonwealth Secretariat. Clearly, Canada did not "prevail upon" the rest of the organization to adopt sanctions against South Africa, as one former Canadian foreign minister has suggested;[30] rather, it was catching up with other Commonwealth members, in particular the Australian Labor Party government of Bob Hawke. In the past, Canada had frequently acted to hold the Commonwealth together by attempting (with considerable success) to bridge the differences between Britain and the organization's "Third World" majority. In this case, however, it was clear that the Commonwealth could be preserved as a credible organization only if it were to take a collective position in support of sanctions – even if this meant isolating Britain. Thus, in keeping with Canada's traditional role, its diplomacy was aimed partly at Commonwealth survival in the new southern African conjuncture.

Much of the positive attention focused on the government's anti-apartheid stand in the mid-1980s was linked to its status as a member of the G-7. As Douglas Anglin has noted, "African states ... look to Canada to exercise leverage on their behalf in Washington and London ... Their hopes in this respect, though not entirely misplaced, appear excessively optimistic."[31] Canada's G-7 status also meant that the government was probably more gently treated by other Commonwealth leaders than it might have been as it retreated from its threat of comprehensive sanctions towards the end of the decade.

As implied above, the Mulroney government had indeed hoped to use its summit connections to encourage a stronger collective Western policy against apartheid, including more sanctions pressure. It was largely unsuccessful in doing so. Mulroney, to his credit, persisted in raising southern Africa at the annual G-7 meetings, beginning with the Venice Summit in 1987. For his troubles, this issue received explicit mention in the "Chairman's Summary on Political Issues" – the least important in the hierarchy of summit documents – through the remainder of the decade. Despite John Kirton's assertion that summit documents "matter in the real world of politics and economics at the national, international and global levels alike,"[32] it is a stretch to view these passing references to South Africa as having any real significance in bringing international pressure to bear on Pretoria. Certainly there was no mention of sanctions – hardly surprising given the well known views of Thatcher, West German chancellor Helmut Kohl, and the two US presidents during this period, Ronald Reagan and George Bush.

With most of the other summit leaders' views clearly diverging from Mulroney's, there was some apprehension in External Affairs that persistent advocacy on southern Africa could become a pointless waste of Canada's limited political capital within this rarefied forum. Furthermore, according to Kim Richard Nossal, it was reported by some officials in Ottawa that the other leaders regarded Mulroney's willingness to advocate a complete break with South Africa in 1985 as a sign of diplomatic immaturity and lack of realism. Had the threat been acted upon, therefore, it could have endangered Mulroney's limited capacity for influence on other key issues, according to this line of reasoning.[33] The weight of this kind of peer pressure was surely formidable, strengthening the hand of those in Ottawa advocating a more restrained policy approach.[34]

Two further aspects of Canada's bilateral diplomacy on South Africa bear noting. First, Canada maintained diplomatic relations with the South African government throughout the Mulroney era. Obviously, the threat to "sever relations absolutely" implied the termination of diplomatic as well as economic links, and a number of activists in Canada, as well as the ANC in exile, argued for this course. In the end, however, even many of the government's sharper critics agreed that officials of the Canadian embassy in Pretoria had played a highly unusual, creative, and useful role on the ground in South Africa.[35] While some, such as Renate Pratt, have argued that the government could have followed the Swedish course of downgrading diplomatic links without losing the benefits of a continued Canadian presence, in general most would agree that the decision not to sever diplomatic relations was the right one.[36]

Second, a source of persistent difficulty for the Mulroney government was its attitude towards the ANC – the principal liberation movement in South Africa. Like most Western countries, Canada had always had trouble working out a satisfactory relationship with southern African liberation movements, most of which (like the ANC) went on to form post-independence national governments. The liberation movements' close links with Soviet bloc countries, their often radical socioeconomic programs, their pursuit of armed struggle in the face of oppressive white minority rule, and their problematic juridical status (neither conventional political parties nor governments) accounted for the coolness of Western relations with them. This set up a vicious circle, in which lack of Western sympathy and support drove such movements to forge even closer links with Soviet bloc countries, reinforcing Western suspicions and further compromising Western policies in the region. Only the Nordic states escaped this cycle, developing close links with these groups buttressed by direct humanitarian assistance from the late 1960s onwards.[37]

Canada's difficulties in forging a more constructive relationship with the ANC persisted through much of the 1980s. In August 1987, Mulroney became the first G-7 leader to meet ANC president Oliver Tambo, who also met with Clark on the same visit to Canada. However, even this apparent breakthrough was significantly compromised by the "cool and low-key," even "churlish," reception Tambo was reportedly given.[38] According to Pratt, "Both Mulroney and Clark indulged in strong anti-communist polemics and pronouncements about the violent nature of the ANC," thus betraying a lack of understanding of both the history of the movement and the impetus behind its limited armed struggle.[39]

What, then, is to be made of Clark's May 1989 claim, which reads: "I do not think there is a country in the world that has a more productive relationship with the African National Congress than Canada does ... a relation that we have put in place"?[40] This statement surely constitutes political hyperbole. Still, it does appear that, under the Mulroney/Clark stewardship, a considerably closer and more effective relationship with the exiled ANC and other ANC-aligned groups did eventually emerge. This was at least partly a consequence of the CFMSA process, in which meetings began with testimony from various internal and external opposition leaders. Such meetings helped foster a much closer understanding between these leaders and Canadian officials, including Clark. This understanding paid dividends for the ANC when it was able to persuade the CFMSA and Canada to maintain Commonwealth sanctions long after other Western governments began to lift theirs.[41] Moreover, the Canadian government, through the International Development Research Centre, became an important supporter of the development of policy positions and capacity by the ANC-aligned "Democratic Movement" in the 1990-94 transitional phase.[42] This leads to consideration of the role of Canadian aid in the run-up to the transition.

Aid

There were two faces to Canadian development assistance in the region that bore on its contribution to the struggle for change: an internal (South African) face and a regional (SADCC) face. Within South Africa, as noted above, much attention was focused on "positive measures" aimed at "reaching into South Africa to aid the victims and opponents of apartheid, to promote dialogue, and counteract South African censorship and propaganda." While some measures were in place throughout the period under review, the resources devoted to them increased significantly after 1987. This trend was at least partly stimulated by the government's need to provide a response to critics of its apparent "sanctions backsliding." In this pre-transition (pre-1990) phase much of this assistance was, in Linda Freeman's words, "dramatic and timely."[43] It included: a major program of support for education and skills training of disadvantaged South Africans; legal and humanitarian aid to political detainees and their families; assistance for small-scale community projects delivered through NGOs; labour education; and a fund supporting a Canadian "Action Plan to Counteract South African Sponsorship and Propaganda" (announced, amidst considerable controversy, at the Toronto meeting of the CFMSA in August 1988). Perhaps most creative was a dialogue fund that eventually amounted to some seven million dollars. Launched in August 1988, it was designed to offer "assistance to the alternative press; funding for events bringing together South Africans of different races to learn about each other and discuss a common future; support for human rights and professional organizations trying to break down the barriers of apartheid; and promotion of the idea of a non-racial future through the arts and popular culture."[44] By most accounts this relatively small fund was able to provide flexible and timely assistance facilitating the work, and occasionally survival, of key opponents of the regime while supporting creative initiatives that helped lay the groundwork for a non-racial future.

In short, Canada's "positive measures" (which persisted, in different forms, through the 1990-94 transition period) have been widely regarded as a useful contribution to the anti-apartheid cause. However, aside from the concern of anti-Apartheid activists in Canada that these measures were being advanced as camouflage for the government's failure to impose new sanctions, Canada's contributions inside South Africa were not particularly outstanding in comparative terms. The fact is that many governments, NGOs, and international organizations were pursuing similar programs of assistance in this period – often for similar reasons.[45] As Freeman shows, while support increased dramatically under Mulroney from about two million dollars in his first year in office to about eighteen million dollars in 1992-93, Canada "remained part of the pack" relative to other major Western donors.[46] It was, in other words, praiseworthy but not, on the whole, exceptional.

Similarly, aid to SADCC in the mid- and late-1980s was stable and fairly generous but not exceptionally so. Support for SADCC became another key test of Western governments' anti-apartheid credentials, given the organization's explicit goal of reducing dependence on South Africa and vulnerability to Pretoria's campaign of regional destabilization.[47] Canada made an early strategic decision that became important to the viability of SADCC when, in 1983, it decided to create a separate SADCC program within the Canadian International Development Agency (CIDA), making southern Africa an institutionalized "region of concentration." Thus, Canada (along with Sweden) was one of the first major donor countries to allocate resources, beyond pre-existing bilateral programs, to SADCC as a regional entity.[48] This decision was an important vote of confidence at a time when a number of other major donors (notably the United States, but also Germany and Japan) were treating it cautiously and sceptically. The decision preceded the election of the Mulroney government, however, so cannot be attributed to its new regional approach.

Quantitatively, Canadian aid to the SADCC region ranked between sixth and tenth in the SADCC donor "league table," placing it in the middle of this group. By contrast, Swedish aid to the region was substantially larger, generally placing it among the top couple of donors.[49] Once again, then, Canada's regional aid program was relatively strong but not extraordinary. It is interesting to note, therefore, that SADCC governments went out of their way to recognize Canada's contribution to the region in the late 1980s, when they asked Canadian representatives to "lead off" the annual SADCC Consultative Conference with donors in 1987 and 1988, and to close the 1989 conference.[50] This would seem to indicate the importance they placed on keeping Ottawa onside as the international momentum towards new pressure on South Africa stalled.

Security Assistance

The provision of "non-lethal" security assistance became a logical and symbolically important corollary to development assistance to the SADCC states. Crudely put, and ethical issues aside, it made little sense to pour money into the rehabilitation of transportation corridors through Mozambique, for example, if this newly rehabilitated infrastructure would immediately be sabotaged by South African-sponsored rebel forces. In the face of this logic the call for security assistance mounted, particularly in the Commonwealth context.[51]

On this issue, Canada and other Western "middle powers" such as Australia and Sweden remained reticent. This contrasted sharply with Britain's relatively early and generous response to such requests. Officials in External Affairs justified this squeamishness in loosely politico-cultural terms: "The Canadian people and Cabinet" were "very worried" about Canada getting involved in security assistance.[52] They seemed to feel that security assistance would offend Canadians' deeply held aversion to the use of violence in settling political disputes. Finally, in September 1988, the government almost surreptitiously announced a two-million-dollar-per-year program of security assistance to be disbursed by CIDA for use in efforts to secure the Nacala and Limpopo railway lines in Mozambique. Shortly thereafter, it quietly trebled Military Training Assistance Program (MTAP) funding for southern African military personnel (see Table 12.1). These developments were, of course, welcome in southern Africa (Robert Mugabe was largely responsible for "breaking" and publicizing Canada's new contribution).[53] Nevertheless, these forms of assistance contrasted sharply with earlier Canadian forms, both in their minimalist quality and in their quiet introduction.

Summary: Assessing Canada's Anti-Apartheid Measures

It is not easy to assess the effects and effectiveness of Canada's various anti-apartheid measures. First, it is difficult to disentangle the role of external pressure and assistance from the more important role of resistance in South Africa itself. Nevertheless, it would be wrong to dismiss the influence of external actions, both in precipitating change and in helping to shape a moderate transition that, in the end, both avoided the bloody chaos many had feared and did not fundamentally threaten Western interests in southern Africa.[54] Whether or not such an outcome, with its relative inattention to apartheid's structural (socio-economic) legacies, serves the best long-term interests of the South African majority is less certain.

More difficult still is the task of situating Canada's significance in relation to the international (particularly Western) effort as a whole. Generally speaking, Canada's record placed it among the front rank of Western countries but only rarely and briefly at its forefront. Moreover, given the limited nature of Canada's links with South Africa and the wider southern African region, and the low profile of its policy in South Africa itself,[55] its overall policy effort is perhaps best characterized as generally constructive but marginal. Moreover, notwithstanding the obvious commitment of key individuals in the government, led by the prime minister himself, even at the height of Canadian engagement the government's approach was consistent with previous and subsequent instances of high profile foreign policy activism on specific "crusades."

More pointedly, any assessment of Canada's policy towards South Africa must hinge on the interpretation of its failure to fulfil the 1985 threat to impose comprehensive sanctions if there was no progress in dismantling apartheid. While it is entirely appropriate to hold any government accountable for its own public commitments, the key unanswered question is whether comprehensive sanctions were the best course of action. I would have two responses to this question. First, the government could have enforced its own sanctions more assiduously, as critics such as Freeman and Pratt carefully detail; moreover, there were almost certainly additional measures that could have been usefully adopted without significantly burdening Canadians. However, particularly with the benefit of hindsight, it also seems clear that partial (versus comprehensive) sanctions were the most appropriate weapon, since they brought enough additional pressure to bear (both materially and psychologically) to help induce change without causing excessive "collateral damage."[56] Therefore, while Canadian policy could have been tougher and more consistent, in the key area of sanctions its basic approach was ultimately the most appropriate one. However, the record as a whole clearly falls short of the exceptional leadership role so often ascribed to Conservative policy on this issue.

Accounting for the Myth of Exceptionalism
One final question remains: why has the myth of Canada's exceptional role on South Africa proven so resilient? Three possible explanations can be advanced. First, it can be argued that the political elite in the Commonwealth and in Canada put extraordinary weight on Mulroney's political courage in repeatedly confronting Thatcher over South Africa and in persisting with his advocacy of this issue at the G-7. Freeman notes the "solidarity and friendships" forged between Mulroney and colleagues such

as Zambia's Kenneth Kaunda and Zimbabwe's Mugabe in the heat of Commonwealth battle, which "took the Canadian government into the post-Apartheid era on a wave of goodwill."[57] Similarly, political colleagues in Canada well understood the courage it took for Mulroney to confront powerful peers whether or not they agreed with his stand. Political courage, in this view, slides easily if somewhat misleadingly into exceptional leadership.

Second, within External Affairs, interpretations of Canada's role were likely coloured by the extraordinary amount of energy and resources devoted to the South African issue – at least relative to what many in the department regarded as far more important priorities. According one participant, Clark "deliberately and systematically devoted an extraordinary amount of time" to this file, making the Southern Africa Task Force "an incredibly lucky unit" and the object of some resentment elsewhere in the department.[58] Thus, it is plausible that a self-justificatory dynamic took hold among the foreign policy professionals: if such extraordinary time and energy were being devoted to this issue, then how could Canada's role be other than extraordinary? It is likely that CIDA personnel engaged with southern Africa would have shared this perception.

Finally, both of these dynamics were embedded within a wider political cultural context: Canadians have generally wished to think of themselves as naturally "good international citizens," particularly on issues of peace and justice. Instances of high profile activism on ethical issues (e.g., peacekeeping, nuclear diplomacy, North-South mediation, landmines, and the International Criminal Court) are constructed as representative of Canada's "natural" vocation in world affairs. By contrast, the many instances in which ethical considerations have been overshadowed by calculations of narrower strategic and/or economic advantage (e.g., soft-pedalling human rights with strategically and/or economically important rights-abusive regimes) are conceived as aberrant. Moreover, the less admirable limitations and retreats surrounding many of the more positive instances of activism are often screened out in popular memory. The danger is that an accurate appraisal of the true strengths and limitations of any given attempt at influence may be occluded, and distorted policy expectations and prescriptions may result. South Africa may be viewed as a key instance of this tendency.

Conclusion

In the final analysis, the Conservative government made a modest but creditable contribution in the international campaign to promote change in apartheid South Africa. Moreover, key policy-makers, including Mulroney himself, displayed a deep personal commitment to the South African issue. However, this does not equate to an exceptional leadership role. To be a successful leader, Cooper, Higgott, and Nossal have argued, one must have a substantial number of willing followers.[59] Concomitantly, one should be able to clearly influence policy outcomes in a preferred direction. On both counts, the Mulroney government's claim to leadership with regard to South Africa is tenuous. Indeed, this case demonstrates the broader challenges of trying to pursue an activist leadership role on global issues, however desirable such a role may be. If Canada's contribution to the demise of apartheid and the transition to majority rule was marginal, even with the high level political will and the relatively generous human and financial resources that underpinned it, we should be under no illusions about the degree of effort and resources such attempts at influence are likely to require on other issues of global justice.

Notes

A French version of this chapter was published in *Études internationales* 31, 2 (juin 2000).

1 Linda Freeman, *The Ambiguous Champion: Canada and South Africa in the Trudeau and Mulroney Years* (Toronto: University of Toronto Press, 1997), 3.

2 Bernard Wood, "Canada and Southern Africa: A Return to Middle Power Activism," *The Round Table* 315 (1990): 280-90. Wood was an early participant in the development of Canada's southern African policy in the 1980s.

3 For example, in an op-ed piece about Commonwealth activism against Nigeria, Barbara McDougall noted that the Commonwealth "reached its zenith in its leadership against apartheid in South Africa, a historic achievement with which every Canadian is familiar. Forced to resign from the Commonwealth in large part because of the influence of Prime Minister John Diefenbaker, South Africa became a pariah nation ... Later, over the objections of British Prime Minister Margaret Thatcher, Prime Minister Brian Mulroney and External Affairs Minister Joe Clark prevailed upon the Commonwealth to introduce wide-ranging economic sanctions against South Africa, a move that once again pushed the rest of the world into taking action." See McDougall, "Why Keep the Commonwealth?" *Globe and Mail*, 14 November 1997.

4 Some scholars characterized the Canadian position as an "enlightened capitalist" one, seeking to save South Africa for the West before it was too late. See, for example, John Saul, "Militant Mulroney? The Tories and South Africa," paper delivered to the Canadian Association of African Studies, Queen's University, Kingston, May 1988.

5 Freeman, *Ambiguous Champion*, esp. chaps. 7-12; Renate Pratt, *In Good Faith: Canadian Churches against Apartheid* (Waterloo: Wilfrid Laurier University Press, 1997), chaps. 6, 8, and 9; also Kim Richard Nossal, *Rain Dancing: Sanctions in Canadian and Australian Foreign Policy* (Toronto: University of Toronto Press, 1994), 243-51.

6 Freeman, *Ambiguous Champion*, 19-29.

7 Wood, "Canada and Southern Africa," 286.

8 SADCC originally included Angola, Botswana, Lesotho, Malawi, Mozambique, Swaziland, Tanzania, Zambia, and Zimbabwe. It was later re-launched as the Southern African Development Community, with the inclusion of post-Apartheid South Africa and several other new members.

9 Clarence Redekop, "Canada and Southern Africa, 1946-75: The Political Economy of Foreign Policy" (PhD diss., University of Toronto, 1977), 782-88; Freeman, *Ambiguous Champion*, 43-79.

10 Freeman, *Ambiguous Champion*, 73-79.

11 David Black, "Australian, Canadian and Swedish Policies toward Southern Africa: A Comparative Study of 'Middle Power Internationalism'" (PhD diss., Dalhousie University,

1991), 255-64. For excellent discussions of the sanctions adopted and their limitations, see Pratt, *In Good Faith*, esp. 187-218; and Freeman, *Ambiguous Champion*, esp. 149-65.

12 External Affairs Canada, *Statements and Speeches*, No. 85/14, "Principles of UN Charter Signposts to Peace," United Nations General Assembly, New York, 23 October 1985.

13 Pratt, *In Good Faith*, 204.

14 Clark argued that voluntary sanctions symbolized the breadth of Canadian societal support for anti-apartheid measures and were therefore preferable to mandatory bans; critics argued that they were vulnerable to lax monitoring and abuse and were symptomatic of the government's questionable resolve.

15 Pratt, *In Good Faith*, 188.

16 Black, "Australian, Canadian and Swedish Policies," 262. For example, they excluded imports of strategic minerals used in making specialty steels in Canada and low-cost dissolving pulp used in the operations of a Cornwall textile mill, along with lucrative exports of sulphur primarily from Alberta. In fairness, all Western countries, even the Nordic countries, avoided such politically salient domestic costs. Moreover, since sustaining support for sanctions in the sanctioning state is a major challenge, avoiding such costs where possible is generally sensible policy. My thanks to Norrin Ripsman for this point.

17 Jon Harkness, "Marshall, Lerner and Botha: Canada's Economic Sanctions on South Africa," *Canadian Public Policy* 16 (1990): 155-60.

18 Freeman, *Ambiguous Champion*, esp. 221-26; and Pratt, *In Good Faith*, 272. The MINORCO take-over bid was ultimately unsuccessful.

19 External Affairs Canada, *Statements and Speeches*, 89/23, "Speech by Joe Clark to the Council on Foreign Relations," 28 September 1989 (emphasis in original).

20 Pratt, *In Good Faith*, 311-12; Black, "Australian, Canadian and Swedish Policies," 265; and Independent Group of Experts, *South Africa: The Sanctions Report* (London: Penguin Books for the Commonwealth Secretariat, 1989), 214.

21 J.H. Taylor has highlighted the latter explanation.

22 United Nations, *The United Nations and Apartheid, 1948-1994* (New York: UN Department of Public Information, 1994).

23 "The Commonwealth Accord on Southern Africa" (from the Nassau CHOGM), item 4.

24 Stephen Chan, *The Commonwealth in World Politics* (London: Lester Crook, 1988), 72.

25 Michael Valpy, "An Interview with Stephen Lewis," *Southern Africa Report* 4 (December 1988): 15. For context, see Freeman, *Ambiguous Champion*, 206-11.

26 Confidential interview, Department of External Affairs, 7 February 1990.

27 Lloyd John Chingambo and Stephen Chan, "Sanctions and South Africa, Strategies, Strangleholds, and Self-Consciousness," *Paradigms* 2 (Winter 1988-89): 112-32. Mulroney took the view that the Front Line States should not be expected to endanger themselves, rightly arguing that the West should bear primary responsibility for putting sanctions pressure on South Africa.

28 External Affairs Canada, *Statements and Speeches*, "Statement by Joe Clark at the Opening Session of the Commonwealth Foreign Ministers Meeting on Southern Africa," Toronto, 2 August 1988.

29 Freeman, *Ambiguous Champion*, 212-33; Pratt, *In Good Faith*, 291-336.

30 McDougall, "Why Keep the Commonwealth?"

31 Douglas Anglin, "Canada and Africa in the 1980s," in *Africa and the Great Powers*, ed. Olajide Aluko (Lanham, MD: University Press of America, 1987), 193.

32 John J. Kirton, "Introduction: the Significance of the Seven-Power Summit," in *The Seven Power Summit*, ed. Peter I. Hajnal (Millwood, NY: Kraus, 1989), xli; see also the "Chairman's Summary on Political Issues" from 1987 (352-53), 1988 (383), and 1989 (428).

33 Nossal, *Rain Dancing*, 250.

34 Freeman argues that the "collapse" began with Mulroney's rebuff at Venice. See Linda Freeman, "Leading from the Rear: Canada and South Africa, 1989," *Southern Africa Report* 5 (December 1989): 6.

35 Freeman, *Ambiguous Champion*, 280. For the unorthodox and admirable activities of Canadian embassy personnel in late-apartheid South Africa, see Heribert Adam and Kogila

Moodley, "The Background to Canada's Activist Policy Against Apartheid: Theoretical and Political Implications," *Journal of Commonwealth and Comparative Politics* 30 (November 1992): 305.

36 Pratt, *In Good Faith*, 344. Downgrading diplomatic relations may, in fact, impose costs in terms of progressive political function on the ground. See Janet L. Graham, "Small Mission in Hard Times: Lagos, 1996-97," in *Diplomatic Missions: The Ambassador in Canadian Foreign Policy*, ed. Robert Wolfe (Kingston: School of Policy Studies, Queen's University, 1998).

37 Black, "Australian, Canadian and Swedish Policies," chap. 8.

38 Linda Freeman, "Where's the Beef? Canada and South Africa, 1987," *Southern Africa Report* 3 (December 1987): 5.

39 Pratt, *In Good Faith*, 280-81; Freeman, *Ambiguous Champion*, 202-4.

40 External Affairs Canada, *Statement* 89/17, "Canada in the World," extracts of statements by Joe Clark to the House of Commons Standing Committee on External Affairs and International Trade, 11 May 1989, 2.

41 Freeman, *Ambiguous Champion*, 247-56.

42 For a critical interpretation, see Heribert Adam and Kogila Moodley, *Democratizing Southern Africa: Challenges for Canadian Policy* (Ottawa: Canadian Institute for International Peace and Security, 1992), esp. 332-43.

43 Freeman, *Ambiguous Champion*, 279, more generally 277-82.

44 Cited in Adam and Moodley, *Democratizing Southern Africa*, 81. For their generally positive assessment of the Dialogue Fund, see ibid., 80-88.

45 Martin Holland, "The Other Side of Sanctions: Positive Initiatives for Southern Africa," *Journal of Modern African Studies* 26 (1988): 201.

46 Freeman, *Ambiguous Champion*, 277 and 282.

47 Destabilization was concentrated in Mozambique and Angola. See John Daniel, "The Truth about the Region," *Southern Africa Report* 14 (August 1999).

48 CIDA, "SADCC CIDA Program Update" (Hull: CIDA, 1990), 20; interview with Douglas Anglin, 24 March 1988.

49 Black, "Australian, Canadian and Swedish Policies," 328.

50 Interview with CIDA official, Hull, 10 August 1989.

51 Black, "Australian, Canadian and Swedish Policies," 287.

52 Interview, March 1988.

53 Pratt, *In Good Faith*, 308-9.

54 David Black, "The Long and Winding Road: International Norms and Domestic Political Change in South Africa," in *The Power of Human Rights: International Norms and Domestic Change*, ed. Thomas Risse, S. Ropp, and Kathryn Sikkink (Cambridge: Cambridge University Press, 1999); and Neta Crawford and Audie Klotz, eds., *How Sanctions Work: Lessons from South Africa* (London: Macmillan, 1999).

55 Adam and Moodley, *Democratizing Southern Africa*, chap. 6.

56 See the views of Tom Lodge, as discussed in Neta C. Crawford, "Trump Card or Theatre: An Introduction to Two Sanctions Debates," in Crawford and Klotz, *How Sanctions Work*, 17-18.

57 Freeman, *Ambiguous Champion*, 210.

58 Interview, Ottawa, February 1990.

59 Andrew F. Cooper, Richard A. Higgott, and Kim Richard Nossal, *Relocating Middle Powers: Australia and Canada in a Changing World Order* (Vancouver: UBC Press, 1993), 116-43.

13
Liberal Internationalism for Conservatives: The Good Governance Initiative
Paul Gecelovsky and Tom Keating

In the foreign policy white paper issued by the Liberal government in 1995, much attention was called to the need for Canada's external policy to reflect and promote Canadian values such as democracy, the rule of law, and human rights. The implication was that this would mark a departure from past practice – one that would distinguish the Liberals from their Conservative predecessors and chart a new course in Canadian foreign policy. The Liberals were a little late. The course had already been set by the Conservatives under Brian Mulroney's leadership, and it was a radically different course than Canadians had travelled in the past. The most dramatic change in policy had occurred in 1990 with the adoption of the values of good governance as a foreign policy priority.

That values should play a role in Canada's involvement in international politics was not a particularly revolutionary development. Foreign policy has always been seen as a reflection of Canadian values, or at least of the values held by those involved in such policy. As Louis St. Laurent, then secretary of state for external affairs, proclaimed in his Gray Foundation Lecture of 1947: "No foreign policy is consistent nor coherent over a period of years unless it is based upon some conception of human values." Foreign policy, while in practice likely "a poor approximation of [the] ideals upon which it may be based," nonetheless has been shaped in part by these values. This has been a consistent aspect of foreign policy, and its importance has been frequently noted. "There is ... a close link between domestic social values and the ethical component of foreign policy. If Canada's liberal humanitarian values are not also reflected in Canada's foreign policy, then popular attachment to them domestically will likely itself decline."[1] What distinguishes this more traditional view of the role of values in foreign policy from that adopted by the Mulroney government in the early 1990s is the belief that these values should be adopted by other political communities around the globe and be used by multilateral associations in assessing the credentials of member governments.

In addition, the adoption of the good governance policy suggested a shift in the government's view of the instruments to be used to promote these values. Canada's traditional approach to such issues in the international realm has been to give priority to peace and order. To the extent that policy-makers have been concerned with good governance, such concerns have been limited to governance at the level of international society or to the setting of standards to which other governments and societies might aspire. Moreover, peace and order were seen to rest as much on respect for state sovereignty and principles of non-intervention as they did on respect for human rights and democratic practices.[2] There were, of course, some apparent exceptions to this practice, such as the government's initial resistance to the admission of non-democratic states into the North Atlantic Treaty Organization (NATO) in the early 1950s and its opposition to South Africa's readmission to the Commonwealth in 1961. For the most part, however, foreign policy reflected a commitment to state sovereignty and a willingness to accept, if not respect, different values and traditions, and different state practices. It also supported the view that interventions, for whatever reasons, constituted violations of international order and should not be condoned. Under the Mulroney government these concerns were set aside as it gave both rhetorical and material support to the promotion of good governance around the globe.

In 1989, the Mulroney government embraced this more ideological and interventionist approach to foreign policy. In charting this new course the Conservatives were, in part, borrowing themes and practices that had been adopted elsewhere and that reflected significant changes in the world at large. There was, however, much in the new policy that was neither borrowed nor reactive but, rather, that reflected the ideas, personalities, and politics of Mulroney and his supporters. There was, in other words, much in the government's good governance policy that was unique; thus, we argue that the Conservatives were the architects of a new foreign policy.

We review the Conservative decision to adopt "good governance" as a policy priority after the 1988 federal election, and we examine the sources of this policy, arguing that it marked a significant shift in the content of Canadian foreign policy. The primary objective here will not be an assessment of the policy's effectiveness or of its long-term influence (though this appears to have been significant). Furthermore, a detailed account of the various mechanisms by which the policy has been implemented lies beyond the scope of this chapter. What we attempt to do is to discern the nature of the shift in policy, identify the primary factors that influenced this change, and discuss some of the implications for Canada's foreign policy in the early 1990s. In our view, the good governance policy stands as one of the distinguishing features of the Conservative government's foreign policy record.

The Mulroney Shift

The initial foreign policy statement issued by the Mulroney government, "Competitiveness and Security," gave little indication that the government would radically alter Canada's international human rights policy from the approach followed by the Trudeau government.[3] With the publication of three documents in 1986 and 1987, the Mulroney government elevated the salience of human rights considerations to a "basic principle," or a "fundamental, integral part" of Canada's foreign policy.[4] Several initiatives were taken to demonstrate the government's commitment to enhancing the place of human rights in Canadian foreign policy, including, inter alia, linking levels of official development assistance (ODA) with a state's human rights record, implementing a training program for Department of External Affairs (DEA) and Canadian International Development Agency (CIDA) officials, creating a human rights unit within CIDA, and developing a manual for human rights reporting. The latter would be used at posts abroad in order to facilitate the preparation of annual reports of the human rights records of all states receiving Canadian aid.

After the initial flurry of activity in 1986-87, human rights concerns, according to Robert M. Campbell and Leslie A. Pal, "languished in a rhetorical fog."[5] Three speeches made by Mulroney in autumn 1991 at Stanford University; at the Commonwealth Heads of Government Meeting (CHOGM) in Harare, Zimbabwe; and at the summit of la Francophonie in Paris, respectively, focused attention on human rights.[6] Along with the reassertion of human rights as an issue of importance to Canada, there was a marked change in the perception of the principle of national sovereignty and its corollary, non-intervention, as a limiting factor in pursuing relations with other states. Mulroney, in his Stanford speech, asserted that a "rethinking" of the principle of national sovereignty had to be undertaken because "problems respect no borders" and because Canada recognized that there are "certain fundamental rights that all people possess – and that, sometimes, the international community must act to defend them."[7] This view was later echoed by Barbara McDougall when she wrote that a "significant" and "irreversible erosion of national sovereignty" had occurred and that for Canada to "remain indifferent to what happens inside other countries" was "absolutely wrong."[8] In adopting this "new look" the Canadian government became an active supporter of interventionist measures in response to what were formerly considered to be the domestic affairs of other states.[9]

Providing content to the "certain fundamental rights" of which Mulroney spoke was the concept of "good governance." An indication of the importance attached to good governance was its inclusion as one of the three "key priorities" in the policy paper released in December 1991 – *Foreign Policy Themes and Priorities*.[10] Included within its ambit was respect for human rights, democratic development, probity in government, priority for basic social programs, poverty alleviation, acceptable levels of defence spending, and the development of market-based economies.

In sum, the adumbration of the good governance policy moved Canadian policy beyond previous expressions of interest in human rights issues in that it focused more directly on how other states governed their societies and economies and asserted both the right and responsibility of external agents to intervene to protect or restore specific political and economic practices. Good governance combined neoliberal economics with liberal democratic politics, resulting in a single development framework. Evidence of this shift is provided by the more interventionist course pursued in response to crises in Haiti and the former Yugoslavia as well as by the adoption of measures in support of democracy in the OAS (see Gordon Mace, Chapter 10; David Black, Chapter 12). The next section examines the main influences that led to this shift in policy.

Identifying the Sources of Good Governance

The good governance policy of the Mulroney government evolved over time. Its origins can be traced to numerous factors both outside and inside Canada. There were a number of critical external developments that eased the way for political leaders in Canada to raise the banner of good governance and encouraged an emphasis on democratic rights and procedures. Challenges to traditional international norms of state sovereignty and non-intervention provided an opportunity for the government to recommend more intrusive measures in support of such practices. Perhaps most important was the change in the bipolar rivalry between the United States and the Soviet Union.

The end of the Cold War was, in part, both a source and a reflection of a broader trend towards democratization in many parts of the world. One of the earliest and most pervasive "lessons" learned from the collapse of communism was the vitality and value of democratic regimes. The democratic peace thesis quickly gained currency in academic and government circles and had a significant influence on many of the latter as well as on certain international institutions. The Mulroney government caught this democratic wave and rode it with a great deal of vigour and persistence. While not alone in doing so, it was among the first and most vocal proponents of this thesis.

Adding a sense of legitimacy to the policies of Western states was the success of indigenous democracy movements in various parts of Africa, Asia, and Latin America during the late 1980s and early 1990s. Transitions to more democratic forms of government had occurred in states such as Benin, El Salvador, Guatemala, Guyana, Mali, the Philippines, South Korea,

Taiwan, and Zambia. By adopting good governance, Western governments were "supporting genuinely popular and intellectual demands" in those states that were swept up in the democratic movement.[11]

The collapse of communism in eastern Europe and the Soviet Union provided the initial opportunity for Western governments to assert themselves unencumbered by competitors. No longer was the threat of "losing" a state to the Soviet Union and its allies an overriding consideration. As Robert Jackson describes it, "the end of the Cold War has increased the international freedom of western democracies to place new conditions of their own choosing on non-western authoritarian states which are in no position to bargain."[12] In this vein governments began to attach "political conditionality" to their relations with non-Western states. Gillies defines political conditionality as "legitimate intervention by aid donors in the domestic affairs of borrowing countries in order to alter the political environment in ways that will sustain human as well as economic development."[13] As this practice increased, whether recipients and donors could agree on the meaning of legitimate intervention was a relevant but untested premise. The use of "increased conditionality has been a striking feature of North-South relations, particularly those involving Sub-Saharan Africa, since the end of the Cold War."[14]

Along with these developments, a number of countries began to look upon the promotion of human rights and democratic development as important foreign policy objectives. In the United States, the US Agency for International Development launched a "democracy initiative" in the early 1990s and saw its budget rise dramatically.[15] In Britain, those states that made changes towards increased "pluralism, public accountability, respect for the rule of law, human rights, and market principles" were to be "encouraged" while those that failed to make these alterations were not to be supported in their "folly."[16] The governments of France, Germany, and the Nordic countries were also active in promoting democratic development and human rights in their foreign policies.

Multilateral organizations such as the World Bank and the Organisation for Economic Co-operation and Development (OECD) also began adopting good governance as a policy objective. It was in the World Bank's 1989 report on the conditions in Sub-Saharan Africa that the concept of good governance made its first appearance. The report argued that Africa's development problems derived from a "crisis of governance"; that is, a failure in the "exercise of political power to manage a nation's affairs." The key to development was for those states who had good governance to assist those that did not. To help states in their transition, in its 1991 report, the Development Assistance Committee of the OECD recommended the inclusion of "support for participatory and democratic development" as an "essential" component of a state's aid policy.[17]

Underlying the adoption of good governance policies by both multilateral organizations and Western states was a general acceptance of a "new orthodoxy" in which the economic reforms called for by structural adjustment programs (SAPs) were married to political reforms along the lines of Western-style democracy.[18] SAPs had been in place since the late 1970s, and, within a decade, the conditions imposed by them had become widely adopted as standard requirements for receiving funding from both multilateral organizations and states. Most often these conditions called for the privatization of state-owned industries, the deregulation of markets, a reduction in government spending, and a devaluation of exchange rates. What was new in the late 1980s and early 1990s was the addition of political considerations and government practices as part of this development discourse. Included in the range of political reforms viewed as necessary were some or all of the following: the adoption of rule of law, the creation of representative institutions, accountable and responsible public administration, and respect for human rights. The addition of political conditions to SAPs marked a change in development thinking in that political reform was no longer viewed as a product of economic development but, rather, was now viewed as a condition of receiving it. Effective economic reforms and full participation in the global market necessitated the adoption of liberal democratic institutions and practices. Thus, in order to establish an environment conducive to the market, both economic and political reforms were necessary. These ideas, and the consensus that supported them in the early 1990s, struck a responsive chord with the Conservative government in Ottawa.

Within this international context, Canadian foreign policy-makers saw both the need and the opportunity to move in the same direction. The need reflected an interest in maintaining credibility with like-minded states and with principal allies such as the United States. It also reflected an interest in providing support for those states that were undergoing the transition to democratic forms of government. More important, this new international focus was consistent with the ideology and policies of the domestic economic program developed by Michael Wilson when he was minister of finance – a program that the Mulroney government had been following since it took office in 1984. Finally, this provided an opportunity for policy-makers to define a new international role for Canadian foreign policy in the emerging post-Cold War system, especially in those institutions in which Canada was an important member, such as the Commonwealth, la Francophonie, and the Organization of American States (OAS).

A combination of developments and pressures within Canada must also be recognized as a significant factor in the government's support for more intrusive international regimes to promote good governance. Within

Canada, the role of the prime minister was critically important in accounting for the emergence of good governance. Mulroney's influence can be seen in three areas. First was his involvement in summit diplomacy, especially at the CHOGM meeting in Harare in 1991, where good governance principles were adopted by the Commonwealth. Mulroney had established his Commonwealth credentials over the South Africa issue at previous CHOGMs and appears to have used these diplomatic credits to win support for the Harare Declaration.

Second, the prime minister took a direct and sustained interest in two international crises that were used to validate important aspects of the good governance initiative. In response to the break-up of the former Yugoslavia, Mulroney was the first international leader to set aside considerations of state sovereignty and call for outside intervention under the auspices of the United Nations. He was also the first leader to take up the cause of democracy in Haiti following the coup d'état that ousted democratically elected president Jean-Bertrand Aristide. While one could identify ulterior motives in both of these cases, Mulroney's response did lend support to the good governance policy and demonstrated the strength of his convictions.

Third, Mulroney was able to support the good governance policy through his powers of appointment. Through a number of critical appointments, he was able to create a coalition in key foreign policy decision-making positions that was in agreement with his approach. Barbara McDougall replaced Clark as secretary of state for external affairs; Michael Wilson replaced John Crosbie as minister of international trade; Marcel Massé replaced Margaret Catley-Carlson as president of CIDA; and de Montigny Marchand replaced J.H. (Si) Taylor as under-secretary of state for external affairs. These changes in personnel can all be viewed, in part, as part of the process of supporting the good governance policy. It is interesting to note that only Monique Landry, minister for external relations and la Francophonie, remained in her position throughout this time. In addition to these changes, the Prime Minister's Office (PMO) assumed a greater role in setting the direction of Canadian foreign policy.

The shuffle of Clark from External Affairs was an indication of Mulroney's increasing dissatisfaction with the direction of Canada's foreign policy. Disagreements over the appropriate measures for Canada to pursue affected the relationship between Mulroney and Clark, with the latter tending to be more cautious than the former. Informing Clark's more cautious approach to foreign policy was a more traditional view of the relationship between the principles of state sovereignty and non-intervention.[19]

Once Clark had been replaced by McDougall, Mulroney was no longer constrained by what one Soviet diplomat called Clark's "rusty old thinking."[20] McDougall had little interest in, or knowledge of, foreign affairs.

She was, as one External Affairs official opined to the *Globe and Mail* at the time, "basically biding her time" as she was "not interested in foreign affairs," had "no intuition into it," and "no particular experience."[21] Further, Clark's position as the "lead minister" within the triad of ministers in the foreign affairs portfolio was assumed not by McDougall but by Wilson. Having held the finance portfolio from 1984 to 1991, and having a close rapport with Mulroney, Wilson was regarded as the more senior and powerful minister. McDougall had served as a junior minister – as minister of state for privatization and minister responsible for the status of women – in the Department of Finance under Wilson. Because during his tenure as finance minister he had had responsibility for Canada's involvement with both the International Monetary Fund (IMF) and the World Bank, Wilson also had a good deal of experience with the conditionality debates taking place within those institutions. Moreover, he was also the minister of industry, science and technology and, thus, had full control over Canada's trade policy (both domestically and internationally). With Wilson taking control of trade and Landry having responsibility for aid, McDougall was searching for some niche within which to make her mark. Soon after assuming the portfolio, she began echoing the prime minister's support of good governance initiatives. Whether this support was born out of conviction or convenience is a matter of debate. Significantly, however, it marked a dramatic shift from the more cautious line that Clark had attempted to pursue.

The return of Marcel Massé to the presidency of CIDA in September 1989 also suggests the prime minister's interest in a more assertive foreign policy. Massé had been the Canadian executive director to the IMF prior to rejoining CIDA (he had been president of CIDA from 1980 to 1982), and it was his experience at the IMF, in particular his work on the economic restructuring of Guyana, that "crystallize[d] many of his ideas" regarding economic development policy. Massé returned to Ottawa with a "fervour" for SAPs, and he was not long at CIDA before Canada was actively supporting these measures. In a speech given in November 1989, he noted that "structural adjustment figures among the priorities for Canadian development assistance" and that SAPs were becoming "more relevant with each day that passes." Later, in March 1991, a staff memo outlined the policy direction that CIDA was to follow under Massé's leadership. It involved "five pillars" of "sustainable development," including: cultural, economic, environmental, political, and social.[22] The similarities between "sustainable development" and "good governance" are readily apparent.

Finally, within External Affairs, the October 1989 replacement of Si Taylor with de Montigny Marchand as deputy minister occurred, in part, because Mulroney believed that the department had "not reacted quickly or imaginatively" to the changes then occurring in the Soviet Union, eastern

Europe, the Middle East, and South Africa. Marchand was to "shake up" DEA in an effort to "provide more innovative foreign policy initiatives."[23]

The influence of members of Parliament can also be cited as an important source of support for a change in policy. In part, the increased attention given to human rights and democratic development was a reaction both to external events and to pressures from domestic constituents and NGOs. Parliament and individual MPs did, however, provide an important channel for these concerns, and, specifically, two parliamentary committees in the mid-1980s served to focus attention on these matters and to press the government to become more assertive. The creation of a subcommittee on international human rights in September 1989 also worked to garner greater awareness of human rights issues within Parliament and Canadian society at large. One of the first indications (outside of its work against apartheid) of the Mulroney government's growing interest in advancing the good governance policy was the establishment of the International Centre for Human Rights and Democratic Development in 1989. The centre was initially recommended in 1985 by the Joint Parliamentary Committee on Canada's International Relations. It was later endorsed by the Winegard Committee's report on development assistance, which was submitted in May 1987.[24]

The centre was designed to "initiate, encourage and support cooperation between Canada and other countries in the promotion, development and strengthening of institutions and programs that give effect to the rights and freedoms enshrined in the International Bill of Rights."[25] The centre received support from the NGO community and from parliamentarians. The bill establishing the centre proceeded through Parliament with little opposition. The primary concern in debates was the significance of the reference to democratic development. Some MPs, noting that the original report had recommended that the centre's title refer to "Institutional Development,"[26] expressed concerns over the emphasis to be given to democracy. Jean-Robert Gauthier claimed that "to promote American or Canadian-style democracy in developing countries is not necessarily a good thing right away," and he was concerned lest Canadians "be accused of imperialism." Howard McCurdy objected to the lack of a clearer definition of democracy, noting that "there are those, particularly to the south of us, who consider that the only form of democracy which has any merit is that which ensures that there will be a totally free enterprise system with no state intervention." Marcel Prud'homme was more critical: "It is the ultimate in arrogance to believe that our kind of system is the kind that applies to every country in the world. True democracy does not necessarily mean for all the world to follow our kind of system and government. Of course we may by having a real democracy in Canada show by example, but we must not be arrogant and tell others that what we do they do."[27] Despite these concerns, the centre began operating in October 1990, with Ed Broadbent, a former leader of the federal New Democratic Party, acting as its first president.[28] The establishment of the centre was both a reflection of the growing demands on the government for greater activity in this area and a new source of pressure for continued action in the future. The nature of the centre and its arm's-length relationship with the government also enabled it to intervene in areas where it might be more difficult for government officials to act. Perhaps most important, the centre demonstrated the government's interest in institutionalizing crucial aspects of the good governance policy within Canadian society.

Unlike previous governments, the Mulroney government, with its good governance policy, demonstrated that it was willing to incorporate measures being advocated by various Canadian NGOs. Certainly many aspects of the policy were closely related to demands emanating from domestic groups for more attention to matters of human rights, development of civil society, and public participation in decision-making abroad. While pressures for a greater concern for human rights and a more humanitarian foreign policy had been emanating from various sectors for a number of years, these converged with other interests (along with the aforementioned external developments in the late 1980s and early 1990s) to precipitate a shift in policy. The domestic context for such a change had been created, in part, by the extensive debate over constitutional reform, especially as this involved debates over a Canadian charter of rights and freedoms. While the Charter of Rights and Freedoms has itself been viewed as a reaction to international developments, it is not unreasonable to assume that it has also had some influence on Canadians' views of the rights situation abroad.[29] At the very least the increased attention paid to human rights issues within Canada made Canadians more rights conscious than they had been previously.

Domestic groups had long been active in promoting a more human rights-oriented foreign policy for Canada.[30] Beginning with the release of a "black paper" in response to the Trudeau foreign policy review, Canadian churches and other NGOs persistently attempted to pressure foreign policy and development assistance policy to take greater account of the violations of human rights around the world. During this period much of the attention of these groups focused on South Africa, the Soviet Union, eastern Europe, and Central America. The volume and frequency of these representations intensified throughout the 1970s and into the 1980s. Representations to the government repeatedly demonstrated the growing political significance of these interests.

Despite their alleged marginalization from foreign policy discussions, these interests came to play a more significant role in the policy-making process under the Mulroney government than they had during previous periods. This was especially evident in a series of parliamentary commit-tees that made an appearance in the 1980s. Canadian NGOs also played a significant role, again with government support, on the international stage in their activities at the United Nations human rights conference in Vienna in 1993. And, despite frequent expressions of frustration at their limited involvement in the formulation of policy, these groups have, as a result of these changes, become an established part of the policy-making process in Canada.[31]

Finally, the articulation of good governance as a "key priority" for Canadian foreign policy represented a way of addressing some of the per-sistent shortcomings in the Mulroney government's international human rights policy. After the initial flurry of activity in 1986-87, Mulroney's rhetorical commitments were not followed through in practice. Various societal groups were becoming more aware of the gap between rhetoric and action in Canada's international human rights policy. Pressure was also maintained through interest groups and individuals making presen-tations to parliamentary committees. Particularly egregious violations of human rights, such as the continued practice of apartheid in South Africa, the Tiananmen Square massacre in China, and the Dili massacre in Indonesia, helped to focus and sustain some pressure on the government to maintain commitments to further human rights internationally.

The adoption of the good governance policy can be regarded, in part, as a way around some of these problems. First, good governance was an active policy in that it attempted to alter the domestic economic and political structures and practices of other governments. Second, it could be argued that almost any Canadian action, or non-action, taken in support of good governance was in conformity with that policy framework. Finally, the various measures designed to implement the good governance policy within CIDA and through the creation of the ICHRDD demonstrated, at some level, the government's commitment to supporting the policy.

Conclusion

The Mulroney government's decision to adopt a policy of good gover-nance can be explained as a result of the convergence of a number of developments and pressures emanating from both the external and the domestic environments. These factors, when combined with the personal inclinations of the prime minister, encouraged a policy that, in substantial terms, marked a significant change from past practice. While the multi-lateralist tactics used by the government to promote the good governance policy were consistent with those employed by previous governments, what was most striking about this policy and its implementation was its substantive content. The policy supported initiatives that were both more interventionist and more substantially demanding (at least rhetorically) than were the policies of previous Canadian governments. Good governance marked a dramatic shift towards the aggressive promotion of human rights, democratization, and market economies abroad.

The foreign policy pursuits of the Conservative government of Brian Mulroney have been frequently criticized as little more than a mirror image of American interests and American policy. From issues as diverse as the Gulf War to a North American trade community, many observers argued that there was little variation between Washington and Ottawa as the two governments moved through the declining years of the Cold War and into the emerging, and self-proclaimed, New World Order. While there are no shortage of examples of issues on which the two governments shared similar policies, perhaps one of the most striking illustrations of a shift towards a more American-type foreign policy orientation was in the area of what came to be referred to as good governance. Yet, what is perhaps most interesting about this policy is that, while it certainly bore a resemblance to American policy, much of it was home-grown. The good governance policy found widespread support in Canada, including many who usually did not find themselves aligned with American global policy. And while it is likely arguable that the good governance policy was supportive of American objectives and thus contributed to the persistence of an American-dominated global order, its sources were not only local in origin, but they also appear to have been at least initially (and primarily) non-material. In other words, the adoption and promotion of the good governance policy was designed by Canadians with the support of Canadians to recast others in the mould of "Canadian values"; that is, liberal internationalism, Conservative-style.

Notes

1 Cranford Pratt, "Canada's Development Assistance: Some Lessons from the Last Review," *International Journal* 49 (Winter 1993-94): 121.
2 Kim Richard Nossal, "Cabin'd, Cribb'd, Confin'd? Canada's Interest in Human Rights," in *Human Rights in Canadian Foreign Policy*, ed. Robert O. Matthews and Cranford Pratt (Kingston and Montreal: McGill-Queen's University Press, 1988), 46-58.
3 T.A. Keenleyside and Patricia Taylor, "The Impact of Human Rights Violations on the Conduct of Canadian Bilateral Relations: A Contemporary Dilemma," *Behind the Headlines* 42 (Winter 1984).
4 Department of External Affairs, *Canada's International Relations: Response of the Government of Canada to the Report of the Special Joint Committee of the Senate and the House of Commons* (Ottawa: Supply and Services Canada, 1986), 23-25; Canadian International Development Agency, *Canadian International Development Assistance: To Benefit A Better World, Response of the Government of Canada to the Report of the Standing Committee on External Affairs and International Trade* (Ottawa: Supply and Services Canada, 1987), 49-56; and CIDA, *Sharing Our Future: Canadian International Development Assistance* (Ottawa: Supply and Services Canada, 1987), 31-32.
5 Robert M. Campbell and Leslie A. Pal, "A World of Difference? Human Rights in Canadian Foreign Policy," in *The Real Worlds of Canadian Politics*, 3rd ed., ed. Robert M. Campbell and Leslie A. Pal (Peterborough: Broadview, 1994), 262, 237.

6   Office of the Prime Minister, "On the Occasion of the Centennial Anniversary Convocation," Stanford University, 29 September 1991; Office of the Prime Minister, "Global Report: World Political Overview," Commonwealth Heads of Government Meeting, Harare, Zimbabwe, 16 October 1991.

7   PMO, "Centennial Anniversary Convocation," Stanford University, 29 September 1991.

8   Barbara McDougall, "Canada and the New Internationalism," *Canadian Foreign Policy* 1, 1 (Winter 1992-93): 1; Department of External Affairs and International Trade, "Fourth Rene Cassin Lectureship in Human Rights," McGill University, 19 March 1992, 3.

9   Tom Keating and Nicholas Gammer, "The 'New Look' in Canada's Foreign Policy," *International Journal* 48 (Autumn 1993): 720-48.

10 Department of External Affairs and International Trade, *Foreign Policy Themes and Priorities: 1991-92 Update* (Ottawa: Policy Planning Staff, December 1991), 16.

11 Adrian Leftwich, "Governance, Democracy, and Development in the Third World," *Third World Quarterly* 14, 3 (1993): 610.

12 Robert H. Jackson, "Morality, Democracy and Foreign Policy," in *Canada Among Nations, 1995: Democracy and Foreign Policy*, ed. Maxwell A. Cameron and Maureen Appel Molot (Ottawa: Carleton University Press, 1995), 52.

13 David Gillies, *Between Principle and Practice: Human Rights in North-South Relations* (Montreal and Kingston: McGill-Queen's University Press, 1996), 22.

14 Jackson, "Morality, Democracy and Foreign Policy," 53.

15 Larry Diamond, *Promoting Democracy in the 1990s*, A report to the Carnegie Commission on Preventing Deadly Conflict (New York: Carnegie Corporation, 1995). See also United States Agency for International Development, *Democracy and Governance Policy Paper* (Washington: US Government Printing Ofice, November 1991).

16 Gillies, *Between Principle and Practice*, 26.

17 Leftwich, "Governance, Democracy and Development," 610.

18 Gerald J. Schmitz, "Human Rights, Democratization, and International Conflict," in *Canada Among Nations, 1992-1993: A New World Order?*, ed. Fen Osler Hampson and Christopher J. Maule (Ottawa: Carleton University Press, 1993), 243.

19 Department of External Affairs and International Trade, "Human Rights and Democratic Development," *Statement* 90/66, 11 November 1990.

20 This was how the then minister-counsellor at the Soviet embassy in Ottawa characterized a speech delivered by Clark in January 1989 on Canada-Soviet relations. See *Toronto Star*, 14 January 1989.

21 *Globe and Mail*, 18 October 1991.

22 Marcia M. Burdette, "Structural Adjustment and Canadian Aid Policy," in Pratt, *Canadian International Development Assistance Policies*, 221; David R. Morrison, *Aid and Ebb Tide: A History of CIDA and Canadian Development Assistance* (Waterloo: Wilfrid Laurier University Press, 1998).

23 *Globe and Mail*, 19 October 1989; see also *Financial Post*, 13 March 1989.

24 *For Whose Benefit? Report of Standing Committee of External Affairs and International Trade on Canada's Official Development Assistance Policies and Programs*, Chairman William Winegard, (Ottawa: Supply and Services Canada, May 1987). The government's response can be found in CIDA, *To Benefit a Better World*.

25 Canada, Parliament, House of Commons, Bill C-147: An Act to Establish the International Centre for Human Rights and Democratic Development, 13 September 1988.

26 Gisele Cote-Harper and John Courtney, "Report to the Right Honourable Joe Clark and the Honourable Monique Landry: International Cooperation for the Development of Human Rights and Democratic Institutions," mimeo, 30 June 1987.

27 House of Commons, *Debates*, 13 September 1988, 19181, 19180; 30 September, 1988, 19837.

28 For early assessments, see Andres Perez, "The International Centre for Human Rights and Democratic Development: A New Approach to Politics and Democracy in Developing Countries?" *Canadian Journal of Development Studies* 13, 1 (1992): 91-102; David Gillies and Marie Cocking, "The Centre for Human Rights: A Distinctive Vision," *International Perspectives* 19, 3 (March 1990): 36.

29 Michael Mandel, *The Charter of Rights and the Legalization of Politics in Canada* (Toronto: Thompson Educational Publishing, 1994); Alan C. Cairns, *Charter versus Federalism* (Montreal and Kingston: McGill-Queen's University Press, 1992), esp. 11-32.

30 For example, Robert O. Matthews, "The Christian Churches and Foreign Policy: An Assessment," in *Canadian Churches and Foreign Policy*, ed. Bonnie Greene (Toronto: James Lorimer, 1990), 161-79.

31 It must, of course, be reiterated that participation does not imply either influence or satisfaction on the part of any of the parties involved. For discussions of the role of domestic groups in foreign policy-making, see Cranford Pratt, "Dominant Class Theory and Canadian Foreign Policy: The Case of the Counter-consensus," *International Journal* 39 (Winter 1993-94): 99-135; and Tim Draimin and Betty Plewes, "Civil Society and the Democratization of Foreign Policy," in *Canada Among Nations 1995: Democracy and Foreign Policy*, ed. Maxwell Cameron and Maureen Appel Molot (Ottawa: Carleton University Press, 1995), 63-82.

Part 3
The Policy-Making Process

14

The Conservatives and Foreign Policy-Making: A Foreign Service View

J.H. Taylor

An illustrious British master of Tory foreign policy, Lord Salisbury, is supposed to have said that "British policy is to drift lazily downstream, occasionally putting out a boathook to avoid a collision."[1] I want to argue in this chapter that such aristocratic languor was not for Canadian Conservatives during the Mulroney era. Both the prime minister, Brian Mulroney, and his secretary of state for external affairs, Joe Clark, believed in setting objectives and pursuing an activist foreign policy. If the other chapters in this book provide academic perspectives, then my purpose in this chapter, as the title suggests, is to provide a foreign service view. I worked for the Mulroney government for nine years – five abroad and four in Ottawa. When the Conservatives came to power in 1984, I was a career foreign service officer with over thirty years experience, holding the appointment of Canada's ambassador to the North Atlantic Treaty Organization (NATO) in Brussels. In the summer of 1985, I was brought back to Ottawa as under-secretary of state for external affairs (in the fall of 1993, the position was renamed deputy minister of foreign affairs). In December 1989, I was appointed ambassador to Japan and served in Tokyo until I retired in 1993. When I speak of events between 1985 and 1989, therefore, I am speaking as someone who was in touch with what was happening as a senior official in Ottawa. When I speak of earlier or later events, I am speaking from the perspective of someone serving abroad.

During forty years in the foreign service, I kept no diaries, copies of official papers I had drafted, or any other official papers, for to do so was officially forbidden. So I write from memory, and I recognize that memory is notoriously inaccurate. People exaggerate the importance of the part they played in events, or, forgetting that "qui s'excuse, s'accuse," they seek to justify what they did. Readers will no doubt be on the watch for such tendencies on my part, as I am myself.

In assessing the Mulroney government's record, it is fairly easy for me to be non-partisan. This is the natural perspective of career public servants.

We were taught from the beginning that the public service was non-partisan. Indeed in my early years in the foreign service, civilians serving abroad did not even have the right to vote. By the time the right to vote was conceded, many of us had either lost the habit or had never acquired it; for my part, I chose not to exercise the right to vote until I retired. Perhaps this was a cranky and eccentric attitude, but I stuck to it.

To be non-partisan is also easy because Canada's foreign policy is so often bipartisan or consensual. Changes of government, it is true, could make a difference. Yet reflecting on Progressive Conservative and Liberal governments back to the government of Louis St. Laurent, I have to say that the advent of a new prime minister or a new minister sometimes made as great a change as did the arrival of a new government, even when the new ministers were from the same party as their predecessors. There is a good case to be made that the most important change in Canadian foreign policy in the immediate post-Second World War period came about when one Liberal, Louis St. Laurent, succeeded another Liberal, Mackenzie King, as prime minister. There was also a sharply marked difference in foreign policy when Lester B. Pearson, a Liberal, was succeeded by Pierre Elliott Trudeau, another Liberal. Change and innovation in foreign policy can have little or nothing to do with party. Sometimes what matters most is the personality and ideas of a particular prime minister or minister.

When I left Ottawa for NATO in 1982, I thought I would never serve in the Ottawa headquarters again. When I was brought home in 1985, it was on three weeks' notice and completely unexpected. Since the 1984 elections, I had paid attention to what the new government was saying about the areas that interested me – NATO and East-West relations. What was going on at headquarters interested me less. I was aware that the new prime minister had said some disobliging things about civil servants and had spoken of giving them "pink slips and running shoes." During the Trudeau years, the Department of External Affairs (DEA) had been the object of endless study and reorganization – almost as if the substance of policy, with all its ambiguities and contradictions, could be managed out of existence if sufficient attention was paid to process. This reorganization fervour had not ceased with the election of the Mulroney Conservatives, and DEA headquarters was in yet another instalment. But these were distant echoes. I was absorbed by the job in Brussels and had been hoping that the new government would keep me there.

The Under-Secretary as Manager
The position to which I was appointed in 1985 has two major responsibilities: the under-secretary is expected both to advise and to manage. In principle, he or she is the senior foreign policy adviser to the government; in practice, he or she is simply one of a number of sources of foreign

policy advice under any government. Some deputy ministers of foreign affairs have scarcely offered foreign policy advice at all but, instead, have preferred to concentrate on managing their department. The management responsibility is not trivial. In the mid-1980s, Canada maintained relations with 145 countries. External Affairs had a large headquarters staff in Ottawa, 150 missions abroad, close to 8,000 employees, annual expenditures of about $830 million, an inventory of property abroad valued at $1.35 billion, and a long-range capital program of about $35 million.[2]

Most deputy ministers try to strike a balance between managing this large and widely scattered organization and providing policy advice. Sometimes they are given an associate to share those tasks, and I was fortunate to have three excellent associate under-secretaries during my time as under-secretary.

One concern I had on the management side was that the apparently endless restructuring of the department in the late 1970s and early 1980s seemed to be producing turmoil and bad feeling rather than greater effectiveness. Because of this, I decided to stop pushing it, so that there was a moratorium for a number of years on further internal change.

Two management innovations of the Conservative period, outside the departmental structure but closely related to it, were (1) the introduction of a chief of staff from the political side into each minister's office and (2) the creation of a special bureau to manage the free trade negotiations. Both of these arrangements worked well so far as DEA was concerned. One reason was the quality of the government's appointments: Jodi White as Joe Clark's chief of staff and Simon Reisman as chief free trade negotiator. Both these innovations subsequently disappeared: the free trade organization (once the negotiations had concluded) and the chief-of-staff system (with the change of government in 1993).

It should be noted that the Conservative government also set up (and subsequently dismantled) special staffs to organize an unprecedented burden of summitry: a francophone summit in Québec, a Commonwealth heads of government meeting in Vancouver, a Goup of Seven (G-7) economic summit in Toronto – all in the space of approximately eighteen months. This responsibility, too, was creditably discharged.

Some may think that such organizational matters are of limited interest; however, they serve to illustrate a fundamental point: this was an effectively functioning government. Unlike its two postwar Conservative predecessors, it was neither chaotic, as the government of John Diefenbaker frequently was, nor too short-lived to make its mark, as the government of Joe Clark had been. On the contrary, the Mulroney government knew how to organize, how to extract appropriate advice from the public service and elsewhere, how to make up its mind between alternatives, and how to see that its instructions were executed. The team of ministers and officials included a number of extremely strong personalities. Not surprisingly, they had their disagreements; but their quarrels never threatened the existence of the government, as they had under Diefenbaker. For the first time since Canada's emergence as a full-fledged international actor, there was a Conservative government in power that was capable of managing foreign policy over the long haul. In this sense, the very existence of the Mulroney government was an innovation.

Certainly the media was always on the hunt for policy disagreements, particularly between Mulroney and Clark, given their historic rivalry. But both men were too shrewd to give the press much satisfaction. As far as I could see, while they had their disagreements, they made an effective and stable foreign policy team for the better part of a decade. Despite some of the early rhetoric, the prime minister never did purge the civil service. Nor was his record markedly different from that of other governments when it came to non-career diplomatic appointments, a matter about which the foreign service is always sensitive. Key areas of the government's foreign policy were entrusted to outstanding public servants who had the confidence of ministers – men and women like Allan Gotlieb, Derek Burney, Sylvia Ostry, and Simon Reisman. With the benefit of hindsight, Brian Mulroney may have had cause to regret several of his high-profile diplomatic appointments, including the appointment of Lucien Bouchard as Canadian ambassador to Paris and Stephen Lewis as Canada's permanent representative at the United Nations in New York. But, at the time, both these ambassadors gave dynamic service. The last thing that could have been said about them was that they were superannuated political hacks or faceless bureaucrats.

All of this is not to suggest that it was something new for a government to be well organized, well staffed, and effective with regard to foreign policy; rather, it is to suggest that it was something new for a Conservative government to fit this description.

Foreign Policy Innovations

But were the Mulroney government's policies new? To paraphrase President Bill Clinton, it all depends on what one means by new. Consider the free trade agreement (FTA). It was the one accomplishment of the Conservative era that has by now been thoroughly debated, and I do not propose to add to Brian W. Tomlin's analysis (Chapter 3) except to ask whether this agreement was new.

It was – and it wasn't. Of course it was not the first free trade agreement with the United States: there had been an earlier agreement between 1854 and 1866, and Sir Wilfrid Laurier lost two elections over the free trade issue, in 1891 and 1911. Mackenzie King had negotiated a modest instalment of free trade in 1935 and considered going further after the Second

World War. The Liberal government of Lester B. Pearson had concluded a crucial sectoral free trade agreement with the Auto Pact in 1965. Various other industrial sectors were then considered for further partial agreements in subsequent years, but nothing came of all this until the Mulroney government espoused free trade and successfully concluded a comprehensive agreement. In short, free trade was not new; it was one of the oldest and most durable issues in Canadian politics.

What, then, was new about free trade in the 1980s? First, for the first time since 1911, a government was prepared to stake its fate on the outcome of an election that turned largely on the issue, except that this time the government won. Second, it was the Conservative party – the party of Sir John A. Macdonald and the National Policy, the party of R.B. Bennett and Imperial Preferences under the Ottawa Agreements, the party of John Diefenbaker and the 15 percent trade diversion – that carried free trade over the bitter opposition of the Liberals – the party of Laurier, King, and Pearson. This was surely one of the most astonishing political reversals in Canadian history.

What about other areas of policy? New elements can be detected in Canada's relations with Africa, and the Conservatives inherited a well established basis for them. Much, but not all, of Canada's policy towards Africa could be framed within the context of the Commonwealth and la Francophonie. But there were also independent African countries in which Canada had interests – countries that had not shared the experience of being British or French colonies. Ethiopia, where Canadians had long been active in the educational system, was one example; Mozambique, a Front Line state during the apartheid era, was another.

The racial issue in South Africa absorbed a very considerable part of the Conservative government's attention, both on the part of ministers and on the part of the prime minister personally. As David Black suggests (Chapter 12), there might have been some resonance of the Diefenbaker government here, since Diefenbaker had led the charge when South Africa was expelled from the Commonwealth. Perhaps in Brian Mulroney's case there was a link with the social consciousness cultivated by his education at St. Francis Xavier University. Perhaps it was that Conservatives were used to being underdogs and had an instinctive feeling for the oppressed. Whatever the causes, there can be no doubt that the majority of Canadians wanted their government to be clearly on the side of ending institutionalized racism in South Africa and that there were few arguments (commercial or otherwise) for treading softly.

Mulroney disliked seeing Britain isolated – or, more correctly, self-isolated – on the apartheid issue within the Commonwealth. But he knew where he stood. At meetings of Commonwealth heads of government, he had strong disagreements with Margaret Thatcher about how best to treat the apartheid regime in South Africa. He had even stronger disagreements with her in private. He believed it would be disastrous if black African leaders were driven to conclude, mistakenly, that no white leader could be counted on to oppose apartheid. As a result, Mulroney worked hard, not only within the context of the apartheid debate, but also in other ways to establish good personal relations with African leaders. For example, through the goodwill of his relationship with Robert Mugabe, president of Zimbabwe, he arranged to finance the provision of grain supplies to Zambia, a country that had been afflicted by drought for some years. This was a spontaneous and personal prime ministerial initiative that came about simply because, while attending a Commonwealth meeting, Mulroney observed how depressed Kenneth Kaunda, president of Zambia, was about the problems facing his country. Moreover, Mulroney was confident enough of his relations with Mugabe that he felt comfortable privately pressing him about specific human rights cases in Zimbabwe.

South Africa was not an issue the prime minister delegated to his foreign minister. On the contrary, both were active on this file. Joe Clark was the chair of the committee of Commonwealth foreign ministers that monitored the issue. He devoted considerable time to consulting private citizens and organizations in order to ensure that the government was in touch with public opinion. He gave detailed attention to strengthening the various sanctions against South Africa. Both he and the prime minister visited the Front Line states. And, in a rather daring move that might easily have backfired, Clark even visited Pretoria to beard the apartheid lion in its den.

Another file with African associations was la Francophonie. Here the issues were as much domestic as foreign, and the prime minister was the principal actor. His intervention brought about an important change. Although the Commonwealth and la Francophonie were never identical twins, in Canadian eyes they had important similarities. However, compared to the Commonwealth, la Francophonie lacked a political dimension. The heads of government of the Commonwealth met every two years, and these meetings helped to demonstrate that contacts at the highest political level within a worldwide multiracial association of sovereign states could be highly serviceable. They redeemed the Commonwealth from the charge that it was no more than the decayed remnants of the British Empire, without contemporary purpose.

How regrettable, then, that a comparable structure did not exist within la Francophonie. This would have come close to doubling the contacts available within the Commonwealth, opening new possibilities for dialogue with more than forty states within which French was an official language or otherwise culturally important. This was the problem – and the answer lay in Canada's hands. Canadians had never been able to agree among themselves on what status was to be accorded Canada's French-speaking provinces at a meeting of heads of government. The Trudeau government had been adamant about rejecting any formula that might have been open to abuse by separatists. The result was an impasse: no formula for federal-provincial participation at francophone summits – hence, no summits.

Brian Mulroney believed that this was an issue that he could solve with Robert Bourassa, then the premier of Québec. A formula was found, the file was unblocked, and the series of francophone summits – the first in Paris, the second in Québec City – was duly inaugurated and has continued ever since. Some may argue that the prime minister conceded too much to the position of the Québec government. Others will maintain that no harm was done and that the strengthening of la Francophonie was well worth the price. Whatever the final judgment, this was clearly an important innovation, and it was clearly one in which the prime minister's role was crucial.

East-West relations is another area where the Conservative role should be examined. During the 1980s, the Soviet Union undertook fundamental reforms under the banners of glasnost and perestroika. It was clear that what was occurring was unprecedented. However, during the 1980s, it was by no means clear whether the reforms would succeed or what might be their final product. The Canadian government was interested in what was going on and took steps to keep itself informed. Joe Clark, for example, held conversations in Ottawa with the Soviet foreign minister, Eduard Shevardnadze, about Soviet intentions. During this period, the prime minister had a number of other foreign policy preoccupations: the free trade negotiations and his responsibilities as the host of three successive summits, to name only the most pressing. Not surprisingly, he found it difficult to envisage going to the Soviet Union himself. For this, he received a certain amount of criticism as the decade drew to a close. The slow Canadian reaction, according to the critics, was a sign that Mulroney, being an unreconstructed Cold War warrior, did not understand what was going on.

I myself never thought that there was much in this criticism. Personally, I would have been glad had the prime minister found time to go earlier than he did – but then, East-West relations formed a large part of my background and interests. Anyway, I had no doubt that the prime minister knew as well as anybody else that the changes in the Soviet Union were important. During the 1980s, there may have been an element in the government's thinking that held that, so long as the Cold War was not entirely liquidated, this was not a field where Canada could hope to make a difference; and Joe Clark always insisted that Canada should concentrate its efforts where it could make a difference.

The prime minister finally went to the Soviet Union late in 1989. He took with him a small army of business leaders and others, demonstrating that the "Team Canada" initiative of the Chrétien years is yet another idea that is not new. On this visit he had long talks with Mikhail Gorbachev about Soviet plans. The Soviet leader gave the impression that he had ideas about how to reconcile glasnost with the existing system. Beyond the level of rhetoric, however, it was not clear how perestroika was going to look in practice.

All this was two years before the Warsaw Pact, the Council of Mutual Economic Assistance, and the breaking apart of the Soviet Union. None of these dramatic events was foreseen at the time. It was clear that, in Gorbachev's mind at least, the Soviet Union would still exist as a socialist state and the leader of a group of socialist countries at the end of the reform process. So if foreign observers, including the Canadian government, were hesitant to rush to judgment about what was going to happen in the Soviet Union, then there were sufficient reasons for caution.

Nor was this the only difficulty. The Soviet Union was obviously going to need heavy foreign financing, and the Canadian government had nothing substantial to contribute. It could (and did) encourage Canadian business leaders to go to the Soviet Union, investigate the possibilities, and assess the risks for themselves. But it was clear that those who decided to invest needed deep reserves of patience as well as of capital. Step by step, however, as the direction and irreversible nature of the changes became clearer, the Canadian government organized itself to help the process of political and economic reform. At this stage, it became more common to hear the reminder, noted by Roy Norton (Chapter 16), that one Canadian in ten had ancestral origins somewhere in central and eastern Europe, and that Canada was, in a sense, closer to the former communist countries than were some of their more immediate western European neighbours. This sensitivity was reflected in such government decisions as the rapid recognition of Ukraine once it voted to declare independence.

The list of changes and new approaches to old problems could be extended. Because Central America was marked by conflict at the time and was the focus of a good deal of concern in Canada, Clark paid an unprecedented series of visits to the countries of the region in order to assess the difficulties for himself. Similarly, he was convinced that relations with the countries of the Pacific Rim could not simply be left as a matter of growing Canadian trade interests in the Pacific, no matter how important those interests had become over the course of the 1980s. He therefore initiated the North Pacific Cooperative Security Dialogue (NPCSD). He was assiduous in fulfilling Canada's responsibilities as a "dialogue partner" in the Association of Southeast Asian Nations (ASEAN). He tried to interest the Japanese and others in adding a modest multilateral dimension to the

NPCSD. For his part, Mulroney cultivated good personal relations, in the context of the G-7, with his Japanese counterparts, notably Nakasone and Kaifu, and he was the first – and so far the only – Canadian prime minister to say publicly and unambiguously that Japan should be made a permanent member of the United Nations Security Council. This was a complex and sensitive question, with much to be said both for and against. While Mulroney was not unaware of these complexities, it was typical of him to overlook the problems in order to set out what he was convinced was the desirable objective.

In much the same way, as Gordon Mace demonstrates (Chapter 10), Mulroney simply cut through – and cut off – years of debate on another complex issue by deciding that Canada should join the Organization of American States (OAS). On Canada-US relations, the thesis that Mulroney did not stand up for Canadian interests would have to also consider his stand on acid rain and the Strategic Defense Initiative (SDI), where the Canadian position would have surely gained an approving smile from Mackenzie King. The Conservative role at successive G-7 summits would also merit consideration.

Conclusion

There is no need to multiply examples. With almost a decade of foreign policy-making under review, it would be impossible to do justice to the range of issues that need to be considered. One conclusion, however, is clear: the Mulroney Conservatives were entirely disinclined to follow the example of Lord Salisbury. Both Mulroney and Clark were activists in international affairs. One may or may not agree with everything they did in foreign policy; one may or may not share a belief in this kind of activist international approach. But the least that can be said for it is that it leaves a rich record – one that richly deserves to be examined.

Notes

1 Quoted in James Morris, *Pax Britannica*, vol. 2: *Climax of an Empire* (London: Faber, 1968), 247.
2 Canada, Department of External Affairs, *Annual Reports* (Ottawa: DEA, 1985-87).

15

Adding Women but Forgetting to Stir: Gender and Foreign Policy in the Mulroney Era

Claire Turenne Sjolander

In June 1999, a conference was held at McGill University to mark the tenth anniversary of the Canada-US free trade agreement (FTA). The invitation list was a veritable "Who's Who" of the free trade players, both Canadian and American. Notable by her absence, however, was Pat Carney, the minister of international trade when that historic agreement was negotiated. Carney was not pleased. She publicly complained, pointing out that John Crosbie, who was appointed trade minister six months after the agreement had been negotiated, was on the panel discussing the negotiation of the FTA: "This is not the only case where men take credit for women's work in history ... It's a sign that women have not come very far in our society that they can be so easily swept under the rug by the old boys." To Desmond Morton, the conference organizer, Carney wrote: "I was the minister involved in negotiating the FTA; John Crosbie was not. To state otherwise, as you are doing, is ... classic historic revisionism and a distortion of history." Although Morton eventually invited her to participate in a panel dealing with the impact of free trade on western Canada, Carney refused to go along, noting that men often "stick women in roles, because of gender or to get rid of them, in places they are not qualified. I know very little of the impact of free trade on Manitoba and Saskatchewan and Alberta." Carney's conclusion was blunt: "history renders women invisible."[1]

Are women as invisible in the foreign policy process as was Carney when it came to the retelling of the free trade story? Are women present? And if women are present, then is foreign policy any different as a result? An examination of gender and Canadian foreign policy provides an alternative (albeit somewhat less customary) vantage point from which to assess the Mulroney era. This chapter proposes two ways of analyzing women, gender, and foreign policy. The first asks Cynthia Enloe's succinct question: "Where are the women?"[2] – where are women (and, by extension, men) found in the practice of Canadian foreign policy? This approach drives us to discover "where women are or are not present and [to] provide some explanation for their absence or presence."[3] Where women are found, however, is merely one part of the picture, since finding women, even an important number of women, does not – and cannot – necessarily lead to the conclusion that hiring or promoting women to positions of authority within the foreign policy apparatus will lead to different policy outcomes.[4] Having said this, however, "finding" the women remains a valuable first step, for "when we examine where women have been included or excluded, recognizing that this is the result of unequal power relations within society which systematically value what is masculine and undervalue what is feminine, we are able to identify the gendered basis of foreign policy."[5]

I therefore begin by identifying where, in Canadian foreign policy, the women were (or were not) during the Mulroney era. At one level, the Mulroney years marked an important departure in the practice of foreign policy in Canada; while Flora MacDonald had been Canada's first female secretary of state for external affairs under the Joe Clark government a half decade earlier, elected women in the Mulroney government occupied many of the foreign policy portfolios. These women included Pat Carney (international trade), Barbara McDougall (external affairs), Kim Campbell (national defence), Flora MacDonald (employment and immigration), Monique Vézina (minister of state for external relations, with responsibility for the Canadian International Development Agency [CIDA]), Monique Landry (external relations), Pauline Browse (minister of state for immigration), and Mary Collins (associate minister of national defence). While there is some obvious significance to having female members of Parliament (MPs) in these positions, I concentrate on identifying where the women were found in the primary bureaucratic apparatus for foreign affairs, the Department of External Affairs (DEA), and on the opportunities and constraints confronting them *as* women. Of course, it is not only those working in External Affairs who have a foreign policy role. An assessment of agencies such as the Department of National Defence or CIDA, however, is beyond the scope of this chapter. The analysis in the first part of this chapter does not specifically address whether the presence of women can or does introduce into foreign policy practices "women-centered ways of framing issues ... [or] feminist agendas,"[6] but it does suggest the possibilities that might (and, by extension, those that might not) exist.

For many theorists, however, the notion of gender is not simply, or even primarily, related to women as biological subjects. As an answer to the question of why "women-centered ways of framing issues and advancing agendas" in Canadian foreign policy often remain unexpressed, providing a focus on women and where they might be found within the foreign policy establishment is, at best, a first step. Understanding gender requires appreciating the fact that gender is socially constructed. As Spike Peterson argues, we need to understand that gender produces "subjective identities through which we see and know the world; and ... that the world is pervasively shaped by gendered meanings. That is, we do not experience or 'know' the world as abstract 'humans' but as embodied, gendered beings."[7] These observations have important implications. More than simply helping us to "find" women, the understanding of gender as a social construct leads us to an analysis of social relations. As Peterson puts it: "Rather than a choice between nature [a feminine construct] *or* culture [a masculine construct], the concept of gender enables us to examine meanings imposed on the body, to understand how women (and men) 'are made not born' ... our construction as feminine and masculine is an ongoing, complex, and often contradictory *process*."[8] While the numbers of women and where they are found in foreign policy is a significant element of this analysis, reflection on gender teaches us that foreign policy is also characterized by particular and often persistent rules and discursive practices. These rules and practices are not simply neutral abstractions whose purpose is to facilitate international life but, rather, gendered constructs that "construct and reproduce notions of masculinity and femininity and associated power differentials."[9] Deborah Stienstra points out that gender as a subject of foreign policy constitutes a set of relationships that influence the making and implementation of policy. But, as she asserts, these are "relationships of domination, where women are defined in terms of men, history is primarily the history of men, and gender usually refers only to women's actions. In foreign policy, current practices, which are primarily defined by men and within a masculine framework, provide the norm for explaining foreign policy."[10]

Gender analyses are not common in the field of foreign policy, and Canadian foreign policy is no exception.[11] With regard to foreign policy statements and policies, the place of and for women is often secondary (if it figures at all). The international system is where the histories of diplomats, soldiers, and heads of state prevail, and these histories are predominantly those of men. A review of the Mulroney era, and some of the key foreign policy documents of this period, reveals the extent to which women are rendered invisible in Canadian foreign policy (just as Carney suggests) and the extent to which foreign policy is gendered as masculine. This provides an important cautionary note to the supposition that rectifying gender imbalances and the discourses and practices to which they give rise is simply a matter of "adding women and stirring." Adding women, and distributing them through the decision-making ranks (stirring), does not guarantee that gendered structures will change.

Despite this cautionary note, I am not arguing that gendered structures are so pervasive that women – as biological subjects – do not matter and cannot make a difference. Moving from the concrete realities facing women to the more abstract notion of gender can "move attention from women's subordination to gender constructions, from the politics and choices of agents ... to gendered structures that passively envelop both women and men."[12] Such a move can make it more difficult to determine ways of emancipating women. The review here attempts to be sensitive to the realities of both the places of women and of the gendered structures, discourses, and practices within which they interact so that real change becomes a possibility. As such, my objective is not to offer a litany of critiques of the failures of the Mulroney government to meet the target of an unrealized ideal; rather, it is to assess the tenure of one government in an ongoing process defined by the social construction of gender relations in the field of foreign policy and to signal the promises for greater emancipatory politics that follow therefrom.

Where Are the Women? Adding and Stirring at External Affairs
To speak of women in the foreign policy apparatus is invariably to speak of the Department of External Affairs. Unfortunately, the department did not welcome women or create a public space that allowed them to flourish. DEA was constituted as a department of men. Sir Joseph Pope, the first under-secretary, set the rules for employment when the department was created in 1909, and these closely followed the guidelines he had proposed to a royal commission on the civil service in 1907: "I recommend that a small staff of young men, well educated and carefully selected, be attached to the department."[13] Pope had not spoken generically when he recommended hiring men, for when he was asked specifically about the employment of women, he went on to say that, "speaking generally, I do not think it desirable, though I know of several exceptions. But I am speaking of general principle, because I find that ... women claim the rights of men and the privileges of their own sex as well."[14]

Not until 1947 was this ban on the hiring of women as officers lifted. The new regime was not greeted with full enthusiasm, however. In 1948, Marcel Cadieux, head of the DEA personnel division, was called on to develop a policy for the selection of foreign service officers, including "the recruitment of girls as foreign service officers."[15] But Cadieux only wanted a "very small number" because "(a) They are very likely to marry and thus create early vacancies and therefore additional problems from the point of view of recruitment; (b) They cannot be sent to all posts as easily as men and their usefulness abroad is not comparable in all missions to that of men, other things being equal."[16]

It is, of course, important to underscore that the Canadian foreign service was not atypical in its hiring practices. Throughout the industrialized world, diplomats were overwhelmingly male. Further, while the ban against women officers had been relaxed, the basic requirement to sit the foreign service exam remained the same – a university degree. In the late 1940s, the pool of women with such qualifications was relatively small, and the department was spared any fear of an onslaught of applications from aspiring female foreign service officers. The roots of a gendered foreign policy, however, were inevitably linked to hiring practices that made little room for women. Foreign policy, by and large, was the business of men.

While during the postwar years single women might have been eligible to be admitted into the foreign service, married women were not. DEA required that female officers resign if they decided to marry, the grounds being that married women could not be posted abroad since their husbands would be either unable or unwilling to follow them into the field.[17] This policy guaranteed that there would be few women in the foreign service and that those who *were* there would be viewed with some degree of condescension. Reflecting this departmental culture, former diplomat John W. Holmes, then with the Canadian Institute of International Affairs, remarked, in a 1965 speech delivered at "Ladies' Night" at the Toronto Board of Trade, that the reason for the low number of women in the foreign service was that few applied. As Holmes put it, "The competition is open to them on equal terms in spite of the fact that they are a risk no insurance company would take. I needn't tell you on Ladies' Night that they are all attractive and marvellous diplomats to boot, but they have a habit of getting themselves attached by marriage to someone else's diplomatic service. It is a particularly lamentable form of dame-drain."[18]

This policy against married women persisted until 1971, fifteen years after a similar ban had been lifted in the public service as a whole. And it was modified only in anticipation of recommendations by the Royal Commission on the Status of Women in Canada that all discrimination against women be ended. The social upheavals of the 1960s had changed much, but they had not yet succeeded in breaking down the conservative and gendered bastion that was External Affairs.

In order to define the context within which women found themselves in the foreign policy apparatus once the Conservative government was elected in 1984, it is important to trace the glacial progress towards women's equal status as foreign service officers. In August 1980, the Trudeau government appointed Pamela McDougall to head the Royal Commission on Conditions of Foreign Service. Her job was, in part, to redefine the relevance and role of the foreign service and, in part, to comment on the lives of people in the foreign service, particularly the rotational staff. The picture McDougall painted of disruptions to family life and the consequent difficulties for children and spouses was certainly disheartening for both men and women. The explicit concern raised by the report regarding the prospects for employment for spouses and the disruptions that postings abroad implied for their careers was at least sensitive to the fact that they might not enjoy the "privilege" of performing a representational role abroad without pay. For all intents and purposes though, the report was constructed around the image of a male foreign service officer with a wife and family rather than around the challenges facing a female officer at home or abroad.[19] These problems of morale were only exacerbated by the 1982 move to create what was called a "new" Department of External Affairs by amalgamating the "old" DEA with the international trade side of the Department of Industry, Trade and Commerce. In short, when they came to office in 1984, the Conservatives found a foreign policy vessel carrying a relatively unhappy crew.

Tracking the situation of women in the foreign service between 1984 and 1993 is not an easy task. Detailed and systematic data on gender breakdown among foreign service officers are difficult to come by, which itself suggests the degree to which the department saw itself as predominantly male. What is clear is that, throughout the period of the Mulroney government, efforts were made to increase the representation of women within the ranks of the foreign service. Some of these efforts followed attempts by the Trudeau government to increase the recruitment of women into the ranks of the foreign service; and, indeed, their numbers did increase during the 1980s and into the 1990s. In 1981 women comprised 8.2 percent of the foreign service (FS) category; by 1998 that number had increased to 28.8 percent.[20] The reason for this increase is apparent in the hiring practices of the department: in 1982, 29 percent of the new cohort of foreign service officers were women; between 1983 and 1988, that figure increased to an average of 33 percent; and in the early 1990s, the percentage of women hired as officers was in excess of 40 percent.[21]

On one level, therefore, the Conservative government acquitted itself well, at least in so far as it continued to press for the hiring of women within the foreign service. The percentage of women hired continued to grow steadily throughout the nine years of Tory rule, arguably leading to the consolidation of a "critical mass" of women necessary to change the practice of foreign policy.[22] As we have seen, however, "adding" women does not, by itself, guarantee that foreign policy is less likely to be gendered masculine. At a minimum, it is necessary to ask whether the addition of women is leavened with serious attention to "stirring"; that is, are women distributed throughout the foreign policy bureaucracy? Here, the numbers are less impressive. In 1982, 5.2 percent (six out of 114) heads of post were women. By 1988, that percentage had increased to 8.3 percent (ten out of 120); by 1994, it had increased to 12.7 percent (fourteen out of 110).[23]

This increase in the number of women serving in ambassadorial posts was almost certainly in response to political pressure on the foreign service to include a greater number of women on the heads of post (HOP) lists sent forward for consideration by Joe Clark as secretary of state for external affairs.[24] Ironically, however, Clark's efforts also caused some in DEA to express concern that women were not necessarily making it to the highest ranks of the foreign service on the basis of merit but, rather, on the basis of gender – a view that was echoed by women as well as by men. The perspective articulated by Marie-Lucie Morin, for example, who, in 1992, was director of the financial and business services division of External Affairs and International Trade Canada (EAITC), as the department had been renamed in 1989, was not an unusual one: "I know that the prime minister and ministers have been making tremendous pressure so that there are more female heads of posts on the list every year, more and more, they want more. And I would say, as a result, you probably have female heads of posts that are being made heads of posts ahead of their years, if anything, for better or for worse."[25]

Ministerial pressure for the appointment of women to senior diplomatic posts needs to be situated within a more carefully sketched context, however. Despite ministerial pressure, and despite the commitment of the prime minister to a 30 percent target for the appointment of women by order-in-council, a detailed analysis prepared by rotational women foreign service officers provides a more nuanced portrait of the situation for women in DEA during the Mulroney years – and a rather less optimistic one than that painted by Barbara McDougall in the Foreword of this volume. This is the most complete snapshot of the department publicly available during this period, and it is significant, in part, because it is taken at the half-way mark of the Conservative government's tenure and, in part, because it was generated by female foreign service officers themselves. At the end of 1988, 15 percent of foreign service officers were women (as opposed to 8.2 percent in 1981), and women began to fight for change. Not surprisingly, given the hiring practices of the 1980s, the greater numbers of women were mostly concentrated at the lower levels: 37 percent of new FS officer recruits were women (FS1D officers), 28 percent of FS officers (category 1) were women, while only 13 percent of FS officers (category 2) were women. In the management categories (EX[FS]), the situation was much worse, with only sixteen of 404 people being women (3.9 percent). The deputy minister was a man, and only two women served as assistant deputy ministers (ADM) – Marie-Andrée Beauchemin (ADM Communications) and Jean McCloskey (ADM Pacific). There were no women directors-general. Despite some high profile women as heads of post abroad, women fared less well in management positions below the level of HOP. By the end of 1988, for example, there were only two women among eighty-one program managers abroad among the political/economic foreign service officers.[26]

The difficulties confronting women within EAITC seemed confirmed by a December 1988 Public Service Commission study conducted on the representation of women in the management categories. External Affairs ranked thirty-second out of thirty-three government departments, behind National Defence but ahead of National Revenue.[27] The Canadian Human Rights Commission selected these three departments to be the focus of its review of equity data and employment systems.[28] The 1990 release of the report of the Task Force on Barriers to Women in the Public Service, launched by Treasury Board president Pat Carney, further emphasized the problems confronting the department and some of the structural barriers to women's advancement in the foreign service. Three sets of barriers were identified:

- *Maternity leave and the promotion system:* DEA introduced maternity leave in 1984, and this was certainly an achievement for women in the foreign service. Yet, as the task force reported, "the promotion system has inherent limitations for women having children."[29] In order to be considered for promotion, a candidate required four performance reviews. Such reviews, prepared annually on a regular timetable, were written only for those who had been in a job for at least six months in any given assignment year. Those on shorter-term assignments, such as those associated with maternity leave, lost their eligibility for a performance review and, thus, for consideration for promotion. As the task force noted acidly: "The only way to avoid this problem is to time your deliveries for August 1, so maternity leave extends over the first half of the assignment year!"[30] And because short-term assignments are rarely challenging and seldom provide an opportunity to acquire new skills, women were doubly disadvantaged by the promotion system.[31]
- *Special, or "stretch," assignments:* The foreign service is rotational: officers mix a series of postings abroad with appointments in Canada. Postings that offer experience and exposure, thus enhancing the prospects for promotion, are coveted. In order to ensure that the rotational staffing system remains flexible enough to function, rotational officers can serve in position that has a higher classification without being promoted to that level (or they can serve in a position with a lower classification without being demoted). Serving in a higher classification is known as a "stretch" assignment, and such assignments are seen as critical to advancement and promotion.[32] However, Margaret Ford noted that disproportionately few women benefited from stretch assignments. While some fifteen males in the political/economic stream received a stretch assignment, and most were eventually promoted to the EX(FS) management category, "no women FS2 officer in the Political/Economic Stream has ever been made a Director in the Department."[33]

• *The corporate culture of the department:* This category is undoubtedly the most sensitive, for its roots are to be found in the old boys' network that once characterized a department in which women were either absent or present only in very small numbers. Despite a changing gender balance, the prevalent attitudes remained those of another era. A corporate culture described as "claustrophobically male"[34] clearly hampers the effectiveness of women's – and some men's – participation in the foreign policy process. Often witnessed in the undervaluing of women's contributions (placing women "where they cannot do too much harm"),[35] this attitude is difficult to separate from the institutional traditions of a once all-male bastion. Barbara Martin, editor of the Professional Association of Foreign Service Officers' newsletter *bout de papier*, commented in 1989 on the shape this corporate culture often took. It included "paternalistic treatment (pats on the head, the cheek, being called 'dear'), exclusion from informal socializing, being deemed 'shrill' or 'aggressive' or 'moody,' in contrast to males who are 'firm' or 'assertive,' having the substance drained from job packages and challenging issues turned over to male colleagues, beliefs that because women have spouses and dependants that they can't provide the quality work that male officers with spouses and dependants can, assumptions that all women answering phones are secretaries, and assumptions that women have less authority."[36] In a profession where plum assignments often depend on an officer's capacity to lobby directors, the network of "old boys" who have served together for years in posts abroad did not enhance the prospects of "stirring" women evenly among the ranks of the foreign service.

What of the women who acted in increasing, albeit still small, numbers as heads of post? The task force reported that female ambassadors were "often show-cased as an indication of progress for women in the Department as a whole,"[37] but the situation beneath the veneer was less encouraging. As one brief submitted to the task force suggested: "in the view of most rotational women officers, management attention seems to have been focussed almost exclusively on ambassadorial appointments for women, with little attention being given to non-ambassadorial level postings and to the all-essential staffing at headquarters."[38] This complaint was echoed by senior women in the department as well; both Ingrid Hall and Lucie Edwards complained about the "Golda Meir syndrome" with regard to the appointment of women to senior ranks in the foreign service. As Hall put it, "you appoint one woman and sit back and don't have to do anything for another ten years."[39] Edwards's assessment was even more pointed: "The department likes to pick on one woman almost per decade and say, 'Look she's doing so outstandingly well, we don't have any problems, this department's doing great.'" In the 1970s, Edwards noted, it was Margaret Catley-Carlson, who eventually became president of CIDA; in the 1980s, it was Louise Fréchette, who eventually became Canada's permanent representative to the United Nations. But as Edwards concluded: "I would like to think ... that we're through that period. What we don't need is a new woman for the '90s. What we need is a critical mass of excellent women moving through the system, so that it becomes very natural and normal and organic for women to be in senior positions in this department."

Moreover, the small number of women in the senior ranks meant that when Jean McCloskey was appointed to another department or overseas large holes were created. For example, when McCloskey was made head of Investment Canada and when, soon after, Louise Fréchette was moved to the United Nations, no women were left on the executive committee of the DEA, and few were available to replace them. As Edwards put it, "[despite] the minister's very real commitment to equality of opportunity and the minister's commitment about women abroad, well, if you lose a Louise Fréchette or if I go abroad ... the number goes down."[40]

Certainly, some women – and the department – argued that, with patience and time, the situation would eventually improve as newly appointed women began to rise through the ranks. The biases against women in the department, however, suggested that the "long haul" would be longer and harder than hiring statistics might suggest. Despite ministerial engagement with the issue, questions remained: "How can Canada be the most outspoken of all countries in the world in our insistence that professional women should comprise at least 30 per cent of international secretariats when women rotational officers comprise only 15 per cent of the Foreign Service Officer complement? ... Why is it that we have more rigorous standards to ensure the equality of women in developing countries and in international secretariats than we do in the Canadian Foreign Service where management can directly influence the outcome?"[41]

The gap between rhetorical commitments internationally and the reality of the situation within the Canadian foreign service was underscored in February 1992, when the Mulroney government decided to reverse the 1981 integration of social affairs (or immigration) officers into DEA from the Department of Employment and Immigration. As part of its effort to have External Affairs "return to basics," this stream, which was 31 percent female, was being transferred back. In March 1992, a group of women officers sent a letter of protest to their minister, Barbara McDougall, pointing out that the proportion of women in DEA would drop to 17 percent once the social affairs stream was moved. This, it was argued, would have an impact on the department's ability to reach its goal of ensuring that women occupied 14.1 percent of management positions by 1996. As they sharply concluded, "There is an embarrassing gulf between our international exhortations and domestic reality ... The traditional male-oriented management style of External Affairs will thus be perpetuated."[42]

That the move of social affairs back to employment and immigration was, in part, perceived as an attack on the situation of women in External Affairs rather than as a piece of bureaucratic restructuring is an important comment on the struggle of women within the foreign service. And, ironically, because the transfer occurred at the end of the Mulroney years, many women in DEA remember the Conservatives for this off-pitch swan song rather than for their other successes in promoting the advancement of women within the department.

Gendered Discourses: The Mulroney Government and Foreign Policy

Finding where women are in External Affairs does not allow us to conclude that foreign policy is, or is not, gendered; instead, we need to focus more explicitly not only on the space for women in the bureaucracy, but also on the government's priorities and policies and how they were framed. Examining a range of government and ministerial statements will help reveal how key issues were framed and the extent to which that framing was gendered. Are women found in foreign policy statements? What is considered important in foreign policy, and what is absent or silenced?

A starting point is the 1985 green paper on foreign policy. Defined as an "aid to the public review ... on the future directions of Canada's international relations,"[43] the green paper provided an overview of the key themes in Canadian foreign policy. As is the case in most foreign policy documents, its language is, at first glance, gender neutral; women are specifically mentioned only once, where their increased participation in the labour force is highlighted as a signpost of changing times.[44] Driven by the exigencies of global economic uncertainties and a resurgent Cold War, *Competitiveness and Security* presents strategies to respond to the prosperity and security that Canada can "no longer take for granted."[45] Throughout the document, the key actor is the state, which acts in the name of an amorphous, ungendered human being. As such, there is no discussion of how the economy has a differential impact on men and women, nor is there any elaboration of a holistic vision of security that is founded on much more than the need to protect against attack and to participate in the global balance of military power.

It is difficult to present an elaborate critique of a document that never aspired to be definitive or comprehensive in its treatment of foreign policy issues. It is also facile to argue that, where the document mentions aid policy or the "Canadian values" of compassion and humanism, it is positing a more "feminine" foreign policy orientation. Yet, as a document defined within a particular era of global politics, *Competitiveness and Security* reveals the priorities of a foreign policy whose language is inherently gendered. Security, and, indeed, economic prosperity, is limited to the security and prosperity of *states*, and it is assumed that such security and prosperity translates unproblematically into that of all "human beings." Furthermore, in proposing state-based solutions (multilateral and bilateral trade regimes or regional security coalitions) to the challenges of security and economic prosperity, there is no acknowledgment that the state participates in creating the insecurities from which it then seeks protection. Finally, the conceptual distinction between the realm of economic policy and the realm of security creates barriers to an understanding of (1) how security is far broader than the conflicts between states amenable to military "solution" and (2) how economic prosperity is influenced by far more than state regulatory regimes and lack of transparency.

To examine the gendered construction of policy in more detail, I will examine two different "policy moments": (1) the debates concerning free trade and (2) the debates concerning the emergence of a post-Cold War world. Interestingly, the key spokespersons for each of these policy moments were both women – Pat Carney as the minister of international trade during the free trade negotiations and Barbara McDougall as secretary of state for external affairs in the early days of the emergence of the post-Cold War world.

As Brian W. Tomlin and Tammy Nemeth (Chapters 3 and 4, respectively) make clear, the decision to negotiate a Canada-US free trade agreement was a germinal moment in the Mulroney foreign policy agenda, and in many respects the FTA was the centrepiece of the Conservative tenure in office. While Crosbie might have been called on to sell the deal once the negotiations were complete, Carney's speeches reveal her equal talents as a salesperson. Describing a bilateral relationship characterized by trade disputes during the early 1980s, she emphasized the positive nature of the trade agreement: "Confronted with this situation [of bilateral trade disputes], the government did not choose the route of vicious trade wars. We chose the positive route. The result is that today we have a free trade agreement that is the envy of our other trading partners. It will give us open and secure access to the biggest market in the world."[46] The free trade initiative "will strengthen and protect the world's largest trading relationship, on which four million Canadian and American jobs depend and ... [will] open up new and exciting opportunities for economic growth in a world vibrant with change, electric with challenge and oppressed by the forces of protectionism."[47] The FTA had simple and ambitious objectives: jobs, economic growth for disadvantaged regions, and protection of social programs and cultural policies. "However, most of all, the great debate is about security and enhancing access to our largest market and our biggest customer, the United States, in a long-term binding treaty."[48]

For Carney, the FTA was not about women, nor did it have any specifically gendered aspects or consequences. Opponents to the agreement were described as having "no vision for Canada and offer no hope for Canadians." Opponents offered only "scare tactics," and these were a "cop-out."[49] The "trauma of change" flowing from the FTA would be no different than that flowing from seven previous rounds of multilateral trade liberalization, and through these "Canadians have not only survived ... we have prospered."[50]

One of the grounds for mobilizing against the FTA was not, however, whether or not Canadians would survive, but whether or not women would survive. The critique brought by the women's movement was simple: free trade was seen as endangering women's jobs and jeopardizing various provisions of the Canadian welfare state. Marjorie Cohen, a spokesperson for the National Action Committee on the Status of Women (NAC), consistently argued that "women will be hard hit because studies show many jobs will be lost in industries with female-dominated workforces."[51] NAC argued that the manufacturing industries most vulnerable to free trade were also those industries with a high proportion of women workers: textiles, the garment industry, footwear, and electrical equipment and food processing plants.[52] The vulnerabilities in these sectors were even more significant given that many of the employees potentially affected were "older-than-average or immigrant women who would have little chance of getting new jobs or being retrained for new professions."[53] Vulnerability in the services sector was equally highlighted as an area of particular – and gendered – concern: "In the last 10 years or so, 80 per cent of the new jobs created in Canada were in the service sector. About 83 per cent of women in the labour force are employed in services. There is reason to fear that over time, under a free trade agreement, many jobs in telecommunications, transport, financial services and elsewhere, could easily be transferred to the United States, thanks to computers and other new technologies."[54]

Concerns about the gendered impact of the FTA did not limit themselves to job losses in vulnerable, and female-dominated, industries. The impact of the Canada-US agreement on social programs was also a concern. As Lise Leduc put it, "We can suppose that social programs that will increase production costs will be contested by Canadians and Canadian industry. One can also suppose that social programs that lower production costs, because some costs will be borne by government programs, will be contested by the Americans. Need I remind you that women are the main users and beneficiaries of these social programs and that they often hold jobs created by such programs?" She expressed similar concerns about the appropriateness of retraining initiatives, particularly given the profile of working women. Women represented 64 percent of workers earning the minimum wage and 70 percent of part-time workers. Women made up only 1 percent of the skilled workers, mechanics, drivers, or non-traditional workers, and the vast majority of women were concentrated across only ten different employment categories. "The analysis of this profile," Leduc concluded, "makes us dubious about this supposed direct access for women to high technology jobs under a free trade agreement. This is why we would like to know what the government intends to do for the retraining of women, particularly." [55]

While it is always difficult to determine specific cause and effect, the FTA, coupled with a recession and a high-interest rate policy, does appear to have been a formula that affected some women particularly harshly. "Government data on employment ... showed a trend over time toward more part-time, low-paid service jobs and less full-time, well-paid, unionized manufacturing work. These same ... sources also indicated women were more likely than men to be looking for jobs through the early 1990s, because many females held part-time but wanted full-time employment."[56] Part-time jobs, however, "only reinforce the assumption that women's work is less valuable than men's, and they fail to bring about any change in the unequal power relations based on gender within Canada."[57] Despite this, the discursive framing of free trade was constructed around creating jobs for Canadians and ensuring the competitiveness of the Canadian market – undifferentiated and ungendered. Women do not exist in the aggregate, however, and a discursive manoeuvre that does not differentiate between types of jobs and categories of workers succeeds in concealing the fact that gender is an important consideration in trade policy. In the economic realities of the late 1980s, as presented in ministerial statements, women participate in the labour market as undifferentiated Canadians, and free trade creates jobs for them. The gendered construction of the economy, which has traditionally placed more value on the work of men than of women, is occluded.[58]

While gender is largely absent in discourses around free trade, such was not the case in discourses around the post-Cold War world order. Here, the issue of women was explicitly raised as part of the broadening of the foreign policy agenda. "In contemporary discussions of foreign policy, familiar subjects such as military security and trade practices have to make room for such new ones as balloting procedures, policing practices and opportunities for the advancement of women."[59] To add women to the discussion in this manner, however, seems to suggest that they are not part of military security and trade practices; rather, it suggests that military security and trade are the preserves of men and that women's concerns are something quite distinct from them. Whatever the intent, raising the question of the "advancement of women" as a separate category – one with which security and trade must share the foreign policy stage – frames women as being "apart" from the familiar or traditional concerns of foreign policy.

Beyond questions of the emancipation of women, the post-Cold War discourse points to the necessity of special provisions for women on the international stage and in international organizations. "Violence against women remains one of the most serious manifestations of human rights abuse. Canada initiated and strongly supports the current work in the UN toward a universal declaration on violence against women."[60] Furthermore, and as has been noted earlier, the Canadian government argued that, in order "to eliminate discrimination, we must also ensure the election and appointment of more women to senior positions in national and international decision-making bodies, including the United Nations."[61] In this formulation, women implicitly become part of the international security agenda; and a concern about "violence against women" implies a transcending of national and international frontiers transforming an issue traditionally defined as a women's issue into an issue of international concern. Women are also actors in international organizations, and their appointment, as women, becomes a focus for international action. While women are absent from the "non-political" sphere of international trade, they do figure in the inherently political arena of foreign policy.

The post-Cold War world order began to change the manner in which security was conceptualized. In 1985, the lead sentence of *Competitiveness and Security*'s discussion of international peace and security issues had defined Canadian security concerns in a straightforward fashion: "The most direct threat to Canadian security derives from the Soviet Union's military capabilities and antipathy to our values, and from the consequent distrust and competition between East and West."[62] The cornerstone of security was articulated clearly: "Nothing is more fundamental to state-hood than the ability to exert control over sovereign territory. And nothing is more fundamental to a state's security than the ability to mount a defence against a potential aggressor."[63] With the end of the Cold War, however, national security was redefined under the rubric of "cooperative security," which encompassed the traditional military threats to national security but also included other concerns, whether or not they had a direct military dimension. These concerns included "transnational threats to security, such as weapons proliferation, drug trafficking, terrorism, and irregular migration" as well as the "challenges and long-term security threats of climate change and related global environmental problems ... [and] the underlying conditions that create a vicious cycle of excessive population growth, underdevelopment, and mass migration."[64] In addition, we find "political establishments that cannot always be termed democratic, with the rule of law only tentatively in place"; "numerous actual or potential ethnic hostilities"; "unrestrained nationalism, rising xenophobia and racism"; and "economic frailty and underdevelopment, rising unemployment and growing economic disparities."[65] In contrast to the Mulroney government's earlier statement, sovereignty is partially problematized under the rubric of cooperative security as the "international community, urged on by Canada and others, is increasingly assuming such functions as electoral supervision, refugee protection, and even the development of democratic institutions – actions that were once considered to fall under the exclusive purview of national governments."[66]

Feminist analyses of security underscore the need to reject a narrow definition constructed around the primacy of the state and military in favour of a more holistic definition that stresses the complex interrelationships between the economy, social justice, environmental integrity, personal security, and freedom from violence in all its forms.[67] The discursive move to cooperative security begins such a transformation of the security discourse, at least in so far as it acknowledges the complex economic and social underpinnings of personal security and, thus, of some elements of national security. While in many respects, given that the state is an instrument of violence against both men and women, a definition of security that is truly responsive to the need for freedom from violence in all its forms would need to transcend the state, the explicit broadening of the security agenda to include non-military dimensions at least begins to respond to feminist critiques. Cooperative security, however, is tension-ridden inasmuch as the state remains the key actor with regard to broadened security dilemmas. In itself, this is not surprising; ministers, and the bureaucracies they represent, are unlikely to dismiss the role of the state in responding to international security concerns, even if the concerns identified within a broadened definition of international security are not amenable to state-directed solutions. In insisting upon a central role for the state, cooperative security has to be viewed through the lens of state-based national security and, thus, cannot in itself fundamentally reorient the bases of the international security structure.[68]

Conclusion: Gender and Canadian Foreign Policy

Where were the women, and did they matter in the formulation of Canadian foreign policy during the Mulroney era? In the case of women in one bureaucratic structure of the foreign policy establishment, it is apparent that the answer is unclear at best. While the Mulroney government in general, and Joe Clark in particular, tried seriously to increase the number of women in the most visible and highest echelons within the foreign service, its efforts were mitigated by DEA's corporate culture, which proved slow, if not resistant, to change. Women in External Affairs did begin to be vocal about the circumstances they confronted during these years, and this in itself is an encouraging sign. Over time, it is likely that an increased effort to recruit women into the foreign service will begin to have an impact on the representation of women within the management positions of the department, and the Mulroney administration can be applauded for its efforts in that direction.

Increasing the number of women does not mean that the gendered nature of foreign policy changes, however, nor does it mean that women figure more explicitly in foreign policy concerns. Trade policy is perhaps the policy least amenable to the inclusion of a serious consideration of the situation of women; as women are aggregated into the general pool of generic Canadians, the ways in which the global economy plays itself out in their lives in gendered ways are obstructed. The more traditional foreign policy agenda, however, has been somewhat less resistant to the incorporation of women, both explicitly (in terms of the security and discrimination concerns that are particular to women) and implicitly (in terms of a broadening of the security agenda to include "non traditional" concerns). In this respect, the Mulroney government took the first steps towards what in the 1990s the Chrétien government called the "human security agenda," although the former did so more cautiously and, in some respects, with a somewhat more circumspect assessment of its possible successes than did the latter.

The road to incorporating women into the foreign policy apparatus is a long one, and the road to incorporating issues of gender into the full range of foreign policy concerns is a longer one still. The challenge is both analytical and empirical. Deborah Stienstra has argued that, in "remaining silent on gendered issues, or including women as outside and insignificant participants of the foreign policy process, traditional Canadian foreign policy analyses are presented as gender neutral."[69] Seeking to highlight the ways in which women and gender have been, and have not been, successfully incorporated into the foreign policy agenda of one government illustrates how much we have left to accomplish; it also illustrates that the journey is not always one that moves forward without going back. As Kathryn McCallion, currently the ADM for Corporate Service in the Department of Foreign Affairs and International Trade, put it in evaluating the Mulroney years: "I think things got better for a while and I think things are on a down trend again. I think people became complacent ... they thought they had reached the beachhead before they actually got there and took for granted [that] once the door was open it would stay open."[70] The Mulroney government assisted in moving forward the process of integrating women and, to a lesser extent, gender into the foreign policy agenda; but one step forward is sometimes followed by two steps back. Adding women is, arguably, the simplest part of a difficult equation; stirring women in so that gendered structures begin to respond to their needs and to the understandings derived from feminist analyses is far more difficult and, indeed, remains a foreign policy challenge that has, as yet, been unanswered.

Acknowledgments
I would like to express my gratitude to Marc Doucet for his able research assistance, as well as to Deborah Stienstra, Heather Smith, and Caroline Andrew for helpful comments.

Notes
1 Jane Taber, "Her Place in History," *Ottawa Citizen*, 22 May 1999, B1. Morton's explanation did himself few favours: "She wasn't slighted. We picked people we thought would be interesting. I'm afraid no one thought of her." Mulroney suggested that Carney's inflexibility about the role she would play kept her away. See Diane Francis, "Carney Wasn't Snubbed: Mulroney," *National Post*, 4 June 1999, A6.
2 Cynthia Enloe, *The Morning After: Sexual Politics at the End of the Cold War* (Berkeley: University of California Press, 1993); and Cynthia Enloe, *Bananas, Beaches, and Bases: Making Feminist Sense of International Politics* (Berkeley: University of California Press, 1990).
3 Deborah Stienstra, "Can the Silence Be Broken? Gender and Canadian Foreign Policy," *International Journal* 50 (Winter 1994-95): 110.
4 As Stienstra puts it, we cannot assume that "biological differences between women and men will *necessarily* lead to different policy practices." See Stienstra, "Can the Silence Be Broken?" 110. Emphasis added.
5 Ibid., 111.
6 Elisabeth Prügl and Mary K. Meyer, "Gender Politics in Global Governance," in *Gender Politics in Global Governance*, ed. Mary K. Meyer and Elisabeth Prügl (Lantham: Rowman and Littlefield, 1999), 5.
7 V. Spike Peterson, "Introduction," in *Gendered States: Feminist (Re)Visions of International Relations Theory*, ed. V. Spike Peterson (Boulder: Lynne Rienner, 1992), 9.
8 Ibid.
9 Prügl and Meyer, "Gender Politics in Global Governance," 5.
10 Stienstra, "Can the Silence Be Broken?" 105.
11 The first monograph on gender and Canadian foreign policy was published in 1999: Edna Keeble and Heather A. Smith, *(Re)Defining Traditions: Gender and Canadian Foreign Policy* (Halifax: Fernwood, 1999).
12 Prügl and Meyer, "Gender Politics in Global Governance," 6.
13 Margaret K. Weiers, *Envoys Extraordinary: Women of the Canadian Foreign Service* (Toronto: Dundurn Press, 1995), 15.
14 Ibid., 15-16.
15 Ibid., 23.
16 Ibid., 22-23.
17 Ibid., 113. This policy persisted whether or not an officer's husband indicated a willingness to accompany his spouse abroad. At the same time, of course, it was assumed that wives would willingly follow husbands anywhere around the world, fulfilling an important representational role that "made them a valuable but unpaid part of the diplomatic service."
18 Weiers, *Envoys Extraordinary*, 101.
19 *Royal Commission on Conditions of Foreign Service* (Ottawa: Supply and Services Canada, October 1981). Most data published in the report do not provide a gender breakdown. And this, perhaps, is not unexpected since in 1981 only 8.2 percent of foreign service officers were women. References to "spouse" were commonly synonymous with "wife" and rarely, if ever, with "husband." Indeed, at least one commentator implied that there was a more nefarious social agenda at work. See the commentary on the report in *International Journal* 37 (1982) by Sir Geoffrey Jackson (386-87): "In general, this women's

lib component of the reports [the Royal Commission staff reports] can be classified as a constructive feminism – though it might be less forced, and somehow more telling, if for 'spouses' we could simply read 'wives' or, for that matter, for 'foreign service community association' read 'diplomatic wives' association,' which is what it seems to mean."

20 Treasury Board of Canada Secretariat, *Employment Statistics for the Federal Public Service, April 1, 1998 to March 31, 1999* (Ottawa: Treasury Board, 1999), 27.

21 Government of Canada, *Reports of Canada on the Convention on the Elimination of All Forms of Discrimination against Women* (Ottawa: Supply and Services Canada, 1983, 1988, and 1994). Article 8 in each report deals with the foreign service.

22 Jill Vickers has argued that a critical mass of 30 percent of women must be reached before "women will really count." See Taber, "Her Place in History," B2.

23 Progress during this era was not always linear, as this pattern might indicate. There was a decrease in the number of women serving as heads of post between 1982 and 1984. Not all of the women appointed as heads of post were rotational foreign service officers; some were political appointments. See *Reports of Canada on the Convention on the Elimination of All Forms of Discrimination against Women*, 1983, 1988, and 1994.

24 "When the Secretary of State for External Affairs directed the inclusion of women in all lists of recommendations for heads of posts, the proportion of women appointed rose from 1.8% in 1984 to 12.6% in 1989." See Report of the Task Force on Barriers to Women in the Public Service, *Beneath the Veneer*, vol. 1 (Ottawa: Supply and Services Canada, 1990), 101. Political commitment to increasing representation of women was clearly an important factor in increasing the numbers of women in high profile and executive positions.

25 Weiers, *Envoys Extraordinary*, 260. Such a perception can all too easily manifest itself in a backlash against women. As a brief to the Task Force on Barriers to Women noted, "there is a ... suspicion that despite the merit nature of the promotion process, there is a 'quota' for women ... And nothing serves to entrench this bias more at the senior levels than forwarding to the Minister initial lists for heads of post that do not contain the names of women and are therefore subsequently rejected. Men are then advised that they have been removed from the lists because of ministerial policy on women. This exacerbates systemic backlash."

26 Margaret Ford, "Women in the Foreign Service: Do They Have Legitimate Career Complaints?" *bout de papier* 7, 3 (1990): 20-21. Ford goes on to point out that "in Washington, our largest and most important Embassy, the most senior woman ranked twenty-eighth on the diplomatic list."

27 Because the DEA had the highest number of management employees of any government department, the low number of women in decision-making positions was particularly consequential.

28 For details, see Ford, "Women in the Foreign Service," 20; and *Beneath the Veneer*, 94-95.

29 *Beneath the Veneer*, 95.

30 Ibid.

31 Ford also noted that the appraisal system discriminated against women since (as with any promotion system) it tended to favour and promote those individuals who have proven successful in the past – in this case, "traditionally a male officer who has functioned well in a predominantly male culture." See Ford, "Women in the Foreign Service," 22.

32 *Beneath the Veneer*, 95.

33 Ford, "Women in the Foreign Service," 21. The Task Force came to similar conclusions.

34 *Beneath the Veneer*, 97.

35 Ibid.

36 Barbara Martin, "Editor's Notebook," *bout de papier* 7, 1 (1989): 2.

37 *Beneath the Veneer*, 97.

38 Ibid., 97. Simon Reisman illustrates this problem. Testifying before the Standing Committee on External Affairs and International Trade, Reisman was asked why, other than Sylvia Ostry, there were so few women on the senior staff negotiating the FTA. He answered that "we tried, within all the realistic possibilities of who was available, to get a team that was reasonably reflective of the whole of Canadian society ... We drew on

those people who are in the departments and agencies who are today doing work in trade and related fields ... So, almost by definition, you were required to go to who was there ... I had women I approached who felt that their career would be better advanced if they stayed where they were." See Canada, Parliament, House of Commons Standing Committee on External Affairs and International Trade, *Minutes of Evidence and Proceedings*, 33rd Parliament, 26 June 1986, 12: 25-12: 26.

39 Weiers, *Envoys Extraordinary*, 128.

40 Ibid., 236-37.

41 Ford, "Women in the Foreign Service," 20.

42 Weiers, *Envoys Extraordinary*, 182-83.

43 Canada, Secretary of State for External Affairs, *Competitiveness and Security: Directions for Canada's International Relations* (Ottawa: Supply and Services Canada, 1985), foreword, iii.

44 Ibid., 29.

45 Ibid., 2.

46 Pat Carney, "Canadian Foreign Policy: Preparing for the 21st Century," speech to Canadian Institute of International Affairs, 25 March 1988, 3.

47 Carney, speech to the Conference on Business's Stake in the Free Trade Negotiations, New York, 19 November 1986, 1.

48 Canada, Parliament, House of Commons, *Debates*, 16 March 1987.

49 Ibid.

50 House of Commons, *Debates*, 9 October 1986.

51 Alan Christie, "Free Trade Impact Said Worse for Women," *Toronto Star*, 25 February 1986, A3.

52 Madelaine Parent, National Action Committee on the Status of Women, testimony before the Standing Committee on External Affairs and International Trade, 30 November 1987, 54: 32.

53 Christie, "Free Trade Impact Said Worse for Women," A3.

54 Parent, testimony before the Standing Committee on External Affairs and International Trade, 54: 34.

55 Lise Leduc, Conseil d'intervention pour l'accès des femmes au travail, National Action Committee on the Status of Women, testimony before the Standing Committee on External Affairs and International Trade, 30 November 1987, 54: 36-37; see also John Temple, "Women Lose in Free Trade," *Sunday Star*, 8 November 1987, A1.

56 Sylvia Bashevkin, *Women on the Defensive: Living through Conservative Times* (Toronto: University of Toronto Press, 1998), 119.

57 Stienstra, "Can the Silence Be Broken?" 119.

58 The fact that Carney did not raise gender with any regularity in her free trade speeches is interesting given that she was the minister who launched the Task Force on Barriers to Women in the Public Service. Her sensitivity to the gendered nature of work and the limits to women's advancement in the civil service would suggest that she would have had a similar understanding of the gendered nature of employment more generally.

59 Barbara McDougall, "Canada and the New Internationalism," *Canadian Foreign Policy* 1 (Winter 1992/93): 2.

60 McDougall, address to the 47th session, UN General Assembly, New York, 24 September 1992, 3.

61 Ibid., 3; see also McDougall, address to the 46th session, UN General Assembly, New York, 25 September 1991, 7.

62 Canada, *Competitiveness and Security*, 37.

63 Ibid., 38.

64 Barbara McDougall, "Introduction," in *Making a Difference? Canada's Foreign Policy in a Changing World Order*, ed. John English and Norman Hillmer (Toronto: Lester Publishing, 1992), xii.

65 Barbara McDougall, "Adapting for Survival: Global Security from Sarajevo to Maastricht to Rio," address to Canadian Institute of Strategic Studies seminar, Toronto, 5 November 1992, 2.

66 McDougall, "Introduction," xiii.

67 Stienstra, "Can the Silence Be Broken?" 123.
68 Nor, in fairness, does it attempt to. Cooperative security is a broadened conception of security that adds on to, but does not challenge, the logic of state-based national security.
69 Stienstra, "Can the Silence Be Broken?" 127.
70 Weiers, *Envoys Extraordinary*, 289.

16
Ethnic Groups and Conservative Foreign Policy

Roy Norton

Some might consider it odd to examine Conservative foreign policy through the lens of ethnic communities. After all, research has consistently shown that ethnic groups enjoy limited influence over Canadian foreign policy: they are, it is commonly said, inadequately "institutionalized" to pursue their objectives; their demands rarely correspond with policies acceptable to governments. By 1984, however, it can be argued that the *potential* for ethnic communities to influence policy outcomes had increased dramatically. First, changes in immigration altered the range of foreign policy interests of Canadians. Sizable new populations from the developing world meant the Conservative government would be pressed on relations with countries to which Canada had not previously accorded much attention.

Second, official policy promoted ethnic group consciousness and cohesiveness. Initiatives such as the 1971 multiculturalism policy and 1982 Charter of Rights and Freedoms stimulated further activism on the part of ethnic groups. Indeed, Stasiulis and Abu-Laban argue that, by the mid-1980s, ethnic minorities had begun to engage in "unprecedented" political involvement; they characterize the 1988 elections as a "watershed for ethno-politics in Canada."[1]

Third, the Conservative election platform had promised to open up the foreign policy-making process. While in Opposition, the Conservatives had criticized Liberal foreign policy-making as "closed" and "elitist." And, in government, they sought to make good on their promise, partly, as Kim Richard Nossal shows (Chapter 18), by giving responsibility for the 1985-86 foreign policy review to a parliamentary committee. This also had an impact on ethnic politics, for it reduced some of the institutional barriers that had limited the scope for ethnic influence on foreign policy.

Fourth, the dramatic changes in world politics during this period galvanized numerous communities in Canada: over a million people who traced their heritage to central and eastern Europe; and tens of thousands of Armenians, Cambodians, Chileans, Chinese, Filipinos, Guatemalans, Haitians, Iranians, Lebanese, Salvadorans, Sikhs, Tamils, and Vietnamese focused on politics in their homelands and frequently demanded that their government provide leadership on human rights issues. As a result, human rights enjoyed a different profile under the Conservatives than it had under the Liberal government of Pierre Elliott Trudeau. While the Liberal government won few plaudits for its human rights policies – Sheldon Gordon, for example, argued that Trudeau had shown an "often appalling indifference" to international human rights violations[2] – the Conservatives, according to Campbell and Pal, "elevate[d] human rights on Canada's foreign policy agenda." One consequence of this was "the simultaneous elevation of human rights NGOs in the policy process."[3] It could be argued that ethnic groups were no less eager than human rights non-governmental organizations (NGOs) to participate in the policy process.

Finally, the 1984 elections changed the shape of electoral politics in Canada. In the past, Canadians of eastern European background had consistently supported the Conservatives, while Canadians from southern Europe, Asia, Latin America, and the Middle East had generally voted Liberal. The 1984 elections marked the first time that a large number of Conservatives were elected in ridings with significant ethnic populations other than eastern European. Traditionally, these ethnic groups had supported Liberal candidates – not , however, due to Liberal responsiveness to their foreign policy concerns. Mulroney regarded the election as an opportunity to win ethnic groups to the party; foreign policy was one avenue by which that could be done.

These, then, are the principal reasons to assume that ethnic group scope to influence foreign policy may have been greater in 1984 than ever before. The purpose of this chapter is to assess whether ethnic groups in fact had the impact on foreign policy that we might have expected. I examine two different groups of ethnic communities in Canada: northeastern European communities (the so-called "Seven Captive Nations") and three "visible minority" communities – Armenians, Haitians, and Sikhs. To discern the political goals of these communities, the means they chose for advocacy, and their ultimate impact on policy-making, I interviewed more than 160 persons between 1995 and 1999. I conducted interviews with ethnic group leaders; those to whom they made representations (members of Parliament [MPs], ministers and their staff, officials); and non-ethnic NGOs, church groups, journalists, pollsters, and others.[4]

Northeastern European Communities

Northeastern Europeans (especially Ukrainians, Estonians, Hungarians, Latvians, and, to a lesser extent, Lithuanians and Poles) had been strong supporters of the Conservatives when they had been in Opposition. These communities were populous: Joe Clark, the External Affairs minister from 1984 to 1991, frequently referred to the "one in ten Canadians who could trace their heritage to eastern Europe."[5] They were also well established, with most northeastern Europeans having immigrated by the 1950s – the exceptions being a Czechoslovakian influx in 1968 and a significant Polish immigration beginning in the late 1970s. These groups were also well integrated into Canadian society; they had spawned some of the "institutionalized" apparatus and relationships considered necessary in order to influence policy outcomes.

Goals

Generally, immigrants from northeastern Europe were strongly anti-communist in orientation, and they expected the Mulroney government to voice that outlook. The three Baltic communities were unambiguous in their demands. They were anxious that Canada's policy of de jure recognition of Estonian, Latvian, and Lithuanian independence be buttressed by concrete signals to the Soviet Union. Each Baltic community wanted the government to recognize an honorary consul representing that state in Canada. Less symbolically, the communities wanted Canada to push at the Conference on Security and Cooperation in Europe (CSCE) for "self-determination rights." Throughout the 1984-93 period, they – along with the Ukrainian, Polish, and Czechoslovak communities – routinely urged that Canada intervene on human rights issues.

After 1989, the expectations of eastern European communities in Canada increased considerably. The Baltic communities wanted the government to help Estonia, Latvia, and Lithuania achieve de facto independence. Ukrainian expectations were even greater. While there had been some differences within the community, as Soviet authority disintegrated the Ukrainian-Canadian community united in pressing for Canadian support for independence. After the 1 December 1991 referendum and presidential election, the community wanted quick recognition; full diplomatic relations; and significant economic, humanitarian, and technical assistance.

The Polish community was also active during this period, but it too was somewhat internally divided. Those who had come to Canada in the 1940s and 1950s wanted Ottawa to take a more active role in the North Atlantic Treaty Organization (NATO) and favoured strong sanctions against Poland. Those who had immigrated in the 1970s and 1980s saw things differently. According to one External Affairs official, recent immigrants had no faith in the Polish government, which they detested, but they saw no point in making life harder for Poles in Poland; rather, they welcomed any step that improved the lot of Poles.

N.F. Dreisziger argues that Hungarian-Canadians were also divided – between those whose principal interest was in exchanges to facilitate the maintenance of Hungarian culture in Canada and those who were hostile to the Hungarian government.[6] However, no formal presentations were made to Parliament on behalf of the Hungarian-Canadian community. One External Affairs official contends that Hungarian-Canadian business leaders saw themselves as important stakeholders in assisting transformations in Hungary.

Nor did the Czechoslovak community speak with one voice. Czechs who immigrated after the Soviet crackdown in 1968 were devoutly anti-Communist. Canadian Slovaks, by contrast, had generally immigrated earlier and, like other integrated communities concerned about cultural retention, may have been more tolerant of cooperation with Prague. The Czechoslovak Association of Canada made presentations to Parliament calling for strong support for NATO and actions to improve respect for human rights. While expressing scepticism about Soviet reforms, they also sought action to promote visits and exchanges and to streamline immigration.

Pressures from these groups often depended on their circumstances. For example, the urgency of appeals from the Hungarian and Czechoslovak populations was somewhat diminished by the liberalizing measures being taken by governments in Budapest and Prague. Likewise, for Canadian Poles, Czechoslovaks, and Hungarians – unlike their Ukrainian and Baltic counterparts – the post-1989 period was one in which economic and commercial goals largely supplanted classic foreign policy preoccupations. There were no issues of recognition or relations; Canada's formal relationships with Poland, Czechoslovakia, and Hungary were well established. Increasingly, the Canadian communities worked with the embassies and consulates of their ancestral countries in Canada, and, as a consequence, demands on the government were much diminished. Indeed, sometimes it proved difficult for community leaders to sustain their organizations. As one leader put it, the transition to democracy deprived these communities of their unifying theme – the fight against communism.

Style of Advocacy

Of the seven "Captive Nations," only the Winnipeg-based Ukrainian Canadian Congress had an Ottawa office. Contact between the Toronto-headquartered Canadian Polish Congress and bureaucrats was undertaken by its Ottawa vice-president. The three Baltic communities and the Czechoslovaks maintained Toronto offices but had no full-time representatives in Ottawa between 1984 and 1993. The volume (and direction) of community representations on foreign policy reflected these differing degrees of "institutionalization." Officials and politicians alike regarded the Ukrainian community as the one that was best organized.

The Baltic communities addressed their concerns equally to MPs and officials. They hosted an annual "Baltic Evening" on Parliament Hill, attracting MPs of all stripes. They also met on a routine basis with the responsible desk officers and divisional directors at External Affairs. The Conservatives initiated an annual consultation, with officials travelling to Toronto to meet Baltic community leaders.

The other communities focused their attention on ministers, MPs, and even senators rather than on officials. This was not a new phenomenon in 1984, although the presence in Cabinet of two senior ministers of eastern European origin (Don Mazankowski and Ray Hnatyshyn), may have served as a "magnet" for western Canadian Poles and Ukrainians. The preference of these groups was to deal with politicians rather than bureaucrats. For their part, elected officials were happy to oblige, since, as one MP put it, *any* meeting with a politician would be covered, along with a photograph, in the community's press.

Nor was there anything new about External Affairs interacting with ethnic communities. Most contact remained responsive – although, in the case of human rights consultations, the department became more proactive. Denis Stairs (Chapter 2) describes the Conservative initiative to hold an annual "officials and NGOs" consultation in preparation for meetings of the United Nations Commission on Human Rights. Some Canadian ambassadors to the region regularly initiated contact with concerned ethnic groups. As the associate under-secretary of state for external affairs, Joe Stanford, told the House of Commons Standing Committee on Multiculturalism in 1988: "There was nothing like this sort of activity even ten years ago."[7] However, whenever possible, External Affairs would try to draw in the minister's office as such meetings were viewed as essentially political.

The government was less than fully comprehensive in its outreach. The Czechoslovak Association of Canada had no formal meetings with either Clark or McDougall. By contrast, the president of the Canadian Polish Congress met Clark on a number of occasions. The deputy prime minister, Don Mazankowski, was the guest speaker at the Congress's biennial general meeting held in Alberta in 1988; Mulroney attended the biennial in Winnipeg in 1992, the first prime minister ever to do so.

Surprisingly, Clark received few foreign policy-related representations in his role as an Alberta MP; the Ukrainians tended to go to Mazankowski. Nonetheless, Clark did address the annual meeting of the Ukrainian Congress in October 1988, and he met periodically with their national leadership. He also met with Estonian, Latvian, and Lithuanian community leaders. When she succeeded Clark in 1991, Barbara McDougall continued to meet periodically with the Baltic and Ukrainian communities. As a Toronto MP, she was physically accessible to Canada's largest concentration of Baltic communities.

These groups also established connections to MPs, contacting them in their ridings and at their Ottawa offices. One Toronto-area Conservative MP described Ukrainians as "more heavily politically involved than most Canadians," noting that the Baltic communities did a disproportionate amount of work during elections. Indeed, the Baltic communities responded to the formation of the Canadian Parliamentary Group for the Baltic Peoples by volunteering to assist MPs who were active in the group.

MPs of all parties acknowledged such support and loyalty by raising the communities' concerns in Parliament. MPs also made representations directly to ministers and officials on behalf of their eastern European constituents. External affairs sought to ensure that those groups that had established a political connection to MPs were, in the words of one official, "kept happy." Not surprisingly, External Affairs also tried to keep the Prime Minister's Office (PMO) happy. One senior official conceded that the Department of External Affairs (DEA) was very conscious that Mulroney had strong views on particular issues, including issues of interest to particular ethnic communities. According to DEA officials, the PMO and the Privy Council Office (PCO) were "constantly relaying" Mulroney's views and instructions, making it important to try to ensure harmony with the External Affairs minister. This was particularly true in the final phase of Mulroney's mandate. According to one official, "every important decision during this time was being referred to the PCO. There was a sense that the PM was driving Canada's policy toward central and eastern Europe, with the objective of pulling these newly liberated countries into the western orbit."

In addition to making representations to ministers, MPs, and officials, ethnic leaders pressed their case before parliamentary committees. The Ukrainian Canadian Congress, the Association of United Ukrainian Canadians, the Canadian Polish Congress, the Hungarian Human Rights Foundation, the Czechoslovak Association, the Baltic Federation in Canada, the Estonian Central Council in Canada, and the Latvian National Federation in Canada all made presentations to one or more of the Special Joint Committee on Canada's International Relations, the Standing Committee on External Affairs and International Trade, and/or the Standing Committee on Human Rights.

Aside from these appearances, the communities generally refrained from publicly pressuring the government, although they did demonstrate at eastern European embassies or consulates. All of the "Captive Nations" communities participated in the annual "Black Ribbon Day" demonstration at Toronto's City Hall alongside other ethnic groups with international human rights concerns.

While no other group lobbied on behalf of these communities, business groups were not hesitant to express concerns about the potential commercial effects of a Canadian focus on human rights. Karel Velan, chair of the Canadian East European Trade Council, made that case to the standing committee during its 1986 hearings on eastern Europe. In 1989, the committee heard the Canada-Polish Business Council call for policies to maximize economic interaction with the region. In 1990, Andrew Sarlos, a prominent Hungarian-Canadian and co-chair of the Central European Development Fund, made the same argument to the committee.

Business interests were not the only counterweight to ethnic demands. Embassies in Ottawa monitored the ethnic press and complained about politicians attending "Captive Nations" events. External Affairs responded, as one official put it, by "pointing out Canadian realities." However, the DEA sought to give no gratuitous offence, since few officials saw any point in needlessly annoying the Soviet Union.

To a certain extent, ethnic groups benefited from the coverage of events in central and eastern Europe. Killings in Baltic capitals, the oppression of Ukrainian dissidents, Polish government repression, the cases of Soviet *refuseniks,* were generally cast in clear "David-and-Goliath" terms. Moreover, over time the groups became increasingly attuned to the need for sophisticated media relations strategies in order to gain attention to their causes and activities.

Policy Outcomes

Most eastern European-Canadians appeared to be pleased with Canada's leadership at the CSCE and on individual human rights cases; one community leader claimed he "always felt Joe Clark was totally in tune with the position [he] was advocating." A senior bureaucrat in External Affairs confirms that Clark's office took the view that it was important to demonstrate sensitivity to ethnic communities' inquiries and to ensure that they were listened to. Moreover, Clark advocated a highly practical, results-oriented approach, often to the chagrin of MPs who embraced a full rhetorical assault on the Soviet Union. To critics, Clark emphasized the emptiness of posturing but, at the same time, conceded candidly that this created a dilemma for policy-makers who, on the one hand, wanted to be hard-headed about the intransigence of the Soviet system, while, on the other hand, being equally hard-headed about the practical effectiveness of measures genuinely open to Canadians.

At the CSCE, however, Canada persistently condemned human rights abuses in central and eastern Europe; in return, the Baltic communities made Canada's ambassador to the CSCE their "Man of the Year," and the Canadian Polish Congress gave him their gold medal. Throughout the CSCE negotiations, Canada was responsible for the rights of minorities and the freedom of people to leave their country. And, bilaterally, Canada pursued the cases of dissidents such as Andrei Sakharov, Anatoly

Shcharansky, and Vaclav Havel – as well as those whose names were known only within particular ethnic communities.

Officials perceive a link between the size of Canada's eastern European communities and the government's decision to create an assistance program to central and eastern Europe. This program began in 1989 as a seventy-two-million-dollar program for Hungary and Poland. The assistance program expanded as more countries became independent – eventually it encompassed the entire region and grew to $4.5 billion. This expansion was not, however, due to any evident response to pressures from ethnic communities. Ethnic groups did not press for aid with anything like the vigour with which they pressed for freedom and independence across eastern Europe.

There was a close link between domestic pressures and the Conservatives' efforts to secure the freedom of the Baltic states. The Conservative government did not oblige Baltic communities' demands for honorary consuls, but it did take other symbolic measures, like "listing" the national days of these communities and adjusting government maps to refer to their countries. After re-election in 1988, however, the government faced a situation fraught with more difficulty. The November 1988 independence resolution taken by Estonia's parliament triggered comparable actions in Latvia and Lithuania. The Soviet response was menacing, and Canada's position became increasingly stern over the next two years. In the course of his frequent interventions in the House, Clark revealed the undertakings he had sought and received from his Soviet counterpart – and stipulated his expectation that they would be respected. Barbara McDougall's press releases adopted an ever more strident tone as the Soviets increasingly threatened the Baltic states.

With Clark's encouragement, MPs became increasingly involved in policy development. Parliamentarians, supported by the government, formally observed Baltic elections. The government agreed to emergency debates in the House and to pro-independence resolutions generated by all-party coalitions of MPs. Parliament proved a useful vehicle by which Canadian sentiment could be transmitted to Soviet authorities without the government having to take actions that could have severely damaged relations with the Soviet Union.

By relying on the House as extensively as it did, the government ensured that Canada's Baltic communities were fully involved in policy development. The approach earned rare plaudits from otherwise partisan opponents. During an Opposition Day debate in May 1990, the New Democratic Party's Bill Blaikie praised Clark for "bring[ing] MPs more into the debate on foreign policy" and for "tak[ing] the House more seriously than some previous ministers of foreign affairs." In March 1991, after a visit to the region, Toronto Liberal MP Jesse Flis told the standing committee that the three Baltic states "cannot thank us enough for the quick and strong action taken by Canada." Those actions included, on 2 December 1991, being the first country to recognize Lithuania and Ukrainian independence. Then – as in the case of the Baltic states – the involvement of domestic communities may have been instrumental.

Visible Minority Communities

Unlike the northeastern European communities, the three "visible minority" communities surveyed here were relatively recent arrivals to Canada. Most Armenians came to Canada in the 1960s – although with a total population of around 60,000, they constituted only about 0.2 percent of Canada's population in 1984. Haitian immigration commenced in 1965, with significant arrivals beginning only in the 1970s. Haitians were barely more numerous than were Armenians. Sikhs – by far the largest of the three "visible minority" communities examined here – arrived mostly in the 1970s and 1980s. All three groups were geographically concentrated in important media centres; by 1984, all had developed some measure of organizational structure.

Goals

The foreign policy demands and rhetoric of Armenian-, Haitian-, and Sikh-Canadians during this period were principally concerned with human rights and democratic development issues. To be sure, the Armenian case fits the "human rights" case least well. The Armenian appeal was cast in human rights terms, but their grievance was historic rather than current. More than one million Armenians had died under the Ottoman Turks between 1915 and 1917; the community wanted the Canadian government to take an international leadership role in characterizing those massacres as "genocide." The new Conservative government thus faced a dilemma: did its commitment to advance human rights internationally include a willingness to jeopardize an important strategic relationship (with NATO partner Turkey) when so doing would not materially affect the human rights condition of any living Armenian?

For a brief time after the devastating Armenian earthquake in December 1988, Armenian-Canadians united to support a different cause – securing as much humanitarian assistance as possible. Later, when issues arose concerning Armenian independence from the Soviet Union, diplomatic recognition and relations, and assistance to the new government in Yerevan, the domestic community was relatively – and surprisingly – silent.

Haitian-Canadians' foreign policy interests were kindled early in 1986. With the exile of "Baby Doc" Duvalier and the formation of a new government, the community demanded that Canada act to help transform Haiti into a democracy. It wanted Ottawa to secure changes to US policy and to persuade the United Nations to become involved: according to one senior official at External Affairs, the Haitian community sought "an extraordinarily activist policy." Aside from immigration and aid-related objectives, however, Haitian-Canadian demands were rarely accompanied by precise policy recommendations; instead, decision-makers were charged with figuring out how to achieve a "free and democratic Haiti."

Just three months before the Conservatives took office, Sikhism's holiest shrine, the Golden Temple in Amritsar, was attacked by the Indian military; some 15,000 Sikhs in Vancouver and 20,000 in Toronto rallied against the Indian government. And one month after the 1984 elections, Indira Gandhi was assassinated by her Sikh bodyguards. From that point onward, Sikhs – and Canadian-Indian relations – were seldom out of the news.

Immigration was a major policy concern for Sikh-Canadians. So were human rights in Punjab and India generally. Sikhs in Canada were highly suspicious of the Indian government and opposed most forms of bilateral cooperation. But the foreign policy issue on which decision-makers were most assertively pressed was also the one on which the community was most profoundly divided: an independent Khalistan.

Style of Advocacy

By 1984, visible minority communities had few of the institutional means for pursuing foreign policy goals. Armenians had fashioned elaborate community structures in Montréal and Toronto – only a small part of whose function was to interact with decision-makers on foreign policy matters. They had no day-to-day presence in Ottawa. The Haitians supported numerous social service organizations in Montréal but did not have a hierarchical leadership with responsibility for foreign policy advocacy. Nor did they have an Ottawa office. The Sikh community proliferated organizations across the country, most of which aggressively advanced particular foreign policy goals. Only the pro-Khalistan World Sikh Organization (WSO) maintained a staffed office in Ottawa throughout this period.

Visible minority group contact with policy-makers was overwhelmingly at the level of MPs and ministers. One Armenian community leader noted that for a long time External Affairs was completely unknown to his community. Clark tried to change that situation by designating a senior official to be "point of contact" with the community. However, because the community "understood politics better than it understood the bureaucracy," according to one leader, it largely continued to target its representations to politicians and their staff. Armenians were methodical in lobbying sitting MPs and party candidates in ridings with sizable Armenian populations; MPs with functional responsibilities, such as committee chairs; and Opposition spokespersons.

Haitians were less thorough in contacting politicians. Indeed, one Liberal MP called them "timid" and "disorganized." They tended to focus only on MPs from the four or five ridings where the community could make ·a difference. Their interaction with External Affairs officials was extremely limited; Canada's ambassador in Port-au-Prince dealt much more with the Montréal community than did Ottawa. In fact, the Conservative government formalized the practice of annual consultations between the community and the ambassador to Haiti.

Relations between Canadian Sikhs and policy-makers were the most complicated of those of any visible minority group. Organizations like the Federation of Sikh Societies of Canada and the Sikh Professional Association of Canada enjoyed routine access to officials – although they, like ethnic groups generally, initiated most of the contact. Other significant groups, such as Babbar Khalsa and the International Sikh Youth Federation, attempted to influence foreign policy by organizing demonstrations but were largely uninterested in talking with decision-makers, bureaucratic or political. The World Sikh Organization tended to be ostracized by External Affairs after December 1987 due to concerns about the nature of their pro-Khalistan activity. Inevitably, the WSO (and other Sikh organizations) concentrated lobbying attention on MPs and Parliament. They did so without any illusions about Parliament's role in foreign policy formulation. One WSO official acknowledges that "a handful of MPs were seen as friends of the Sikhs. They didn't turn us away – even if they didn't necessarily do anything for us."

Armenian-Canadian leaders also appeared before parliamentary committees. Parliamentarians did not receive testimony from the "moderate" Armenian Democratic Liberal Organization; rather, officials heard exclusively from the Armenian National Committee of Canada. That was not significant as long as genocide was the community's preoccupation. It became important with Armenia's independence, given the Armenian National Committee's near-hostility to the Armenian government of Levon Ter Petrosian.

Unlike Armenians and Sikhs, Haitians never appeared before parliamentary committees. Parliament, however, came to them. After an aborted Haitian election in November 1987, Clark named a three-person all-party parliamentary group to travel to Haiti. Before doing so, the members of this group met in Montréal with eighteen different organizations.

MPs raised foreign policy issues of concern to these communities in both the House and in committee. Only concerning Haiti, however, did the government seem to welcome the questions: in the House, Mulroney chose not to respond to questions about Armenian- or Sikh-related matters, but he was happy to respond to questions about Haiti, and his comments reflected extensive personal involvement in the issue. Of the three visible minority communities, only the Haitians felt they had a direct conduit to the prime minister (particularly through André Arcelin and, subsequently, his wife, Nicole Roy-Arcelin, who was elected as a Conservative MP in 1988). Mulroney's interest was understood at External Affairs – and that by itself was sufficient to overcome departmental hesitation about the resources required relative to the likely policy returns.

We can better understand the prime minister's enthusiasm for the Haitians' objectives (and relative lack of interest in the Armenian and Sikh causes) by examining the activities of each group. In a partisan sense, the Haitians were among the least "aligned" of any visible minority community. While the ridings in which they lived had almost all been held by Liberals prior to 1984, their electoral participation was low, and the community had not really been courted by the Liberal establishment. Their partisan loyalty thus was winnable, and they were obvious targets for a Conservative leader anxious to root his party in Québec.

By contrast, while the Armenian community took pains to endorse some non-Liberal candidates, most Montréal Armenians had for years been resolute supporters of the Liberal party. This is not to say that the community's loyalty would not have shifted to the Conservatives had their "genocide" demand been met. Theirs is a classic example of a case in which a single foreign policy action could have caused a highly activist community to realign itself politically.

While Sikh-Canadians were probably the most politically active visible minority community, with rare exceptions they had been more inclined to support Liberals or New Democrats than Conservatives. Again, however, had the Conservatives adopted an aggressive rhetoric accusing India of systematic human rights violations, the allegiance of all but the pro-Khalistan die-hards might have been won.

Of these three visible minority communities, only the Haitians enjoyed the support of a broad societal coalition. It was not an alliance cobbled together by Haitian leaders per se; rather, these leaders stood aside and surrendered much of the direction of the "Haitian democracy" movement to elements of society more experienced with policy advocacy. Armenian and Sikh leaders, on the other hand, freely admit that their communities were almost totally ineffective with regard to magnifying their influence through coalitions.

Media perceptions of the three visible minority communities account significantly for the breadth of the Haitians' appeal and the narrowness of that of the Armenians and the Sikhs. Notwithstanding the fact that Haitians had consistently been victims of racism, the Québec and national media highlighted their campaign for democracy in Haiti, portraying the coup leaders in negative terms.

Armenian-Canadians endured none of the racism that plagued Haitians or Sikhs – but, like the Sikhs, on the issue of terrorism, their entire community suffered from "guilt by association." And Armenians bore the additional burden that, because their principal policy goal focused on events that had occurred seven decades ago, no current images were available to the electronic media that might have helped them broaden popular support for their cause.

Sikh-Canadians faced a different set of challenges. Indira Gandhi's assassination, the Air India bombing in June 1985, and the arrival of refugee claimants on the shores of Nova Scotia in 1987 – all contributed to negative perceptions of the community; partisan hyperactivity in the Liberal party nominating process in 1988 compounded the problem.

Policy Outcomes

The government reneged on its 1984 campaign commitment to "recognize" the Armenian genocide; Clark admitted to the community that the Conservatives had erred in making the promise. Although Paul McCrossan, a Conservative MP whose Scarborough constituency had a sizable Armenian population, led an effort to arrive at a formulation that the community and the government could accept, the negotiations failed. On the other hand, the government did commit considerable emergency aid to assist victims of the 1988 Armenian earthquake. However, Canada did not recognize the independence of Nagorno-Karabakh; it did not open a full embassy in Yerevan; and it did not provide disproportionate assistance to the newly independent Armenia. The Conservatives did initiate an ongoing dialogue with the community at the officials' level, and Clark was the first External Affairs minister to visit Toronto's Armenian Community Centre.

Those Sikh-Canadians promoting an independent Khalistan failed abjectly; that portion of the community wanting Canadian action against human rights abuses in India met greater success. The Mulroney government's representations to the Indian government were often cited as proof that the Sikh community had been effective. As one official put it, "The simple repetition of the line in India – and the fact we meant it – had an impact. Our credibility was enhanced ... because of the obvious political price being paid at home." However, there was some disappointment in the Sikh community that the Conservatives did not publicly press India on human rights matters; and there was some scepticism concerning the assurances of External Affairs that these representations were being made to New Delhi privately.

On a key immigration objective, the Sikh community enjoyed unambiguous success. Processing times for applicants from India had been exceptionally slow, and the government allocated the resources to begin ameliorating the situation. Canadians of South Asian origin, however, had lobbied in unison for that change. On other, more "political," immigration-related objectives (a Canadian consulate in Punjab, acceptance by Canada of refugee applicants from Punjab), Sikh-Canadians were completely disappointed. Sikhs wanting a cooling in the Canada-India relationship also met with failure. Bilateral agreements (including an extradition treaty) were signed; ministers made several reciprocal visits; and considerable energies were expended to strengthen commercial relations. Canada and India cooperated in multilateral contexts, particularly in the effort to end South African apartheid.

Concerning policy and process outcomes of interest to Haitian-Canadians, the picture is much different. After the 1991 coup, Canada was at the centre of an international political and diplomatic effort to restore democracy to Haiti. The prime minister was in frequent touch with George Bush and Bill Clinton as well as with the French and Venezuelan presidents. Mulroney raised the issue at the Group of Seven (G-7) and la Francophonie summits, and he insisted that Canada take the lead at the United Nations. Indeed, Haiti ended up consuming a disproportionate share of External Affairs' resources, at least, in the words of one official, "relative to a rational assessment of Canadian interests at stake." Most of those interviewed concurred that the high level of activity reflected the effectiveness of this group.

Did Ethnic Groups Influence Conservative Foreign Policy?

The evidence suggests that northeastern European communities were able to secure greater attention to their goals from the Mulroney government than they had from the Trudeau government. There was a concern in the Mulroney Cabinet that the Department of External Affairs was unsympathetic to some of the concerns of particular communities, notably those from the Baltics. DEA adhered to the accepted state-to-state model of international relations, making it problematic for Canada to be talking to the Baltic communities. However, the consultative process fostered by the Conservatives accelerated change and achieved at least two purposes: (1) it reinforced among ethnic communities a view that they had a legitimate role to play; and (2) it confirmed to those conducting foreign policy that their constituency had expanded.

As we have seen, however, not every group felt appropriately consulted. Ministerial time, as always, was at a premium. The culture at External Affairs did not change overnight: officials made highly individualistic judgments about the priority they should attach to outreach efforts. Nonetheless, as Don Page, the official who coordinated the department's input to the 1985-86 foreign policy review, wrote, it was obvious that "in this new [ethnic] environment ... Canadian foreign policy would be asked to expand beyond its well-worn parameters to include these new priorities."[8]

Outreach took different forms under the Conservatives than it did under the Liberals. More than its predecessor, the Conservative government used Parliament to craft foreign policy positions, particularly concerning Haiti and the Baltic states. A parliamentary solution was sought in the Armenian case, even if unsuccessfully. Clark valued both Parliament's representative function, seeing it as a barometer of the foreign policy priorities of Canadians, and the fact that MPs were much more accessible to ordinary Canadians than were officials. This, in turn, meant more people became more genuinely involved.

Involving Parliament did not mean ceding decision-making authority to parliamentarians. The Sikh case demonstrates that MPs, however supportive of an ethnic community they might have been, had next to no influence on policy outcomes (even though, according to some Conservatives, there was more support in the Conservative caucus for the Sikh community than for any other save the Jewish community). One Conservative believes that was simply because "Sikhs work their MPs."

The Sikh case is instructive. No matter that the community was divided and that a majority of its adherents probably did not support an independent Khalistan. Pro-Khalistan advocates constituted the most publicly outspoken portion of the community, and the government was firmly opposed to their agenda. Clark told the House on 10 March 1988 that "the activities of a small, militant minority in the Sikh community represent the most serious internal security threat that Canada faces today." There were also national unity considerations. Speaking to the Standing Committee on Justice, Clark said: "For elected Canadian officials to support the advocates of Khalistan today would be the equivalent to endorsing the foreign interference in our affairs which Canadians found so objectionable only 20-odd years ago."[9] In a similar fashion, the Armenian case suggests that there were concerns about "rewarding" terrorist activity, and, in the end, the Conservatives took seriously the "national security" implications of a move that risked alienating Turkey from its NATO partners. Furthermore, they were not disposed to break with the US administration on this issue.

The government responded to Sikh community pressures by routinely raising human rights matters with Indian authorities. Likewise, it responded to the demands of eastern European- and Haitian-Canadians by elevating human rights and democratic development goals in its policies towards regions of concern to those communities. As Gecelovsky and Keating argue (Chapter 13), the pursuit of human rights and good governance by the Mulroney Conservatives "was a radically different course than Canadians had travelled in the past."

Ethnic communities generally place human rights issues at or near the top of their foreign policy agenda. By emphasizing human rights, the government not only responded to ethnic groups, it also encouraged them. But it did not always do so in a way preferred by ethnic communities. For example, while Sikh-Canadians wanted actions that would embarrass Indian authorities, the Conservative government believed that public hectoring would be counterproductive. It generally felt the same regarding the Soviet and eastern European governments, which is why a "two-track" policy was pursued, with an aggressive posture employed in the multilateral CSCE context, and a more pragmatic, results-oriented approach applied bilaterally. Only in the case of the Haitians did the government embrace the rhetoric of the domestic group.

The near-frenetic activity to facilitate Ukrainian independence definitely reflected an awareness of Ukrainian-Canadian objectives. Charlotte Gray dismisses the government's rapid recognition of Ukrainian independence as simply being "driven by the presence of one million Canadians of Ukrainian origin."[10] While her number is inflated, the point is uncontested. Ukrainian-Canadians were overjoyed by Ottawa's quick move, and some of the Ukrainian community's animosity towards the government (lingering from the naming of the Deschènes Commission of Inquiry on War Criminals in Canada in 1985) may have dissipated as a result. Gray declares her cynicism – but does not offer reasons why it was *wrong* for the government to take actions of a largely symbolic nature, that consumed minimal resources, that did little to jeopardize Canadian relations with what remained of the Soviet Union (but that certainly enhanced relations with the new Ukrainian government), and that happened to please a sizable number of Canadians. This was *not* a departure; it is highly likely that a government less responsive to Ukrainian-Canadians would, ultimately, have taken the same actions as did the Conservatives.

Perhaps because the Haitian community was so comparatively small no evident cynicism greeted the government's hyperactive response to Haiti's crises. To be sure, the government realized partisan gains that probably extended beyond that particular ethnic community. By acting as it did, the Mulroney government may have solidified Haitian identification with the "federalist camp" in the battle with separatists over Québec's future. By exerting leadership in the wake of the September 1991 coup dislodging Aristide, McDougall was able to show that she was in charge of her portfolio (after finding herself in bad odour with the PMO after her response to the August 1991 coup attempt in Moscow). And, as noted by one senior official, the kind of high level diplomacy required to restore Aristide "played to the PM's personal style; [he] liked to operate himself on the international scene, or to have his immediate entourage act on his behalf." There were, however, ample foreign policy-related reasons for the Conservatives to energetically embrace the Haiti issue. In addition to its "fit" with its human rights/democratic development agenda, by attaching so much importance to Haiti the government was able to: help revitalize the Organization of American States (and validate its decision to join that body), infuse la Francophonie with additional purpose (and find a francophone analogue to their Commonwealth-related activism on South Africa), and help guide the "post-Cold War" United Nations towards an enhanced role in resolving regional conflicts.

It is ironic that the least "institutionalized" ethnic community examined here happened to receive the greatest amount of government attention. According to one official, one of the reasons for this was that a number of Canadian interests were affected in the Haitian case. An additional explanation can be found in the fact that, for reasons of geography, language, and the US-Haiti relationship, Canada was a great power in the case of Haiti. Canadian actions were likely to be meaningful. To a lesser extent, that condition also applied in the Ukrainian case – where, precisely because of Canada's large Ukrainian population, G-7 and other Western nations were somewhat disposed to defer to Canadian leadership.

Conclusion: A Departure?

Guiding the chapters of this book has been one overarching question: did the Conservative government's approach to foreign policy represent a policy departure? When applied to ethnic groups, the answer is a qualified "yes." The "yes" must be qualified because it is impossible to say how a different government would have responded to the world confronting the Mulroney Conservatives. Concerning the ethnic groups examined here, some might argue that, rhetoric aside, the *substantive* response of a Turner Liberal government to demands of the sort that came from the Armenian and Sikh communities would have been no different from that of the Mulroney Conservative government. Had they been re-elected in 1984, the Liberals might have pursued as activist a policy towards Haiti, the Baltic states, and Ukraine. While such a proposition seems doubtful, it, of course, cannot incontrovertibly be proven wrong.

However, there can be little doubt that, in their approach to ethnic groups and foreign policy, the Conservatives displayed some of the creativity and drive that tends to come from those who are "new" to the policy arena. Mulroney was deeply interested in the intricacies of many foreign policy issues, and he was keen to immerse himself in finding a resolution to them. Likewise, Clark had a lot to prove in the job. As a result, he worked prodigiously and drove his department to be "on top" of every issue and always to generate ideas for ways in which Canada could "make a difference." Issues previously deemed peripheral – like those advanced by many ethnic communities – secured scrutiny because he insisted they be taken seriously.

Finally, the Conservative approach represented a departure in terms of *process*: the Mulroney government differed from the Trudeau government in ways that were intrinsic to the Conservative view of policy-making. First was its propensity to consult. Indeed, this book is replete with examples of consultative processes implemented by the Mulroney government. The Conservative party was itself a perennial outsider to government. It drew support from many Canadians who were part of no establishment and whose contact with foreign policy-makers had been limited. Ethnic groups fit perfectly within the category of Canadians whom Clark profoundly felt had been "closed out" of the process of making Canada's foreign policy. He was determined to open up that process; and ethnic communities generally benefited from the government's disposition to consult.

Second, the Conservatives tended to use Parliament, and one of the effects of doing this was the promotion of greater consultation due to the fact that ethnic groups saw the legislature as the "policy arm" closest to them. But this was not simply a device to help broaden the range of consultation. For almost all of the previous twenty-one years, Parliament had been the preferred forum for Conservatives. Without formal access to the advice tendered by Canada's highly professional public service, it was the caucus that determined policy. As a skilled parliamentarian and effective consensus builder, Clark – more than his predecessors – trusted the institution to generate policy ideas that reflected the current priorities of Canadians in every part of the country. On Haiti, on the Baltic states, and on other issues, ethnic groups benefited from the fact that the Conservative government invited Parliament to play a meaningful role.

Finally, there is the Mulroney government's emphasis on human rights and democratic governance. One of Mulroney's Cabinet colleagues suggests that the prime minister came to the Haiti file "out of a visceral human rights interest." And the Conservatives were less obsessed than were their predecessors with international "order": they were prepared, as Michaud and Nossal have observed with reference to Ukraine (Chapter 1), to be the "first Canadian government to ... encourage the idea of the disintegration of a federal state." The caucus, perhaps especially its western Canadian component, was committed to measures to promote democratic development. In that regard, the Conservatives may have been influenced somewhat by right-wing rhetoric from the United States – rhetoric to which the Liberal government had been largely impervious.

And so, from 1984 onward, the objective shared overwhelmingly among ethnic groups – the international promotion of human rights and democratic governance – was precisely the one to which the Mulroney government was giving voice. Rather than being told why Canada could not interfere in the internal affairs of other countries, ethnic communities were now being invited to hold their government accountable to policy standards akin to those they had been advocating themselves. In short, on style and specifics, on consultation, on the role of Parliament, and on the place of human rights and democratic governance in the panoply of policy priorities, the Conservative era represented a considerable departure from the Liberal era.

Notes

1 Daiva K. Stasiulis and Yasmeen Abu-Laban, "The House the Parties Built: (Re)constructing Ethnic Representation in Canadian Politics," in *Ethnocultural Groups and Visible Minorities in Canadian Politics: The Question of Access*, ed. Kathy Megyery (Toronto: Dundurn Press, 1991), 19; and Daiva K. Stasiulis and Yasmeen Abu-Laban, "Ethnic Activism and the Politics of Limited Inclusion in Canada," in *Canadian Politics: An Introduction to the Discipline*, ed. Alain-G. Gagnon and James P. Bickerton (Peterborough: Broadview Press, 1990), 584.

2 Sheldon Gordon, "The Canadian Government and Human Rights Abroad," *International Perspectives* (November/December 1983): 9; likewise, Kathleen Mahoney claimed that, under Trudeau, human rights were "on the periphery of foreign affairs." See Kathleen Mahoney, "Human Rights and Canada's Foreign Policy," *International Journal* 47 (Summer 1992): 556.

3 Robert M. Campbell and Leslie A. Pal, *The Real Worlds of Canadian Politics: Cases in Process and Policy*, 3rd ed. (Peterborough: Broadview Press, 1994), 217, 229.

4 The following were interviewed between November 1995 and October 1999: André Arcelin, Alice Basarke, Girair Basmadjian, Bill Bauer, Eric Bergbusch, Patrick Boyer, Pauline Browes, Joe Clark, Jesse Flis, Derek Fraser, Louise Fréchette, Stan Gooch, John Graham, Graham Green, Peter Hancock, Levon Hasserjian, Paul Heinbecker, Ramon Hnatyshyn, David Hoff, Keder Hyppolite, Jim Judd, Zuhair Kashmeri, Jan Kaszuba, Monique Landry, Laas Leivat, Marek Malicki, Barbara McDougall, Maria Minna, Graham Mitchell, Reid Morden, Harjot Oberoi, André Ouellet, T.S. Puréwal, Gobinder Randhawa, John Reimer, John Robinson, Milo Suchma, J.H. Taylor, Frantz Voltaire, Andrew Witer, and Gerald Wright.

5 According to the 1981 Census, there were 529,615 Canadians of Ukrainian origin; 254,485 Poles; 132,000 Hungarians; 82,000 Czechs and Slovaks; and 50,300 Estonians, Latvians, and Lithuanians. Only the Polish population grew significantly between 1984 and 1993. See Jean R. Burnet with Howard Palmer, *"Coming Canadians": An Introduction to a History of Canada's Peoples* (Toronto: McClelland and Stewart, 1988), 42.

6 N.F. Dreisziger with M.L. Kovacs, Paul Brody, and Bennett Kovrig, *Struggle and Hope: The Hungarian-Canadian Experience* (Toronto: McClelland and Stewart, 1985), 228.

7 Canada, Parliament, House of Commons Standing Committee on Multiculturalism, *Minutes of Proceedings and Evidence*, 26 June 1988.

8 Don Page, "Populism in Canadian Foreign Policy: The 1986 Review Revisited," *Canadian Public Administration* 37 (Winter 1994): 584.

9 House of Commons, Standing Committee on Justice, *Minutes of Proceedings and Evidence*, 16 June 1988.

10 Charlotte Gray, "New Faces in Old Places: The Making of Canadian Foreign Policy," in *Canada Among Nations, 1992-93: A New World Order?* ed. Fen Osler Hampson and Christopher J. Maule (Ottawa: Carleton University Press, 1994), 23.

17
Bureaucratic Politics and the Making of the 1987 Defence White Paper

Nelson Michaud

Following the general elections on 4 September 1984, many bureaucrats in Ottawa were convinced, given the negative comments made by the Progressive Conservatives while they were in Opposition, that the new government under Brian Mulroney was going to regard them as little more than a stronghold of Liberal party sympathizers. There is, indeed, some evidence that the new government lacked confidence in the impartiality of its bureaucracy,[1] and many key officials from the Trudeau era were side-lined immediately after the 1984 election. On the other hand, many of these bureaucrats were back in key positions not long afterwards, exercising considerable influence during the Conservative era.[2] Other chapters in this book make clear that the bureaucracy played an important role in many of the initiatives and departures pursued by the Mulroney government, a conclusion also supported by other research.[3]

In this chapter, I attempt to go one step further by trying to measure the level of influence the bureaucracy had on the Mulroney government's foreign policy decisions. I do this by reconstructing the relationship between bureaucracy and the Cabinet in one case study – the June 1987 white paper on defence. At the time, the white paper was portrayed as a clear departure from Liberal defence policies. The *Globe and Mail* referred to an "abrupt turn" and a "decisive reversal."[4] The *Toronto Star* described the exercise as "a 180° turn in our defence policy."[5] Moreover, analysts such as Dan Middlemiss referred to it as a "bold blueprint for change."[6]

Such evaluations suggest that the white paper can be considered as one of the possible departures from Liberal policies that this book seeks to analyze. Conversely, many aspects of the policy were dropped one after the other soon after its adoption. Why was this generally perceived departure from Liberal policy so short-lived? To answer this question, I first postulate that the fate of a policy is, in large measure, determined by the control that its instigators manage to exercise when the time comes to actually implement it. I argue that the officials who were successful in securing approval for the white paper lost control of the policy at the implementation phase, leading to its eventual collapse. To show how this happened, I analyze the interaction between bureaucrats, military officials, and politicians, first using a framework developed by Albert Legault,[7] which puts this interaction within a broad political context. I then analyze the interaction per se by turning to two analytical models: (1) Graham Allison's bureaucratic politics model and (2) Vincent Lemieux's structuration of power framework.[8] Used in conjunction, these two approaches help to reveal how the white paper was formulated and how and why it failed.

The Defence White Paper: A Policy Departure?

The 1987 white paper on defence was issued many months behind schedule. Thus, when it was finally published, there was a need to present it as the result of a lengthy and carefully thought out exercise. In keeping with Conservative election promises to bridge the gap between defence commitments and defence capabilities, it advocated a considerable increase in defence spending.[9] Indeed, of the five defence white papers issued by Canada in the last five decades, four articulated policies aimed at reducing the resources, size, and role of Canadian forces.[10] The 1987 paper was the only one to advocate increasing the defence budget and the only one that embraced a strong antagonistic stance.

The presentation of the 1987 white paper was also orchestrated in order to reflect a clear departure from previous policy statements. All those close to the process confirmed that special care was taken to ensure that the look of the document reflected the "true meaning of the policy," as one official put it.[11] Photographs, graphs, tables, and charts were included in the text to produce a document that was the most colourful defence white paper ever produced by a Canadian government. Likewise, the communication plan accompanying the document called for a national tour by the minister in order to sell the policy to attentive publics and to Canadians in general, although the opposition parties portrayed this as an attempt by the minister to avoid defending his policy in the House of Commons.[12] Ignoring these expected criticisms, Perrin Beatty travelled across the country, arguing, as he had done in his House of Commons speech when he tabled the white paper, that this was part of the transformation the Conservative government was bringing about in defence policy.[13]

The strategy was not as successful as had been anticipated. As Norrin Ripsman demonstrates in Chapter 7, the new policy quickly came under attack not only from the expected quarters – the peace movement and the Liberal Opposition – but also (and more surprisingly) from within the government itself.[14] Many features of the policy were quickly abandoned. As a result, the 1987 white paper had virtually no lasting effect. Some have argued that the white paper collapsed because of a thaw in East-West relations; others have pointed to a difficult domestic financial situation in which deficit fighting was the unquestionable credo. The departure factor, although unquestionably present, was not as important as it was then portrayed, which is in accordance with Ripsman's finding regarding continuity. To use Denis Stairs's image, in this instance, the Conservatives were, in fact, engineers who wanted to be perceived as architects. Therefore, the desire to be seen as departing from Liberal policy cannot be regarded as the prime factor in explaining the fate of the white paper. Better explanations may be found in the dynamic that characterized the exchanges between the bureaucracy and the executive.

The Policy Context

It is important to put the white paper into a broader context in order to understand the pulling and hauling games that occurred during the policy formulation process. Figure 17.1 synthesizes the framework Legault suggests for reading both the exchanges and their context and for identifying the sources of influence pertaining to defence policies.[15] This framework consists of external factors (matters related to foreign policy and to security) and domestic factors (influence of the "social pyramid" and of the "political pyramid" that is defined as having the Cabinet at its apex, the parliamentary institutions at its base, and the "bureaucratic and administrative controls of the departments, financial control of the treasury, control by the public service, and, last but not least, judiciary control" at its heart).[16]

Figure 17.1

Potential sources of influence on defence policy

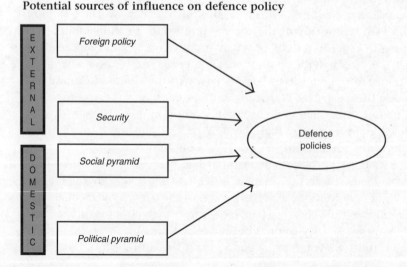

Foreign Policy

Foreign policy played an important part in the evolution of the white paper. External Affairs took the lead in the first part of the project. Internal departmental factors, such as the numerous ministers that rotated through the Department of National Defence (DND) during this period may provide an explanation not only for the late publication of the white paper, but also for DND's lack of leadership (which, of course, was advantageous to External Affairs).[17] Erik Nielsen, the minister who held the portfolio the longest (February 1985 to June 1986), had actually tried to speed up the process: he asked that a green paper on defence be dropped on the grounds that defence was not a matter for that kind of public debate, and he urged that the department proceed directly to a white paper. However, Nielsen had many other responsibilities that, in the end, prevented him from paying full attention to the development of the white paper.[18] In this, Nielsen may also have been influenced by foreign policy questions, specifically, Clark's release of a foreign policy green paper. Indeed, the External Affairs document touched on numerous defence issues: it defined Canada as a "three-ocean" country, it defended the necessity of "protecting our national sovereignty," and it made reference to the priority to be given to national defence.[19]

Thus, the lead was clearly taken by the foreign policy-makers, and national sovereignty became the cornerstone upon which the new defence policy was to be built. The impact of national sovereignty grew even stronger when Clark defended Canadian claims over the Northwest Passage, an incident discussed by Rob Huebert (Chapter 6). Sovereignty was also featured in the two reports tabled by the Special Joint Committee of the Senate and the House of Commons, co-chaired by Member of Parliament (MP) Tom Hockin and Senators Jean-Maurice Simard and Jacques Flynn.

Other foreign policy aspects may have influenced the content of the white paper, including the foreign policy impact of decisions related to the role Canadian forces would play in Europe. Canadian troops were still based in Germany, and Canada was committed to the defence of the northern flank of the North Atlantic Treaty Organization (NATO) and the reinforcement of Norway. However, the chief of defence staff proposed a new plan for Canada in Europe – one that would limit Canadian involvement to the northern flank.[20] When word of this proposal reached other capitals, political pressure was reportedly put on Canada. Britain was fiercely opposed to the idea, and Chancellor Helmut Kohl of Germany, having conscription problems in his own country, did not look favourably upon a withdrawal of the Canadian military. It was not a question of numbers as much as a question of abandoning what was perceived to be a powerful symbol of resistance to American military hegemony.

Canada's reaction to developments in East-West relations following the watershed Reykjavik Summit between Ronald Reagan and Mikhail Gorbachev can also be considered as another foreign-policy-related factor. Despite the recognition of some "encouraging signals" coming out of Moscow, official Canadian policy towards the Soviet Union was, to say the least, cautious. Relations between Canada and the Soviet Union were not helped by charges of spying in 1988, at which time officials from the Soviet Embassy were declared persona non grata by the Mulroney government. Officials in the DND were even more conservative than were those in External Affairs – an attitude that led to interesting confrontations in terms of security assessment, as we will see.

The Security Agenda

Two different readings of the strategic situation prevailed at the time the white paper was formulated. The common reading in DND circles was strongly influenced by Cold War assumptions. Perrin Beatty, for example, was issuing warnings about the Soviet threat in a speech to the Empire Club in Toronto in January 1987.[21] Likewise, to those who pointed to the Gorbachev initiatives in East-West relations, the Canadian chief of defence staff, General Paul Manson, replied that there was "little evidence so far that Moscow is serious about restraint."[22]

These statements seem surprising, but it should be noted that officials argue that one should be wary of a "hindsight interpretation" of the end of the Cold War. They point out that one should recall that the white paper was prepared between 1984 and 1986 (even though it was not published until 1987) and that the end of the Cold War can be dated somewhere between November 1989 and December 1991, depending on which event is chosen – the fall of the Berlin Wall, Germany's reunification, or the collapse of the Soviet Union.

Other officials had a softer reading of events. As Till has clearly demonstrated,[23] the Soviet threat was quite different in 1987 from what it had been three or four years earlier. Moreover, while bureaucrats in Ottawa were putting the final touches on the defence white paper, their counterparts in Washington and Moscow were ironing out the details of an agreement to eliminate middle-range nuclear missiles in Europe,[24] the fruits of the Reykjavik Summit.

This dual vision dominated debate over the white paper. Although the Cold War reading prevailed, a perception of détente finally materialized. Should we consider this to be the element that brought down the white paper? The modification of the strategic balance as a result of the collapse of the Soviet Union and the emergence of a single superpower no doubt had its effect on the implementation of the white paper, which was crafted during the Cold War. However, the different visions that have prevailed from the security point of view, and that were strongly expressed in the bureaucratic pulling-and-hauling games that occurred within the political pyramid, may have played a more important role than the evolving world context within which they occurred.

The Social Pyramid

Four sets of actors can be identified within the social pyramid: the electorate, the military-industrial lobby, peace groups, and the Conservative party. As many students of Canadian foreign policy have noted, it is difficult to establish a direct link between public opinion and defence policies.[25] The explanation may be, as Albert Legault has suggested, that only specialized publics are advocates on defence matters.[26] This is in agreement with William D. Coleman and Grace Skogstad, who argue that the key determinants in the social pyramid are these "policy communities."[27] However, when a new government proposes policies that are perceived to be fundamentally different from those that went before, we might face an exception to this general rule. Was this the case?

My research suggests that there was little to no influence from three out of these four groups. The first group, the electorate, did not have much influence. It is true that, in September 1984, the electorate voted for the Conservatives. However, one cannot conclude that this represented specific approval of the new defence orientation, not least because defence policy was not often mentioned during the campaign; the Conservatives committed themselves to only a few defence promises, such as publishing a new defence white paper and reversing the Trudeau government's decision to close the Canadian Forces Base (CFB) at Chatham.[28]

As for the second group, the military-industrial lobby, while some have argued that it wields prominent influence,[29] others suggest it does not.[30] The interviews I conducted for this research confirm the latter view. The similarities between the wishes expressed at parliamentary hearings by representatives of this group and the eventual content of the white paper seem more a result of coincidence of interests than of influence.

As for the third group, the peace lobby, which is located at the opposite end of the ideological spectrum from the military-industrial lobby, although the Hockin-Simard/Flynn Committee's report indicates that seventy-five of these organizations appeared before them,[31] these groups did not influence the content of the white paper.[32]

With regard to the fourth group, the Conservative party, it is clear that partisan pressures did influence the content of the white paper. From Robert Borden on, the Conservatives had a history of being close to the needs of the military. Both Legault and Bland argue that the white paper reflected pressures from within the Conservative caucus,[33] an assessment shared by the media at the time.

The litmus test of partisan influence may be found in the promises of the 1984 election campaign, when the Conservatives committed themselves to giving priority to defence policy. The first three major promises were to bring the distinctive colours back to each component of the armed forces (a clear departure from the Liberal tradition), to keep CFB Chatham operational, and to modernize the North Warning System. Presenting the Canadian public with a new defence policy was to be part of a second round of promises. The first three items were dealt with early in the mandate, but with the 1988 election in sight, a white paper was needed. This being the case, the 1987 white paper can be seen as a highly partisan project, the fulfilment of an electoral promise to please two groups of "natural" Tory supporters: (1) right-wing, law-and-order voters and (2) the business community.[34]

Although we can identify the partisan factor as important for the emergence of defence policy, a question remains: What was the weight of the partisan influence in the *crafting* of this policy? J.H. Taylor (Chapter 14) points out that differences in foreign policy tend to be more acute when there is a change of leadership within the governing party than when there is a change of governing party. The possibility that such a dynamic existed in the mid-1980s suggests that special attention should be given to the political pyramid.

Bureaucracy, the Military, and Politicians: A Bureaucratic Politics Analysis

All of the actors involved in the policy-making process sought to defend their agenda, from bureaucrats involved in foreign and defence policymaking, to military officials who assessed the security parameters, to politicians engaged with their party's commitment. In other words, elements were in place for an intense bureaucratic struggle.

The Analytical Framework

Graham Allison's bureaucratic politics model provides the best framework for analyzing this internal debate over the future of Canadian defence policy.[35] By focusing on "actors in position," it reaches the heart of the decision-making process. Allison rejects explanations based solely on the rational approach, for it "obscures the persistently neglected fact of bureaucracy: the 'maker' of a government policy is not one calculating decision-maker, but rather a conglomerate of large organizations and political actors who differ substantially about what their government should do and who compete in attempting to affect both governmental decisions and the actions of the government."[36] Rationality plays a role but only as a component of a more complex process.

In Allison's terms, policies are "intra-national political resultants: *resultants* in the sense that what happens is not chosen as a solution to a problem but rather results from compromise, conflict, and confusion of officials with diverse interests and unequal influence; and *political* in the sense that activity from which decisions emerge is best characterized as bargaining along regularized channels among individual members of government."[37] This framework, therefore, considers the interaction of actors involved in the decision-making process.

Over the years, one of the persistent criticisms of Allison's framework has been that it is notoriously difficult to operationalize. In order to use Allison's model, I have relied on Lemieux's notion of the "structuration of powers,"[38] since it also considers "actors in position," one of Allison's key postulates. Lemieux's approach consists of "slicing" the decision process into different "episodes," which have influenced the outcome, and "inter-episodes," which are necessary for the understanding of the process but do not influence the outcome. For each episode, two actors are identified and their stance before and after their interaction is assessed so that it corresponds to a vector[39] expressing the amount of influence exercised. A reading of the combined vectors, representing the whole process, allows us to determine the type of influence exercised. The necessary data for the verification of the hypotheses came from two sources: (1) documentary analysis (official documents, some of them released under the Access to Information Act; parliamentary debates transcripts; and media analysis) and (2) personal interviews with those involved in the policy formulation process.[40]

The Political Pyramid and Bureaucratic Politics

It is possible to identify twenty-one policy episodes within three periods (see Table 17.1). The first period occurred when the Tories were in Opposition, were preparing their platform, and were formulating their defence policy. The second was a "planning period," which began the day after the 1984 election and ran until the end of June 1986, when Mulroney announced a major mid-term shuffle of his Cabinet and appointed Perrin Beatty as minister of national defence. The third period covers Beatty's mandate as minister and ends with the tabling of the white paper in the House of Commons on 5 June 1987.

These episodes result in an intricate network of interactions among players in both the social and the political pyramids. While it is not possible to detail each relationship here, it is possible to consider the results as a whole. The key "actors in position" involved in the process were the minister of national defence, the Department of National Defence, the secretary of state for external affairs, the minister of finance, and the prime minister.

Table 17.1

Policy episodes

Proposition period:
Episode 1: The Tory Opposition formulates its defence policy.
Episode 2: The leader of the Opposition, Brian Mulroney, agrees to the policy.
Episode 3: Election night.

Planning period:
Episode 4: The government is organized.
1st inter-episode: Robert Coates heads the Department of National Defence.
2nd inter-episode: Coates resigns.
Episode 5: Erik Nielsen is appointed minister of national defence.
Episode 6: Joe Clark tables his green paper on Canada's foreign relations.
3rd inter-episode: Special Committee of the Senate and the House hears witnesses.
4th inter-episode: Consideration of the other parliamentary committees' mandate.
Episode 7: Standing Committee on External Affairs and Defence studies NORAD renewal.
Episode 8: Harvie Andre appointed associate minister of national defence.
Episode 9: Clark calls for Canadian sovereignty: the *Polar Sea* affair.
Episode 10: Mulroney commits himself to a deadline for the white paper.
Episode 11: Special Committee final report tabled.

Building-up period:
Episode 12: An expected Cabinet shuffle.
Episode 13: Beatty makes the process a priority.
Episode 14: DND prepares the basis for the policy.
Episode 15: DND puts on a demonstration for Beatty in Lahr.
Episode 16: Operation Brave Lion.
5th inter-episode: DND opens the consultation process.
Episode 17: The government announces its foreign policy.
Episode 18: Broad outlines of defence policy drafted.
Episode 19: Michael Wilson's budget of 18 February 1987 makes defence commitments.
Episode 20: Defence policy is debated at departmental level.
Episode 21: Defence policy is debated at Cabinet level and adopted.
6th inter-episode: Defence white paper is assembled.
Epilogue: Beatty announces the policy as approved by Cabinet.

When examining the evolution of this policy, it is important to keep in mind that there were strong bureaucrats in DND, especially an assistant deputy minister committed to the renewal of the Canadian Forces. The relationship between DND and its minister varied considerably, depending on who occupied crucial senior policy positions. For instance, the relationship between the chief of defence staff, General Gérard Thériault and

Robert Coates was strained, and reports of their differences even found their way into the press.[41] However, since the white paper was not under consideration at that time, the acrimony between the two had little impact on its eventual outcome.

More important was the relationship between Erik Nielsen and the two chiefs of defence staff who served under him, Thériault and his successor, General Paul Manson. Nielsen was a veteran of the Second World War, which meant that DND was favourably disposed towards him. And, as minister, Nielsen enjoyed his responsibilities.[42] Key initiatives were discussed during his tenure: sometimes he convinced his officials, sometimes they convinced him. For instance, it was Nielsen who wanted to proceed directly with a white paper rather than going through the green paper process. And it was he who decided, against Thériault's advice, that Canadian troops would remain in Germany. Finally, it was Nielsen who insisted that his officials consider the importance of national sovereignty as a defence objective. On the other hand, when his officials pushed acquiring nuclear-propelled submarines, Nielsen did not object – to the surprise of some of his key military advisors – and asked for a feasibility study.[43] The fact that he was the MP for Yukon, a riding bordering the Northwest Passage, may help explain his reaction to this proposal. In any case, it is clear that the officials and the minister mutually influenced each other.

The situation was quite different with Beatty. In fact, on a scale of assertiveness, Beatty was opposite to Coates, with Nielsen ranking somewhere in between. In government circles it was well known that Beatty was much more open to other people's ideas than were either Coates or Nielsen. This situation is well illustrated by Episodes 14, 15, and 16, when DND officials were preparing information for their new minister. In order to convince him of the importance of their suggestions, they organized a visit to Lahr, Germany, where the minister witnessed, first-hand and from an operational standpoint, the needs being expressed by his officials. This was followed by Operation Brave Lion, a NATO military exercise in which Canada was going to practice the defence of the Northern Flank in Norway. However, because the DND was so under-resourced, Operation Brave Lion turned out to be a major failure. This demonstrated to the minister the need for the long shopping list that DND wanted to put in the white paper, and it prompted his crusade to muster support from his Cabinet colleagues.

One of the opponents of the white paper's aggressive stance was Joe Clark, secretary of state for external affairs. First, Clark's attitudes towards the Soviet Union differed markedly from those of the white paper. Second, Clark was concerned about the impact of the proposed acquisition of nuclear-powered submarines on Canadian-American relations, for the administration in Washington was clearly not happy with that proposal.[44] On many occasions, both at interdepartmental meetings and at the Cabinet committee he chaired, Clark is reported to have strongly voiced his opposition to the white paper. For the sake of peace, however, he decided to let it go forward, although he did so, according to one official, "knowing that it would not take long before a reconsideration would be in order."

Given Clark's objections, how can we explain how the white paper was approved by Cabinet? Was Beatty, by himself, able to convince Clark to drop his objections? A look at other actors may shed some light on this question. One of the key factors that affected the evolution of defence policy during this period was the federal government's financial situation. Nielsen alluded to this stumbling block before the Standing Committee on External Affairs and Defence.[45] Harvie Andre, Nielsen's associate minister and the person responsible for steering the defence budget through the estimates process, was even more blunt: "If we could examine our defence policy without monetary constraint, it would be much easier."[46] In an exchange with NDP critic Derek Blackburn, Andre emphatically suggested that the real problem lay with the minister of finance, Michael Wilson.

Indeed, Wilson was the key actor. As the minister responsible for balancing the budget,[47] Wilson was the final voice in the negotiations. And all indications are that he was opposed to lavish defence spending and succeeded in blocking Andre's initiatives. However, he failed to counter Beatty's much more expensive proposals in the white paper. Did this indicate that, in Cabinet, Beatty's influence was stronger than Wilson's?

In such circumstances, the final arbiter would have been the prime minister. Given that the white paper was approved by Cabinet, one may conclude that Beatty succeeded in convincing Mulroney to ask Wilson to step aside and let the policy go. There is no doubt that the partisan argument – that is, the necessity to publish a white paper in order to fulfil an electoral commitment that he himself had made – had some weight in Mulroney's final decision. However, there are indications that he was somewhat reluctant to go with such an extravagant defence policy. I have already noted his remarks, ten days after the tabling of the document. And these should come as no surprise, given that he had already hinted that he hesitated over releasing the white paper. In a media scrum, the prime minister declared that "the paper was postponed because of economic realities and is being scaled down."[48] Why, then, did he approve the release of the 1987 white paper?

It is possible that Beatty was able to convince enough of his Cabinet colleagues to tip the scale in his favour. Another possibility, however, is that the Privy Council Office (PCO) played an important part in shaping Cabinet-level support for the white paper. The official at National Defence

Headquarters who was really behind the white paper was Robert Fowler, who had been made assistant deputy minister (policy) only a few weeks before Beatty was appointed minister. Fowler had already had a long career at External Affairs. He was then moved to the PCO and, thence, to DND. Was it possible that Fowler used his contacts at External Affairs and, more important, at the PCO to influence the course of events? After all, the PCO's prime responsibility is to advise the prime minister and to coordinate Cabinet work, another important feature in this pulling-and-hauling game. It is, therefore, possible that it was not Beatty who was able to convince Mulroney to publish the white paper but, rather, a high-ranking civil servant. Unfortunately, to this date I have found no evidence to support this hypothesis; in fact, many of the people interviewed clearly indicated that the PCO had no influence in the process (which would be, to say the least, unusual).

Regardless of who had the greater weight in this debate, it is clear that the defence policy was fiercely discussed and that the phrase "pulling and hauling" is apt. This is the most important conclusion of my review of the political pyramid. Another important conclusion is that the players who had lost the inning that ended with the publication of the white paper did not believe that they had lost the game.

Conclusion: Lack of Control?

Many of the policies outlined in the white paper were never implemented. Some might suggest this was simply because they were bad policies to begin with and that it would have been bad politics to implement them. Such an explanation, however, is too easy; bad policies are, from time to time, implemented. Other people point to the changing state of world politics. There is no doubt that some political objectives outlined in the defence policy may have become obsolete within a short period of time. However, the logistical needs addressed by the white paper were also put in limbo, although some of them are still to be addressed.

More important, a review of relationships within the political pyramid indicates that there was no one dominant player; as a consequence, pulling-and-hauling games were undertaken by several different actors. Those actors who lost a first inning often bounced back to win later on. For example, External Affairs managed to take the lead with its own green paper, but Department of National Defence was able to gather enough support in Cabinet to get its wish-list policy through. However, this support came from those who were quite prepared to kill their neighbour's initiative in order to preserve their own; thus, when the time came to try to fit DND's wishes into the evolving financial and security environments, there were not enough actors to defend most parts of this eroded policy. In other words, this fierce pulling-and-hauling game resulted in an interesting paradox: the government lost control of the policy, even though different actors managed to control some parts of the policy process. It was this lack of overall control that may well have been the reason for the non-implementation of several aspects of the 1987 white paper. Concretely, when the time came to "defend Defence," nobody was in a position to prevent the collapse of huge parts of the program outlined in the white paper: new coalitions of actors were formed, and it was easy to weaken the position of people interested in defending a specific aspect of the policy without weakening the policy as a whole.

What role did the "departure" factor play in the collapse of the white paper? It can be argued that, when one examines the policy-making process in detail, the only role it played was related to the discomfort that newness can bring. In light of the diminishing threat from the Soviet Union, why would it be necessary to adopt a fundamentally new policy since the one already in place (based on the 1971 white paper) was crafted at the time of another détente? The departure factor can, therefore, be considered as a scapegoat, as the perfect excuse for a dismissal that, in fact, had its roots in a general lack of interest with many aspects of the white paper. The 1987 white paper was simply a matter of bad planning on the part of engineers who wanted to be perceived as architects.

Notes

This chapter is based, in part, on my doctoral thesis, "Genèse d'une politique syncopique: la défense du Canada et le Livre blanc de 1987," Université Laval, 1998. I wish to thank Vincent Lemieux and Albert Legault for their advice, and Gordon Mace, Louis Bélanger, Kim Richard Nossal, Réjean Pelletier, Denis Stairs, and J.H. (Si) Taylor for their comments and suggestions on earlier versions. A more detailed analysis of the key episodes was published in the *Canadian Journal of Political Science* (June 2001).

1   Donald J. Savoie, *Thatcher, Reagan, Mulroney: In Search of a New Bureaucracy* (Toronto: University of Toronto Press, 1994), 225; for a more detailed and nuanced view, see Jacques Bourgault, *La satisfaction des ministres du gouvernement Mulroney face à leurs sous-ministres 1984-1993* (Ottawa: Centre canadien de gestion, 1998), rapport de recherche no 22.
2   Michel Vastel, *Bourassa* (Montréal: Éditions de l'Homme, 1991).
3   Nelson Michaud and Louis Bélanger, "Canadian Institutional Strategies: New Orientations for a Middle Power Foreign Policy?" *Australian Journal of International Affairs* 54 (April 2000): 97-110.
4   Jean Edward Smith, "Beefed Up Defence Program: Part of Ottawa's Abrupt Turn," *Globe and Mail*, 29 June 1987, A7.
5   Carol Goar, "A 180° Turn in Our Defence Policy," *Toronto Star*, 6 June 1987, B1, B5.
6   Dan W. Middlemiss, "Canadian Defence Policy: An Uncertain Transition," in *Canada Among Nations, 1989: The Challenge of Change*, ed. Maureen Appel Molot and Fen Osler Hampson (Ottawa: Carleton University Press, 1990), 120.
7   Albert Legault, "Les processus décisionnels en matière de politique de défense," *International Journal* 42 (1987): 645-74.
8   Graham T. Allison and Philip Zelikow, *Essence of Decision: Explaining the Cuban Missile Crisis*, 2nd ed. (New York: Addison Wesley Longman, 1999); Vincent Lemieux, *La struc-*

turation du pouvoir dans les systèmes politiques (Sainte-Foy: Les Presses de l'Université Laval, 1989).

9 Progressive Conservative Party of Canada, *Honour the Commitment* (Ottawa: PC Party, 1984); on the "commitment-capability gap," see Peter C. Newman, *True North: Not Strong and Free* (Markham: Penguin, 1983); D.W. Middlemiss and J.J. Sokolsky, *Canadian Defence: Decisions and Determinants* (Toronto: Harcourt, Brace, Jovanovich, 1989).

10 Canada, *White Paper on Defence* (Ottawa: Queen's Printer, 1964); *White Paper on Defence* (Ottawa: Queen's Printer, 1971); *White Paper on Defence, 1994* (Ottawa: Supply and Services Canada, 1994).

11 Confidential interview.

12 Canada, Parliament, House of Commons, *Debates*, 8 June 1987.

13 House of Commons, *Debates*, 5 June 1987, 6779.

14 "Defence Plans Are Far from Firm, Mulroney Hints," *Toronto Star*, 16 June 1987, A10. This headline appeared only ten days after the tabling of the policy in the Commons.

15 Legault, "Les processus décisionnels."

16 Ibid., 645; my translation.

17 From mid-September 1984 to the end of June 1986, there were six ministers and associate ministers of defence: Robert Coates, Joe Clark, Erik Nielsen, Perrin Beatty, Harvie Andre, and Paul Dick.

18 This conclusion is confirmed by many of those whom I interviewed. Nielsen was deputy prime minister; minister responsible for reviewing government programs; and, for a time, acting minister of transport and acting minister of fisheries and oceans. In addition, he had the non-official, but no less demanding, tasks of disciplining the caucus and the Cabinet as well as of advising the prime minister on sensitive political issues.

19 Canada, Secretary of State for External Affairs, *Competitiveness and Security* (Ottawa: Supply and Services Canada, 1985).

20 Michel C. Auger, "Quartier général," *L'Actualité*, mars 1986, 36-42.

21 Department of National Defence, Notes for a Speech by the Honourable Perrin Beatty, Minister of National Defence, at the Empire Club, Toronto, 16 January 1987.

22 "Soviets Pose Threat, Defence Minister Says," *Globe and Mail*, 16 January 1987, A5.

23 G. Till, "The Soviet Navy, the North Atlantic and Canada," in *Canada and NATO: Uneasy Past, Uncertain Future*, ed. Margaret O. Macmillan and D.S. Sorenson (Waterloo: University of Waterloo Press, 1990), 90-91.

24 P. Mélandri, *Reagan: Une biographie totale* (Paris: Laffont, 1988).

25 For example, Denis Stairs, "Publics and Policy-Makers: the Domestic Environment of Canada's Foreign Policy Community," *International Journal* 26 (1971): 224; Denis Stairs, "Public Opinion and Foreign Policy in Canada," *International Journal* 33 (1978): 129-49; Robert W. Reford, "The Public and Public Policy: The Impact of Society on the Canadian Security Policy Process," in *Canada's International Security Policy*, ed. David B. Dewitt and David Leyton-Brown (Scarborough: Prentice Hall, 1995); J.S. Finan and S.B. Flemming, "Public Attitudes toward Defence and Security in Canada," in ibid.; Geoffrey Pearson, "Canada, NATO, and the Public Mood," in *Canada and NATO: Uneasy Past, Uncertain Future*, ed. Margaret O. Macmillan and D.S. Sorensen; and Gordon Mace et Michel Roussel, "Les groupes d'intérêt et la politique étrangère canadienne: le cas de l'Amérique centrale," *Études internationales* 21, 3 (1990): 499-523.

26 Legault, "Les processus décisionnels," 646.

27 William D. Coleman and Grace Skogstad, ed., *Policy Communities and Public Policy in Canada: A Structural Approach* (Toronto: Copp, Clark, Pitman, 1990). By contrast, Percheron and Memni define this as "political competence." See Anick Percheron, "La socialisation politique: défense et illustration," in *Traité de science politique*, vol. 3: *L'action politique*, ed. Madeleine Grawitz et Jean Leca (Paris: Presses universitaires de France, 1985), 201; Dominique Memni, "Participation et comportement politique:

L'engagement politique," in *Traité de science politique*, vol. 3: *L'action politique*, ed. Madeleine Grawitz et Jean Leca (Paris: Presses universitaires de France, 1985), 312.

28 These promises were contained in the main speech on defence that Mulroney delivered on 1 August 1984 in Newcastle, New Brunswick, across the Miramichi River from CFB Chatham. See Jeff Sallot, "Tories Would Boost Forces by about 10%: Mulroney," *Globe and Mail*, 2 August 1984, A7.

29 H. Peter Langille, *Changing the Guard* (Toronto: University of Toronto Press, 1990); Ann Denholm Crosby, *Dilemmas in Defence Decision-Making: Constructing Canada's Role in NORAD, 1958-1996* (London: Macmillan, 1998).

30 J. Treddenick, "Economic Significance of the Canadian Defence Industrial Base" in *Canada's Defence Industrial Base*, ed. David G. Haglund (Kingston: Ronald P. Frye, 1988), 42; Albert Legault, "Les autres engagements internationaux du Canada en matière de défense," in *Les Politiques de défense du Canada dans les années 1980* (Sainte-Foy: Centre québécois des relations internationales, 1981); Ernie Regher, *Arms Canada: The Deadly Business of Military Exports* (Toronto: Lorimer, 1987), 722.

31 Special Joint Committee of the Senate and the House of Commons on Canada's External Relations, *Interdependence and Internationalism* (Ottawa, Supply and Services, 1986), 175-82.

32 Middlemiss and Sokolsky, *Canadian Defence*, 226.

33 Legault, "Les processus décisionnels," 653; Douglas L. Bland, "The Canadian Defence Policy Process and the Emergence of a Defence Industrial Preparedness Policy," in Haglund, *Canada's Defence Industrial Base*, 239.

34 Business Council on National Issues, *Canada's Defence Policy: Capabilities versus Commitments* (Ottawa: BCNI, 1984), 54-55.

35 Graham T. Allison, "Conceptual Models and the Cuban Missile Crisis," *American Political Science Review* 43, 3 (1969): 689-718; Graham T. Allison, *Essence of Decision; Explaining the Cuban Missile Crisis* (Boston: Little Brown, 1971); Graham T. Allison and Morton H. Halperin, "Bureaucratic Politics: A Paradigm and Some Policy Implications," in *Theory and Policy in International Relations*, ed. Raymond Tanter and R.H. Ullman (Princeton: Princeton University Press, 1972), 40-79; Allison and Zelikow, *Essence of Decision*, 2nd ed.

36 Allison and Halperin, "Bureaucratic Politics," 42.

37 Allison and Zelikow, *Essence of Decision*, 294-95 (italics in original).

38 Vincent Lemieux, *La structuration du pouvoir dans les systèmes politiques* (Sainte-Foy: Les Presses de l'Université Laval, 1989). For applications, see Vincent Lemieux, "La structuration du pouvoir dans les organisations universitaires," *Politiques et management public* 12, 2 (1994): 135-49; and Vincent Lemieux, *Éléments d'une théorie politique des voix* (Sainte-Foy: Université Laval, Laboratoire d'études politiques, 1995).

39 Sixteen identified vectors allow one to measure decision-making processes that could involve as much as four interactions between two actors in a single episode. See Lemieux, *La structuration*, 18.

40 A total of twenty-seven interviews were conducted with politicians (including Mulroney, Clark, Coates, Dick, Andre, and Beatty), with senators and chairs of committees and caucus, and with civil servants (including Chiefs of Defence Staff Thériault and Manson, Vice-Chief Vance, deputy ministers Dewar [DND] and Si Taylor [DEA], and ADMs Robert Fowler and Ken Calder).

41 Joe O'Donnell, "Forces Chief Faces Probe over Jet Trip," *Toronto Star*, 22 June 1985, A1, A4.

42 Although his memoirs do not make much mention of his time as minister. See Erik Nielsen, *The House Is Not a Home* (Toronto: Macmillan Canada, 1989), 250-51.

43 See House of Commons, Standing Committee on Defence, *Proceedings*, 1985, vol. 25, 32.

44 The opposition of the US Navy had more to do with domestic political concerns than with foreign policy concerns. The navy was worried that its funding could be put in jeopardy if the mishandling of such high-tech toys resulted in an accident in the Arctic and provoked public opposition.

45 House of Commons, Standing Committee on External Affairs and National Defence, *Proceedings*, 1985, vol. 7, 19.

46 House of Commons, Standing Committee on Defence, *Proceedings*, 1986, vol. 6, 5.

47 In the 1983 leadership race, both Wilson and Mulroney had made deficit fighting a primary goal of their economic platforms. See Brian Mulroney, *Where I Stand* (Toronto: McClelland and Stewart, 1983); Michael Wilson, *Focus on Canada/Point de vue sur le Canada*. Leadership program, mimeo, 1983.

48 Canadian Press, "Defence Review Scaled Down, PM Says," *Globe and Mail*, 1 May 1986, A9.

18
Opening Up the Policy Process: Does Party Make a Difference?
Kim Richard Nossal

Does party make a difference to the process by which foreign policy is made? The other chapters in this book focus on the degree to which the Progressive Conservative government of Brian Mulroney represented a departure from previous practice with regard to different aspects of Canada's external relations – in both policy and process. The purpose of this chapter is to explore one aspect of the foreign policy process during this period – the degree to which Conservative foreign policy was marked by changes in the way that foreign policy decision-makers, notably the ministers in Cabinet, dealt with both the public and Parliament.

Roy Norton (Chapter 16), in discussing the role of ethnic groups in the foreign policy process, argues that one of the reasons for the pattern we saw in the relations between the Mulroney Conservatives and ethnic groups in Canada was the tendency of the Conservatives to consult those outside the state apparatus. Norton suggests that this was a function of the party's "outsider" status in Ottawa. Don Page, a scholar of Canadian foreign policy who spent a number of years in the Department of External Affairs (DEA) before returning to academia, makes a comparable point about the way in which the Mulroney government dealt with Parliament and the public. Page uses the term "populist" to describe the Conservative approach to the foreign policy process.[1] Although he does not explicitly define what he means by populism in a Canadian context, he clearly uses the term in its traditional, late nineteenth-century American sense; that is, he uses it to describe a political party that claims to represent the interests and the views of "the people," usually defined as the "common people" or the "ordinary people." I seek to extend Norton's analysis and to assess Page's characterization and, in so doing, to determine whether the practices of the Mulroney government can be considered "populist." I also examine whether these practices reflected the particularities of the Progressive Conservative party and its leadership or whether, as Denis Stairs argues in Chapter 2, the opening up of the policy process that we saw during the Conservative years was all part of a "trajectory," a response to the "insistent imperatives arising from circumstances."

The Mulroney Conservatives as Populists?

At first blush, it may seem strange to characterize the Mulroney Conservatives as populists with regard to foreign policy, for the dominant image in the public memory holds precisely the opposite: the foreign policy of the Mulroney era is commonly said to be elitist, closed, and marked by a propensity to ignore the public and members of Parliament.

This common memory owes a certain debt to the Liberal party, for this was the essence of the Liberal critique of Conservative foreign policy articulated in the run-up to the 1993 general elections and coordinated by Lloyd Axworthy, the party's External Affairs critic. Axworthy's wide-ranging critique of Conservative foreign policy focused squarely on the putative elitism of the Mulroney government. The Conservatives, Axworthy argued, were "unwilling to carry on a serious dialogue with the Canadian people on foreign policy issues," rarely consulting either the public or their elected representatives in Parliament on important foreign policy decisions.[2] This critique was also reflected in the Liberal election platform in 1993 – the so-called Red Book. Canadians, the Red Book stated, do not want an elitist foreign policy: "They do not want Canadian foreign policy to be determined solely through special personal relationships between world leaders." Instead, the Red Book argued, Canadians want a "democratic" foreign policy process: "Canadians are asking for a commitment from government to listen to their views, and to respect their needs by ensuring that no false distinction is made between domestic and foreign policy."[3]

The Liberal party was forthright in its promise that there would be a more "democratic" foreign policy should Jean Chrétien be the next prime minister: "We need a foreign policy decided in a more democratic, open way," the Liberal platform stated. "There must be consent of Canadians on important initiatives; there must be a clear role for Parliament in making decisions. There must be more involvement by our NGOs [nongovernmental organizations] [and] business interest groups in defining our role in the globe."[4]

Of course, the clear implication of the Liberal critique was that the Mulroney Conservatives had been pursuing a deeply elitist and undemocratic foreign policy. The reference in the Red Book to foreign policy by "special personal relationships" was a scarcely disguised criticism not only of Mulroney's close personal relations with Presidents Ronald Reagan and George Bush, but also of the prime minister's avid international summiteering, which, as Andrew F. Cooper reminds us (Chapter 11), was often interpreted by Canadians as little more than self-serving status-seeking.

Likewise, the Liberal promise to pursue an "open" foreign policy implied that Conservative foreign policy was undemocratic and "closed" – a policy that ignored the public and either by-passed Parliament or relegated it to a position of no consequence.

In fact, the Liberal critique relied heavily on public perceptions that, by 1993, had grown so negatively disposed towards the Mulroney Conservatives that certain events were forgotten, ignored, or reinterpreted. Moreover, after October 1993, there was an additional complication: so decimated was the Progressive Conservative caucus that there was little capacity to correct the historical record. One can see this dynamic most clearly with regard to the question of the holding of foreign policy debates in the House of Commons. During the election campaign, the Liberals had criticized the Mulroney government for its refusal to give Parliament a role in debating foreign policy and its willingness to despatch Canadian forces abroad without first securing the approval of Parliament. This line was reiterated when the first foreign policy debate in the thirty-fifth Parliament (1993-97) – on Canadian participation in the Bosnian peacekeeping mission – was held in the House of Commons in January 1994. Numerous members of Parliament (MPs) – on both sides of the House – congratulated the Chrétien government for holding a foreign policy debate; a commonly stated sentiment was that it was such a refreshing change from the Mulroney years, when, it was claimed, there had been *no* debates on foreign affairs.[5] Needless to say, such assertions, when made by those who had sat as MPs in either the thirty-third Parliament (1984-88) or the thirty-fourth Parliament (1988-93), must have been either the result of exceedingly poor memory or simple disingenuousness, for in fact MPs during the Mulroney era had had numerous opportunities to participate in foreign policy debates on a wide range of issues. During this period, debates were held on South Africa, the crisis in Central America, the Tiananmen massacre, and free trade – not to mention the unprecedented marathon three-day debate on the Gulf War in January 1991.[6]

But after 1993 keeping the historical record accurate was difficult, given that only two of the 155 Conservative MPs from the thirty-fourth Parliament were returned by the voters (and neither of them were particularly interested in foreign affairs). The loss of official party status not only brought with it the loss of research capabilities that might have allowed the record to be corrected, but, more important, the loss of opportunities for intervention on the part of the two Conservative members, both of whom were seated in relative obscurity up by the curtains at the back of the chamber.

In other words, the willingness of Liberals to be purposely forgetful, the lack of historical memory on the part of the new members from the Bloc Québécois and the Reform party, and the inability of the Conservative rump to correct faulty memories all combined to leave an enduring impression that the Mulroney Conservatives never involved Parliament in the foreign policy process and that it had an undemocratic, elitist foreign policy. However, as I go on to argue, in fact the Mulroney government, to an unprecedented degree, involved both the public and MPs in the foreign policy process.

Bringing the Public In: Famine in Ethiopia

It is useful to begin with the Mulroney government's first foreign policy crisis – the famine in Ethiopia.[7] This suddenly appeared on the Canadian (and international) political agenda in October 1984, scarcely a month after the new government had been sworn in. The Mulroney government's response to this crisis revealed some of the initial impulses of the Conservative approach that we would see manifest themselves in many (though by no means all) other foreign policy areas.

Needless to say, the Ethiopian famine itself did not suddenly appear: since the early 1980s the Food and Agriculture Organization (FAO) had been issuing urgent appeals to the international community for assistance to combat the famine in Ethiopia, which had been aggravated by the combination of a massive and prolonged drought and the country's collapse into civil war. But the response had been negligible: in 1983, the Trudeau government, for example, had considered and then rejected a proposal from the minister of agriculture for a twenty-million-dollar emergency relief scheme on the grounds that the situation was not sufficiently grave.[8] But when video images of the famine were broadcast on television around the world in October 1984, they had a powerful and galvanizing effect on many countries. In Canada, they prompted what the *Globe and Mail* termed "a sudden outpouring of emotion and money."[9] Offers of assistance poured into Ottawa from individuals, groups, and institutions from across Canada – "a quite remarkable demonstration of interest by ordinary Canadians," as Joe Clark, the secretary of state for external affairs, put it later.[10]

The response of the new government, in power for less than a month, represented a number of policy departures. First, instead of turning to established line departments – External Affairs or the Canadian International Development Agency (CIDA) – to organize and coordinate the Canadian contribution to famine relief, Mulroney, in essence, created a new ad hoc layer of political administration. David MacDonald, a former Conservative MP and minister in the Clark government, was appointed as Canadian emergency coordinator/African famine to organize the Canadian contribution to the Ethiopian relief effort, and he was given resources to establish an office separate from the line departments.

Second, the Mulroney government established a special financial facility for famine relief: by the middle of November, a special fund for Africa, amounting initially to fifty million dollars, had been created. But this was a relief fund with a difference: in an effort to both reflect the number of Canadians donating to the relief effort and to encourage public participation, the government pledged that it would match donations from ordinary Canadians dollar for dollar up to fifteen million dollars. That initial pledge turned out not to be enough. As large numbers of Canadians organized fund-raising activities over the winter of 1984-85, the government was prompted to contribute nearly thirty-six million dollars in matching funds.

Third, the government also closely involved the NGO community with the process of organizing the relief effort. While the Canadian government had, for a number of years, allocated funds to NGOs as a means of implementing its development assistance policies, in the Ethiopian relief effort, MacDonald was charged with bringing the NGOs into the process of making program allocation decisions. To orchestrate the relief effort, an umbrella coalition, Africa Emergency Aid, was created; MacDonald and a CIDA representative had seats on this group's board, but the NGO community held a majority. As Morrison notes, this arrangement "broke new ground."[11] Finally, as the worst aspects of the crisis passed and donations fell, MacDonald sought to bolster the commitment of Canadians to the long-term concern for African development by holding a series of community meetings across the country. Entitled Forum Africa, these meetings culminated in the National Forum Africa, which was held in Ottawa in February 1986.

It should be noted that MPs played a role in the work of the relief operation. In particular, the Standing Committee on External Affairs and National Defence held hearings on the famine relief effort in April 1985, recommending that MacDonald's tenure be extended for an additional year and that the government continue making matching funds available.

While the crisis itself was, at least for Canadians, relatively short-lived, by the spring of 1985 it could be argued that its legacy was longer-lived. First, this legacy reflected the willingness of the Conservative government to try to open up the policy process by establishing what were termed "partnerships" with a broader public. It is no coincidence that the key players in this process were Clark and MacDonald, for the government's approach to Ethiopia was, in part, an echo of what Clark's short-lived 1979 government had sought to do in the case of the Vietnamese boat people when it encouraged the public to become personally involved in sponsoring refugees from Indochina.[12] Second, the Conservative response to the Ethiopian crisis in 1984-85 and the coordinating activities of MacDonald not only laid the groundwork for the increased involvement of NGOs in the policy-making and policy-implementation processes, but, just as important, they moved many parliamentarians who had been participants in the process. One in particular, William Winegard, chair of the House of

Commons Standing Committee on External Affairs and International Trade, would be galvanized to try to reform Canada's development assistance programs (see Michaud and Nossal, Chapter 19). Finally, this episode served to entrench the idea of an appropriate role for ordinary Canadians in the policy-making process, a conception that would be central to the process of reviewing foreign policy that began to unfold in 1985.

Bringing Parliament In: Reviewing External Policy

When the Progressive Conservatives came to power in September 1984, one of the priorities of the new government was to subject the foreign and defence policies that they had so ardently criticized over the summer election campaign to a full review. During the election campaign, the Conservatives had sought to distance themselves from the foreign policy orientations of the Liberals under Pierre Elliott Trudeau, but the Conservative platform on foreign and defence policy issues was ruggedly minimalist, consisting of a few basic promises frequently repeated.

Once in power, however, the new government clearly needed to put some substance onto this slender frame. In the Speech from the Throne that opened the thirty-third Parliament in 1984, the government announced that it was going to do what Trudeau had done fifteen years earlier: foreign and defence policy would be subjected to a substantive review. However, unlike the Trudeau exercise of the late 1960s or the CIDA-initiated review of development assistance policies of the mid-1970s, two of the three Conservative policy reviews in the international sphere were conducted not by officials who had little input from outside the foreign and defence bureaucracies,[13] but, rather, thanks to Secretary of State for External Affairs Joe Clark, involved a central role for MPs as well as input from NGOs and ordinary citizens alike.

To achieve this, Clark put out a green paper to catalyze the public debate.[14] In June 1985, the government created a Special Joint Committee on Canada's International Relations, with membership from both the House of Commons and the Senate, and gave it both the authority and the resources to allow it to conduct a wide-ranging review. Its work was conducted in two phases: over the summer of 1985, it was tasked with examining whether to accept the US invitation to join the research phase of the Strategic Defense Initiative (SDI) and whether to enter free trade negotiations with the United States. The committee held public hearings on these two issues in Halifax, Montréal, Ottawa, Toronto, Winnipeg, Calgary, and Vancouver; it received submissions from nearly 700 individuals and organizations, and it heard from over 300 witnesses.

The second phase of the committee's work focused on the broad review of foreign policy. In the fall of 1985 the committee organized panels of expert witnesses on a variety of policy issues, and then, in January 1986, the committee began to travel across the country to hold public hearings. In all, forty-five hearings were held in fifteen Canadian cities covering every province and the two territories. The committee received written submissions from 245 individuals and 287 organizations. At the hearings, the committee heard the presentation of 161 briefs by organizations. An innovative departure involved the provision made to listen to "ordinary" Canadians: citizens were invited to present a five-minute statement to the committee; in all, the members listened to 131 of these brief statements.[15]

This public process was deemed so effective and useful from a policy perspective that the Mulroney government used it to conduct an assessment of development assistance policies. The responsibility for the review was given to the House of Commons Standing Committee on External Affairs and International Trade, chaired in the thirty-third Parliament by William Winegard. The Winegard committee, like its special committee counterpart, issued a discussion paper to galvanize debate. It held hearings in eight Canadian cities and heard from over 100 witnesses. The committee also received nearly 300 formal written briefs and, according to the Winegard report, "thousands of letters."[16] Significantly, its report embraced a distinctly reform-oriented set of recommendations, which David R. Morrison termed a "refreshing approach."[17]

This pattern of public consultation and parliamentary involvement was not used consistently across the government. The review of defence policy did not follow the pattern established for the foreign policy review (although that had been the original intention). As Nelson Michaud shows (Chapter 17), although a defence review had been initiated in the fall of 1984, no green paper ever emanated from the Department of National Defence; and when Perrin Beatty was appointed minister in 1986, he decided to go right to a white paper, with parliamentary hearings to be held ex post facto by the new Standing Committee on National Defence (SCOND), which was created in 1986 by splitting the Standing Committee on External Affairs and National Defence. However, in the meantime, the government was making a number of decisions – increasing troop strength in Europe, modernizing the North American Aerospace Defence Command (NORAD) facilities, and purchasing a low-level air defence system – that would have an impact on Canada's defence posture. However, as Middlemiss and Sokolsky remind us, these decisions were taken "without a great deal of parliamentary discussion or involvement."[18]

While recognizing that the commitment to bringing Parliament into the foreign policy process was not uniformly embraced across the government, we should nonetheless put the parliamentary practices of the Mulroney Conservatives into a broader context. For although, early in the first mandate, one political scientist was moved to predict that Mulroney enjoyed the exercise of power so much that he would be unlikely to encourage parliamentary committees to be independent,[19] in fact the Mulroney government appointed a special committee on the reform of the House of Commons, headed by a veteran Conservative MP, James McGrath. In June 1985, the McGrath committee issued its report, arguing that the reforms it was recommending were intended to give MPs "a meaningful role in the formation of public policy and, in so doing, to restore the House of Commons to its rightful place in the Canadian political process."[20] Among its approximately sixty recommendations was a series of recommendations for the reform of the committee system that would result in freeing committees from the centralized control of Cabinet ministers. While the embrace of these reforms did not result in a dramatic increase in the influence of committees over the policy process, there can be little doubt that, during the Mulroney era, committees enjoyed a greater policy role than they had before 1984.

This portrait suggests a government in which some ministers were committed to opening up the policy process by involving MPs more directly in policy formulation – at least within the relatively unforgiving constraints of the Westminster system – and by giving "ordinary" Canadians an opportunity to participate directly in foreign policy. Joe Clark was clearly one such minister: both Page and Morrison, for example, attest to the importance of Clark's personal commitment to opening up the process.[21] And certainly Clark's approach to some issues was unusual: in the case of South Africa, there can be little doubt that some of the measures taken by the Conservative government – such as the establishment of a "registry" to allow institutions and individuals to register their own protests against apartheid, the provision of assistance to extra-parliamentary opposition, or Clark's urging "the whole country" to write letters of protest to those Canadian companies that were not complying with the government's "code of conduct" for firms doing business in South Africa – were not only highly innovative but also marked a considerable departure from previous practice.[22] If "populism" means a willingness to try to involve as many "ordinary" people in the policy process as possible or practicable, then we can conclude that, when it came to foreign policy, the Mulroney Conservatives had an evident populist streak.

How might we assess this populist streak in Conservative foreign policy-making? Denis Stairs argues that the participation of members of Parliament and members of the public in the foreign policy and development assistance reviews did represent a significant innovation. Certainly both the process and the scope of the inquiries was, as the Special Joint Committee itself asserted, an "unprecedented" exercise in Canada. However, Stairs also notes that we have to put the desire of the Mulroney government to consult with Canadians within a broader political context. He argues that the pattern of consultations launched by the Conservatives was "simply part of a longer-term trajectory" that had its beginnings in the Trudeau years.[23] Stairs suggests that such factors as the widening of the international agenda, instantaneous electronic communications, a new transnational NGO politics, and the growth of participatory politics within Canada all contributed to the Conservative government doing what it did. He concludes that the process is "ultimately independent of party."

Stairs is right to point to the existence of a trajectory: the "domesticated" foreign policy process in the 1970s was indeed remarkably more open than it had been in the late 1960s, when Franklyn Griffiths was analyzing the closed nature of the foreign policy process[24] and when policy-makers saw nothing untoward in a review of foreign policy being conducted entirely by the bureaucracy. And there can be no denying that the foreign policy process opened up even further in the 1980s. In short, we can identify a secular development – a trajectory, just as Stairs claims.

On the other hand, it can be argued that the way in which governments have chosen to "open" the policy process has not developed in such a linear way and, indeed, is not as independent of party as Stairs suggests. If Stairs were correct, then we should expect that the Liberal government that replaced the Conservative government in 1993 would have not only continued the innovations introduced in the 1980s but, indeed, would have intensified them. In other words, if a trajectory were in fact at work, then we should have seen the further strengthening of parliamentary committee autonomy and an increased use of MPs to develop foreign policy initiatives on a range of issues. We should have seen the intensification of the practice of trying to involve "ordinary" Canadians in the formulation and implementation of policy. We should have seen the proliferation of such unusual schemes as a state-sponsored campaign of writing protest letters to Canadian corporations engaged in international activities deemed to offend public sensibilities or government matching funds to encourage ordinary Canadians to donate to worthy international causes.

Yet it is clear that the ways in which the Conservatives sought to involve both the public and MPs in the foreign policy process between 1984 and 1993 differed considerably not only from the Trudeau Liberal approach of the 1970s and early 1980s (which we might expect if Stairs were correct), but also, and more important, from the Chrétien Liberal approach of the 1990s (which we would *not* expect if Stairs were correct). In other words, to see whether or not a trajectory is at work, we need to examine how the Chrétien government chose to "democratize" Canadian foreign policy in the 1990s.

Bringing in Civil Society Organizations: The Chrétien Era

A brief examination of the history of opening up the foreign policy process since 1993 reveals several trends. First, the involvement of MPs in foreign policy development does not appear to have intensified since the end of the Mulroney era. It is true that the Chrétien government adopted the Conservative model of appointing a special joint committee of Parliament to undertake a review of foreign policy, and, indeed, unlike the Conservatives, the Liberals appointed a special committee on defence.[25] However, we have not seen an increase in the importance of Parliament with regard to the policy process. Indeed, on at least one occasion, it can be argued that the Liberal government actually diminished the role of parliamentarians: originally, MPs were not going to be invited to the 1994 National Forum, which was to be the centrepiece of the Liberal effort to "democratize" Canadian foreign policy. Although that decision was reversed, incredibly, the MPs and senators who did attend the forum were not permitted to say anything.[26]

While the special joint committees completed their work, and the Standing Committee on Foreign Affairs and its two committees continued to put out reports on foreign policy issues, it can be argued that the level of activity remains static. Certainly we have not seen an increase in the autonomy of parliamentary committees; and some MPs have expressed concern about the failure of their reports to have an impact, the limited amount of time that ministers devote to appearing before the committee, and high turnover rates in committee membership. Moreover, some MPs have argued that, as of 1993, committees returned to being as dominated by the executive as they had been prior to 1984. This is because some of the McGrath reforms of the mid-1980s, which were intended to bolster committee autonomy, were abandoned in 1993, constituting what Michael M. Atkinson and David Docherty term a "relatively brief experiment, lasting only for the duration of the Mulroney era."[27]

More important, some foreign policy-makers have openly expressed the view that Parliament is no longer the most appropriate political institution for the articulation, aggregation, and intermediation of views on foreign policy issues between civil society and the state. For example, Robert J. Lawson, who worked in Foreign Affairs on the landmines issue, has argued that there are "serious weaknesses" in the notion that Parliament is the most effective institution for defining the interests of "Canadians as a whole."[28] Lawson's concerns mirror Maxwell Cameron's argument, which doubts the possibility of an effective legislature without an informed citizenry. Cameron goes on to contend that the way to ensure an informed citizenry is to establish a "triangulation" between the state apparatus, "the public," and non-governmental organizations.[29]

And, indeed, the focus of opening up the policy-making process since 1993 has been on NGOs – though, increasingly, Canadian state officials have taken to using the language of "global civil society" to describe these actors. Steve Lee, head of the Canadian Centre for Foreign Policy

Development (CCFPD) – a government-financed organization established in 1996 by Lloyd Axworthy (after he became minister of foreign affairs) to "help integrate public participation into government policy-making" – defines civil society as "citizens acting in public space, for the public good."[30] Civil society organizations (CSOs), then, are "those organizations formed for collective purposes primarily of the state and the marketplace. They therefore include NGOs but encompass labour unions, professional associations, organized religion, community self-help groups, and even recreational groups."[31]

However they might be defined by Ottawa officials, CSOs have been central to all the important democratizing initiatives and activities of the Chrétien Liberals. They have been the core participants at the annual national forums on foreign policy, which have been held since 1994. CSOs have been central to the activities of the Canadian Centre for Foreign Policy Development and the many regional and functional forums, conferences, and round tables on different international issues organized by the CCFPD after 1996. And, most important of all, CSOs were crucial partners in Lloyd Axworthy's effort to secure an international ban on anti-personnel landmines – an effort known as the "Ottawa Process." All of the accounts of the Ottawa Process are clear on the deeply symbiotic relationship between the NGOs, which provided crucial backing for the Canadian initiative at crucial moments, and the Canadian government, which afforded the NGOs unprecedented access to the policy-making process.[32] For his part, Axworthy clearly stated his own view of the proper role of CSOs in the foreign policy-making process: "One can no longer relegate NGOs to simple advisory or advocacy roles ... They are now part of the way decisions have to be made. They have been the voice saying that governments belong to the people, and must respond to the people's hopes, demands and ideals."[33]

Conclusion

For all of the talk of "the people," however, it is not at all clear that what we saw in the years after 1993 was the intensification of the populist practices evident in the Conservative era, when the government tried to bring "ordinary" Canadians into the foreign policy process. On the contrary, what we saw was a foreign policy process that privileged elites over "ordinary" Canadians.[34] Ordinary people were not flown to Ottawa for national forums; ordinary people were not consulted by the CCFPD; ordinary people were not brought into the policy process by the minister of foreign affairs. On the contrary, an examination of the activities undertaken by the Chrétien government, activities supposedly intended to "democratize" the foreign policy process (e.g., the National Forums on Canada's International Relations, the CCFPD conferences and round tables, the "partnerships" with NGOs), reveals that organized interests, rather than "ordinary" individuals, were the primary target.

A comparison between the approaches to foreign policy-making on the part of the Mulroney Conservatives and the Chrétien Liberals reveals substantial differences in political philosophy. It can be argued that, in foreign policy-making, the Conservatives were generally inclined towards opening up the policy process by embracing a populism intermediated by Parliament, while the Liberals were generally inclined towards opening up the policy process by bringing a wider range of "civil society" groups into the process by forging "partnerships."

Such a conclusion suggests that a "trajectory" has, indeed, been at work over the last forty years but only as a steady secular trend towards greater openness. And one can argue, as does Denis Stairs, that such a general trajectory is independent of party. However, one can also argue that party can, and did, make a difference as to how Cabinet ministers dealt with expanding pressures for public and parliamentary participation.

Notes

1 Don Page, "Populism in Canadian Foreign Policy: The 1986 Review Revisited," *Canadian Public Administration* 37 (Winter 1994): 573-97.
2 *Liberal Foreign Policy Handbook* (Ottawa: Liberal Party of Canada, May 1993); see also Lloyd Axworthy, "Canadian Foreign Policy: A Liberal Party Perspective," *Canadian Foreign Policy* 1, 1 (Winter 1992/93): 14; Kim Richard Nossal, "The Democratization of Canadian Foreign Policy?" *Canadian Foreign Policy* 1, 3 (Fall 1993): 95-108.
3 Liberal Party of Canada, *Creating Opportunity: The Liberal Plan for Canada* (Ottawa: Liberal Party of Canada, 1993), 105, cited in Page, "Populism in Canadian Foreign Policy," 574.
4 *Liberal Foreign Policy Handbook*, cited in Denis Stairs, "The Public Politics of the Canadian Defence and Foreign Policy Reviews," *Canadian Foreign Policy* 3, 1 (Spring 1995): 91.
5 Canada, Parliament, House of Commons, *Debates*, 25 January 1994, 134, 282.
6 Kim Richard Nossal, "Quantum Leaping: The Gulf Debate in Australia and Canada," in *The Gulf War: Critical Perspectives*, ed. Michael McKinley (Sydney: Allen and Unwin, 1994), 48-71. On parliamentary debates during the Mulroney era, see Kim Richard Nossal, *The Politics of Canadian Foreign Policy*, 3rd ed. (Scarborough: Prentice Hall Canada, 1997), 275-76.
7 David R. Morrison, *Aid and Ebb Tide: A History of CIDA and Canadian Development Assistance* (Waterloo, ON: Wilfrid Laurier University Press, 1998), 234-35.
8 *Sunday Star*, 4 November 1984, cited in ibid., 234.
9 *Globe and Mail*, 6 November 1984, cited in ibid.
10 Cited in Maureen Appel Molot and Brian W. Tomlin, "The Conservative Agenda," in *Canada Among Nations, 1985: The Conservative Agenda*, ed. Maureen Appel Molot and Brian W. Tomlin (Toronto: James Lorimer, 1986), 9.
11 Morrison, *Aid and Ebb Tide*, 235.
12 Howard Adelman, *Canada and the Indochinese Refugees* (Regina: Weigl Educational, 1982); Gerry Dirks, "World Refugees: The Canadian Response," *Behind the Headlines* 45 (May/June 1988): 1-18.
13 Bruce Thordarson, *Trudeau and Foreign Policy: A Study in Decision-Making* (Toronto: Oxford University Press, 1972); J.L. Granatstein and Robert Bothwell, *Pirouette: Pierre Elliott Trudeau and Canadian Foreign Policy* (Toronto: University of Toronto Press, 1990).
14 Canada, Secretary of State for External Affairs, *Competitiveness and Security: Directions for Canada's International Relations* (Ottawa: Supply and Services Canada, 1985).

15 Canada, Special Joint Committee of the Senate and of the House of Commons on Canada's International Relations, *Independence and Internationalism: Report of the Special Joint Committee* (Ottawa: Queen's Printer, June 1986), 1-4. For an excellent insider account of the actual process of the parliamentary review, see Page, "Populism in Canadian Foreign Policy."

16 Canada, House of Commons, Standing Committee on External Affairs and International Trade, *For Whose Benefit? Report of the Standing Committee on External Affairs and International Trade on Canada's Official Development Assistance Policies and Programs* (Ottawa: Queen's Printer, 1987), xiii.

17 Morrison, *Aid and Ebb Tide*, 279.

18 D.W. Middlemiss and J.J. Sokolsky, *Canadian Defence: Decisions and Determinants* (Toronto: Harcourt Brace Jovanovich Canada, 1989), 103.

19 W.M. Dobell, "Foreign Policy in Parliament," *International Perspectives* (January/February 1985): 11.

20 Canada, Parliament, Special Committee on the Reform of the House of Commons, *Report* (Ottawa: Queen's Printer, June 1985), 1.

21 Page, "Populism in Canadian Foreign Policy," 595; David R. Morrison, "Canada and North-South Conflict," in *Canada Among Nations, 1987: A World of Conflict*, ed. Brian W. Tomlin and Maureen Appel Molot (Toronto: James Lorimer, 1988), 155.

22 Kim Richard Nossal, *Rain Dancing: Sanctions in Canadian and Australian Foreign Policy* (Toronto: University of Toronto Press, 1994), 91-110.

23 Indeed, Stairs was one of the first students of Canadian foreign policy to identify the beginnings of this trajectory in the mid-1970s. See Denis Stairs, "Public Opinion and External Affairs: Reflections on the Domestication of Canadian Foreign Policy," *International Journal* 33 (Winter 1977-78): 126-49.

24 Franklyn Griffiths, "Opening Up the Policy Process," in *An Independent Foreign Policy for Canada?* ed. Stephen Clarkson (Toronto: McClelland and Stewart, 1968), 110-18.

25 For accounts of these reviews, see Stairs, "Public Politics"; and Heather A. Smith, "Seeking Certainty and Finding None: Reflections on the 1994 Canadian Foreign Policy Review," *Canadian Foreign Policy* 3, 1 (Spring 1995): 117-24; and Robert J. Lawson, "Construction of Consensus: The 1994 Canadian Defence Review," in *Canada Among Nations, 1995: Democracy and Foreign Policy*, ed. Maxwell A. Cameron and Maureen Appel Molot (Ottawa: Carleton University Press, 1996), 99-117.

26 This story circulated after the forum and was eventually confirmed by John English, who was a Liberal MP, during the thirty-fifth Parliament. See John English, "The Member of Parliament and Foreign Policy," in *Canada Among Nations, 1998: Leadership and Dialogue*, ed. Fen Osler Hampson and Maureen Appel Molot (Toronto: Oxford University Press, 1998), 79.

27 Michael M. Atkinson and David C. Docherty, "Parliament and Political Success in Canada," in *Canadian Politics in the 21st Century* (5th ed.), ed. Michael Whittington and Glen Williams (Toronto: Nelson Canada, 1999), 22.

28 Robert J. Lawson, "Construction of Consensus: The 1994 Canadian Defence Review," in Cameron and Molot, *Canada Among Nations, 1995*, 102.

29 Maxwell A. Cameron, "Democratization of Canadian Foreign Policy: The Ottawa Process as a Model," *Canadian Foreign Policy* 5, 3 (Spring 1998): 147-65.

30 Steve Lee, "A Note from the Canadian Centre for Foreign Policy Development," *Canadian Foreign Policy* 7, 1 (Fall 1999): iii.

31 Alison Van Rooy, "How Ambassadors (Should) Deal with Civil Society Organizations: A New Diplomacy?" *Canadian Foreign Policy* 7, 1 (Fall 1999): 148. Van Rooy estimates that there are 20,000 such CSOs in Canada.

32 On the Ottawa Process, see Maxwell A. Cameron, Robert Lawson, and Brian W. Tomlin, eds., *To Walk without Fear: The Global Movement to Ban Landmines* (Toronto: Oxford University Press, 1998); David A. Lenarcic, *Knight-Errant? Canada and the Crusade to Ban Anti-Personnel Land Mines* (Toronto: Irwin, 1998); Maxwell A. Cameron, "Global Civil Society and the Ottawa Process: Lessons from the Movement to Ban Anti-Personnel Mines," *Canadian Foreign Policy* 7, 1 (Fall 1999): 85-102.

33 Address by Axworthy to the Oslo NGO Forum on Banning Anti-Personnel Landmines, 10 September 1997, cited in Cameron, "Democratization of Foreign Policy," 163.
34 For an elaboration of this argument, see Nossal, "Democratization of Canadian Foreign Policy?"; and Nossal, "The Democratization of Canadian Foreign Policy: The Elusive Ideal," in Cameron and Molot, *Canada Among Nations, 1995*, 29-43.

19
Diplomatic Departures? Assessing the Conservative Era in Foreign Policy

Nelson Michaud and Kim Richard Nossal

Did the Progressive Conservative government of Brian Mulroney take Canadian foreign policy in substantially different directions during its nine years in power? To what extent did the Conservatives depart from Canadian traditions in international affairs? How innovative or unusual were the foreign policy initiatives undertaken between 1984 and 1993?

For many, the answers to these questions are self-evident: foreign policy during the Mulroney era was merely an adjunct to American global policy; Mulroney himself was little more than a craven toady who embarrassed the country by his fawning behaviour. More ominously, he was a cat's paw for American-based multinationals. As prime minister, Mulroney merely played out his former role as president of Iron Ore Company, carrying out a grand Conservative plan to sell the country out to the Yanks, dismantling all that was distinctively Canadian, and, in the process, subordinating Canadian interests to those of the United States. In this view, the Conservatives abandoned the traditional bases of Canada's post-Second World War foreign policy (which were put in place by Lester B. Pearson, secretary of state for external affairs from 1948 to 1957) and betrayed Pearson's peacekeeping traditions by applauding the American invasion of Panama and following the Americans into the Gulf War. In short, the foreign policy approach of the Conservatives was just like its domestic policies – Reaganesque and Thatcherite, after the two leaders Mulroney so obviously admired, and whose terms of office overlapped his own.

Such a public remembrance is perhaps not surprising, given that, many years after his departure from public life, Mulroney continues to be a deeply unpopular figure in Canada. As a result, the public memory of the Conservative era tends to be largely defined by the viscerally negative sentiments that Mulroney's public persona inspired among so many Canadians during the years he was prime minister. While this politico-psychological phenomenon is interesting in itself, and deserving of further study,[1] there is little doubt that this dislike has had an impact on how foreign policy in the Mulroney era is remembered.

However, a more dispassionate look at the Conservative era yields a somewhat different analysis. The contributions to this volume lead us to conclude that there are no straightforward or unqualified answers to the questions we asked at the beginning of this chapter. On the one hand, the studies above suggest that the more simplistic portrayals of Conservative foreign policy – that it was a pale imitation of the conservative global policies embraced by Thatcher and Reagan – by and large miss the mark. On the other hand, these departures need to be put into context.

First, the chapters above provide ample evidence that, in the nine years that Mulroney was prime minister, the Conservative government he headed embraced foreign policy stances and initiatives that, more often than is admitted, departed markedly from the Reagan/Thatcher line. Indeed, the accounts above make clear that the Mulroney government was consistently willing to articulate – and defend – a Canadian conception of interests that often sharply opposed the interests of the United States and/or Britain. Here, one might immediately think of the distinctive Canadian position towards the American Strategic Defense Initiative (SDI) or the opposition to Britain's stance on apartheid. In short, Conservative foreign policy may not have been distinctly conservative, as Denis Stairs quite rightly observes in Chapter 2, but it was distinctly Canadian.

Moreover, the account here also demonstrates that the Mulroney Conservatives departed from many of the tenets of Canada's foreign policy that had been faithfully followed under a succession of Liberal governments since the Second World War; indeed, their foreign policy often marked a departure from that pursued by the Conservative governments of John G. Diefenbaker and Joe Clark. The Mulroney government also embraced initiatives in foreign policy that had been anathema – or simply unthinkable – to previous prime ministers and previous governments, Liberal or Conservative.

These diplomatic departures occurred in a number of different policy areas. In Canadian-American relations, the decision to negotiate a free trade agreement with the United States was, as Brian Tomlin (Chapter 3) shows, the clearest example of a dramatic reversal of a historic trend that stretched back to the aftermath of the 1911 elections. Likewise, Tammy Nemeth (Chapter 4) suggests that the continentalization of energy policy also represented a new orientation for Canadian policy. The successful effort to settle the long-running conflict with the United States over Canadian sovereignty of Arctic waters, examined by Rob Huebert (Chapter 6), reflected a clear departure from the policies of previous governments. The free trade deals reflected a new orientation towards the western hemisphere more generally. The decision to pursue an activist role in attempts

to negotiate an end to the Central American conflict was one manifestation of this. Another, as Gordon Mace (Chapter 10) suggests, was the decision to join the Organization of American States and to use Canadian
membership to revitalize it.

The Conservative government also trod a new path in multilateral diplomacy beyond the hemisphere. Of particular importance was Mulroney's
personal willingness to extend the "beau risque" – an attempt to concili-
ate federal politics with the aspirations of Québec – to the realm of international affairs, a process outlined by Luc Bernier (Chapter 9). The
promising gamble worked: Mulroney's ability to forge an agreement with
the provincial Liberal government of Robert Bourassa resulted in the creation of a francophone summit – a forum that had been impossible while
Trudeau was in power. And Andrew Cooper (Chapter 11) shows the degree
to which Mulroney's personal diplomacy at the UN social conferences of
the 1990s represented a departure from the policies of previous governments, even if it was one often prompted by political opportunism.

There were also departures in defence policy. One was the 1987 defence
white paper, a hawkish document distinctly unlike anything before (or
since) in Canadian security policy. But, as Nelson Michaud (Chapter 17)
demonstrates, those who secured the acceptance of the defence white
paper lost control of its implementation, with the result that other actors
in the policy-making process – that is, those who were more concerned
about the federal deficit – prevailed. After 1987, to use Norrin Ripsman's
suggestive metaphor, eyes were no longer so wide and pockets were even
emptier (Chapter 7). One by one the promises of the white paper were
abandoned. The efforts to cut spending led to another policy departure:
the withdrawal of Canadian forces from Europe, which brought to an end
a forty-year commitment that had been embraced by five prime ministers.

In peacekeeping, the departures were no less pronounced, as Manon
Tessier and Michel Fortmann (Chapter 8) demonstrate. Mulroney was the
first prime minister in forty years to have approved the use of Canadian
forces for combat operations against Iraq in Kuwait; the Conservative government took a bold approach to humanitarian intervention, approving
the use of Canadian forces for a mission in Somalia that marked a radical
departure from the traditions of "first-generation" peacekeeping. And the
withdrawal from the UN peacekeeping force in Cyprus represented the
end of a mission that had stretched over nearly three decades.

In environmental matters, the Conservative government might have
been as forthright in its efforts to grapple with the threat of acid rain as
had been the Trudeau government; indeed, eventually the Mulroney government's tactics on acid rain looked remarkably like those pursued by the
Trudeau government from 1980 to 1984. But, as Heather Smith (Chapter
5) shows, Mulroney's embrace of a "green" foreign policy in the early 1990s

– exemplified by his personal diplomacy at the UN Conference on the Environment and Development in Rio de Janeiro – represented a new aspect of Canadian diplomatic activism.

On the issue of human rights, the Conservative government pursued an approach that was markedly different from that of the Trudeau government. As David Black (Chapter 12) and Paul Gecelovsky and Tom Keating (Chapter 13) suggest, the Mulroney government's human rights policy was activist and interventionist, willing to press for a variety of rights in a variety of contexts. While the Mulroney government's activism on apartheid in South Africa is usually held up as the exemplar of its activist approach, and one that is, as Black argues, usually very much overblown, it can nonetheless be argued that Conservative activism on behalf of human rights and good governance in countries as varied as China, Sri Lanka, Indonesia, Russia, and Yugoslavia did represent a new direction for Canadian policy. Likewise, the promotion of the rights of women and children is indicative of an expansive definition of human rights activism. The argument here is not that the Mulroney government was a paragon on the issue of the protection and defence of human rights during this period; numerous criticisms can be (and have been) levelled at the Conservatives for inconsistencies and contradictions in their human rights policies. Rather, the argument is that the attention given to human rights after 1984 represented an important departure from Canadian government practice to that point.[2]

Finally, the explorations of the foreign policy process under the Conservatives suggest some differences from previous practice. J.H. Taylor (Chapter 14), who served as the deputy minister in the Department of External Affairs for part of this period, attests to some of those differences. Claire Turenne Sjolander (Chapter 15) demonstrates the degree to which there were some differences in the Conservative approach to incorporating gender not only with regard to the foreign policy process, but also with regard to policy (although, as she notes, steps forward tend to be accompanied by steps backward). Both Roy Norton (Chapter 16) and Kim Richard Nossal (Chapter 18) argue that, during the Conservative era, we saw an opening up of the policy-making process, with ethnic groups and the public being brought more generally into the making of foreign policy.

In short, this rereading suggests that Conservative foreign policy was more multidimensional than public memory admits. It suggests that the Conservative government was willing to defend a Canadian conception of interests against the interests of the United States, contradicting the popular view that the Mulroney Conservatives simply sold Canada out at every turn. Finally, it demonstrates that, while the Mulroney Conservatives did not radically alter all aspects of Canada's foreign policy, they did, in fact, abandon a number of established lines of external relations that, since the Second World War, a succession of federal governments had followed.

However, as we noted, these departures must be put into context. The different studies in this volume suggest that Denis Stairs is not at all wrong to argue that, in foreign policy, the Mulroney Conservatives were more "engineers" than "architects," that, as he puts it, they dealt with "insistent imperatives arising from circumstance" rather than with designing fresh policies. In short, Stairs stresses that any assessment of Conservative "diplomatic departures" must pay careful attention to the importance of structural conditions when attempting to explain the foreign policy of a government like Canada's, which persistently needs "engineers" more than it does "architects."

Moreover, all of the contributions to this book illustrate the degree to which foreign policy during the Conservative era was subject to the inertia inherent in the practice of Canadian diplomacy. This is hardly surprising, given the highly bureaucratized nature of the Canadian state, the homogenizing nature of Canadian brokerage politics, and Canada's location as a middle power within the international system. Thus, as Stairs reminds us, we should not be suprised that the change of government in 1984 did not result in a radical shift in foreign policy, for the Progressive Conservatives were not able to start with a clean slate; they were never able to write their own foreign policy agenda; and they could not avoid dealing with the dossiers left behind by the Liberals.

And even if we can see clear evidence of departures from the polices of previous governments, it is important to remember that these departures were not carefully planned. Regardless of whether they were architects or engineers, the Conservatives came to office equipped with neither architectural plans nor engineering drawings. Only in the area of the policy process can we see a predilection for a populist approach to public and parliamentary input, a reading that contradicts the Liberal charge, made during the 1993 election, that the Conservative approach to foreign policy-making was elitist. However, with regard to policy, as we argued in the introduction, there were few signs of a coordinated approach. Certainly, from the Conservative foreign policy pronouncements in 1983 and 1984 it was not possible to predict that, by 1993, the Mulroney government would have embraced so many innovations and departures in external policy.

Moreover, it would be inaccurate to suggest that foreign policy under the Conservatives was shaped by a world vision that drew its inspiration from Ronald Reagan in the United States and/or Margaret Thatcher in Britain. Although it has been popular to caricature the Mulroney government as Reaganesque or Thatcherite, such labels simply do not adequately capture the vision of world politics that guided the Mulroney government.[3] Mulroney's approach to world politics, as well as that of both his secretaries of state for external affairs – Joe Clark and Barbara McDougall – had much more in common with the characteristics of what John W. Holmes used to call "middlepowermanship" – an abiding concern for moderate diplomacy directed at the peaceful resolution of the conflicts that will always arise in international relations.[4] In this, they reflected a more general and persistent political culture of Canadian foreign policy, which, as Denis Stairs has argued, puts a premium on manifesting in international affairs the same brokerage politics demanded by Canadians at home.[5]

Finally, the diplomatic departures we can see so clearly during this period were not always brought into being by the Mulroney government. In other words, this was by no means the Conservative transformation of Canadian foreign policy; rather, much of the transformation in foreign policy during the Conservative era was quite ad hoc – a response by the government in Ottawa to the exigencies of the moment, an attempt to respond to pressures from both domestic and external sources at a tumultuous time in global politics. At the same time, however, there can be little doubt that the diplomatic departures of the Conservative era ended up changing the face of Canada's external relations – with the United States, with the hemisphere, with the Asia Pacific, with Europe, and, indeed, with the rest of the world.

Notes

1 For a preliminary journalistic exploration of this theme, see Michael Valpy, "Mr Mulroney's Makeover," *Globe and Mail*, 10 October 1998, D1.
2 Indeed, Jennifer Ross argues that the origins of the "human security" agenda embraced by Lloyd Axworthy, Canada's foreign minister from 1996 to 2000, can be traced back to the Conservative era. See Jennifer Ross, "Is Canada's Human Security Policy Really the 'Axworthy' Doctrine?" *Canadian Foreign Policy* 8 (Winter 2001): 75-93.
3 As even staunch academic critics of the Mulroney Conservatives will readily admit. See, for example, Andrew B. Gollner and Daniel Salée, "A Turn to the Right? Canada in the Post-Trudeau Era," in *Canada under Mulroney: An End-of-Term Report*, ed. Andrew B. Gollner and Daniel Salée (Montreal: Véhicule Press, 1988), 15.
4 John W. Holmes, *Canada: A Middle-Aged Power* (Toronto: McClelland and Stewart, 1976).
5 See Denis Stairs, "The Political Culture of Canadian Foreign Policy," *Canadian Journal of Political Science* 15 (December 1982): 667-90.

Appendix A
Chronology of Events, 1984-93

4 September 1984	Canadian general election – Progressive Conservative majority: 211 PCs (50% of popular vote), 40 Liberals (28%), 30 NDP (19%)
17 September 1984	Mulroney government sworn in; Joe Clark appointed secretary of state for external affairs; James Kelleher in international trade, Robert Coates in national defence. John Turner is leader of the Opposition
31 October 1984	Indian prime minister Indira Gandhi assassinated
6 November 1984	US presidential elections: Republican President Ronald Reagan re-elected
18 November 1984	Donald Macdonald, chairman of the Royal Commission on the Economic Union and Development Prospects for Canada, calls for a "leap of faith" and the embrace of free trade with the United States
11 December 1984	Bill establishing "Investment Canada" introduced in House of Commons
31 December 1984	United States withdraws from UNESCO
12 February 1985	Robert Coates forced to resign; Joe Clark acting minister of national defence
27 February 1985	Erik Nielsen appointed minister of national defence
10 March 1985	Soviet leader Konstantin Chernenko dies, succeeded by Mikhail S. Gorbachev
17-18 March 1985	"Shamrock Summit," Québec City
2-4 May 1985	Bonn G-7 summit
23 June 1985	Air India bombing
6 July 1985	"Baie Comeau" sanctions against South Africa announced
1-11 July 1985	Polar Sea transits the Northwest Passage
5 September 1985	Report of the Royal Commission on the Economic Union and Development Prospects for Canada (Macdonald Commission) released
7 September 1985	"Polite no" to the US request for Canadian participation in the Strategic Defense Initiative announced
10 September 1985	New Arctic waters policy announced
26 September 1985	Mulroney announces that he has phoned Reagan asking him to initiate free trade talks
1 October 1985	Canada makes formal request for free trade negotiations with the United States
20-22 October 1985	Commonwealth Heads of Government Meeting, Nassau, Bahamas

8 November 1985	Simon Reisman appointed Canada's chief negotiator for free trade
22 February 1986	First Francophone summit, Paris
19 March 1986	Second annual Canada-US summit, Washington; NORAD renewed for five years
14 April 1986	US bombs cities in Libya
4-6 May 1986	Tokyo G-7 summit
30 June 1986	Cabinet shuffle: Pat Carney to international trade, Perrin Beatty to defence
25 September 1986	Uruguay Round of multilateral GATT negotiations launched (completed December 1993)
11-12 October 1986	Reagan and Gorbachev summit in Reykjavik, Iceland
4 December 1986	Government statement on foreign policy tabled
25 January 1987	German elections: Christian Democratic Union chancellor Helmut Kohl re-invested
5 April 1987	Third annual Canada-US summit, Ottawa
3 June 1987	Meech Lake Accord on constitutional amendment signed by first ministers
5 June 1987	White paper on defence published
8-10 June 1987	Venice G-7 summit
11 June 1987	British elections: Prime Minister Margaret Thatcher wins third consecutive majority
2-4 September 1987	Second Francophone summit, Québec City
3 October 1987	Canadian and American officials reach agreement on a free trade accord
13-17 October 1987	Commonwealth Heads of Government Meeting, Vancouver
8 December 1987	Intermediate-Range Nuclear Forces (INF) Treaty signed by Reagan and Gorbachev
2 January 1988	Mulroney and Reagan sign the Canada-United States Free Trade Agreement
11 January 1988	Canada-United States Arctic Cooperation Agreement signed
31 March 1988	John Crosbie replaces Carney at international trade
8 April 1988	Agreement reached for withdrawal of Soviet troops from Afghanistan
27-28 April 1988	Fourth Canada-US summit, Washington
8 May 1988	French presidential elections: Socialist candidate François Mitterrand re-elected
24 May 1988	Bill C-130, implementing the FTA, introduced into the House of Commons
19-21 June 1988	Toronto G-7 summit
28 September 1988	Reagan signs legislation implementing the FTA after it passes the House of Representatives (9 August) and the Senate (19 September)
29 September 1988	Nobel Peace Prize awarded to UN peacekeeping forces
8 November 1988	US presidential elections: Republican candidate George Bush elected
21 November 1988	Canadian general election – Progressive Conservative majority: 169 PCs (43% of popular vote); 83 Liberals (32%); 43 NDP (20%)
5-9 December 1988	Montreal mid-term review of the Uruguay Round of multilateral trade negotiations
30 December 1988	Legislation implementing the FTA given Royal Assent after passing the Senate (30 December) and the House of Commons (24 December)
1 January 1989	Canada-United States Free Trade Agreement comes into effect

1 January 1989	Canada begins two-year term on UN Security Council
30 January 1989	Bill McKnight replaces Beatty as minister of national defence
24-26 May 1989	Francophone summit, Dakar, Senegal
4 June 1989	Beijing massacre
28 June 1989	Department of External Affairs renamed External Affairs and International Trade Canada (EAITC)
14-16 July 1989	Paris G-7 summit
3 October 1989	100 officers of the Royal Canadian Mounted Police join military peacekeepers, and officials from Elections Canada join the UN Transition Assistance Group (UNTAG) deployed in Namibia
19-24 October 1989	Commonwealth Heads of Government Meeting, Kuala Lumpur, Malaysia
9 November 1989	Berlin Wall is breached
13 November 1989	Canada becomes 33rd member of the OAS
20 December 1989	United States invades Panama
2 February 1990	African National Congress legalized by South Africa
10 February 1990	Nelson Mandela released from jail
22 June 1990	Meech Lake Accord defeated
23 June 1990	Liberal leadership convention: Jean Chrétien succeeds John Turner as leader of the Liberal party and leader of the Opposition
9-11 July 1990	Houston G-7 summit
11 July 1990	Oka/Kahnawake crisis begins
30-31 July 1990	Second APEC summit, Singapore
2 August 1990	Iraq invades Kuwait
6 August 1990	US deploys forces to Saudi Arabia in response to Iraqi invasion of Kuwait (Operation Desert Shield)
29-30 September 1990	World Summit for Children, New York
3 October 1990	Germany is reunited
19-21 November 1990	Second CSCE summit, Paris, marks the formal end of the Cold War
27 November 1990	John Major succeeds Margaret Thatcher as Conservative leader and prime minister of Britain
16 January 1991	US-led coalition begins air attacks against Iraq (Operation Desert Storm)
17 January 1991	German elections: Helmut Kohl re-invested as chancellor
19 April 1991	Seventh NORAD renewal
21 April 1991	Cabinet shuffle: Clark to constitutional affairs, Barbara McDougall to external affairs, Michael Wilson to trade, Marcel Masse to national defence
21 May 1991	Rajiv Gandhi, former prime minister of India, assassinated
25 June 1991	Croatia and Slovenia declare independence; civil war breaks out in Yugoslavia
1 July 1991	Warsaw Pact dissolved
15-17 July 1991	London G-7 summit
31 July 1991	US and USSR sign Strategic Arms Limitations Treaty
18-21 August 1991	Attempted coup in USSR
30 September 1991	Coup d'état in Haiti overthrows president Jean-Bertrand Aristide
16-22 October 1991	Commonwealth Heads of Government Meeting, Harare, Zimbabwe
12 November 1991	Dili massacre, East Timor
12-14 November 1991	APEC summit, Seoul, South Korea
19-21 November 1991	Francophone summit, Chaillot, Paris

25 December 1991	Soviet Union declared dissolved by Mikhail Gorbachev
1 January 1992	Boutros Boutros-Ghali (Egypt) begins term as sixth UN secretary-general
21 February 1992	Security Council approves the deployment of a peacekeeping force for Yugoslavia (UNPROFOR)
9 April 1992	British elections: John Major leads Conservatives to fourth consecutive majority
3-14 June 1992	UN Conference on Environment and Development (Earth Summit), Rio de Janeiro
17 June 1992	UN secretary-general Boutros Boutros-Ghali publishes *An Agenda for Peace*
6-8 July 1992	Munich G-7 summit
26 October 1992	Referendum on Charlottetown constitutional accord defeated
3 November 1992	US presidential elections: Democratic candidate Bill Clinton elected
8 December 1992	US Marines land in Somalia, beginning Operation Restore Hope
11 December 1992	Mulroney government announces that Canada will withdraw from the peacekeeping mission in Cyprus by June 1993
14-15 December 1992	Canadian troops arrive in Somalia
17 December 1992	NAFTA signed by Mexico, Canada, and the United States
4 January 1993	Kim Campbell replaces Marcel Masse as minister of national defence
13 June 1993	Progressive Conservative leadership convention: Kim Campbell elected leader
14-25 June 1993	World Conference on Human Rights, Vienna
25 June 1993	Kim Campbell sworn in as prime minister, Perrin Beatty in External Affairs, Tom Hockin in trade, Tom Siddon in national defence
7-9 July 1993	Tokyo G-7 summit
16-18 October 1993	Francophone summit, Mauritius
21-25 October 1993	Commonwealth Heads of Government Meeting, Nicosia, Cyprus
25 October 1993	Canadian general election – Liberal majority: 177 Liberals (41% of popular vote); 54 Bloc Québécois (13%); 52 Reform (19%); 9 NDP (7%); 2 PCs (16%)
1 November 1993	Maastricht Treaty comes into force; European Community becomes European Union
5 November 1993	Chrétien government sworn in; André Ouellet appointed minister of foreign affairs; EAITC renamed Department of Foreign Affairs and International Trade (DFAIT). Lucien Bouchard of the Bloc Québécois is leader of the Opposition

Appendix B
Photo Gallery

Prime Minister Brian Mulroney and Pierre-Marc Johnson, premier of Québec, Ottawa, 10 October 1985 (Courtesy of National Archives of Canada/Andy Clark)

Secretary of State for External Affairs Joe Clark at the United Nations General Assembly, 22 September 1987 (UN/DPI/Saw Lwin)

Mulroney and US President Ronald Reagan at the Shamrock Summit, Québec City, 18 March 1985 (Courtesy of National Archives of Canada/ Peter Bregg)

Minister of National
Defence Erik Nielsen
with US Secretary
of Defense Caspar
Weinberger, Ottawa,
10 October 1985
(Courtesy of DND)

DFAIT photos are repro-
duced with the permission
of the Minister of Public
Works and Government
Services Canada, 2001.

Pat Carney, minister of international trade (Courtesy of DFAIT /Denis Drever)

John Crosbie, minister of international trade, speaking on the free trade issue in the House of Commons, Ottawa, 17 May 1988 (Courtesy of CP Picture Archive/ Chuck Mitchell)

Mulroney and US President George Bush, Washington, 20 May 1992 (Courtesy of National Archives of Canada/Bill McCarthy)

Environment Minister Jean Charest and Mulroney with a delegate at the Earth Summit, Rio de Janeiro, 12-13 June 1992 (Courtesy of National Archives of Canada/Ken Ginn)

Derek Burney, Canada's ambassador to the United States, pointing out the new Canadian embassy on Pennsylvania Avenue to Clark, Washington (Courtesy of DFAIT/ Denis Drever)

Clark and South African leader Nelson Mandela, after Mandela's release from prison in 1990. (Courtesy of DFAIT/ Denis Drever)

Secretary of State for External Affairs Barbara McDougall with UN Secretary-General Boutros Boutros-Ghali, UN Headquarters, 15 January 1992 (UN/DPI/ M. Grant)

Mulroney and British Prime Minister Margaret Thatcher at the Commonwealth Heads of Government Meeting, Vancouver, 13-17 October 1987 (Courtesy of National Archives of Canada)

Minister of National Defence Perrin Beatty visiting troops during Operation Brave Lion, Norway, September 1986 (Courtesy of DND)

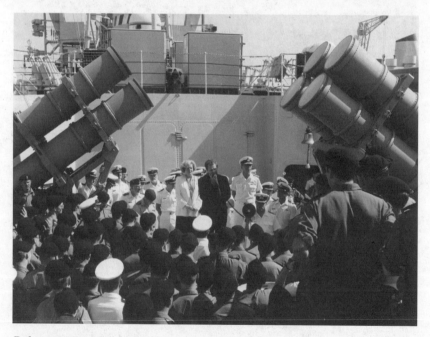

Defence minister Bill McKnight and Associate Minister of National Defence Mary Collins addressing crew on HMCS *Terra Nova* prior to its departure for the Persian Gulf, 24 August 1990 (Courtesy of DND)

Minister of National Defence Bill McKnight in Qatar during Operation Desert Shield, 15 November 1990 (Courtesy of DND)

Minister of National Defence Marcel Masse (centre); on right is Gen. John de Chastelain, Chief of Defence Staff, later appointed Canadian ambassador to the United States; on left is Manfred Woerner, secretary-general of NATO. NATO Headquarters, Brussels, 28 May 1991 (Courtesy of DND)

Minister of National Defence Kim Campbell with crew of an Aurora CP-140, Charlottetown, 12 February 1993 (Courtesy of DND)

James Kelleher, Mulroney's first minister of international trade, 1984-86

Appendix C
Foreign Policy Appointments, 1984-93

Cabinet Ministers

Prime Ministers
Brian Mulroney   17 September 1984 to 25 June 1993
Kim Campbell   25 June 1993 to 5 November 1993

Secretaries of State for External Affairs
Joe Clark   17 September 1984 to 21 April 1991
Barbara McDougall   21 April 1991 to 25 June 1993
Perrin Beatty   25 June 1993 to 5 November 1993

Ministers of International Trade
James Kelleher   17 September 1984 to 30 June 1986
Pat Carney   30 June 1986 to 31 March 1988
John Crosbie   31 March 1988 to 21 April 1991
Michael Wilson   21 April 1991 to 25 June 1993
Tom Hockin   25 June 1993 to 5 November 1993

Ministers of National Defence
Robert Coates   17 September 1984 to 12 February 1985
Joe Clark   12 February 1985 to 27 February 1985
Erik Nielsen   27 February 1985 to 30 June 1986
Perrin Beatty   30 June 1986 to 30 January 1989
Bill McKnight   30 January 1989 to 21 April 1991
Marcel Masse   21 April 1991 to 4 January 1993
Kim Campbell   4 January 1993 to 25 June 1993
Tom Siddon   25 June 1993 to 5 November 1993

Associate Ministers of National Defence
Harvie Andre   20 August 1985 to 30 June 1986
Paul Dick   30 June 1986 to 30 January 1989
Mary Collins   30 January 1989 to 25 June 1993

Ministers of State for External Relations
(Responsible for CIDA and Francophonie Affairs)
Monique Vézina   17 September 1984 to 30 June 1986
Monique Landry   30 June 1986 to 4 January 1993
Monique Vézina   4 January 1993 to 25 June 1993

Ministers of Employment and Immigration

Flora MacDonald	17 September 1984 to 30 June 1986
Benoît Bouchard	30 June 1986 to 31 March 1988
Barbara McDougall	31 March 1988 to 21 April 1991
Bernard Valcourt	21 April 1991 to 5 November 1993

Deputy Ministers

Clerks of the Privy Council

Gordon Osbaldeston	10 December 1982 to 12 August 1985
Paul Tellier	12 August 1985 to 17 June 1992
Glen Shortliffe	17 June 1992 to 28 March 1994

Under-Secretaries of State for External Affairs

Marcel Masse	27 October 1982 to 1 September 1985
J.H. (Si) Taylor	1 September 1985 to 1 December 1989
Raymond Chrétien (acting)	1 December 1989 to 1 January 1990
De Montigny Marchand	1 January 1990 to 23 September 1991
Reid Morden	23 September 1991 to 15 August 1994

Deputy Ministers of National Defence

Daniel Bevis (Bev) Dewar	1 November 1981 to 29 May 1989
Robert R. Fowler	29 May 1989 to 26 June 1995

Chiefs of Defence Staff

Gen. G.C.E. Thériault	1 July 1983 to 11 July 1986
Gen. Paul D. Manson	11 July 1986 to 8 September 1989
Gen. John de Chastelain	8 September 1989 to 29 January 1993
Admiral John Anderson	29 January 1993 to 1 January 1994

Presidents of CIDA

Margaret Catley-Carlson	1 September 1983 to 1 September 1989
Marcel Massé	1 September 1989 to 11 February 1993
Jocelyne Bourgon	11 February 1993 to 18 July 1993
Huguette Labelle	18 July 1993 to 18 May 1999

Deputy Ministers of Employment and Immigration
(Citizenship and Immigration as of June 1993)

Gaétan Lussier	30 April 1982 to 6 September 1988
Nick Mulder (acting)	6 September 1988 to 16 September 1988
Arthur Kroeger	16 September 1988 to 1 October 1992
Ruth Hubbard	1 October 1992 to 10 February 1993
Nick Mulder	10 February 1993 to 25 June 1993
Jean-Jacques Noreau	25 June 1993 to 27 November 1995

Bibliographical Essay

Unfortunately, there are relatively few books that deal with Canadian foreign policy during the Conservative period. To be sure, there are numerous references to the Mulroney government's external policy in the textbook literature; there is a large periodical literature in scholarly journals, much of which is cited in the endnotes to the chapters above; and a number of dissertations have been written on particular aspects of foreign policy during this period (listed on the National Library of Canada website, <www.nlc-bnc.ca>). But the general historical record is limited, and what has been published tends to focus on domestic politics rather than foreign policy. The following brief review offers a guide to what is available for those interested in further reading on the Mulroney era.

Memoirs

Mulroney himself has not yet written his memoirs (reportedly because he believes it necessary to wait in order to be able to put his prime ministership in proper perspective: see Michael Valpy, "Mr Mulroney's Makeover," *Globe and Mail*, 10 October 1998, D1; and Michel Vastel, "La revanche de Mulroney," *L'Actualité*, 15 December 1998, 18-23). Peter C. Newman was given access to Mulroney's papers, with the idea of producing an authoritative history of the Conservative years, but the book he eventually wrote, *The Canadian Revolution, 1985-1995: From Deference to Defiance* (Toronto: Viking, 1995), falls far short of an overall history of the Conservative era.

A number of Mulroney's ministers, however, have written memoirs: Erik Nielsen, *The House Is Not a Home* (Toronto: Macmillan of Canada, 1989); Lucien Bouchard, *À visage découvert* (Montréal: Boréal, 1992); Andrée Champagne, *Champagne pour tout le monde!* (Montréal: Stanké, 1995); Kim Campbell, *Time and Chance: The Political Memoirs of Canada's First Woman Prime Minister* (Toronto: Doubleday Canada, 1996); and John Crosbie, *No Holds Barred: My Life in Politics* (Toronto: McClelland and Stewart, 1997). Jean Charest, who served as leader of the Conservative party before he moved to head the Liberal party of Québec, also contributed to this literature with *My Road to Québec* (Montréal: Éditions Pierre Tisseyre, 1998) – published in French as *Jean Charest*. The most recent addition to the genre is Pat Carney's *Trade Secrets: A Memoir* (Toronto: Key Porter, 2000). But, with the exception of Carney, most do not focus on foreign policy. Hugh Segal's autobiography, *No Surrender: Reflections of a Happy Warrior in the Tory Crusade* (Toronto: HarperCollins, 1996), devotes only two pages to foreign policy. Nor does Senator Jacques Flynn, who co-chaired the Special Joint Committee on Canada's International Relations, say much about foreign policy in his own autobiography, *Un bleu du Québec à Ottawa* (Sillery: Septentrion, 1998). None of the secretaries of state for external affairs during this period – Joe Clark, Barbara McDougall, and Perrin Beatty – has written their memoirs.

Biographies

The only major biography of Mulroney comes to an end on 17 September 1984, the day he was sworn in as prime minister: John Sawatsky, *Mulroney: The Politics of Ambition* (Toronto: Macfarlane, Walter, and Ross, 1991). Two books cover Mulroney's rise to power: L. Ian MacDonald, *Brian Mulroney: The Making of the Prime Minister* (Toronto: McClelland and Stewart, 1984); and Rae Murphy, Robert Chodos, and Nick auf der Maur, *Brian Mulroney: The Boy from Baie-Comeau* (Toronto: James Lorimer, 1984). A very slim collection of Mulroney's speeches was published to coincide with the 1983 leadership convention: Brian Mulroney, *Where I Stand* (Toronto: McClelland and Stewart, 1983). All these titles were also published in French: Sawatsky, *Mulroney: Le pouvoir de l'ambition* (Montréal: Libre expression, 1991); MacDonald, *Mulroney: De Baie Comeau à Sussex Drive* (Montréal: Éditions de l'Homme, 1984); Murphy, Chodos, and auf der Maur, *Brian Mulroney* (Montréal: Boréal Express, 1984); Mulroney, *Telle est ma position* (Montréal: Éditions de l'Homme, 1983).

The two main contenders for the Conservative leadership in 1993, Kim Campbell and Jean Charest, have had books written about them: Frank Davey, *Reading "Kim" Right* (Vancouver: Talonbooks, 1993); Murray Dobbin, *The Politics of Kim Campbell: From School Trustee to Prime Minister* (Toronto: James Lorimer, 1993); Robert Fife, *Kim Campbell: The Making of a Politician*, (Toronto: HarperCollins, 1993); Henri Motte et Monique Guillot, *Jean Charest: l'homme des défis* (Montréal: Balzac-LeGriot, 1997); André Pratte, *L'énigme Charest* (Montréal: Boréal, 1998). Foreign policy issues are not discussed at length, although the books on Campbell dedicate a chapter to her tenure as minister of national defence.

Domestic Politics

There are several personalized, and largely negative, accounts of Mulroney's time as prime minister. For the often unflattering "kiss-and-tell" exposé by Mulroney's press secretary, Michel Gratton, see *"So What Are the Boys Saying?" An Inside Look at Brian Mulroney in Power* (Toronto: McGraw Hill Ryerson, 1987). Investigative reporter Stevie Cameron's *On The Take: Crime, Corruption and Greed in the Mulroney Years* (Toronto: Macfarlane, Walter and Ross, 1994) is a chronicle of corruption and patronage during the Conservative era. The book's sales reflected Mulroney's lingering unpopularity among Canadians: it sold over 200,000 copies, while William Kaplan's *Presumed Guilty* (Toronto: McClelland and Stewart, 1998), an investigation of the charges against Mulroney over the Airbus affair (which presented a solid case for exoneration) was not a best-seller.

On the Mulroney government's constitutional initiatives, see Andrew Cohen, *A Deal Undone: The Making and Breaking of the Meech Lake Accord* (Vancouver: Douglas and McIntyre, 1990); and Peter Russell, *Constitutional Odyssey* (Toronto: University of Toronto Press, 1993). The electoral politics of the period are well covered by Robert Bernier, *Gérer la victoire? Organisation, communication, stratégie* (Boucherville: Gaëtan Morin, 1991); Richard Johnston, et al., *Letting the People Decide: Dynamics of a Canadian Election* (Montreal and Kingston: McGill-Queen's University Press, 1992); and Alan Frizzell, Jon H. Pammett, and Anthony Westell, *The Canadian General Election of 1993* (Ottawa: Carleton University Press, 1994).

Assessments of domestic policies during the Conservative era may be found in David Bercuson, J.L. Granatstein, and William Young, *Sacred Trust? Brian Mulroney and the Conservative Government in Power* (Toronto: 1986); this book also has several chapters on foreign policy. By contrast, see Andrew B. Gollner and Daniel Salée, eds., *Canada under Mulroney: An End-of-Term Report* (Montreal: Véhicule Press, 1988); Stephen McBride and John Shields, *Dismantling a Nation: Canada and the New World Order* (Halifax: Fernwood, 1993); and George Radwanski and Julia Luttrell, *The Will of a Nation: Awakening the Canadian Spirit* (Toronto: Stoddart, 1992). These books do not cover foreign affairs beyond the free trade agreement.

Foreign Policy

There are only two books specifically devoted to an examination of the foreign policy of the Mulroney Conservatives. Both are written by journalists, and both make no claim to scholarly objectivity: Lawrence Martin, *Pledge of Allegiance: The Americanization of Canada in the Mulroney Years* (Toronto: McClelland and Stewart 1993); and Marci McDonald, *Yankee Doodle Dandy: Brian Mulroney and the American Agenda* (Toronto: Stoddart, 1995).

Among scholarly works, the collection edited by André Donneur and Panayotis Soldatos, *Le Canada à l'ère de l'après-guerre froide et des blocs régionaux: une politique étrangère de transition* (North York: Captus Press, 1993) provides a general analysis of the Conservative era but finishes before the end of this period. The best historical survey of the foreign policy of the Mulroney period comes in parts – the annual *Canada among Nations* series edited by scholars at the Norman Paterson School of International Affairs, Carleton University. The first volume in the series covered 1984, the year that the Mulroney Conservatives came to power. See Brian Tomlin and Maureen Appel Molot, eds., *Canada Among Nations, 1984: A Time of Transition* (Toronto: James Lorimer, 1985). Editors and subtitles for the other eight volumes that cover the Mulroney years are: Molot and Tomlin, *1985: The Conservative Agenda*; Tomlin and Molot, *1986: Talking Trade*; Molot and Tomlin, *1987: A World of Conflict*; Tomlin and Molot, *1988: The Tory Record*; Molot and Fen Osler Hampson, *1989: The Challenge of Change*; Hampson and Christopher J. Maule, *1990-91: After the Cold War*; Hampson and Maule, *1992-93: A New World Order?*; Hampson and Maule, *1993-94: Global Jeopardy*.

Two general long-range analyses of Canadian foreign policy include surveys of the Mulroney years but come to opposite conclusions. Arthur Andrew's negative portrayal of the "fall" of Canada as a middle power during the Conservative years – *The Rise and Fall of a Middle Power: Canadian Diplomacy from King to Mulroney* (Toronto: James Lorimer, 1993) – stands in marked contrast to Costas Melakopides's positive overview of Mulroney's "constructive internationalism": *Pragmatic Idealism: Canadian Foreign Policy, 1945-1995* (Montreal and Kingston: McGill-Queen's University Press, 1998).

Otherwise, foreign policy explorations focus on particular issues. The free trade agreement is covered by G. Bruce Doern and Brian Tomlin, *Faith and Fear: The Free Trade Story* (Toronto: Stoddart, 1991); Michael Hart, Bill Dymond, and Colin Robertson, *Decision at Midnight: Inside the Canada-U.S. Trade Negotiations* (Vancouver: UBC Press, 1994); and Gordon Ritchie, *Wrestling with the Elephant: The Inside Story of the Canada-U.S. Trade Wars* (Toronto: Macfarlane Walter and Ross, 1997). Allan Gotlieb, Canada's ambassador to Washington for most of the 1980s, has left a brief but insightful memoir that focuses on Canadian-American relations more generally: *'I'll Be with You in a Minute, Mr Ambassador': The Education of a Canadian Diplomat in Washington* (Toronto: University of Toronto Press, 1991).

Mulroney's policies towards South Africa are the focus of Linda Freeman's *The Ambiguous Champion: Canada and South Africa in the Trudeau and Mulroney Years* (Toronto: University of Toronto Press, 1997). James Rochlin, *Discovering the Americas: The Evolution of Canadian Foreign Policy towards Latin America* (Vancouver: UBC Press, 1994), traces the evolution of Canadian approaches to the hemisphere, culminating with the Conservative period. Regionalization has also been covered in Gordon Mace and Jean-Philippe Thérien, eds., *Foreign Policy and Regionalism in the Americas* (Boulder: Lynne Rienner, 1996); and Gordon Mace, Louis Bélanger et al., eds., *The Americas in Transition: The Contours of Regionalism* (Boulder: Lynne Rienner, 1999). David R. Morrison's history of Canada's development assistance policies, *Aid and Ebb Tide: A History of CIDA and Canadian Development Assistance* (Waterloo, ON: Wilfrid Laurier University Press, 1998), contains extensive coverage of the Conservative era and complements Jean-Philippe Thérien's *La quête de développement: horizons canadiens et africains* (Montréal: ACFAS, 1988).

There are no works devoted specifically to the defence policy of the Mulroney government, but a number of general studies cover the Conservative period: André Donneur and Jean Pariseau, *Regards sur le système de défense du Canada* (Toulouse: Presses de l'Institut de politiques de Toulouse, 1989); Albert Legault and Michel Fortmann, *Une diplomatie de l'espoir* (Québec: Les Presses de l'Université Laval/Centre québécois des Relations internationales, 1989), translated into English and published as *A Diplomacy of Hope: Canada and Disarmament, 1945-1988* (Montreal and Kingston: McGill-Queen's University Press, 1992); Desmond Morton, *Une histoire militaire du Canada 1608-1991* (Sillery: Septentrion, 1992); and Ann Denholm Crosby, *Dilemmas in Defence Decision-Making: Constructing Canada's Role in NORAD, 1958-96* (London: Macmillan, 1998).

Contributors

Luc Bernier is a professor at the École nationale d'administration publique and author of *De Paris à Washington: la politique internationale du Québec* (1996).

David R. Black is associate professor of political science and coordinator of international development studies, Dalhousie University. He is the co-author (with Andy Knight and Claire Turenne Sjolander) of *Turbulence and Transition: Towards a Critical Understanding of Canadian "Foreign Policy" in a Changing World* (forthcoming).

Andrew F. Cooper is professor of political science, University of Waterloo, and author of *Canadian Foreign Policy: Old Habits and New Directions* (1997).

Michel Fortmann is a professor in the Department of Political Science, Université de Montréal and director of the Programme d'études de sécurité conjoint Université de Montréal/McGill University.

Paul Gecelovsky is an adjunct professor in the Department of Political Science, University of Windsor. His interests include human rights and the role of ideas in Canadian foreign policy.

Rob Huebert is an assistant professor in the Department of Political Science and the Centre for Military and Strategic Studies, University of Calgary.

Tom Keating is professor of political science, University of Alberta, and author of *Canada and World Order* (1993); at present he is conducting research on the promotion of democracy and human security in Canadian foreign policy.

Gordon Mace is a professor in the Department of Political Science and at the Graduate Institute of International Studies of Laval University. His most recent book, in collaboration, is *The Americas in Transition: The Contours of Regionalism* (1999).

Hon. Barbara J. McDougall, OC, is president and chief executive officer of the Canadian Institute of International Affairs; between 1991 and 1993, she served as Canada's secretary of state for external affairs.

Nelson Michaud teaches international relations and Canadian political institutions at École nationale d'administration publique (Université du Québec). He is a member-researcher at the Institut québécois des hautes études internationales and a research fellow at the Centre for Foreign Policy Studies, Dalhousie University. His research interests include foreign policy analysis, decision- making processes, and the media and foreign policy. He has published in refereed journals in Canada, Britain, and Australia.

Tammy L. Nemeth is a doctoral student in history at the University of British Columbia. Her thesis concerns Canadian-American energy relations from 1958 to 1988 and the drift towards a continental energy policy.

Roy Norton is executive director of international relations and chief of protocol for the Government of Ontario. His doctoral dissertation focuses on the involvement of visible minority communities in the Canadian foreign policymaking process, and in 1999 it was awarded the Distinguished Dissertation Award by the Association for Canadian Studies in the United States.

Kim Richard Nossal is professor and head of the Department of Political Studies, Queen's University, Kingston. He is the author of *The Politics of Canadian Foreign Policy* (1997).

Norrin M. Ripsman is assistant professor of political science at Concordia University. He is the author of *Democracies and Peacemaking: Domestic Structure, Executive Autonomy and Peacemaking After Two World Wars* (forthcoming).

Claire Turenne Sjolander is associate professor and chair of the Department of Political Science at the University of Ottawa. She is author (with David Black and W. Andy Knight) of *Turbulence and Transition: Towards a Critical Understanding of Canadian "Foreign Policy" in a Changing World* (forthcoming), and she is editor (with Heather Smith and Deborah Stienstra) of *Gendered Discourses, Gendered Practices: Feminists (Re)write Canadian Foreign Policy* (forthcoming).

Heather A. Smith is an assistant professor of international studies at the University of Northern British Columbia, co-author of *(Re)Defining Traditions: Gender and Canadian Foreign Policy* (Halifax: Fernwood, 1999), and editor (with Claire Turenne Sjolander and Deborah Stienstra) of *Gendered Discourses, Gendered Practices: Feminists (Re)write Canadian Foreign Policy* (forthcoming).

Denis Stairs is McCulloch professor in political science at Dalhousie University; he specializes in Canadian foreign and defence policy, Canada-US relations, and similar subjects.

J.H. Taylor, OC, was under-secretary of state for external affairs from 1985 to 1989 and was Canada's ambassador to Japan from 1989 until his retirement from Canada's foreign service in 1993.

Manon Tessier is an official with the Department of Foreign Affairs and International Trade. Her interests lie in Canadian foreign policy and international peacekeeping, and she is the author, with Albert Legault, of *Canada and Peacekeeping: Three Major Debates* (1999).

Brian W. Tomlin is professor of international affairs and director of the Centre for Negotiation and Dispute Resolution at Carleton University. He is the co-author of *The Making of NAFTA: How the Deal Was Done* (2000).

Index

Note: References to photographs are printed in italics.

Acid rain, 7-8, 12, 73-75
Africa Emergency Aid, 280
African National Congress, 175, 185
Agence de coopération culturelle et technique, 131, 136
aid. *See* development assistance
Air Defence Modernization Program, 102, 110n5
Air Defense Initiative, 102
Air Defense Master Plan, 104
Air Quality Agreement (1991), 75, 80
Alaskan oil, 63, 68
Alberta: and energy policy, 60, 65
Allison, Graham, 261, 266-67
Amritsar massacre, 250
Andre, Harvie, 270
Anglin, Douglas, 184
Anti-Apartheid Register, 179, 283
anti-ballistic missile treaty, 106
anti-submarine warfare, 100, 102, 105
apartheid, 5, 28, 35, 291, 293; Anti-Apartheid Register, 179, 283; Bank of Nova Scotia, 176-77; Bush on, 184; Canadian policy, 173-91; at CHOGM, 215-16; Clark on, 182; Diefenbaker and, 174; Eminent Persons Group, 182; Front Line States, 183; and G-7 Summit, 184, 189; Kohl on, 184; McDougall on, 191n3; MINORCO loan, 176-77; Mulroney on, 18, 41n14, 176; Mulroney and Thatcher, 182; Reagan on, 184; Southern Africa Task Force, 190; Thatcher, 175, 182, 184; Trudeau and, 174-75; UN Security Council, 175; US Congress and, 180
Arcelin, André, 252

Arctic Cooperation Agreement (1988), 91-94, 96
Arctic waters: 84-97, 291; Arctic Waters Pollution Prevention Act, 89; ICJ reservation 86, 89-90; Inuit 95; northern patrol flights 87-89, 98n22; Special Joint Committee report, 94-95; sovereignty, 20; straight baselines, 86-87; summit negotiations, 93. *See also Manhattan; Polar Sea*
Aristide, Jean-Bertrand, 200, 256
Armenian Democratic Liberal Organization, 251
Armenian National Committee of Canada, 251
Armenian-Canadians, 249-54
Asian Regional Forum, 17
Association of Southeast Asian Nations, 218
Association of United Ukrainian Canadians, 246
Atkinson, Michael M., 285
Atlantic Accord, 61
Atmospheric Environment Service, 77, 81
Axworthy, Lloyd, 36, 277, 286

Babbar Khalsa, 251
"back-in" provision of National Energy Program, 61
Baltic Federation in Canada, 246
Bank of Nova Scotia: apartheid, 176-77
Barre, Raymond, 135
Beatty, Perrin, 100, 107, 261, 267, 268, 269, 282, *308;* on Soviet Union, 264
Beauchemin, Marie-Andrée, 226
Beijing massacre. *See* Tiananmen massacre
Bennett, R.B., 215
Biafra, 21
Black, Conrad, 162
Blackburn, Derek, 270

Blaikie, Bill, 248
Bloc Québécois, 278
Borden, Robert, 3, 265
Bouchard, Lucien, 73, 167, 214
Bourassa, Robert, 140n19, 217
Boutros-Ghali, Boutros, *306; Agenda for Peace*, 124
Brezhnev, Leonid, 107
British North America Act (1867), 132
Broadbent, Ed, 203
Brock, William, 51, 54
Browse, Pauline, 221
Bruce, Jim, 81
Brundtland Commission, 77
Brydges, Tom, 81
bureaucratic politics model, 261; and 1987 defence white paper, 266-71
Burney, Derek , 48, 55, 57, 214, *305;* Arctic negotiations, 93; international conferences, 166; on Québec, 141n26; Shamrock Summit, 52; trade policy review, 52-53, 54
Bush, George H., 4, 11, 109, 142, 145, 163, 254, 277, *304;* acid rain, 75; apartheid, 184; free trade with Mexico, 153; New World Order, 16; UNCED 79
Business Council on National Issues, 31, 50, 52
Buteux, Paul, 109
Byrd, Robert, 23n21

C.D. Howe Institute, 51
Caccia, Charles, 74
Cadieux, Marcel, 133-34, 223
Cameron, Maxwell, 285
Camp David Accords, 117
Campbell, Kim, 221, *310*
Canada-Polish Business Council, 247
Canada-US Air Quality Agreement, 75, 80
Canadian Air Sea Transportable (CAST) Brigade Group, 103
Canadian Airborne Regiment, 16
Canadian-American relations. *See* United States
Canadian Centre for Foreign Policy Development, 285-86
Canadian Coast Guard, and Arctic waters, 85-97
Canadian East European Trade Council, 247
Canadian Federation of Independent Business, 31
Canadian Forces: Arctic policy, 87-88; Canadian Airborne Regiment, 16; distinctive uniforms, 266; in Europe, 108; Operation Brave Lion, 268, 269

Canadian International Development Agency, 167, 201; aid to South Africa, 187; and Ethiopia famine, 279; human rights unit, 196
Canadian Laws Offshore Application Act, 87
Canadian Manufacturers' Association, 31, 50
Canadian Parliamentary Group for the Baltic Peoples, 246
Canadian Polish Congress, 244-47
"Captive Nations," 243-49
Carney, Patricia (Pat), 54, 61, 221, 227, *303;* free trade conference, 220; on trade and security, 231-32; women in public service, 239n58
Cartagena Protocol, 145
Catley-Carlson, Margaret, 15, 200, 229
Central European Development Fund, 247
Charest, Jean, 167, *305*
Charter of Rights and Freedoms, 203, 241
Chloroflurocarbons, 76-77, 81
Chrétien, Jean, 6, 36, 82, 218, 236, 277; and Québec, 138
churches, and human rights, 203
Ciaccia, John, 137
civil society organizations, 286. *See also* non-governmental organizations
Clark, Joe, 6, 268, 291, 295, *302, 305, 306;* African National Congress, 185; Anti-Apartheid Register, 283; and apartheid, 173, 182; appointment of women, 221, 226, 235; Arctic waters, 84, 87, 93, 95; Armenian-Canadians, 250, 253; chair of Commonwealth Committee of Foreign Ministers on Southern Africa, 176, 216; and Commonwealth, 181; as constitutional affairs minister, 15, 200; and 1987 defence white paper, 269-70; Ethiopia famine, 279-80; ethnic groups, 243, 245, 247, 251; as External Affairs minister, 257; foreign policy process, 283; green paper on foreign policy, 263, 281; and Mexico, 139; North Pacific Cooperative Security Dialogue, 17, 218; and Parliament, 255, 258; as prime minister, 10, 213; Québec's international activities, 134; sanctions, 180, 192n14; on Sikh-Canadians, 255; and Soviet Union, 217; Tiananmen massacre, 18; Vietnamese "boat people," 280
climate change, 77-79
Clinton, Bill, 214, 254
Coates, Robert, 11, 268

Cohen, Marjorie, 232
Cold War: impact of, 34, 197, 254-65
Coleman, William D., 265
Collins, Mary, 221, *308*
Colonial Laws Validity Act (1865), 132
"commitment-capability gap," 101-2
Commonwealth of Nations, 18, 175,
   181, 196, 199; apartheid, 215-16;
   Commonwealth Committee of Foreign
   Ministers on Southern Africa, 176,
   182, 183, 186, 216; Commonwealth
   Heads of Government Meetings: Nassau
   (1985), 182; Vancouver (1987), 181;
   Kuala Lumpur (1989), 183; Harare
   (1991), 200
Competitiveness and Security. See green
   paper on foreign policy
Comprehensive Anti-Apartheid Act, 180
Conference on the Environment
   (Stockholm 1972), 39
Conference on Security and Cooperation
   in Europe, 17, 243, 247
Consolidated Gold Fields, 180
Constitution Act (1982), 132
Contadora Group, 146
Convention on Biological Diversity, 169
Convention on Long-Range
   Transboundary Air Pollution, 74
Conventional Forces in Europe (CFE)
   agreement, 107
Council for Canadians, 85
Council of Mutual Economic Assistance,
   218
Crees, 137
Crofton, Pat, 11
Crosbie, John, 31-32, 167, 200, 220, *304*
cruise missile testing, 104
Cyprus: peacekeeping mission in, 115-16;
   withdrawal from, 121-22
Czechoslovak Association of Canada,
   245, 246
Czechoslovak-Canadians, 243-49

D'Aquino, Thomas, 50, 57
de Chastelain, Gen. John, 123, *309*
de Gaulle, Charles, 128, 134-35
defence policy, 13-15, 33, 104; 1971
   defence white paper, 100, 103; 1987
   defence white paper, 13, 33, 88, 101,
   104, 109, 117, 123, 260-72, 292;
   bureaucratic politics 266-71; "commitment-capability gap," 101-2; parliamentary committees and, 124, 282
Derwinski, Edward, 93
Deschènes Commission of Inquiry on
   War Criminals in Canada, 256

development assistance, 37; to central
   and eastern Europe, 248; to Ethiopia,
   280; to South Africa, 178
Development Assistance Committee, 198
Dialogue Fund (South Africa), 178
Diefenbaker, John G., 40, 114, 129, 215,
   291; as prime minister, 213, 214;
   apartheid ,174; on Soviet Union, 10
Dili massacre, 19, 204
Dobson, Wendy, 51
Docherty, David, 285
Doucet, Fred, 52
Dreiziger, N.F., 244
Duvalier, Jean-Claude "Baby Doc," 249

Eagleberger, Lawrence, 111n18
Economic Council of Canada, 31
Edwards, Lucie, 228-29
Elections Canada, 118
eminent persons group, 182
energy policy, 59-69; interest groups and,
   65-66
Energy, Mines and Resources Canada, 78
English, John, 288n26
Enloe, Cynthia, 220
environment, 71-82; acid rain, 7-8, 12,
   73-75; Arctic waters, 89; Convention
   on Long-Range Transboundary Air
   Pollution, 74; Department of, 77;
   Helsinki Protocol on Sulphur Dioxide,
   75; policies, 292. *See also* UN
   Conference on the Environment and
   Development
Estonian Central Council in Canada, 246
Estonian-Canadians, 243-49
Ethiopia, famine in, 15, 279-80
ethnic groups, 241-59; statistics on, 259n5
Exclusive Economic Zone, 89
Export Development Corporation, 178
External Affairs, Department of: Arctic
   waters policy, 89-90; corporate culture,
   228, 235, 254; ethnic groups, 246, 254;
   free trade, 52; Québec, 133-34; reorgan-
   ized, 52, 225; statistics on, 213; women
   in, 223-30

Faure, Edgar, 135
Federation of Sikh Societies of Canada, 251
Finance, Department of, 51; and defence
   policy, 108-9, 270
Flis, Jesse, 248
Food and Agriculture Organization, 279
Ford, Margaret, 227
Foreign Extraterritorial Measures Act, 20
Foreign Investment Review Agency, 7,
   30-31, 48

Fowler, Robert, 271
Framework Convention on Climate
  Change, 78-79
France, and Québec, 135
Francophonie, la, 17, 199, 216-17, 257
Fréchette, Louise, 229
free trade, 45-57; elite views 31; gendered
  impact of, 232-33; impact on Canadian-
  Latin American relations, 151-53; and
  Israel, 149; and Mexico, 153-54;
  Mulroney on, 8-9, 32, 55; North
  American Free Trade Agreement, 28,
  146, 154; and Ontario, 54; and Québec,
  54, 136-37; sectoral free trade, 8, 31
Freeman, Linda, 187, 189
Front Line States, 183, 215; Mulroney
  on, 192n27

G-7 Summit, 18, 72; apartheid, 184, 189
Gabon affair, 135-36
Gandhi, Indira, 250, 253
Gandhi, Rajiv, 182
Gauthier, Jean-Robert, 202
Geldenhuys, Deon, 19
gender: and Canadian foreign policy,
  220-37; and free trade 232-33
General Agreement on Tariffs and Trade,
  50, 162
Gérin-Lajoie, Paul, 129
Giscard d'Estaing, Valéry, 135
Gobeil, Paul, 131
"Golda Meir syndrome," 228
good governance, 18-19, 194-205
Gorbachev, Mikhail, 107, 101, 163, 218,
  264
Gordon, Sheldon, 242
Gotlieb, Allan, 7, 11, 214
Granatstein, J.L., on Shamrock Summit,
  22n6
Grant, George, 40
Gray Lecture, 194
Gray, Charlotte, 256
green paper on foreign policy (1985), 38,
  230, 234, 271, 281
Green Plan, 73, 78, 82, 170
Grenada: American intervention in, 145
Gulf conflict (1990-91), 16, 109, 278

Haiti: Jean-Bertrand Aristide, 200, 256;
  crisis in, 20; "Baby Doc" Duvalier, 249;
  Haitian-Canadians 249-54
Hall, Ingrid, 228
Halliday, Tony, 51
Halstead, John, 109
Hare, Kenneth, 81
Havel, Vaclav, 248
Hawke, Bob, 163, 184

heads of post, women as, 226
Helms-Burton legislation, 145
Helsinki Protocol on Sulphur Dioxide, 75
Hnatyshyn, Ray, 245
Hockin, Thomas, 11, 14, 71, 94-95, 263
Hockin-Simard committee. See Special
  Joint Committee on Canada's
  International Relations
Holmes, John W., 28, 32, 224, 295
Hong Kong: Mulroney on, 18
"hub-and-spoke" trade arrangements,
  153-54
human rights, 293; parliamentary sub-
  committee on, 202
Human Rights Commission, 227
"human security agenda," 236, 295n2
Hungarian Human Rights Foundation, 246
Hungarian-Canadians, 243-49
Hussein, Saddam, 109
Hydro-Québec, 137

Icebreakers, 86; Polar 8, 90-91, 95-96;
  Polar Sea, 20, 84-97, 268
"ice-covered areas article," 89
immigration, from Punjab, 253-54
Imperial Preferences, 215
India, Canadian relations with, 253-54
Indonesia, sanctions against, 19
Industry, Trade and Commerce,
  Department of, 48; reorganized, 52
interest groups. See non-governmental
  organizations
Intermediate-Range Nuclear Forces (INF)
  Treaty, 107
International Centre for Human Rights
  and Democratic Development, 202-3
International Control Commission, 125n4
International Court of Justice, 86, 89-90
International Criminal Court, 190
International Development Research
  Centre, 186
International Energy Agency, 62, 65, 66,
  68
International Monetary Fund, 201
International Sikh Youth Federation, 251
Inuit, 95
Investment Canada, 30
Iraq, invasion of Kuwait, 109
Iron Ore Company of Canada, 29, 290
Israel: Mulroney on, 9; free trade agree-
  ment, 149

Jamieson, Don, 175
Johnson, Daniel, 140n19
Johnson, Pierre-Marc, 301
Judicial Committee of the Privy Council,
  132

Kaunda, Kenneth, 190, 216
Kelleher, James, 10, 51, 52, 54, *310*
Khalistan, Sikh advocacy of, 250, 253
Khrushchev, Nikita, 10
King, W.L. Mackenzie, 138, 162, 212, 214
Kingdon, John, 45; model of policy
   process 46-48
Kipling, Margaret, 69
Kohl, Helmut, 14, 263; and apartheid 184
Korean Air Lines flight 007, 9
Kuwait, Iraqi invasion of, 109

Labour Conventions case, 132
landmines initiative, 286
Landry, Bernard, 131
Landry, Monique, 167, 200, 201, 221
Latin American Economic System, 146
Latvian National Federation in Canada,
   246
Latvian-Canadians, 243-49
Laurier, Sir Wilfrid, 3, 214
Lawson, Robert J., 285
"leap of faith," 12, 52; and Mulroney, 56
Leduc, Lise, 232
Lee, Steve, 285-86
Lemieux, Vincent, 261
Lesage, Jean, 130
Lévesque, René, 131, 135
Lewis, Stephen, 11, 181, 182, 214
Liberal party, foreign policy promises, 277
Lipsey, Richard, 51
Lithuania: recognition of, 249
Lithuanian-Canadians, 243-49
long-range patrol aircraft, 108
Lougheed, Peter, 54, 57

Macdonald, David, 10, 279-80
Macdonald, Donald S., 12, 45, 52;
   Macdonald Commission: *see* Royal
   Commission on the Economic Union
   and Development Prospects for Canada
MacDonald, Flora, 10; as secretary of
   state for external affairs, 221
Macdonald, Sir John A., 215
MacKenzie, General Lewis, 123
Mandela, Nelson, *306*
Manhattan voyage, 86, 89, 90
Manson, Gen. Paul, 264, 269
Marchand, de Montigny, 200, 201
Martin, Barbara, 228
Martin, Lawrence, 3-4, 21
Masse, Marcel (minister of national
   defence), 108, 109, *309*
Massé, Marcel (president of CIDA), 15,
   200, 201
maternity leave, External Affairs, 227
Mazankowski, Don, 101, 108, 245

McCallion, Kathryn, 236
McCloskey, Jean, 226, 229
McCrossan, Paul, 253
McCurdy, Howard, 202
McDonald, Marci, 3-4, 21
McDougall, Barbara J., *306;* apartheid
   191n3; and Baltic communities 245,
   248; and foreign policy 200-1; as for-
   eign minister, 168-69, 221, 256, 295;
   good governance, 19; on "new interna-
   tionalism" 35-36; on non-intervention
   119-20; on sovereignty 19, 196; and
   1991 Soviet coup 168-69; and Vienna
   conference 168-69; women in External
   Affairs, 221, 226, 229, 231
McDougall, Pamela, 224
McGrath, James, 283
McKnight, Bill, 107, *308, 309*
McMillan, Tom, 77, 78
McMurtry, Roy, 10
Mexico: air quality agreement, 75; Clark
   and, 139; free trade, 146, 153-54;
   Québec office in, 134, 139
Middlemiss, Dan, 260
Military Training Assistance Program,
   178, 188
MINORCO, loan to, 176-77
Mitchell, George, 23n21
Mitterrand, François, 136
Montreal Protocol on Substances that
   Deplete the Ozone Layer, 75, 77
Morin, Claude, 128
Morin, Jacques-Yvan, 131
Morin, Marie-Lucie, 226
Morrison, Alex, 123
Morrison, David R., 280, 282
Morton, Desmond, 123, 200
Mugabe, Robert, 188, 190, 216
Mulroney, Brian, *301-307;* African
   National Congress, 185; on apartheid,
   41n4; 176; Arctic sovereignty, 20; on
   Baltic states, 10; Biodiversity Treaty, 79;
   on Canadian-American relations, 8;
   1987 defence white paper, 270; Clark,
   200, 214; Conrad Black on, 162; ethnic
   groups, 252-54; foreign policy aspirations, 3; foreign policy populism, 276-
   87; free trade, position on, 8-9, 32, 55;
   on Front Line States, 192n27; gender,
   220-37; good governance, 19, 194-204;
   and Hong Kong, 18; on humanitarian
   intervention, 16; on Israel as "ally," 9;
   as leader of the opposition, 6-10; leadership style, 161-63; Liberal critique of,
   277; Mexican-American free trade talks,
   153-54; negotiations on Arctic policy,
   93-94; on peacekeeping, 123; public

opinion on, 291-91; and Québec, 129, 292; relations with US presidents 12, 277; at Rio, 164-66; and St. Francis Xavier University, 215; Stanford University speech, 119; on sovereignty, 19, 196, 200; and Soviet Union, 217; and summit diplomacy, 163-66, 213; and Thatcher on apartheid, 182; and UN dues, 123; and world conferences, 160-71
Multicultural Affairs, Department of, 168
Multinational Force and Observers, 116, 117-18

National Action Committee on the Status of Women, 232
National Defence, Department of: 1987 white paper, 34; peacekeeping, 121; polar icebreaker, 90
National Energy Program, 7, 40n3, 48, 60-61; "back-in" provision, 61
National Forum Africa, 280
National Forum on Canada's International Relations, 285, 286
National Policy, 215
Navy: Arctic deployments, 88-89
non-governmental organizations, 15l, 277; energy policy, 65-66; Ethiopian famine, 280; foreign policy review, 281-82; human rights, 203-4, 242
Nielsen, Erik, 11, 268, *303;* and 1987 defence white paper, 263; responsibilities of 273n18; on sovereignty, 269
Nigerian civil war, 21
"Nixon shocks," 150
Non-Proliferation Treaty, 108
Noriega, Manuel, 145
North American Aerospace Defence Command, 33, 100, 105, 116, 282
North American Free Trade Agreement, 13, 14, 28, 146, 154
North Atlantic Treaty Organization, 14, 33, 100, 194, 243; Canadian commitment to, 263; Norway, commitment to, 103; withdrawal of Canadian forces from Europe, 35
North Pacific Cooperative Security Dialogue, 17, 218
North Warning System, 95, 106, 110n5, 266
Northwest Passage 84-97, 106, 263; international law, 92
Norway: Canadian commitment to, 103
nuclear-powered submarines, 34, 106, 269-70; and US Navy, 274n44

Office franco-québécois de la Jeunesse, 133
Official Development Assistance, 196

Omnibus Trade and Competitiveness Act (US), 150
Ontario: and free trade, 54
"Open regionalism," 155-56
Operation Brave Lion, 268, 269
Organisation for Economic Cooperation and Development, 198
Organization of American States, 5, 17, 20, 142-59, 197, 199, 219, 292; Canadian human rights policy, 257
Organization of Petroleum Exporting Countries 65, 69
Ostry, Sylvia, 214, 238n38
Ottawa Process, 286
Ozone depletion, 75-77

Page, Don, 254, 276
Panama: American intervention in, 109, 145
Pan-American Union, 143
Parenteau, Roland, 138
Park, Anne, 168
Parliament: foreign policy debates, 278; parliamentary committees, 15, 31, 38, 124, 246, 280, 282; subcommittee on human rights, 202; use of, 258. *See also* Special Joint Committee on Canada's International Relations
Parti Québécois, 129, 131, 140n19
peacekeeping, 16, 113-25, 292; "first-generation," 126n12; public opinion on, 120; "second-generation," 119-20
Pearson, Lester B., 16, 114, 134, 212, 214, 290
Peterson, Spike, 222
Petrosian, Levon Ter, 251
Peyrefitte, Alain, 135
Polar 8 icebreaker, 90-91, 95-96
Polar Sea, 20, 84-97, 268
Polish-Canadians, 243-49
Pope, Sir Joseph, 223
Pratt, Renate, 176, 185, 189
Prime Minister's Office, 166, 200, 246
Privy Council Office, 166 246; Arctic policy 85-86, 89-90; 1987 defence white paper, 270-71
Professional Association of Foreign Service Officers, 228
Progressive Conservative party: "Blue Tories," 10-11; change of leadership, 6; impact on 1987 defence white paper, 265-66; impact on foreign policy, 5, 39-40, 294-95; leadership race, 9; "Red Tories," 10
protectionism, US, 49-50, 150, 151
Prud'homme, Marcel, 202

public opinion: on defence policy, 265-66; on free trade, 54; on Mulroney, 290-91; on peacekeeping, 120, 124
Public Service Commission, 227

Québec, 292; Catholic Church in, 129; and Chrétien, 138; délégation-générale in Paris, 129; federal-provincial relations, 131-34; foreign policy of, 128; and France, 134-36; and free trade, 54, 136-37; Gabon affair, 135-36; Mexico, 134, 139; Mulroney and, 128, 136, 139; *Office franco-québécois de la Jeunesse*, 133; Trudeau and, 128, 138; and United States, 136-37
Quiet Revolution, 128, 129-31, 135

Ramphal, Sonny, 182
Reagan, Nancy, 4
Reagan, Ronald, 4, 18, 145, 163, 264, 277, 294, *302;* Arctic policy, 93-94; apartheid, 184; and Trudeau, 8
Reciprocity Treaty (1911), 3; and 1911 election, 9
Redekop, Clarence, 175
Reform party, 278
Regan, Gerald, 50
Regional Economic Expansion, Department of: attitude towards free trade, 52
Regional Industrial Expansion, Department of, 11
Reisman, Simon, 213, 214; on women in FTA negotiations, 238-39n38
Reykjavik summit, 101, 107, 264
Rio Treaty, 144
Roche, Douglas, 10, 38
Royal Commission on Conditions of Foreign Service, 224, 237n19
Royal Commission on the Economic Union and Development Prospects for Canada (Macdonald Commission), 12, 31, 45, 52, 139
Royal Commission on the Status of Women in Canada, 224
Roy-Arcelin, Nicole, 252

Sakharov, Andrei, 247
Salinas de Gotari, Carlos, 153
sanctions: against Indonesia, 19; against South Africa, 175-76, 177-79; Clark on, 180, 192n19; Thatcher on, 182
Sarlos, Andrew, 247
sectoral free trade, 8, 31
security, 33-35, 254-65; energy and, 62-63; gendered analyses of, 233-35
Shadwick, Martin, 120
Shamrock Summit, 4, 11, 32, 52, 163; acid

rain, 75; air defence, 102; Arctic negotiations, 92-93; Granatstein on, 22n6
Shcharansky, Anatoly, 248
Shevardnadze, Eduard, 217
Shultz, George, 93
Sikh Professional Association of Canada, 251
Sikh-Canadians, 249-54
Simard, Jean-Maurice, 14, 71, 94-95, 263
Simpson, Jeffrey, 113, 124
Single European Act, 150
Skelton, O.D., 143
Skogstad, Grace, 265
Somalia: Canadian Airborne Regiment in, 16; Commission of Inquiry, 124; peacekeeping mission, 16, 120, 124
South Africa. *See* apartheid
Southern Africa Task Force, 190
Southern African Development Coordination Conference, 174, 186-87, 191n8
sovereignty: Arctic sovereignty, 20, 84-97; Conservatives on, 196; Foreign Extraterritorial Measures Act, 20; McDougall on, 19, 119-20, 196; Mulroney on, 19, 196, 200; Special Joint Committee on, 263
Soviet Union, coup in, 168-69; Conservative views on, 34; McDougall and, 168-69
Special Joint Committee on Canada's International Relations (Hockin-Simard committee), 202, 246; on Arctic sovereignty, 94-95, 202, 263; on environment, 71-72; and foreign policy process, 281-82, 283; on peacekeeping, 115, 117; report, 38; Strategic Defense Initiative, 14
St. Francis Xavier University, and Mulroney, 215
St. Laurent, Louis, 194, 212
Standing Committee on External Affairs and International Trade (Commons), 15
Standing Committee on External Affairs and National Defence (Commons), 38, 246; and Ethiopia famine, 280
Standing Committee on National Defence (Commons), 282
Standing Committee on National Defence and Veterans Affairs (Commons), 124
Standing Committee on Foreign Affairs (Senate), 31, 124
Stanford University speech, 196
Stanford, Joe, 245
Statute of Westminster (1931), 132
Stevens, Sinclair, 11
Stienstra, Deborah, 222, 236

straight baselines, 86-87
Strategic Arms Reduction Talks (START)
    Treaty, 107
Strategic Defense Initiative, 13, 102, 105,
    219, 281, 291; Mulroney on, 14;
    Special Joint Committee on, 14
Strategic Petroleum Reserve, 63
structural adjustment programs, 199,
    201
submarines, nuclear-powered. *See*
    nuclear-powered submarines
Suez crisis, 16
Supreme Court of Canada, 132

Tambo, Oliver, 185
Task Force on Barriers to Women in the
    Public Service, 227
Taylor, J.H. (Si), 21, 200, 201
"Team Canada," 218
Thatcher, Margaret, 7, 18, 215, 294, *307;*
    apartheid 175, 184; at Nassau CHOGM,
    182
Thériault, Gérard, 268, 269
Third Option, 32, 41n6, 49, 50, 146, 149,
    152
"30 Percent Club," 74
Tiananmen massacre, 18, 204, 278
Tolba, Mostafa, 77
Toronto Group (on CFCs), 76-77, 81
Trade and Tariff Act (US), 149
trade: economic blocs, 151, 156; "hub-
    and-spoke" arrangements, 153-54;
    Imperial Preferences, 215. *See also* free
    trade; sanctions
Trading with the Enemy Act (US), 20
Trudeau, Pierre Elliott, 6, 51, 212; acid
    rain, 74; apartheid, 174-75; defence
    policy, 100, 103-5; Eagleberger on,
    111n18; foreign policy review, 281; la
    Francophonie, 217; human rights, 242;
    ICJ reservation, 89; *Manhattan* voyage
    86; OAS, 142; peace initiative, 8, 34,
    105; peacekeeping, 114; and Québec,
    128, 138
Turner, John, 45

Ukraine: independence of, 218, 243, 256;
    recognition of, 20-21, 249
Ukrainian Canadian Congress, 244, 246
Ukrainian-Canadians, 243-49
UN Commission for Human Rights, 38,
    245
UN Conference on the Environment and
    Development (Rio de Janeiro 1992), 17,
    79, 160, 293
UN Conferences on Law of the Sea, 86
UN Environment Program, 76, 77

UN Forces in Cyprus (UNFICYP), 116;
    Canadian withdrawal from, 121-22
UN Operation in Somalia (UNOSOM),
    120
UN Protection Force (UNPROFOR), 12
UN Security Council, 118, 219; and
    apartheid, 175; reform of, 37
UNITAF (Unified Task Force), 16. *See also*
    Somalia
United States: Arctic policy 91-94;
    Québec 136-137; US Agency for
    International Development, 198; US
    Coast Guard 85, 93; US Congress, and
    apartheid, 180; US Navy 106; nuclear-
    powered submarines, 274n44; protec-
    tionism, 49-50; relations with Canada,
    8, 11-13, 28-33; Trading with the
    Enemy Act, 20; US Trade
    Representative, 50, 150
Universal Declaration on Human Rights,
    20

Velan, Karel, 247
Versatile Shipyards, 91
Vézina, Monique, 10, 221
Vienna Convention for the Protection of
    the Ozone Layer, 76
visible minority groups, 249-54

Warsaw Pact, 107, 218
Waverman, Leonard, 59
Weinberger, Caspar, 14, 105, 303
Western Accord, 54, 61
white paper on provincial international
    relations, 132
White, Jodi, 213
Wilson, Michael, 49, 51, 101, 107, 200,
    268; 1987 defence white paper, 270;
    foreign policy, 201; Polar 8 cancella-
    tion, 91
Winegard, William, 11, 15, 202, 280;
    development assistance review, 282
Woerner, Manfred, *309*
Wood, Bernard, 174, 182
World Bank, 198
World Commission on Environment and
    Development, 72
World Conference on Human Rights
    (Vienna 1993), 18, 160
World Metereological Organization, 77
World Sikh Organization, 250, 251
World Summit for Children (New York
    1992), 17, 160

Yugoslavia: civil war in, 16; Canadian
    peacekeeping, 120, 123; Mulroney on,
    200; UNPROFOR, 120